Frommer's®

Prague & the Best of
the Czech Republic

9th Edition

by Mark Baker

WILEY

John Wiley & Sons, Inc.

ABOUT THE AUTHOR

Mark Baker is a long-time American expat who lives in Prague. He's one of the original editors of *The Prague Post* and was for years a correspondent and editor for Radio Free Europe/Radio Liberty, based in Prague. He's now a freelance writer and reporter. He's the author of *Frommer's Prague Day by Day*, and coauthor of *Frommer's Eastern Europe* and *Frommer's Poland*.

Published by:

JOHN WILEY & SONS, INC.

111 River St.
Hoboken, NJ 07030-5774

ISBN 978-1-118-08609-4 (paper); ISBN 978-1-118-26168-2 (ebk); ISBN 978-1-118-23673-4 (ebk); ISBN 978-1-118-22340-6 (ebk)

Editor: Jamie Ehrlich
Production Editor: Erin Geile
Cartographer: Andrew Murphy
Photo Editor: Richard Fox
Production by Wiley Indianapolis Composition Services

Front Cover Photo: Charles Bridge in Prague © Doug Pearson / Jon Arnold Images Ltd / Alamy Images
Back Cover Photo: Malostranske Namesti in Prague's Old Town © Frank Chmura / Prisma Bildagentur AG / Alamy Images

For information on our other products and services or to obtain technical support, please contact our Customer Care Department within the U.S. at 877/762-2974, outside the U.S. at 317/572-3993 or fax 317/572-4002.

Wiley also publishes its books in a variety of electronic formats. Some content that appears in print may not be available in electronic formats.

Manufactured in the United States of America

5 4 3 2 1

CONTENTS

10 DAY TRIPS FROM PRAGUE 189

11 THE BEST OF BOHEMIA 210

12 THE BEST OF MORAVIA 257

13 PLANNING YOUR TRIP TO PRAGUE & THE CZECH REPUBLIC 276

14 USEFUL TERMS & PHRASES 293

Index 299

LIST OF MAPS

HOW TO CONTACT US

In researching this book, we discovered many wonderful places—hotels, restaurants, shops, and more. We're sure you'll find others. Please tell us about them, so we can share the information with your fellow travelers in upcoming editions. If you were disappointed with a recommendation, we'd love to know that, too. Please write to:

Frommer's Prague & the Best of the Czech Republic, 9th Edition
John Wiley & Sons, Inc. • 111 River St. • Hoboken, NJ 07030-5774
frommersfeedback@wiley.com

ADVISORY & DISCLAIMER

Travel information can change quickly and unexpectedly, and we strongly advise you to confirm important details locally before traveling, including information on visas, health and safety, traffic and transport, accommodations, shopping, and eating out. We also encourage you to stay alert while traveling and to remain aware of your surroundings. Avoid civil disturbances, and keep a close eye on cameras, purses, wallets, and other valuables.

While we have endeavored to ensure that the information contained within this guide is accurate and up-to-date at the time of publication, we make no representations or warranties with respect to the accuracy or completeness of the contents of this work and specifically disclaim all warranties, including without limitation warranties of fitness for a particular purpose. We accept no responsibility or liability for any inaccuracy or errors or omissions, or for any inconvenience, loss, damage, costs, or expenses of any nature whatsoever incurred or suffered by anyone as a result of any advice or information contained in this guide.

The inclusion of a company, organization, or website in this guide as a service provider and/or potential source of further information does not mean that we endorse them or the information they provide. Be aware that information provided through some websites may be unreliable and can change without notice. Neither the publisher nor author shall be liable for any damages arising herefrom.

FROMMER'S STAR RATINGS, ICONS & ABBREVIATIONS

Every hotel, restaurant, and attraction listing in this guide has been ranked for quality, value, service, amenities, and special features using a **star-rating system.** In country, state, and regional guides, we also rate towns and regions to help you narrow down your choices and budget your time accordingly. Hotels and restaurants are rated on a scale of zero (recommended) to three stars (exceptional). Attractions, shopping, nightlife, towns, and regions are rated according to the following scale: zero stars (recommended), one star (highly recommended), two stars (very highly recommended), and three stars (must-see).

In addition to the star-rating system, we also use **seven feature icons** that point you to the great deals, in-the-know advice, and unique experiences that separate travelers from tourists. Throughout the book, look for:

special finds—those places only insiders know about

fun facts—details that make travelers more informed and their trips more fun

kids—best bets for kids and advice for the whole family

special moments—those experiences that memories are made of

overrated—places or experiences not worth your time or money

insider tips—great ways to save time and money

great values—where to get the best deals

The following abbreviations are used for credit cards:

AE American Express	DISC Discover	V Visa
DC Diners Club	MC MasterCard	

TRAVEL RESOURCES AT FROMMERS.COM

Frommer's travel resources don't end with this guide. Frommer's website, **www.frommers. com,** has travel information on more than 4,000 destinations. We update features regularly, giving you access to the most current trip-planning information and the best airfare, lodging, and car-rental bargains. You can also listen to podcasts, connect with other Frommers.com members through our active-reader forums, share your travel photos, read blogs from guidebook editors and fellow travelers, and much more.

THE BEST OF PRAGUE & THE CZECH REPUBLIC

B
ests by their very nature are highly personalized affairs. One person's best might be a classical concert in a baroque church, while another person might relish a night of jazz in a club that's been around since the '50s. Fortunately, Prague has a wide selection of bests that are sure to cater to a range of interests, whether they be in music, art, architecture, nature, or just a glass of good beer. Here are some of my suggestions.

THE most UNFORGETTABLE TRAVEL EXPERIENCES

- **Stroll Across Charles Bridge at Dawn or Dusk:** The silhouettes of the statues lining the 650-year old crown jewel of Czech heritage hover like ghosts in the still of the sunrise skyline. Early in the morning, you can stroll across the bridge without encountering the crowds that appear by midday. With the changing light of dusk, the statues, the bridge, and the city panorama take on a whole different character. See "Walking Tour 1: Charles Bridge & Malá Strana (Lesser Town)" in chapter 7.

- **Make Your Own Procession Down the Royal Route:** The downhill jaunt from Prague Castle, through Malá Strana (Lesser Town), and across Charles Bridge to Old Town Square, is a day in itself. (If you want more exercise, start in the Old Town and walk up to the castle.) The trip recalls the route taken by the carriages of the Bohemian kings; today, it's lined with galleries, shops, and cafes. See "Walking Tour 3: Staré Město (Old Town)" in chapter 7.

- **Take a Slow Boat Down the Vltava River:** You can see many of the most striking architectural landmarks from the low-angle and low-stress vantage point of a rowboat you pilot yourself. Make the trip in the evening for something even more special. See "Sightseeing Options" in chapter 6 o **Get Lost in Prague's Old Town:** It happens to everyone, even people who have lived here for years. You think you're taking a shortcut down a back alley, and soon you're on a street you've never seen before and have no idea where you are. Old Town's winding lanes were carved out long before cities had rectilinear street grids, and that's a big part of the city's charm. See chapter 6.

o **Catch a Performance of Smetana's Moldau Symphony:** Or any other piece of classical music, for that matter. Prague's Gothic spires and baroque cupolas provide the perfect backdrop for a classical concert, opera, or ballet, and the city's symphony halls and churches are just as beautiful as the music itself. See chapter 9, "Prague Nightlife."

o **Have a Cold One in the City That "Invented" Beer:** I'm not talking about Prague here, but the western Bohemian city of Plzeň (Pilsen) that's the birthplace of modern lager. It's why we call beer "pilsner" or simply "pils." They're still making beer there and you can tour the brewery. If you can't make it to Plzeň, stop in at just about any pub in the country for some of the best beer you'll ever drink. See chapter 11, "The Best of Bohemia."

o **Step into History at Karlštejn Castle:** A 30-minute train ride southwest of Prague puts you in the most visited Czech landmark in the environs, built by Charles IV (Karel IV in Czech—the namesake of Charles Bridge) in the 14th century to protect the Holy Roman Empire's crown jewels. This Romanesque hilltop bastion fits the image of the castles of medieval lore, though the exterior is more impressive than inside. See chapter 10.

THE best SPLURGE HOTELS

o **U Zlaté studně** (U zlaté studně 4, Prague 1; ℭ 257-011-213): Recently selected as one of the world's leading small hotels, the "Golden Well" impresses on every level. This reconstructed 17th-century town house sits just below Prague Castle, and many of the rooms afford stunning views out over Malá Strana and Old Town. See p. 53.

o **Hotel Aria** (Tržiště 9, Prague 1; ℭ 225-334-111): This reconverted baroque town house plays on Prague's musical heritage, with each of its beautifully appointed rooms named after a composer or performer. Some rooms look out over the Vrtbovská garden. Don't leave without having dinner or a drink on the rooftop terrace. See p. 57.

o **Falkensteiner Hotel Grand Spa Marienbad** (Ruská 123, Mariánské Lázně; ℭ 354-929-396): If there's one hotel in Mariánské Lázně that comes close to capturing the glamour of the early '60s French New Wave film *Last Year at Marienbad*, it would be this palace that sits atop a long hill at the end of Ruská street. Unlike many other spa-town hotels, there's no whiff of "hospital" here; it's pure luxury. See p. 225.

o **Hotel Mandarin Oriental** (Nebovidská 1, Prague 1; ℭ 233-088-888): This local branch of the international luxury chain occupies a sublime location in a converted monastery in a quiet corner of Malá Strana. This is no cookie-cutter chain; each room is funky and wonderful in its own unique way. See p. 57.

o **Grandhotel Pupp** (Mírové nám. 2, Karlovy Vary; ℭ 353-109-111): The Pupp, built in 1701, is one of Europe's oldest grand hotels. It's so "grand," in fact, it was used as a location setting in the 2006 James Bond film *Casino Royale*. There's no

better abode from which to enjoy the country's most glamorous spa resort. See p. 217.

o **Four Seasons Hotel Prague** (Veleslavínova 2a, Prague 1; 𝄐 **221-427-000**): Arguably the number one luxury hotel in Prague's Old Town, with many rooms having a river view of Prague Castle and Charles Bridge. The house restaurant, Allegro, won a Michelin star 2 years running, a first in all of central Europe. See p. 59.

o **Hotel Budweis** (Mlýnská 6, České Budějovice; 𝄐 **389-822-111**): České Budějovice's newest four-star entry is a stylish, modern hotel fashioned from the town's former grain mill. Many of the original architectural details have been retained, such as the exterior brickwork and wood-beamed ceilings and gleaming parquet floors throughout. See p. 238.

o **Hotel Comsa Brno Palace** (Šilingrovo nám. 2, Brno; 𝄐 **532-156-777**): Arguably Brno's nicest hotel, it occupies a stunningly restored 19th-century town palace, within easy walking distance of the Špilberk Castle or the city center. The four-story atrium will take your breath away. See p. 264.

o **Hotel Savoy** (Keplerova 6, Prague 1; 𝄐 **224-302-430**): This opulent but tasteful small hotel suggests London more than Prague. Enjoy afternoon tea in the library, where you can read by a crackling fire. See p. 53.

o **Hotel Paříž** (U Obecního domu 1, Prague 1; 𝄐 **222-195-195**): This restored Art Nouveau hotel recalls 1920s Prague, one of the wealthiest cities on earth at that time. It's across from another remodeled gem, the Municipal House (Obecní dům). See p. 61.

THE best MODERATELY PRICED HOTELS

o **Hotel Lahofer** (Veselá 13, Znojmo; 𝄐 **257-216-337**): One of the country's smartest and best-run small hotels just happens to be in the small Moravian border town of Znojmo. The Lahofer occupies a renovated town house dating back to the 13th century, just a block from the main square. The hotel is owned by the Lahofer winery, and there's a small wine shop in the reception area. See p. 274.

o **K+K Hotel Central** (Hybernská 10, Prague 1; 𝄐 **225-022-000**): Okay, it's absurd to put a four-star luxury hotel in the moderate category, but this stunningly restored Art Nouveau palace frequently discounts rates over its website, so it's always worth a click to see what's available. See p. 65.

o **Hotel Cloister Inn** (Konviktská 14, Prague 1; 𝄐 **224-211-020**): This freshly restored hotel in a former convent offers a comfortable room at a fair price in Old Town near Jan Hus's 15th-century Bethlehem Chapel. See p. 62.

o **Pension Větrník** (U Větrníku 40, Prague 6; 𝄐 **220-612-404**): This family-run romantic hideaway is reachable in about 25 minutes by tram from the city center. See p. 68.

o **Czech Inn** (Francouzská 76, Prague 10; 𝄐 **267-267-600**): This place calls itself a hostel, but "budget boutique" would be more accurate. Great breakfasts, an upscale modern interior, a bank of convenient computers in the lobby for surfing, and friendly receptionists make this a great choice if saving money is the prime consideration. See p. 61.

o **Hotel Konvice** (Horní ul. 144, Český Krumlov; 𝄐 **380-711-611**): The Konvice wins perennial—justifiable—rave reviews for coziness, cleanliness, and location, just a block from Český Krumlov's main square. Room no. 11 has two separate bedrooms and a castle view from the terrace. Several other rooms have drop-dead castle views too. See p. 246.

○ **Hot ýlek & Hospoda u malého Vítka** (Radniční 27, Český Krumlov; ✆ 380-711-925): If you can't get in at the Konvice (above), here's another impossibly cute hotel in Český Krumlov. This one occupies a Renaissance-era house that's been remodeled top to bottom by a skilled woodcarver. Each of the rooms is snug and clean and has been named after a popular Czech cartoon character. See p. 247.

○ **Hotel Absolutum** (Jablonského 476, Prague 7; ✆ 222-541-406): This is a sleek, modern hotel, with designer-style rooms at reasonable prices. The location, across the street from the Holešovice train and metro station, won't win a beauty contest, but it's convenient for getting to the center. See p. 67.

THE most UNFORGETTABLE DINING EXPERIENCES

○ **La Degustation** (Haštalská 18, Prague 1; ✆ 222-311-234): How could you ever forget a full seven-course meal that seems to unfold without end over a long evening, interspersed with unexpected appetizers and bottles and bottles of wine? It's a meal you'll talk about for years to come (but remember not to have a big lunch beforehand). See p. 82.

○ **Kavárna Obecní dům** (náměstí Republiky 5, Prague 1; ✆ 222-002-763): This reinvigorated Art Nouveau cafe at the **Municipal House** has re-created the grandeur of Jazz Age afternoons. See p. 91.

○ **Grosseto Marina** (Alšovo nábřeží, Prague 1; ✆ 605-454-020): This popular Italian restaurant occupies a big boat anchored off the Old Town side of the Vltava, just near the Mánes Bridge. If it's a dramatic backdrop you're seeking, the views out over Malá Strana and Prague Castle can't be topped. See p. 84.

○ **Sansho** (Petrská 25, Prague 1; ✆ 222-317-425): 2011 was a banner year for restaurant openings, and none made a bigger splash than this minimalist Asian-fusion place in Nové Město. Head chef Paul Day cut his culinary teeth at London's award-winning Nobu and brought with him a philosophy of mixing the best of East and West in an understated setting that puts the focus on the food. See p. 87.

○ **U modré kachničky** (Nebovidská 6, Prague 1; ✆ 257-320-308): The "Blue Duckling," on a narrow Malá Strana street, comes close to refining standard Czech dishes into true Bohemian haute cuisine. This series of small dining rooms with vaulted ceilings and playfully frescoed walls is packed with antique furniture and pastel-flowered linen upholstery. Request a table upstairs in a romantic nook not far from the wafting piano music. See p. 79.

○ **Angus Aberdeen Steakhouse** (Pražská 23, Plzeň; ✆ 371-580-069): Plzeň is blessed with several good places to eat, but if you've got just one meal to spend here, blow off the brewery restaurant and have an unforgettable steak on a marvelous riverside terrace. See p. 231.

○ **Šenk Na Parkánu** (Veleslavínova 4, Plzeň; ✆ 377-324-485): This very likeable and popular Czech pub is conveniently situated just next door to Plzeň's Beer Museum, and serves the same wicked good unfiltered, nonpasteurized beer you were served at the end of the beer tour. See p. 231.

o **Masné Krámy** (Krajinská 29, České Budějovice; ✆ 387-201-301): České Budějovice's fabled watering hole, named after the town's former meat market, underwent a thorough face-lift a couple of years ago that left it much cleaner and still serving the same great—and cheap—Czech tavern food. See p. 240.

o **Koishi** (Udolní 11, Brno; ✆ 777-564-744): The Czech Republic's best sushi restaurant just happens to be in Brno. In fact, some reviewers put Koishi among the country's top 10 restaurants in all categories. The specialties here are nigiri and maki sushi, but there's also a wide range of other types of fish, steaks, and even pastas to satisfy all palates. See p. 266.

o **Bakeshop** (Kozí 1, Prague 1; ✆ 222-316-823): Yes, it's pricey for a bakery, particularly one in central Europe, but who can resist those loaves of sourdough bread, muffins straight from the oven, cookies, and brownies, not to mention the range of lunch items like sandwiches, salads, and big bowls of chili? Eat at the counter along the window or take it with you. See p. 86.

THE best MUSEUMS

o **Šternberk Palace** (Hradčanské nám. 15, Prague 1; ✆ 233-090-570): The country's best collection of European art, ranging from Byzantine-era icons straight through to Rembrandt, El Greco, Goya, and van Dyck. See p. 108.

o **Alfons Mucha Museum** (Panská 7, Prague 1; ✆ 221-451-333): Posters, decorative panels, objets d'art, and excerpts from sketchbooks, as well as oil paintings from this well-known Art Nouveau master, are displayed at the baroque Kaunický Palace near Václavské náměstí. See p. 110.

o **St. George's Convent** (Jiřské nám. 33, Prague 1; ✆ 257-531-644): I never thought I'd have a weakness for 19th-century landscape paintings, but these are spectacular. While the Czech Republic lacks rugged mountains (not to mention a seashore), it's blessed with some of the most beautiful rolling countryside in Europe, and the painters displayed here knew how to capture that. See p. 108.

o **Veletržní Palác** (Veletržní at Dukelských hrdinů 47, Prague 7; ✆ 224-301-111): Prague's museum of art of the 20th and 21st centuries is an underrated gem, filled with masterworks by Klimt, Munch, Schiele, and Picasso. But the real treats here are works by the Modernist Czech painters from the 1920s and '30s. See p. 108.

o **Jewish Museum** (U Starého hřbitova; enter from Široká 3, Prague 1; ✆ 221-711-511): This "museum" is not just one building but a series of preserved synagogues and the Old Jewish Cemetery, which together bear witness to 7 centuries of Jewish life in this tiny part of Prague. The admission fee is regrettably high, but the memory of all those jagged tombstones jutting upward in that crowded plot will last a lifetime. See p. 105.

o **Museum of the Ghetto** (Terezín; ✆ 416-782-225): This is a sobering space that tells the shocking tale of how the Nazis deceived the world into thinking their "Final Solution" was actually building vacation homes for Jews. How did the Nazis get away with it, and how did the world allow them to? See p. 206.

o **Bone Church (Kostnice)** (Sedlec, near Kutná Hora; ✆ 728-125-488): Three words: creepy, creepy, creepy. Thousands of human bones from the Middle Ages were used in the 19th century to construct this "gothic" interior of a rather ordinary looking (from the outside) church not far from Kutná Hora. You'll finally understand the term "bone chilling." See p. 200.

THE best THINGS TO DO FOR FREE (OR ALMOST)

○ **Having a Cup and a Debate at the Kavárna Slavia** (Národní at Smetanovo nábřeží, Prague 1; © 224-218-493): The reincarnation of Prague's favorite Communist-era dissident cafe retains its former Art Deco glory. The cloak-and-dagger interactions of secret police eavesdropping on political conversations may be gone, but there's still an energy that flows with the talk and java at the Slavia—and it comes with a great view. See p. 91.

○ **Crossing the Charles Bridge at Night:** At night, the bridge takes on a completely different persona. The crowds thin out (a little), and musicians, street performers, and flower people come here to sit under the statues and sing or just hang out. Why not join them? See chapter 9 for more nightlife options.

○ **Enjoying New Year's Eve in Český Krumlov:** At midnight in Bohemia's Český Krumlov, the Na Plášti Bridge at the castle overlooking the town turns into a mini–United Nations, as revelers from all over gather to watch and light fireworks, see who can uncork the champagne the fastest, and just plain celebrate. See "Český Krumlov" in chapter 11, p. 241.

○ **Exploring Antiques Shops:** If you like old stuff, you'll enjoy finding something "out of this world" in many of Prague's antiques shops (*starožitnosti*) or bookstores selling more-or-less-old publications (*antikvariáts*). See chapter 8, "Prague Shopping" (p. 158), for shopping suggestions.

○ **Have a Beer at Letná:** In summer, you'll find the city's best beer garden on the far eastern edge of Letná Park, across the river from Old Town. While the beer's not free (too bad!), it's not all that expensive either, and you're free to sit at one of the picnic tables or along the park benches. The views down to Old Town are simply superb. See "Other Top Sights" in chapter 6.

○ **Treat Yourself to a Svařák:** *Svařák,* short for *svařené víno,* is the Czech version of mulled wine, a traditional Christmastime treat that's best drunk outside in the freezing cold from a plastic or Styrofoam cup. Vendors on Old Town Square start selling the stuff in early November and *svařák* season lasts through the new year or longer. Okay, it's not free, but a good-size cup of the stuff will only set you back about 40Kč.

○ **Drop in at the Castle:** To be sure, the full-price ticket to all the castle sights can set you back a pretty *koruna.* But there's no cost to enter the castle complex itself and simply walk around. It's even better at night, when the crowds thin out and you have those views down to Malá Strana and Old Town to yourself. See p. 94.

○ **Feed the Swans:** The bread won't exactly be free, but it's worth a couple of crowns to buy some rolls and head down to the river (for the best swan sightings, try the banks on the Malá Strana side just south of the Malostranská metro station along the street U Lužického semináře). The Vltava is home to hundreds of white swans (if not more), but be careful with the bread, since the birds might bite.

THE best ACTIVITIES FOR FAMILIES

○ **Ride a Big Boat down the Vltava:** For those not willing to test their navigational skills or rowing strength in their own boat, large tour boats offer similar floating views, many with meals. Be sure to check the direction of your voyage to be certain it travels past the castles and palaces. See "Sightseeing Options" in chapter 6.

○ **Picnic at Vyšehrad:** Of all the parks where you can picnic, the citadel above the Vltava standing guard over the south end of the Old Town is the calmest and most interesting spot close to the center. Its more remote location means less tourist traffic, and the gardens, city panoramas, and national cemetery provide pleasant walks and poignant history. See "Other Top Sights" in chapter 6.

○ **Spend a Day at the Zoo:** Prague's zoo has improved immensely in recent years, after the 2002 flood severely damaged the grounds and even killed several animals. There's been lots of new investment, and the setting by the river is great. Check out some of the biggest collections of giraffes and great apes in central Europe. See "Other Top Sights" in chapter 6.

○ **Gaze at the Stars:** For budding astronomers, Prague has two treats in store. A real live observatory on Petřín Hill is open on clear nights in summer or winter for checking out the moon, Jupiter, Saturn, and even some other galaxies. The planetarium in Stromovka park is an indoor stellar spectacle. See "Other Top Sights" in chapter 6.

○ **Hop Aboard the Oldtimer:** That's Prague's endearing name for Tram 91, a vintage streetcar from a bygone era that still plies the rails on Saturdays and Sundays during the summer. Hop aboard at any stop, buy a ticket from the conductor, and ride for as long as you want. See "Sightseeing Options" in chapter 6.

○ **Visit the Technical Museum:** Older kids will enjoy a visit to Prague's National Technical Museum, a kind of miniature Smithsonian Institution, crammed with planes, trains, and automobiles. It re-opened in 2011 after a multiyear renovation and is better than ever. See "Other Museums & Galleries" in chapter 6.

○ **Get Lost in a Mirror Maze:** There are lots of offbeat attractions on Petřín Hill in addition to the mock "Eiffel Tower." The mirror maze is an old-fashioned house of mirrors—more disorienting for adults than it is for kids! But fun for all. See "Sightseeing Options" in chapter 6.

THE most ROMANTIC EXPERIENCES

○ **Český Krumlov:** If you have time for only one excursion from Prague, make it Český Krumlov. This living gallery of Renaissance-era buildings housing many galleries, shops, and restaurants is 167km (104 miles) south of Prague. Above it towers the second-largest castle complex in the country, with the Vltava River running underneath. No wonder UNESCO named this town a World Heritage Site. See "Český Krumlov" in chapter 11.

○ **Holding Hands on the Charles Bridge:** This is a no-brainer, but the real trick is to choose the right moment. In summer, shoot for an evening stroll just as the sun is setting behind Prague Castle. In winter, pray for snow, and then go out at night as the flakes swirl around and muffle the sounds of the city.

- **Take a Long Ride on the Metro:** There must be something in the air down there or about those long intervals between stations (especially along the C line), but Czechs (particularly young couples) love to hold hands, kiss, and generally push the PDA envelope on the metro. As they say, "when in Rome . . ."
- **Dine on the River:** Several of Prague's best restaurants are perched right next to the Vltava or command stunning views out over it (see chapter 5, "Where to Eat in Prague," for some suggestions). Or do the ultimate romantic thing and actually dine *on* the river. Buy a bottle of "Bohemia Sekt" (domestic sparkling wine) and a picnic lunch from Bakeshop (p. 86), and rent a paddle boat from one of the rental outlets on the island across from the National Theater.
- **Visit Your Local Pub:** I know that it's bad form to kiss in a pub. Not only does the beer play tricks with your judgment, but you also risk the rest of the bar jangling their keys (a polite enjoinder to "get a room"). On the other hand, if you're lucky, the setting and the beer will conspire to create a moment that seems so right, the only logical response will be an amorous one. See chapter 9, "Prague Nightlife," for a list of good Czech pubs.
- **Spend an Afternoon at Stromovka Park:** This is Prague's most secluded park and no one will look askance as you spread out your blanket, uncork a bottle of wine, and start whispering sweet nothings into your partner's ear. In fact, look around, everyone else seems to be doing the same thing. See "Other Top Sights" in chapter 6.

THE best CZECH BEER

- **Pilsner Urquell:** I can hear the catcalls already. Yes, this is the biggest brewer in the country (it's a little like choosing "Budweiser" as the best American beer), but Pilsner Urquell really might be the Czechs' best. It still wins lots of national beer prizes, and the signature bitter taste and smooth follow-through of its main 12-degree lager still sets the standard for beers around the world.
- **Budvar:** Possibly my personal favorite, since I like beers to have a slightly sweet (but not too much so) taste. By the way (and no slight to the good folks in St. Louis, Missouri), this is the original "Budweiser" and hails from České Budějovice (known as "Budweis" in German).
- **Staropramen:** Prague's home brewery would never have made this list in the old days—the quality was too inconsistent. But "Staro" is now owned by the giant InBev group (which also owns Bass Ale and Stella Artois, among other big names) and surprisingly it's gotten better, not worse.
- **Kozel:** This bitter brew has long been a favorite of Prague's rowdy expat drinkers, who admire the brand's signature label depicting a goat just as much as the taste. Now Kozel is owned by the Pilsner Urquell group and has lost a little of its cachet. The standard Kozel golden lager seems to be getting harder and harder to find, but the very good Kozel dark is available at nearly all Pilsner Urquell pubs.
- **Krušovice:** This is another decidedly bitter brew that seems to divide beer drinkers down the middle between those who love it and those who can only tolerate it. Count me among the former. It's brewed in the middle of hop country and seems to taste all the fresher for it.
- **Smaller names:** As I compile this list, I can just hear the beer snobs sigh. For convenience sake, I've listed the big national brewers here—the ones that are easy to find at pubs around Prague. Of course, the big brewers are just half the story, and

not necessarily the most interesting half. As you're walking around town, look for the following smaller labels: **Svijany, Primátor, Bernard,** and **Klášter** (among others). These are some of the brighter stars of the emerging generation. One place to find these and others smaller labels is the **Prague Beer Museum.** See "Czech Pubs" in chapter 9. To find a good selection of hard-to-find bottles from smaller brewers, check out **Galerie Piva** in Malá Strana and **Pivní Galerie.** See "Beer, Wine & Spirits" in chapter 8.

PRAGUE & THE CZECH REPUBLIC IN DEPTH

Prague continues to climb up the list of Europe's (and the world's) most visited cities, attracting around 4 million foreign tourists annually. That figure puts it somewhere in the middle of the Top 10 for Europe, behind classic destinations like London, Paris, and Rome, but comparable to other popular hot spots like Amsterdam, Barcelona, and Berlin. It's far and away central Europe's biggest tourist draw, outpacing Kraków, Budapest, and even Vienna.

That's quite an achievement for a city that, in many ways, is still adjusting to the epic changes of a little more than 2 decades ago, when peaceful protesters toppled a corrupt Communist regime that had ruled the country since nearly the end of World War II.

For visitors, Prague's growing popularity can be a double-edged sword. The sheer number of people, particularly over the Easter holidays and in midsummer, puts a noticeable strain on the city's infrastructure, resulting in crowded tram and metro cars, clogged streets, and overburdened restaurants and hotels. On a more personal level, the crowds detract—at least a little—from the city's ineffable mystery and charm. Alas, those days when one could boast of "discovering" this central European gem are probably over for good.

But the changes by no means have all been for the bad. Over the past decade, visitors have pumped literally billions of dollars into the local economy, funding major, long-overdue renovations of historical sights like Prague Castle, Charles Bridge, and Old Town Square. Tourism income has fueled the emergence of some of Europe's most beautiful hotels and pensions, many occupying renovated Renaissance and baroque town houses that had gone derelict for decades before.

Similarly, the restaurant scene is more vibrant than ever, thanks at least partly to visitors, who have pushed Praguers to try foods and cuisines that range far beyond traditional pork, sauerkraut, and dumplings. Tourists have also fueled the city's growing number of concerts, cultural events, and music clubs. It's no exaggeration to say they've played a big part in transforming the annual Prague Spring music festival into one of the world's great celebrations of classical music.

Maybe the best effect of the city's growing international popularity is simply energy. Without its thousands of visitors every day, Prague would be quainter for sure, but far quieter—a beauty, but still a backwater. Try to keep that in mind as you're standing in the middle of Old Town Square on a hot sunny day surrounded by hundreds of fellow travelers all taking part in what feels like a global street party. Prague has always been at the geographic heart of Europe, and now it's at its spiritual heart as well.

PRAGUE & THE CZECH REPUBLIC TODAY

The Czech Republic at the close of 2011 found itself in a situation that's become distressingly familiar in recent years: struggling with both a dysfunctional government and a weak economy.

For most of the past 20 years since the fall of Communism, the country has had it relatively easy. Helped by a massive influx of tourist dollars, billions more in foreign investment, and a post-revolutionary president, the late Václav Havel, admired around the world, the Czech Republic was arguably the most successful of the former Eastern bloc states. The country was among the first former Soviet satellites to be brought into the NATO military alliance (1999) and entered the European Union in the first wave of Eastern expansion in 2004.

But then the global economic crisis came along at the end of 2008, and things started to go south fast (see "Economy," below). Though Czechs appear to have escaped the worst of the downturn, they nonetheless felt the global chill in trade and investment; the years from 2009 to 2011 marked the economy's worst period since the 1989 Velvet Revolution that overthrew Communism. One casualty of the crisis appears to be plans to adopt the euro. The Czechs were never enthusiastic about the E.U.'s common currency, but now any plans to use the euro have been put on indefinite hold.

To make matters worse, the Czech Republic's two main political parties are again at each other's throats as this book goes to press (see "Domestic Politics," below). Political infighting brought the government down in the middle of 2009 (inconveniently coming as the country held the E.U.'s rotating presidency), and throughout much of 2011, a rash of corruption scandals threatened to bring down the fragile center-right government that had been stitched together from the ashes. Fortunately for short-term visitors, none of this is likely to matter much. The Czechs have seen their share of unstable governments and the country continues to soldier on.

Not even the weak economy could prevent Prague from embarking on its most ambitious series of capital investments since the building of the metro in the 1970s and '80s. Everywhere you look these days, you see cranes, backhoes, and scaffolding.

The main train station, Hlavní nádraží, is in the midst of a multiyear rebuilding phase until 2014 that's hoped to clean it up and make it a more attractive gateway to the nation's capital. Cultural authorities meantime have shut down the National Museum at the top of Wenceslas Square for a long renovation (until at least 2015).

The biggest project of all, and one of the costliest construction feats now underway in the entire E.U., is the Blanka Tunnel in Letná, north of the Old Town across the Vltava River, and the extension of metro line A (green) eventually to Prague Airport (by 2016 or later). The Blanka tunnel will stretch several miles underground and one day will form part of an ambitious ring-road system to route vehicles away from the city center. For visitors, the immediate effect of all the building is the near-constant rerouting of tram and bus lines. Take all transportation advice in this guide with a grain of salt. They are accurate as this book goes to press, but tramlines can change from day to day.

Domestic Politics

While the average visitor isn't likely to notice, the Czech Republic is blessed (if that's the right word!) with perhaps Europe's most dysfunctional government (and with Poland, Slovakia, and Hungary in the mix, which says a lot). The two main parties, the center-right Civic Democratic Party (ODS) and the center-left Social Democratic Party (ČSSD), are locked in constant battle, though neither party commands a sufficient majority to form a stable government on its own. The result has been a succession of weak coalitions involving one or the other main party and linking smaller parties with often-contradictory aims.

At press time, it was a dysfunctional center-right coalition that held sway, with a predictable number of corruption scandals that threatened each week to bring the government down. None of this strikes the average Czech as unusual in any way. The country has been beset by unstable governments since the Velvet Revolution and continues to thrive in spite of it.

Added to this volatile mix is President Václav Klaus, the man who succeeded Václav Havel as president in 2003. Apart from having the same first name, Klaus bears absolutely no resemblance to his predecessor. He's carved out a niche as a right-wing iconoclast, firmly anti-E.U. in his politics and a strong opponent of climate-change legislation or anything else that in his eyes smacks of "Bolshevism." Though he's far to the right of most of his countrymen, he continues to enjoy broad support.

Economy

The global economic downturn of 2009 to 2011 hit the high-flying Czech economy disproportionately hard. Before the crisis, the economy was growing on the order of 5% to 6% a year. This level of growth was considered necessary if the country hoped to catch up with western Europe in a generation. During the worst years of the economic crisis, the economy actually contracted, not expanded.

While you're not likely to notice it while strolling through Prague, the Czech economy is actually highly industrialized. Exports include automobiles and big-ticket capital goods like trams, trains, and buses. Orders for all these dried up as the downturn swept across Europe and the rest of the world.

Still, the Czech Republic appears to be weathering the storm better than its peers in central Europe. There was no run on the Czech crown, for example, comparable to the Hungarian forint. Indeed, the crown held its own with respect to the euro and strengthened against the U.S. dollar. Prague, with its reliance on tourism, was partially buffered from the economic malaise, but the capital too suffered from a drop in the number of visitors. Many restaurants and shops dependent on the tourist trade suffered, and several properties went belly up. Hotels responded by discounting room rates to a fraction of their pre-crisis levels. While 2011 saw a slight rebound in hotel prices, it was still possible on some nights to book a four-star room in the center of town for under US$100. These deals could very well be on offer in 2012 too.

One note of caution: Because of the economic difficulties, some of the properties listed in this book may no longer be in business by the time you read this. At press time, it was impossible to predict with any accuracy who might and might not survive.

2 | LOOKING BACK: PRAGUE & CZECH HISTORY

The Beginning

The word "Bohemia," now used to describe the westernmost province of the country, comes from an ancient Celtic tribe, the *Boii*, who once lived on the territory of the modern-day Czech Republic. The Boii settled here some 300 years before Christ in the land around the Vltava River. The Latin term *Bohemia* (land of the Boii) became etched in history.

Those early years were marked by strife between local Celtic tribes and Germanic tribes, like the Marcomanni, who managed to expel the Boii around 100 B.C., only to be chucked out in turn by the Huns by A.D. 450. The Huns were then expelled by a Turkic tribe, the Avars, a century later.

Shortly after this began the great Slavic migration of peoples westward from parts of Asia across the Carpathian Mountains into Europe. The westernmost of these Slavic tribes tried to set up a kingdom in Bohemia. The farming Slavs often fell prey to the nomadic Avars, but in 624 a Franconian merchant named Samo united the Slavs and began expelling the Avars from central Europe.

The Great Moravian Empire

Throughout the 9th century, the Slavs around the Morava River consolidated their power. Mojmír I declared his Great Moravian Empire—a kingdom that eventually encompassed Bohemia, Slovakia, and parts of modern-day Poland and Hungary—as a Christian organization still outside the boundaries of the Holy Roman Empire.

In 863, the Greek brothers Cyril and Methodius arrived in Moravia to preach the Eastern Christian rite to a people who didn't understand them. They created a new language, mixing Slavic with a separate script, Cyrillic. When Methodius died in 885, the Moravian rulers reestablished the Latin liturgy, though followers of Cyril and Methodius continued to preach their faith in missions to the east. Ultimately the Slavonic rite took hold in Kiev and Russia, where the Cyrillic alphabet is still used, while western Slavs kept the Latin script and followed Rome.

The Great Moravian Empire lasted about a century—until the Magyar invasion of 896—and not until the 20th century would the Czechs and Slovaks unite again under a single government. After the invasion, the Slavs living east of the Morava River swore allegiance to the Magyars, while the Czechs, who lived west of the river, fell under the authority of the Holy Roman Empire.

Bohemia Looks to the West

Bořivoj, the first king of the now-separate Bohemia and Moravia, built Prague's first royal palace at the end of the 9th century on the site of the present Prague Castle on Hradčany Hill. In 973, a bishopric was established in Prague, answering to the archbishopric of Mainz. Thus, before the end of the first millennium, the German influence in Bohemia was firmly established.

The kings who followed Bořivoj in the Přemyslid dynasty ruled over Bohemia for more than 300 years, during which time Prague became a major commercial area along central Europe's trade routes. In the 12th century, two fortified castles were built at Vyšehrad and Hradčany, and a wooden plank bridge stood near where the stone Charles Bridge spans the Vltava today. Václavské náměstí (Wenceslas Sq.) was a horse market, and the city's 3,500 residents rarely lived to the age of 45. In 1234, Staré Město (Old Town), the first of Prague's historic five towns, was founded.

Encouraged by Bohemia's rulers, who guaranteed German civic rights to western settlers, Germans founded entire towns around Prague, including Malá Strana (Lesser Town) in 1257. The Přemyslid dynasty of the Czechs ended with the 1306 death of teenage Václav III, who had no heirs. After much debate, the throne was offered to John of Luxembourg, husband of Václav III's younger sister, a foreigner who knew little of Bohemia. It was John's firstborn son who left the most lasting marks on Prague.

Prague's First "Golden Age"

Charles IV (Karel IV) took the throne when his father died fighting in France in 1346. Educated among French royalty and fluent in four languages (but not initially Czech), Charles almost single-handedly ushered in Prague's first golden age (the second occurred in the late 16th c.). Even before his reign, Charles wanted to make Prague a glorious city. In 1344, he won an archbishopric for Prague independent of Mainz. When he became king of Bohemia, Charles also became, by election, Holy Roman Emperor.

During the next 30 years, Charles transformed Prague into the bustling capital of the Holy Roman Empire and one of Europe's most important cities, with some of the most glorious architecture of the day. He commissioned St. Vitus Cathedral's construction at Prague Castle as well as the bridge that would eventually bear his name. He was most proud of founding Prague University in 1348, the first higher-education institution in central Europe, now known as Charles University. In 1378, Charles died of natural causes at age 62.

The Protestant Reformation and the Hussite Wars

While Charles IV was the most heralded of the Bohemian kings, the short reign of his son Václav IV was marked by social upheaval, a devastating plague, and the advent of turbulent religious dissent.

Reformist priest Jan Hus drew large crowds to Bethlehem Chapel, where he preached against what he considered the corrupt tendencies of Prague's bishopric. Hus became widely popular among Czech nationals who rallied behind his crusade against the German-dominated establishment. Excommunicated in 1412 and charged with heresy 2 years later, Hus was burned at the stake on July 6, 1415, in Konstanz (Constance), Germany, an event that sparked widespread riots and ultimately civil war. Czechs still commemorate the day as a national holiday.

The hostilities began simply enough. Rioting Hussites (followers of Jan Hus) threw several Roman Catholic councilors to their deaths from the windows of Prague's New Town Hall (Novoměstská radnice) in 1419, a deed known as the "First Defenestration." It didn't take long for the pope to declare a crusade against the Czech heretics. The conflict widened, and by 1420, several major battles were being fought between the peasant Hussites and the Catholic crusaders, who were supported by the nobility.

- **Princess Libuše** (pre–9th c.) Fabled mother of Bohemia. Legend holds that the clairvoyant Libuše, the daughter of Bohemian philosopher Krok, stood on Vyšehrad Hill and foretold that on this land a great city would stand. She and Prince Přemysl Oráč declared the first Bohemian state, launching the Přemyslid dynasty, which lasted from the 10th to the 12th century.

- **St. Wenceslas (Svatý Václav;** ca. 907–35) Patron saint of Bohemia. Prince Wenceslas was executed at the site of the present-day city of Stará Boleslav—on the orders of his younger brother, Boleslav, who took over the Bohemian throne. A popular cult arose proclaiming the affable and learned Prince Wenceslas as the perpetual spiritual ruler of all Czechs. A statue of him at the top of the square was erected in 1912.

- **Charles IV (Karel IV;** 1316–78) Bohemian king, Holy Roman Emperor, and chief patron of Prague. Born to John of Luxembourg and Eliška, the sister of the last Přemyslid king. Charles ascended the throne in 1346, and during his reign he made Prague the seat of the Holy Roman Empire and one of Europe's most advanced cities. He also inspired several key sites through the country, including Prague's university (Univerzita Karlova), stone bridge (Karlův most), largest New Town park (Karlovo nám.), and the spa town of Karlovy Vary.

- **Master Jan Hus** (1369 or 1370–1415) Religious reformer, university lecturer, and Czech nationalist symbol. Hus questioned the authority of the pope and called for the formation of a Bohemian National Church. From his stronghold at Bethlehem Chapel in Old Town, he declared that the powerful clergy should cede their property and influence to the people. In 1414, he was summoned to explain his views before the Ecclesiastic Council at Konstanz in Germany but was arrested on arrival. He was burned at the stake as a heretic on July 6, 1415, a day considered the precursor to the Hussite Wars and now a Czech national holiday. His church lives on today in the faith called the Czech Brethren.

- **Bedřich Smetana** (1824–84) Nationalist composer. After studying piano and musical theory in Prague, Smetana became one of Bohemia's most revered composers, famous for his fierce nationalism. His *Vltava* movement in the symphony *Má Vlast (My Country)* is performed on the opening night of the Prague Spring Music Festival. His opera *The Bartered Bride* takes a jaunty look at Czech farm life.

- **Antonín Dvořák** (1841–1904) Neo-Romantic composer and head of Prague Conservatory. Dvořák is best known for his symphony *From the New World*, which was inspired by a tour of the United States. His opera about a girl trapped in a water world, *Rusalka*, remains an international favorite; it became a popular film in Europe, starring Slovak actress Magda Vášáryová.

- **Franz Kafka** (1883–1924) Writer. Kafka was a German-Jewish Praguer who for much of his adult life worked in relative obscurity as a sad Prague insurance clerk. In works such as *The Metamorphosis*, *The Castle*, and *Amerika*, Kafka described surreal and suffocating worlds of confusion. Now many use the adjective *Kafkaesque* to mean "living in absurdity."

- **Tomáš G. Masaryk** (1850–1937) Philosopher, professor, and Czechoslovakia's first president. Educated in Vienna and Leipzig, Masaryk spent decades advocating Czech statehood. In 1915, he made a landmark speech in Geneva calling for the end of the Habsburg monarchy. He received the backing of President Woodrow Wilson at the end of World War I for a sovereign republic of Czechs and Slovaks, which was founded in October 1918. He served nearly 17 years as president of the new republic.

- **Alexander Dubček** (1921–92) Government leader. Though he's not a Czech, Dubček is a key figure in the history of Prague and the country. A Slovak Communist, he became the first secretary of the Communist Party in January 1968, presiding over the "Prague Spring" reforms. After he was ousted in the August 1968 Soviet-led invasion, Dubček faded from view, only later to stand with Havel to declare the end of hard-line Communist rule in 1989. He returned to become speaker of Parliament after the Velvet Revolution but was killed in a car accident in 1992.

- **Václav Havel** (1936–2011) Author, dissident, ex-president. Absurdist playwright in the 1960s, Havel became a leading figure in the prodemocracy movement Charter 77 and the first president after leading the Velvet Revolution. See the box "Václav Havel & the 1970s," p. 21.

Among other famous Czechs are Oscar-winning film director **Miloš Forman** *(Amadeus, One Flew Over the Cuckoo's Nest)* and **Milan Kundera,** the author of *The Unbearable Lightness of Being* and other widely admired works about 20th-century Czech life. Kundera is now a French citizen and bitterly refuses to make a public return to his homeland, after having left during the dark days of Communist "normalization."

The Czech Republic is the homeland of many supermodels. Former Wonderbra icon **Eva Herzigová** hails from the blue-collar northern Bohemian industrial berg of Litvínov—whose smokestacks are about as far removed as you can get from the catwalks. Model, actress, and writer **Paulina Pořízková** is from the town of Prostějov; recently crowned the "Sexiest Woman Alive," **Karolína Kurková** is from Děčín, near the German border; and tsunami survivor and activist **Petra Němcová** is from Karviná, in Moravia.

With U.S. businessman Donald Trump back in the news, mention should be made of his ex-wife, **Ivana Trump,** who was born in the town of Zlín, to the east of Prague in Moravia. The woman who first defined the term "Velvet Divorce" was a skier on the Czechoslovak National Team and a model before marrying "The Donald" in 1977 (divorcing in 1991). Her first novel, *For Love Alone*, took place partly in Bohemia.

A schism split the Hussites when a more moderate faction, known as the Utraquists, signed a 1433 peace agreement with Rome at the Council of Basel. Still, the more radical Taborites continued to fight, until they were decisively defeated at the Battle of Lipany a year later.

Rudolf II & the Second "Golden Age"

Following this period of hostility, the nobility of Bohemia concentrated its power, forming fiefdoms called the Estates. In 1526, the nobles elected Archduke Ferdinand king of Bohemia, marking the beginning of Roman Catholic rule by the Vienna-based Habsburg family, which continued until the end of World War I.

Habsburg Emperor Rudolf II ascended to the throne in 1576 but uncharacteristically for a Habsburg chose to live in Prague rather than Vienna. This led to what became Prague's second golden age. Rudolf invited the great astronomers Johannes Kepler and Tycho Brahe to Prague and endowed the city's museums with some of Europe's finest art. The Rudolfinum, which was recently restored and houses the Czech Philharmonic, pays tribute to Rudolf's opulence.

Rudolf was relatively tolerant to the city's Jews, even hiring for a time the head of the Jewish community, Mordechai Maisel, to manage his financial affairs. Many of the splendors of Prague Jewish quarter, Josefov, were built during this time.

Rudolf brought many benefits to Prague but ultimately failed to resolve the ever-present split between Catholics and Protestants, setting the stage for the coming Thirty Years' War in Europe, a conflagration that eventually torched the entire continent and had no peer in terms of destruction until the world wars of the 20th century.

Prague has the dubious distinction as being the place where the war started. Conflicts between the Catholic Habsburgs and Bohemia's ever-present Protestant nobility came to a head on May 23, 1618, when two Catholic governors were thrown out of the windows of Prague Castle, in the Second Defenestration. The war lasted until 1648, with the defeat of the Swedish army on the Charles Bridge (you can still see war damage on the side of the Old Town Bridge Tower). The war came to an end with the Peace of Westphalia.

The Battle of White Mountain & the Austrian Occupation

The Thirty Years' War was a tragic setback for the Czechs and the Czech nation. One of the early decisive battles, presaging the Habsburg Catholics' sweeping victory in the Czech lands, was fought in 1620 on a hill in western Prague known as "Bílá Hora" (White Mountain).

The Czechs were ruled by their Protestant king, Frederick V of Palatinate. But Frederick was a lackluster commander-in-chief and the Habsburgs won decisively in a battle that lasted just 2 hours. The immediate repercussions were severe. The Austrians arrested some 47 Bohemian noblemen and publicly executed 27. Today, you'll find 27 crosses on the ground of Old Town Square to commemorate the executions. Following the battle, Frederick was run out of town to be forever known mockingly as the "Winter King," since he lasted just one winter on the throne. The Habsburgs went on to rule over the Czech lands for the next 300 years.

Vienna's triumph was Prague's loss, and the empire's focus shifted back to Vienna. Fresh waves of immigrants turned Prague and other towns into Germanic cities. By the end of the 18th century, Prague was dominated by Germans and the Czech language was on the verge of dying out.

Into the 20th Century & the Founding of Czechoslovakia

In the 19th century, the Industrial Revolution drew Czechs from the countryside into Prague, where a Czech national revival began.

As the economy grew, Prague's Czech population increased in number and power, eventually overtaking the Germans by around midcentury. In 1868, the Czech people threw open the doors to the gilded symbol of their revival, the neo-Renaissance National Theater (Národní divadlo), with the bold proclamation NÁROD SOBĚ ("The Nation for Itself") inscribed over the proscenium. Then, in 1890, at the top of Wenceslas Square, the massive National Museum Building (Národní muzeum) opened, packed with exhibits celebrating the rich history and culture of the Czech people.

As Czech political parties continued to call for more autonomy from Vienna, Archduke Ferdinand and his wife, Sophie, were assassinated in 1914 in Sarajevo, setting off World War I later that same year. Meanwhile, a 65-year-old philosophy professor named Tomáš G. Masaryk seized the opportunity to tour Europe and America, speaking in favor of creating a combined democratic Czech and Slovak state.

As the German and Austrian armies wore down in 1918, the concept of "Czechoslovakia" gained international support. U.S. President Woodrow Wilson backed Masaryk on October 18, 1918, in Washington, D.C., as the professor proclaimed the independence of the Czechoslovak Republic in the Washington Declaration. On October 28, 1918, the sovereign Republic of Czechoslovakia was founded in Prague. Masaryk returned home in December after being elected (in absentia) Czechoslovakia's first president.

The "First Republic": 1918–38

The 1920s ushered in an exceptional but brief period of freedom and prosperity in Prague. Czechoslovakia, its industrial strength intact after the war, was one of the 10 strongest economies in the world. Prague's capitalists lived the Jazz Age on par with New York's industrial barons. Palatial Art Nouveau villas graced the fashionable Bubeneč and Hanspaulka districts, where smart parties were held nonstop.

The Great Depression gradually spread to Prague, however, drawing sharper lines between the classes and nationalities. As ethnic Germans in Czech border regions found a champion in the new German Chancellor Adolf Hitler in 1933, their calls to unify under the Third Reich grew louder.

In 1938, Britain's Neville Chamberlain and France's Edouard Daladier, seeking to avoid conflict with the increasingly belligerent Germans, met Hitler and Italy's Benito Mussolini in Munich. With the signing of the "Munich Accord," they agreed to cede the Bohemian border areas (which Germans called the "Sudetenland") to Hitler on September 30 and marked one of the darkest days in Czech history. Chamberlain returned to London to tell a cheering crowd that he'd achieved "peace in our time." But within a year, Hitler had absorbed the rest of the Czech lands and installed a puppet government in Slovakia. Soon Europe was again at war.

World War II

During the next 6 years, more than 130,000 Czechs were killed, including more than 80,000 Jews. Though Hitler ordered devastation for other cities, he sought to preserve Prague and its Jewish ghetto as part of his planned museum of the extinct race.

The Nazi concentration camp at Terezín, about 48km (30 miles) northwest of Prague, became a way station for many Czech Jews bound for death camps at Auschwitz and points east. Thousands died of starvation and disease at Terezín even though the Nazis managed to dress it up as a "show" camp for Red Cross investigators. Meanwhile, the Czechoslovak government in exile, led by Masaryk's successor, Edvard Beneš, tried to organize resistance from friendly territory in London. One initiative came in May 1942, when Czechoslovak paratroopers were flown in to assassinate Hitler's lead man in Prague, Reich Protector Reinhard Heydrich. The paratroopers managed to set a charge to blow up Heydrich's motorcade as it passed along a road north of Prague. Heydrich survived the initial blast, but died in the hospital days later. Hitler retaliated by ordering the total liquidation of a nearby Czech village, Lidice, where 192 men were shot dead and more than 300 women and children were sent to concentration camps. Every building in the town was bulldozed to the ground. The paratroopers, Jozef Gabčík and Jan Kubiš, and some of their civilian helpers, were hunted down by Nazi police and trapped in the Cyril and Methodius church on Resslova Street in Nové Město near the Vltava. They reportedly shot themselves to avoid being captured. The debate still rages on whether the assassination brought anything but more terror to occupied Bohemia.

Communism Comes to the Czech Lands

The final act of World War II in Europe played out where the Nazis started it, in Bohemia. As U.S. troops liberated the western part of the country, Gen. George Patton was told to hold his troops at Plzeň and wait for the Soviet army to sweep through Prague because of the Allied Powers' agreement made at Yalta months before. Soviet soldiers and Czech civilians liberated Prague in a bloody street battle on the last days of the war. Throughout Prague you can see small wall memorials on the spots where Czechs fell battling the Germans.

On his return from exile in England, Edvard Beneš ordered the expulsion of 2.5 million Germans from Czechoslovakia and the confiscation of all their property. Many thousands of Germans were killed in reprisal attacks. The "Beneš Decrees" are still an occasional bone of contention between the Czech and German governments. Meanwhile, the Czechoslovak government, exhausted and bewildered by fascism, nationalized 60% of the country's industries, and many looked to Soviet-style Communism as a new model. Elections were held in 1946, and Communist leader Klement Gottwald became prime minister after his party won about one-third of the vote.

Through a series of cabinet maneuvers, Communists seized full control of the government in a bloodless coup in February 1948, and Beneš was ousted. Little dissent was tolerated, and a series of show trials began, purging hundreds of perceived threats to Stalinist Communist authority. Another wave of political refugees fled the country. The sterile, centrally planned Communist architecture began seeping into classical Prague.

1968 & The Prague Spring

In January 1968, Alexander Dubček, a career Slovak Communist, became first secretary of the Czechoslovak Communist Party. Long before Mikhail Gorbachev, Dubček tinkered with Communist reforms that he called "socialism with a human face." His program of political, economic, and social reform (while seeking to maintain one-party rule) blossomed into a brief intellectual and artistic renaissance known as the "Prague Spring."

Václav Havel & the 1970s

In 1976, during the worst of "normalization," the Communists arrested a popular underground rock band called the Plastic People of the Universe on charges of disturbing the peace. This motivated some of Prague's most prominent artists, writers, and intellectuals, led by playwright Václav Havel, to establish Charter 77, a human-rights advocacy group formed to pressure the government—then Europe's most repressive—into observing the human rights principles of the 1975 Helsinki Accords. In the years that followed, Havel, the group's perceived leader, was constantly monitored by the secret police, the StB. He was put under house arrest and jailed several times for "threatening public order."

Increasingly nervous about what seemed to them a loss of party control, Communist hard-liners in Prague and other eastern European capitals conspired with the Soviet Union to remove Dubček and his government from power. On August 21, 1968, Prague awoke to the rumble of tanks and 200,000 invading Warsaw Pact soldiers claiming "fraternal assistance." Believing that they'd be welcomed as liberators, these soldiers from the Soviet Union, Poland, East Germany, Bulgaria, and Hungary were bewildered when angry Czechs confronted them with rocks and flaming torches. The Communist grip tightened, however, and Prague fell deeper into the Soviet sphere of influence. Another wave of refugees fled. The following January, a university student named Jan Palach, in a lonely protest to Soviet occupation, doused himself with gasoline and set himself afire in Wenceslas Square. He died days later, becoming a martyr for the dissident movement. But the Soviet soldiers stayed for more than 2 decades during the gray period the Communists called "normalization."

The Velvet Revolution & Beyond

Just after the Berlin Wall fell, and with major change imminent in the rest of central and eastern Europe, thousands of students set out on a chilly candlelit march on November 17, 1989. As part of their nonviolent campaign, they held signs calling for a dialogue with the government. Against police warnings, they paraded from the southern citadel at Vyšehrad and turned up National Boulevard (Národní třída), where they soon met columns of helmeted riot police. Holding their fingers in peace signs and chanting, "Our hands are free," the bravest 500 sat down at the feet of the police. After an excruciating standoff, the police moved in, squeezing the students against buildings and beating them with clubs.

Although nobody was killed and the official Communist-run media presented the story as the quiet, justified end to the whims of student radicals, clandestine videotapes and accounts of the incident blanketed the country. By the next day, Praguers began organizing their outrage. Havel and his artistic allies seized the moment and called a meeting of intellectuals at the Laterna Magika on Národní, where they planned more nonviolent protests. Students and theaters went on strike, and hundreds of thousands of Praguers began pouring into Wenceslas Square, chanting for the end of Communist rule. Within days, factory workers and citizens in towns throughout the country joined in a general strike. On Wenceslas Square, the protesters jingled their keys, a signal to the Politburo that it was time to go. By the end of the year, the Communist government fell and on New Year's Eve, Havel, joined by

Dubček, gave his first speech as president of a free Czechoslovakia. Because hardly any blood was spilled, the coup was dubbed "the Velvet Revolution."

The 1990s brought both democracy and free-market capitalism to the country, with the early phases marked by wild corruption sprees, when the whole of Eastern Europe was known as "the Wild East." Czechoslovakia as a country was unable to resist the pressures of freedom as Slovaks stepped up their demands for an independent state. Czechoslovakia split peacefully into the independent Czech and Slovak republics on January 1, 1993.

Prosperity eventually returned to the country by the end of the 1990s and the Czechs realized a long-held foreign policy goal in 2004 of joining the European Union. One major setback came in 2002, with the tragic flooding of the Vltava that inundated large parts of Malá Strana and other riverside districts, but luckily spared much of the Old Town. The damage ran into the billions of euros, but the city managed to turn the tragedy into a boon, using the reconstruction effort to rebuild large sections of the city, like Smíchov, Holešovice, and Karlín, that had been neglected for decades. Much transformation work still needs to be done and corruption remains a chronic problem, but the general consensus is that the Czechs have somehow clawed their way back into the Western family of nations and this time may be there to stay.

ART & ARCHITECTURE

Prague wears its history on its sleeve. Spared large-scale destruction during World War II, the city's medieval core remains largely intact. For history buffs, a walk down nearly any street in the Old Town is a real-life power-point presentation on 8 centuries of history. A little knowledge of architecture goes a long way toward helping to decode it.

ROMANESQUE

Romanesque architecture dates from the turn of the first millennium and is the style of the oldest buildings still standing in Prague. Romanesque exteriors are often circular (a rotunda), and the interiors are starker and simpler than Gothic. Prague's finest Romanesque building is **St. George's Basilica** at the Prague Castle complex (see chapter 7, p. 147). Look past the building's misleading 17th-century facade to find a starkly beautiful stone interior with a lovely vaulted ceiling.

GOTHIC

Ask any Praguer what his or her favorite architectural style is and chances are he or she will say Gothic. It's no wonder. Gothic's signature soaring towers, spires, and buttresses are deeply connected to Prague's rise in the 14th century as one of Europe's great cities and its brief but impressive period as capital of the Holy Roman Empire under Charles IV.

In Prague's heyday, the best architects of the time came here to build Charles's vision for a capital worthy of the empire. These included Petr Parléř, who oversaw the building of **St. Vitus Cathedral** (p. 98), and Benedikt Ried, whose soaring ceiling in the **Vladislav Hall** (p. 98) at Prague Castle is consider a highpoint of late Gothic. Ried was also involved in building Kutná Hora's great **St. Barbara's Cathedral.**

Great Gothic buildings read like a greatest hits collection of the city's architecture. In addition to St. Vitus and the Old Royal Palace, there's the **Týn Church,** the **Old Town Hall and Astronomical Clock,** and even the foundations of **Charles**

Bridge itself (but not the statues—they came later). See chapter 6 for more on these structures.

RENAISSANCE

Bohemia also participated in the great European renaissance of the 16th century, with its emphasis on classical and mythical figures, and above all harmony and symmetry in architectural design. Renaissance came to Prague via the Habsburgs and the nobility and their love of Italian style.

Renaissance buildings are easy to spot; just look for the trademark *sgraffito*—geometric or figurative designs etched into a building's stucco exterior. The **Schwarzenberg Palace** on Hradčanské náměstí, across from the entrance to Prague Castle, is the city's best example of Renaissance architecture.

BAROQUE

Baroque architecture is inevitably linked to the twin triumphs of the Austrian Habsburg Empire and the Roman Catholic Church following the 1620 Battle of White Mountain and efforts to indoctrinate the Czechs with over-the-top displays of power and wealth. You can forget the architectural adage "less is more." With baroque, more is definitely more. Signature elements include big cupolas, marble columns, ornately painted frescoes, and all manner of marble and gold.

The most important baroque buildings in Prague are doubtless the **St. Nicholas Cathedral** in Malá Strana (p. 103) and the bright pink **Kinský Palace** on Old Town Square, as well as many of the palaces in Malá Strana. The baroque period was an intensively active one; many church interiors in Prague (regardless of the exterior style) have lavish baroque interiors.

19TH-CENTURY NEOCLASSICAL & OTHER "NEOS"

The 19th century saw the reemergence of the Czech nation, and 19th-century buildings are invariably tied up with Czech nationalism. Unfortunately, the century was a relatively boring period for architectural invention. Prague architects took their cues from Vienna, which was in the thrall of "historicism"—basically copying historic styles such as Gothic, Classic, and Renaissance and appending the prefix "neo" to the front.

Landmark buildings from this time include the neo-Renaissance **National Theater, National Museum,** and **Rudolfinum** (p. 178). This is also when Prague received all those Gothic spires that inspired its nickname of "City of a Thousand Spires." During the latter part of the 19th century, "neo-Gothic" was all the rage.

ART NOUVEAU & "CUBISM"

The turn of the 19th century elicited a strong reaction from Prague architects, tired of the sterility of the previous decades. Art Nouveau, with its wavy lines, florid designs, and conscious ornamentation, was everything neoclassical was not. Prague Art Nouveau emerged as a synthesis of the prevailing Parisian style mixed in elements of the more subdued Viennese Secession style. Today, buildings of both types can be found in the city center.

The best example of the Parisian variant is the **Obecní Dům** (Municipal House), just off of Náměstí Republiky (p. 112). For Secession, check out the **turn-of-the-19th-century apartment buildings** in Josefov, along Pařížská and around the former Jewish quarter. You can't help but notice the inlaid jewel- and tile-work embedded into the facades like a finely crafted jewelry box.

Cubism came a few years later and like Art Nouveau was a reaction to the sterility of the 19th century. Cubism was a purely Czech invention that never caught on outside the country's borders; nevertheless, the Cubist effects are striking. Check out the facade on the **House at the Black Mother of God,** just off of Celetná in the Old Town (p. 113).

2 FUNCTIONALIST & COMMUNIST

These styles bear a superficial resemblance, but in fact have nothing to do with each other. Functionalism was a style that arose in the 1920s, greatly influenced by Germany's Bauhaus, that sought to strip away all unnecessary ornamentation from a building, leaving in its place clean, horizontal lines and spare but pleasing boxy shapes.

Arguably, the best Functionalist building in Prague is the 1928 **Veletržní palác** in Holešovice, originally built as an exhibition space for trade fairs and now housing the National Gallery's Museum of 20th and 21st Century Art.

Communist style, by contrast, came after World War II with the ascendancy of the Communist regime. These buildings are boxy too, but the boxes reflect more a lack of imagination and money than any conscious style choice. One of the more celebrated (and controversial) Communist buildings is the 1975 **Kotva** department store, built in Brutalist style, just off of Náměstí Republiky in the Old Town.

The brief exception to the uniformity of Communist architecture came with 1950s' Socialist-Realist style, where architects tried consciously to imitate Stalin's tastes. One of the very few examples of Socialist Realist architecture in Prague is the former **Hotel International** in Dejvice (now home to the **Crowne Plaza Hotel**).

Art in the Czech Republic

The Czech contribution to painting and the visual arts has not been as profound as in other areas, like literature, film, and architecture. Czech painters, in general, didn't break out in a big way until the 19th century and the coming of the Czech National Revival movement, with painters like Mikuláš Aleš and Antonín and Josef Mánes. The best of these mainly realist and landscape paintings can be found in the Museum of Czech 19th-Century Art at St. George's Convent in the Prague Castle complex (see chapter 6, p. 108). The Art Nouveau style of the early 20th century saw the emergence of the country's first (and possibly only) household name in painting, Alfons Mucha. Mucha's work can be viewed in the stained-glass windows at St. Vitus Cathedral, as well as at the Obecní Dům and at the Alfons Mucha Museum in Nové Město (New Town; see chapter 6).

The first decades of the 20th century, the early Modern period, saw an explosion of Czech talent working in styles like Cubism, Constructivism, and Surrealism. Check out painters such as Bohumil Kubišta, Josef Šíma, and the female Surrealist Toyen at the National Gallery's Museum of 20th and 21st Century Art in Holešovice (p. 108).

World War II and the Communist takeover put an end to much of this output and for several years, Czech painters were constrained to working in the "Socialist-Realist" style (essentially mimicking Soviet art and extolling the virtues of workers, peasants, and the Communist Party).

Against this relatively modest backdrop, it may come as a surprise that one of the biggest names in contemporary art these days is a Czech, David Černý, whose irreverent, tongue-in-cheek murals, statues, and installations have been exhibited around the world. Černý first came to fame in the early 1990s, when he painted a Russian tank—an official monument to commemorate the country's liberation after World War II by the Soviet Union—the very unmilitary color pink. Since then, he's gone on to do several more public installations around Prague that mostly mock the powers that be or are meant to question modern assumptions. The best of these include an installation of giant babies crawling up the Žižkov TV tower (possibly meant to suggest our dependence on the media for sustenance); a hanging statue of St. Wenceslas astride an upside-down horse (perhaps mocking Czechs' uncritical worship of their own history) inside the Lucerna shopping arcade (p. 118); and a statue of two men urinating together into a basin shaped like the Czech Republic (possibly a comment on the self-deprecating nature of Czechs or perhaps their propensity to urinate outside whenever or wherever the urge strikes) just near the entrance to the Hergetova Cihelna restaurant (p. 78).

Černý's most notorious and best-known installation is doubtless "Entropa," mounted in Brussels in 2009 to coincide with the Czech Republic's holding of the rotating European Union presidency. In an obvious breach of E.U. decorum, the installation viciously lampooned each of the E.U.'s 27 member states, depicting Germany, for example, covered in highways zigzagging vaguely in the shape of a swastika, or Romania as a Dracula theme park. Depending on your point of view, it was either deeply insulting or a brilliant send-up of European stereotypes. Neither the Czech government nor the bureaucrats in Brussels were amused and Bulgaria, portrayed by Černý as a squat toilet, even demanded that the installation be taken down. It was removed at the end of the Czech presidency in mid-2009 and has yet to find a permanent home.

PRAGUE & THE CZECHS IN POP CULTURE

Czech contributions to Western culture are not widely recognized outside the country's borders. That's a shame since despite being a relatively small country, the output in film, literature, and music has been nothing short of remarkable.

Film

Czech filmmaking has a long tradition, but the heyday came in the mid-1960s when a group of young directors made quirky films that managed to capture both the pathos of life under Communism and the Czechs' innate pluck and humor under adverse circumstances. These "New Wave" films, as they were called, took the world by storm, garnering two Oscars for best foreign film and several other nominations.

Jiří Menzel and Miloš Forman were the leading directors at the time. An easy-to-find example of this period's work (with English subtitles) is Menzel's Oscar-winning *Closely Watched Trains*, a snapshot of the odd routine at a rural Czech train station during the German occupation of World War II.

Forman made his splash with a quirky look at a night in the life of a town trying to have fun despite itself. *The Fireman's Ball* shows Forman's true mastery as he captures the essence of being stone-bored in a gray world, yet he still makes it thoughtful and funny. Of course, this was made before Forman emigrated to the big budgets of Hollywood and first shocked Americans with *Hair*. He then directed the Oscar-winning *One Flew Over the Cuckoo's Nest* and *Amadeus*. For *Amadeus*, Forman sought

Five Czech Films to Rent on DVD

A list of great Czech and Czechoslovak films could well run to several dozen, but these five convey a good flavor of Czech life over the decades, complete with ample doses of the Czech sardonic wit seen as necessary to making sense of it all. All five are available with English subtitles through services such as Amazon (www.amazon.com) or Netflix (www.netflix.com).

1. *Loves of a Blonde* (1966). Miloš Forman's New Wave masterwork artfully combines the tender sadness of unrequited love and the frustrations felt by a group of single women stuck in dead-end jobs in a Communist-Czechoslovak factory town.

2. *Amadeus* (1984). Forman's absorbing Oscar-winning Mozart drama was partly filmed in Prague, an homage to the city that appreciated Amadeus's genius long before Vienna and the rest of the world caught on.

3. *Closely Watched Trains* (1965). Jiří Menzel charmed the world with this Oscar-winning tragicomedy about Miloš, a young man with "issues" who only discovers his manhood in a futile act of resistance against the Nazis in World War II.

4. *The Unbearable Lightness of Being* (1988). Imperfect yet highly watchable adaptation of the Milan Kundera novel of the same name manages to capture something of Czech humor under adverse circumstances in the days before the Warsaw Pact invasion of 1968.

5. *Czech Dream* (Český sen; 2004). Offbeat documentary is a brilliant send-up of consumer capitalism and shows what can happen when a new shopping center offers impossibly low prices. The problem is, as the title implies, it's just a "dream."

authenticity, so he received special permission from the Communists to return to Prague; while filming, he brought back to life the original Estates' Theater (Stavovské divadlo), where Mozart first performed.

Czech-based directors after the New Wave mostly disappeared from view, but one stunningly brave film was made in 1970, as the repressive post-invasion period known as "normalization" began its long, cold freeze of talent. In *The Ear (Ucho)*, director Karel Kachyňa presents the anguished story of a man trapped in an apartment wired for sound, subject to the Communist leaders' obsession and paranoia with Moscow. That *The Ear* was made in the political environment of the time was astounding. That it was quickly banned wasn't. Fortunately, local TV has dusted off copies from the archives, and it has begun playing to art-house audiences again.

The film about Prague probably most familiar to American audiences is *The Unbearable Lightness of Being*, based on the book by émigré author Milan Kundera. Set in the days surrounding the 1968 Soviet invasion, the story draws on the psychology of three Czechs who can't escape their personal obsessions while the political world outside collapses around them. Many Czechs find the film disturbing, some because it hits home, others because they say it portrays a Western stereotype.

Nowadays, modern Czech directors are trying to get back some of that old mojo, but with only hit-and-miss successes. The father-and-son team of Zdeněk and Jan Svěrák did manage to win the Best Foreign Film Oscar in 1996 for *Kolja*, the bittersweet tale of an abandoned Russian boy grudgingly adopted by an aging Czech bachelor on the cusp of the 1989 revolution. Other important younger directors include Jan Hřebejk, who tends to make tough, unsympathetic films about modern life, like his 2004 *Horem Pádem* (Up and Down), and Petr Zelenka, who's made a series of offbeat, cult films that while all very different nevertheless manage to capture some of the absurdity of the 1960s' New Wave, such as 2002's *Rok dábla* (Year of the Devil), and *Knoflíkáři* (Buttoners).

The latest trend in Czech filmmaking appears to be setting films during the World War II Nazi occupation and the bleak period that came immediately after. The year 2010 saw no less than three big-budget films that dealt in some way with wartime Prague and its aftermath: *Tři sezóny v pekle* (3 Seasons in Hell), *Protektor,* and Jan Hřebejk's *Kawasakiho růže* (Kawasaki Rose). In 2011, audiences were treated to an absorbing and well-done motion picture on the tragedy at Lidice, called *Lidice,* starring Czech leading man Karel Rodan. Many of the best Czech films are available on DVD through Netflix or Amazon.

Prague has also become a popular location for shooting major motion pictures. Producer/actor Tom Cruise and director Brian De Palma chose it for the stunning night shots around Charles Bridge in the early scenes of *Mission: Impossible* (1996). During shooting, a verbal brawl broke out with Czech officials, who jacked up the rent for use of the riverside palace that acts as the American Embassy in the film (the palace is actually claimed by the von Liechtenstein family). Though Cruise vowed at the time never to return to Prague, he was back in 2010 to film the fourth installment of the Mission Impossible franchise, *Mission Impossible IV.*

Books
FICTION

Any discussion of Czech literature outside of the Czech Republic usually begins and ends with Milan Kundera, a brilliant novelist and essayist, whose earlier novels (at least) manage to be both fun reads and high-brow literature at the same time. Kundera began writing in 1960s, but chose to move to Paris in the mid-'70s after his biting satire of life in Communist Czechoslovakia ran afoul of the official view. Unfortunately, this choice to leave rather than stay and tough it out, paired with an attitude that seems to grow haughtier with every passing year, has turned nearly the whole country against him, and Czechs are now in the ironic position of loathing their only world-recognized literary genius. Nearly all of Kundera's early works are worth a read, but *The Unbearable Lightness of Being, The Book of Laughter and Forgetting,* and *The Joke* stand out as masterpieces.

In addition to Kundera, Czechoslovakia turned out several other writers of the first rank during the Communist period whose works are still readily available in English translation. Czechs themselves are unanimous in their praise for Bohumil Hrabal, noted for his wit, sense of humor, and feel for the Czech "everyman." Hrabal died in 1997 when he fell (so they said officially) out of a fifth-story window while trying to feed pigeons. His death was eerily similar to the fate of a character in one of his stories. He had two internationally acclaimed hits: *Closely Watched Trains* (also translated as *Closely Observed Trains,* on which the Menzel film was based), and *I Served the King of England.* When then-President Bill Clinton visited Prague in 1994, he asked to have a beer with Hrabal in the author's favorite Old Town haunt, the pub U Zlatého tygra (at the Golden Tiger).

Five Czech Books for the Plane or Backpack

Though publishers have dropped the ball in recent years when it comes to publishing English translations of Czech literature, fortunately there's a good body of work available in English, including most of the classics from the Communist period. Here is a highly subjective list of five "musts."

1. *The Joke*, Milan Kundera. Kundera's first novel was written in his country's brief period of relative freedom in the mid-1960s and tells the story of Ludvík, an enthusiastic young Communist whose sarcastic sense of humor puts him at odds with the party faithful and changes his life forever. Funny and moving in equal measure.

2. *I Served the King of England*, Bohumil Hrabal. Far more than Kundera, Czechs identify with Hrabal and his themes of quirkiness, absurdity, and human folly. This is his most accessible book in English and describes the hilarious rise and fall of an ambitious waiter during the Nazi occupation and the years immediately after.

3. *Life With a Star*, Jiří Weil. Weil wrote two classics on the fate of

Jews in Nazi-occupied Prague during World War II. This book tells the story of a young Jewish banker who goes undercover to save his life. The other, *Mendelssohn is on the Roof*, is equally gripping.

4. *The Good Soldier Švejk*, Jaroslav Hašek. Humorous tale of a Czech army recruit who'll do anything to avoid military service in the Austrian army during World War I, including acting the half-wit. Or maybe he really is that stupid? Czechs laugh, too, but tend to resent the portrayal; after reading it, at least you'll understand all those restaurants named "Švejk" around the country.

5. *The Castle*, Franz Kafka. Kafka is more widely appreciated than read, but give this book or his short-story collections a try to understand the complexities of modern life as viewed by a prescient German-speaking Jewish insurance salesman in the years during and after World War I. The ending is unsatisfying but chilling.

Another popular writer from this period, Ivan Klíma, is best known for his poignant short stories about Czech life in 1960s and '70s, collected in works like *My First Loves* and *My Merry Mornings*. He has also written several novels after 1989 that deal with the moral ambiguities of moving from Communism to capitalism. Of these, perhaps *Judge on Trial* remains the best.

Younger Czech writers have had a difficult time of it breaking onto the international stage. Part of the reason for this is economic—there just isn't the market in English that there used to be when Czechoslovakia was part of the Soviet bloc. That situation may be improving, however, and the past couple of years have seen two big translations in English of popular, contemporary Czech works of fiction: Petra Hůlová's *Pamět' mojí babičce* (in English as *All This Belongs To Me*) and Miloš Urban's *Sedmikosteli* (Seven Churches). The latter is a highly recommended, offbeat thriller that takes place amid the medieval churches of Prague's Nové Město.

Jaroslav Hašek wrote perhaps the best-known Czech novel of all time: *The Good Soldier Švejk*, a post–World War I satire about a simpleton soldier who wreaks havoc in the Austro-Hungarian army during the war.

No reading list would be complete without reference to Franz Kafka, Prague's most famous novelist, who wrote his originals in his native German. *The Collected Novels of Franz Kafka,* which includes *The Castle* and *The Trial,* binds his most claustrophobic works into a single volume.

NONFICTION

If it's contemporary philosophy you want, there is, of course, the philosopher ex-president. Several of Václav Havel's essays and books are available in English translation. For essays, try either *Living in Truth* or *Open Letters,* both containing works he wrote mainly in the 1970s and '80s about moral life in a Communist state. His best essay, "The Power of the Powerless," explained how the lethargic masses were allowing their complacency with Communism to sap their souls. *Disturbing the Peace* is an autobiographical meditation on childhood, the events of 1968, and Havel's involvement with Charter 77. His first recollections about entering politics are in "Summer Meditations," a long essay written during a vacation. Havel's most recent work *To the Castle and Back* (2008) recounts his ups and downs in high office as president of Czechoslovakia and later the Czech Republic from 1989 to 2003. Havel died on December 18, 2011, at the age of 75.

For an epic intellectual tour of the long, colorful, and often tragic history of the city, try the 1997 release of *Prague in Black and Gold* by native son and Yale literature professor Peter Demetz. His follow-up book, *Prague in Danger* (2008), is an absorbing history of Prague life during the Nazi occupation interwoven with poignant tales of Demetz's own family.

Music

Czechs have bequeathed the world at least three household names in classical music: **Antonín Dvořák, Bedřich Smetana,** and **Leoš Janáček,** as well as heaps of pop tunes that are mostly unknown beyond the country's borders but still fun to listen to.

Dvořák is best known to visitors for his *Symphony No. 9 (From the New World),* which was written during his stay in the United States in the 19th century and was so beloved it was taken to the moon by astronaut Neil Armstrong during his Apollo mission in 1969.

Smetana wrote probably the best-known piece of Czech classical music, the *Moldau Symphony* (Vltava), whose ominous low notes (like thunder rolls) will be instantly recognizable to any classical music lover. Smetana's composition was part of six symphonic poems entitled *Má Vlast* (My Homeland) that sums up perfectly in bars and measures Czechs' yearning for their own national identity in the 19th century.

Janáček, an early 20th century composer from Moravia, will be less familiar to most, but better known perhaps to hard-core opera lovers for compositions such *Kát'a Kabanová* and *The Cunning Little Vixen.* His works mix traditional Moravian folk melodies with modern impulses to create music that initially sounds discordant but soon grows on you.

Czech popular music came into its own in the 1960s with singers like Karel Gott (who is still going strong well into his 70s), Marta Kubišová, and Helena Vondráčková. Czech pop at the time was heavily influenced by Western bands like The Beatles, but nevertheless retains something of the naive hope and optimism of those days before the 1968 Warsaw Pact invasion when it seemed Czechoslovakia might actually break free of Communism.

Modern Czech popular music mimics international trends in rock, pop, electronic, and hip-hop. Some of the more popular bands include Čechomor (beautifully rendered folk ballads), Kabát (hard-core rock), Kryštof (catchy pop), and Support Lesbiens (tongue-in-cheek pop sung in English, and, yes, the misspelling is intentional).

EATING & DRINKING

Czech food is filling and hearty, and when it's done well is reminiscent of a good home-cooked meal. Not surprisingly, given the country's long period as part of the Austro-Hungarian Empire, Czech cuisine borrows heavily from its neighbors. The schnitzels, strudels, and goulashes you'll see on menus here have all been gently appropriated but often given a local twist. Czech goulash, for example, is milder than its Hungarian cousin and comes in a number of variations depending on whether the main ingredient is beef or pork. Schnitzels are typically built around fried chicken or pork instead of veal, normally the heart of a Viennese schnitzel.

If there's a uniquely Czech contribution in all of this, it's likely to be the bread or potato dumplings, *knedliky*, that accompany many main dishes. These are essentially big balls of dough prepared in boiling water that come sliced and (hopefully) steaming hot to your plate. They are great for soaking up the extra gravy or sauce from the goulash.

Traditional Meals

STARTERS

Traditional Czech meals invariable start out with a soup, often beef or chicken broth or maybe something heartier like *kulajda,* a potato-mushroom cream soup, seasoned with dill and a shot of vinegar to make it slightly sour. The herb soups are often the most piquant part of the meal, but the meat-based broths, whether chicken or beef, are frequently served without filtering the heavy renderings.

Appetizers are often passed over to get to the main course, but traditional starters are likely to include salads, ham rolls, and sometimes imported dishes like beef Carpaccio or smoked salmon.

MAIN COURSES

No self-respecting Czech restaurant could open its doors without serving at least some version of the three national foods: *vepřo, knedlo,* and *zelo* (pork, dumplings, and cabbage). The **pork** *(vepřové maso)* is usually a shoulder or brisket that is roasted and lightly seasoned or breaded and fried like a schnitzel *(řízek).* Unlike German sauerkraut, the **cabbage** *(zelí)* is boiled with a light sugar sauce. The **dumplings** are light and spongy if made from flour and bread *(houskové knedlíky),* or dense and pasty if made from flour and potatoes *(bramborové knedlíky).* This "VKZ" combo cries out for an original **Budweiser (Budvar), Kozel,** or **Pilsner Urquell** beer to wash it down.

Other standard main courses include *svíčková na smetaně,* slices of beef that are baked and served in a vegetable-based cream sauce served over tender, spongy, sliced dumplings; roast beef *(roštěná);* baked chicken *(grilované kuře);* and smoked ham and other spicy cured meats *(uzeniny).*

A local favorite is **cmunda,** found at the pub U medvídků (p. 184): a steaming potato pancake topped with sweet boiled red cabbage and spicy Moravian smoked pork. Also popular is **wild game,** such as venison, goose, rabbit, and duck, and the more exotic, like the wild boar goulash served at U modré kachničky (one of the better Czech-centric restaurants; p. 79). Czech sauces can be heavy and character-less but occasionally they are prepared with daring doses of spice.

There's also usually a good selection of indigenous freshwater fish, such as trout, perch, and carp, the Christmas favorite. People worry about the safety of waterways, but most fish served in Prague come from controlled fish farms. Since the country has no coastline, you'll find most **seafood** at the more expensive restaurants, but a growing selection of salmon, sea bass, shark, and shellfish is shipped in on ice.

Beer

Beer, called *pivo*, is the Czech national beverage. It's a perfectly acceptable accompaniment to either lunch or dinner (and occasionally even breakfast). You'll find it not only at the lowliest pubs but also the finest restaurants. Indeed, wherever Czechs congregate, you can be sure there will be a pub or a beer stand somewhere nearby. And it's not just a guy thing either; it's very popular with women too.

Beer goes back a long way. It's been served in pubs for centuries, often made by monks who lived off the proceeds. The earliest incarnations bore only a faint resemblance to what we consider beer nowadays. Modern-day Pilsner-style pale lager was first brewed in the western Bohemian city of Plzeň (or *Pilsen*, hence the name) in 1842, and the beer industry hasn't looked back since. That brewery, Pilsner Urquell, by the way, is still going strong. See p. 229 for a tour of the Pilsner Urquell brewery.

Typical Czech beer is not exactly the same as you're used to back home. Czech beer tends to be heavier and hoppier than standard American or English lagers, and even a bit zippier than German beers. There are also not as many varieties here. While Czechs do dabble occasionally in dark beer (*tmavé pivo*), stouts, and porters, the main diet invariably consists of the pale Pilsner-style beers known locally as "light" beer (*světlé pivo*). That said, you won't find American-style "light," or low-calorie, beer. Instead, beer is sold according to degree (a technical term that refers to the amount of malt extract used in brewing). The two most common strengths are 10-degree (often confusingly written as 10%—though it doesn't mean 10% alcohol content) and 12-degree. Ten degree beers typically contain less alcohol (about 4% by volume as opposed to 4.5% for a standard 12-degree beer).

Ordering a Beer in a Czech Pub

Ordering a beer Czech-style is simple and takes just a few words to master. After sitting down at a pub or restaurant, when the barman or waiter comes to take your order, simply say *pivo prosím* (beer, please) and indicate with your fingers how many you want. A thumb is one, a thumb and index finger is two, and so on in order. The next question, invariably, will be "large or small?" *Velké* (vel-keh) means "large" and refers to a half liter (about 16 oz.); *malé* (mall-eh) means "small," or a third of a liter (about 10 oz.). It will be taken for granted that you want the golden Pilsner-style lager; so if you'd like a dark beer, make a point of saying *"tmavé"* (tuh-*mah*-veh). The last question might be what octane you want. If you'd like the lighter, less-alcoholic 10-degree beer, say *"desítku"* (des-seet-koo). Standard 12-degree brew is *dvanáctku* (duh-vah-naht-skoo). After you've finished, if you'd like another, say *ještě jedno* (yesht-ye yed-no) for "one more." If you'd like to pay up and move on, say *zaplatím prosím* (zah-plaht-*eem* pro-*seem*), which translates awkwardly as "I will pay now, please."

Wine

Wine, called *víno*, is not quite as storied as beer in the Czech Republic. Nearly all the drinkable wines come from a small grape-growing area in southern Moravia, just across the border from the Austrian *Weinviertel*. For years, the big wineries were mostly state-owned and suffered from overproduction. Now, smaller vintners are setting up shop and quality is on the rise. Many Prague restaurants stock the better Czech varieties, and so don't be afraid to dabble. Czech wines have the virtue of being much cheaper than imported wines, and the quality is getting closer every year.

Czech wines come in both white and red, with most of the better bottles in white. Popular whites include *Tramín* (better known abroad by its German name, "Gewürztraminer"), Sauvignon, and *Rulandské bíle*, which seems to sound better as "Pinot Blanc"). The best reds include *Frankovka* (sometimes known abroad as "Blaufränkisch") and *Rulandské červené* ("Pinot Noir").

In Prague, at least, wines take a distinct back seat to beer. That situation is reversed in Moravia, where wine and beer seem at least equally appreciated. On hot days in the summer, though, Praguers do enjoy sitting back with a *bilý střík*, a glass of white wine cut with soda water. In winter, a cup of mulled wine, called *svařené víno* (or *svařák* for short), is great for cupping your hands around during a chilly stroll of Prague's Christmas market. In season, you'll find it at vendors everywhere. Also, in the fall, look out for *burčák*, young wine that's still in the process of fermenting. It looks and tastes like juice but packs a powerful wallop.

WHEN TO GO
The Best Times to Go

Spring and fall are considered high season in Prague. Of the two, spring is the more beautiful. The chestnut trees begin to flower in early April and if you're blessed with a few sunny days, you're going to think you died and went to heaven. Fall (Sept–Oct) can be pleasant as well, with long, warm days and usually reliably sunny weather. Avoid travel over the Christmas, New Year's, and Easter holidays, when the city fills to brimming with tour groups from Germany and Italy. Midsummer (July–Aug) is considered shoulder (in-between) season. On the plus side, hotels usually discount prices 20% or more. On the minus, summers can be surprisingly iffy weather-wise. Some years bring weeks of hot sunshine; others, day after day of cold rain. You might also consider coming during the off season: January and February and from November to mid-December. Yes, it's cold and often rainy or snowy, but the crowds thin out and you finally feel like you have this beautiful city to yourself.

Weather

Spring and fall generally bring the best weather for touring, with warm days and cool nights. Summers can be hit or miss, with some years bringing lots of rain and others weeklong stretches of hot sunshine. Winters can be cold and unusually long, sometimes lasting into April or even May. Rain is a possibility any time of year, so be sure to pack an umbrella.

Prague's Average Temperatures & Rainfall

	JAN	FEB	MAR	APR	MAY	JUNE	JULY	AUG	SEPT	OCT	NOV	DEC
HIGH (°F/°C)	34/1.1	36/2.2	46/7.8	54/12.2	64/17.8	69/20.5	72/22.2	73/22.8	65/18.3	54/12.2	41/5	36/2.2
LOW (°F/°C)	24/–4.4	25/–3.8	32/0	36/2.2	45/7.2	51/10.5	54/12.2	53/11.6	48/8.8	39/3.8	32/0	28/–2.2
RAIN (IN./CM.)	0.8/2	0.7/1.8	1/2.5	1.4/3.6	2.3/5.8	2.7/6.9	2.6/6.6	2.5/6.4	1.6/4.1	1.2/3	1.1/2.8	0.9/2.3

Holidays

Public holidays include: New Year's Day (Jan 1); Easter Monday (Mar or Apr); Labor Day (May 1); Liberation Day (May 8); Sts. Cyril & Methodius Day (July 5); Death of Jan Hus Day (July 6); St. Wenceslas Day (Sept 28); the Founding of the Czechoslovak Republic (Oct 28); the Student Demonstrations of 1989 (Nov 17); Christmas (Dec 24–25); and St. Stephen's Day (Dec 26).

Calendar of Events

Prague has an active cultural calendar year-round. For an exhaustive list of events, check our website at http://events.frommers.com.

SPRING

The **Prague Spring Music Festival** (www.festival.cz) held in late spring (late May, early June) is a world-famous, 3-week series of symphony, opera, and chamber performances. **Prague Khamoro** (www.khamoro.cz), usually held at the end of May or early June, is a celebration of Roma (gypsy) culture. **Febiofest** (www.febiofest.cz), in March, is one of the largest noncompetitive film and video festivals in central Europe. Many of the films are shown in English or with English subtitles. The **One World** film festival (www.jedensvet.cz), also in March, brings together the best human rights and documentary films of the past year. Many of the screenings are in English. Late spring (late May to early June) brings the annual **Prague Fringe Fest** (www.praguefringe.com), a week of offbeat music, happenings, and theater at scattered venues around town.

SUMMER

The summer kicks off with the **Prague Writers' Festival** (www.pwf.cz) in June. A handful of contemporary writers from around Europe and the United States, including usually a couple of big names, hold readings, booksignings, lectures, and happenings. **Tanec Praha** (Dance Prague; www.tanecpraha.cz) is an international dance festival in June that focuses on contemporary dance and movement theater. **United Islands** (www.united islands.cz) festival, usually a long weekend in June, is a carnival of jazz, rock, folk, and house music spread out over several islands in the Vltava River.

FALL

The **Prague Autumn Music Festival,** in late September and early October, is similar to the spring festival but the focus is more on orchestral music, bringing some of Europe's best ensembles to play at Prague's Rudolfinum. The weeklong **Prague International Jazz Festival** (www.jazzfestivalpraha.cz), usually in November, attracts some big names in jazz. Performances are usually held in the Lucerna Music Hall and the city's oldest jazz venue, Reduta.

WINTER

The **Christmas** season begins on St. Nicholas Eve (Dec 5), when children traditionally dress as **St. Nicholas,** the devil, or an angel. The annual **Prague Christmas Market** in Old Town Square gets going about then. Stalls hawk all manner of food, mulled wine, ornaments, and cheap gifts in a festive atmosphere that toes a fine line between traditional and tacky. New Year's Eve is literally a blowout, and the entire town comes out to light firecrackers on Old Town Square, Wenceslas Square, and Charles Bridge. Watch your head, as every year hundreds of people are injured by errant bottle rockets.

RESPONSIBLE TRAVEL

Prague and the Czech Republic have been relatively slow to encourage and adopt sustainable tourism practices. Part of the blame, like everything else, goes to Communism. For 40 years from 1948 to 1989, industries, roads, and vast public housing tracts were built up with scant concern for their effect on the environment. By the time of the Velvet Revolution in 1989, the city and country were on a downward ecological spiral. Large areas in the north of the country had been destroyed by strip mining and acid rain produced by rampant coal burning. In Prague, the air was unbreathable during winter inversions, when slow-moving high-pressure systems would trap dirty air in the lower atmosphere. On those days, children would be bused out of the city to camps in the countryside. The city was still pumping raw sewage into the Vltava River.

The good news is that the city authorities have taken big steps toward cleaning up the air and the river. Much of the city is now heated by natural gas, not coal, leaving the air much cleaner in the winter months—though a huge increase in car ownership has mitigated some of these gains. Sewage is now treated before it's released into the river. The water is still too polluted to swim in, but every year brings an improvement in water quality.

Much remains to be done. Auto exhaust, for one, is still a significant source of air pollution. In the outlying areas, property developers have transformed large swaths of land into residential and office complexes, destroying green areas and adding more roads and cars to the mix.

Cultural Impact of Tourism

On a subtler note, the massive increase in tourism in the past 20 years has contributed to a form of cultural environmental damage; once thriving urban areas in the center have been transformed into largely tourist-only zones. Souvenir shops, selling cheap glass and T-shirts, have forced out legitimate shops and services, with high rents having pushed ordinary Czechs into other parts of town.

There are signs that the national and municipal authorities are aware of the problems, but are still at odds at how best to solve them while keeping the city's economy, particularly its very important tourism industry, on track. The 2009–11 global economic recession didn't help matters.

While there is not much you can do as a short-term visitor, it's at least good to be aware of the impact your trip is having on the culture. In general, when shopping, try to avoid the tacky souvenir shops in the center, especially along Karlova Street, that traffic in cheap, mass-produced items like factory-made puppets, Russian nesting dolls, and fake KGB hats that are not made locally and have little connection to the Czech Republic. Seek out instead the smaller stores, away from the action, that offer genuine, high-quality Czech made goods, like handmade puppets and jewelry from Czech garnets. In the shopping section, I identify some of these places. A small but growing number of hotels have adopted sustainable practices, such as curbing unnecessary water use and recycling, but there's still much room for improvement on this front. For further information on steps the Czech government is taking toward protecting the environment, turn to the website of the **Czech Ministry of the Environment** (www.mzp.cz).

The not-for-profit **Friends of Czech Greenways** (www.pragueviennagreenways. org) is a foundation dedicated to promoting eco-friendly tourism by building up an infrastructure of hiking, biking, and water routes around the country, including several projects in Prague.

In addition to the resources for Prague listed above, see www.frommers.com/planning for more tips on responsible travel.

TOURS

Escorted General-Interest Tours

Several international travel agencies offer travel packages that focus exclusively on Prague and the Czech Republic or offer Czech destinations as part of a "Central European" or "Eastern European" tour. A few of the best are described below.

U.S.-based **Kensington Tours** (300 Delaware Ave., Ste. 1704, Wilmington, DE 19801; ✆ **888-903-2001;** fax 866-613-7599; www.kensingtontours.com) offers a luxury "Five Days in Prague" tour that includes day trips to Karlovy Vary and Kutná Hora, and a 10-day discovery tour that includes Budapest and Vienna.

U.S. operator **Tauck's** (✆ **800-788-7885;** www.tauck.com) offers a 2-week eastern European tour that includes Prague, Warsaw, Budapest, and Vienna. Another tour, called "A Week in Imperial Europe," focuses on the capital cities of central Europe.

The Czech domestic operator **Čedok** (Na Příkopě 18; ✆ **221-447-242;** www.cedok.com) offers several highly rated Czech packages, including to the best-known castles in Bohemia and to the country's UNESCO-listed cities.

Adventure & Wellness Trips

The Bohemian and Moravian countryside is covered with bike paths and organized bike trips have become very popular. These usually include airport pickups, hotels along the way, bike and helmet rentals, and a van to carry your belongings as you cycle. One of the most popular rides is the 400km (250 miles) run from Prague to Vienna along mostly dedicated bike paths and country roads. The Czech-based **Greenways Travel Club** (✆ **519-511-572;** www.gtc.cz) maintains a list of organized bike trips, including the Prague-Vienna trail and several specialty bike tours that mix cycling with exploring the beer region of southern Bohemia or the wine region of southern Moravia.

Food & Wine Trips

Trips that combine sightseeing with wine-tasting or eating and/or cooking are only starting to get going in the Czech Republic. Čedok, Greenways Travel Club (see above), and other operators run tours to the wine areas of southern Moravia.

The U.S.-based operator **Ipswich Tours** (8 Herrick Dr., Ipswich, MA 01938; ✆ **877-356-5163;** fax 978-356-0382; www.ipswichtours.com) runs a 15-day "Gourmet" tour of the Czech Republic, Poland, and Hungary that combines traditional sightseeing with a special emphasis on local foods.

For more information on Package Tours and for tips on booking your trip, see www.frommers.com/planning.

SUGGESTED ITINERARIES

This "old crone"—Prague—has claws. Indeed, writer Franz Kafka described it this way—he allegedly tried to leave his hometown on several occasions, but each time the city's haunting atmosphere and architecture kept pulling him back. Don't panic—even after a stretch of mesmerizing days walking the streets of Staré Město (the Old Town) and Malá Strana (Lesser Town), you'll probably still be able to bring yourself to get back on your plane and fly home. Nevertheless, memories of the city are likely to linger long after you leave.

Unlike many other urban destinations in Europe, Prague's impact lies more with impressions, rather than traditional sites like museums. While there are plenty of good museums here too, the biggest draws are the city's mood, architecture, and atmosphere. These are best enjoyed while slowly wandering through Prague's city center. With that in mind, it's best to keep your itinerary loose.

Of the "must-sees," well, there are only a handful. Certainly, the Charles Bridge rates as number one, but try to time your visits for sunrise and sunset to glimpse the grand architecture of Prague Castle and the Old Town skyline at their best. Prague Castle, too, qualifies as an obvious must, but here as well you might want to save your exploration for the evening hours, when the crowds thin out and the lights of the Old Town below come alive. Old Town Square is another site that can't be missed. This, coincidentally, was Kafka's old neighborhood, and for nearly his entire life, he rarely lived more than a couple of blocks away from this square.

The Prague itinerary sketched out below is suited for a 3-day stay, with the first day devoted to hitting the musts. The second day is more relaxed to fill in the gaps. The third day is open for a picnic, a day trip, or simply to museum- (or bar-) hop.

Neighborhoods in Brief

Prague was originally developed as four adjacent self-governing boroughs: Hradčany, Malá Strana, Staré Město, and Nové Město, plus a walled Jewish ghetto, Josefov, adjacent to Staré Město. Central Prague's neighborhoods have maintained their individual identities along with their medieval street plans.

Hradčany (Castle District) The Castle District dominates the hilltop above Malá Strana. Here you'll find not only the fortress that remains the presidential palace and national seat of power, but also the seat of religious authority in the country, St. Vitus Cathedral, as well as the Loreto Church, Strahov Monastery, and the European masters branch of the National Gallery. You can take a scenic walk down the hill via Nerudova or through the lush Petřín

Hill gardens. (See "Walking Tour 2: Prague Castle," in chapter 7.)

Malá Strana (Lesser Town) Prague's storybook Lesser Town was founded in 1257 by Germanic merchants who set up shop at the base of the castle. Nestled between the bastion and the Vltava River, Malá Strana is laced with narrow, winding lanes boasting palaces, and red-roofed town houses (see "Walking Tour 1: Charles Bridge & Malá Strana [Lesser Town]," in chapter 7). The parliament and government and several embassies reside in palaces here. Kampa Park, on the riverbank just south of Charles Bridge, forms the southeastern edge of Lesser Town. Nerudova is the steep, shop-lined alley leading from the Lesser Town Square (Malostranské nám.) to the castle. Alternate castle routes for the strong of heart are the New Castle Stairs (Nové zámecké schody), 1 block north of Nerudova, and the Old Castle Stairs (Staré zámecké schody), just northwest from the Malostranská metro station. Tram no. 22 will take you up the hill toward the castle if you don't want to make the heart-pounding hike.

Staré Město (Old Town) Staré Město was chartered in 1234, as Prague became an important stop on trade routes. Its meandering streets, radiating from Old Town Square (Staroměstské nám.) are still big visitor draws. Old Town is compact, bordered by the Vltava on the north and west and Revoluční and Národní streets on the east and south. You can wander safely without having to worry about straying into danger. Once here, stick to the cobblestone streets and don't cross any bridges, any streets containing tram tracks, or any rivers, and you'll know that you're still in Old Town. You'll stumble across beautiful Gothic, Renaissance, and baroque architecture and find some wonderful restaurants, shops, bars, cafes, and pubs. For a detailed walking tour, see "Walking Tour 3: Staré Město (Old Town)," in chapter 7.

Josefov Prague's Jewish ghetto, entirely within Staré Město, was surrounded by a wall before almost being completely destroyed to make way for more modern 19th-century apartment buildings. The Old-New Synagogue is in the geographical center of Josefov, and the surrounding streets are wonderful for strolling. Prague is one of Europe's great historic Jewish cities, and

exploring this remarkable area will make it clear why. For details, see "Walking Tour 4: Josefov (Jewish Quarter)," in chapter 7.

Nové Město (New Town) Draped like a crescent around Staré Město, Nové Město is where you'll find Václavské Náměstí (Wenceslas Square), the National Theater, and the central business district. When it was founded by Charles IV in 1348, Nové Město was Europe's largest wholly planned municipal development, and the street layout has remained largely unchanged from those times. It's hard to believe now, but Nové Město was once as majestic as Old Town (Staré Město), but many of the ancient structures were razed in the late 19th century to make way for more modern buildings. There are just a handful of tourist attractions here, but the neighborhood is filled with good hotels and restaurants.

Outlying Areas The four core neighborhoods are surrounded on all sides by attractive, mostly residential neighborhoods, with fewer attractions for visitors but plenty of hotels, restaurants, clubs, and pubs. **Vinohrady,** to the east of Nové Město, is filled with graceful town houses and leafy streets and is the neighborhood of choice for the city's upwardly mobile. There's a big beer garden here (Riegrovy sady) that's a fun destination on a warm summer night, plus many of the city's best dining spots. **Žižkov,** just north of Vinohrady, has a long tradition of being a hard-drinking, working-class neighborhood. Nevertheless, lower rents here have drawn an arty, alternative crowd in recent years. Žižkov is home to Pálac Akropolis, still the best venue in town for live rock and alternative music. **Dejvice, Letná,** and **Holešovice,** across the river and north of Staré Město, are mostly residential areas. Dejvice, with its pre–World War II mansions, is home to many embassies. Letná has a great park and a lovely beer garden in its own right. Holešovice is home to the city's best modern art collection at the Veletržní Palác and has some great nightlife spots. **Smíchov,** south of Malá Strana, is a formerly poor section of town that's found a new lease on life in the form of trendy hotels, shopping centers, and office parks. There are still lots of down-home pubs here, as everywhere in Prague.

Prague at a Glance

NEIGHBORHOODS
Castle District **1**
Jewish Quarter **4**
Lesser Town **3**
New Town **12**
Old Town **5**

INFORMATION
Castle Information
Office **2**
Prague Welcome
Office **6**

TRANSPORTATION/MAIL
Florenc Bus Station **9**
Main Post Office **10**
Main Train Station **11**
Masaryk Station **8**

.·🚇·. Metro
━🗼━ Royal Route
═══ Pedestrian passage
▨▨▨ Steps

Finding an Address

Don't worry about getting lost—everyone does temporarily, even lifelong Praguers. If you're pressed for time and can't enjoy an aimless wander, you'll find that street signs are emblazoned on red Art Nouveau frames, usually bolted to buildings. House numbers generally increase as you get farther from the Vltava or the square from which the street begins.

Note that Prague street names always precede the numbers, like Václavské nám. 25. Ulice (abbreviated ul. or often omitted) means "street," třída (abbreviated tr.) means "avenue," náměstí (abbreviated nám.) is "square" or "plaza," most is "bridge," and nábřeží is "quay."

Prague is divided into 10 postal districts whose numbers are routinely included in addresses. The districts forming the main tourist areas are listed below with their corresponding neighborhoods.

Prague 1 Hradčany, Malá Strana, Staré Město, Josefov, northern Nové Město.
Prague 2 Southern Nové Město, Vyšehrad, western Vinohrady.
Prague 3 Eastern Vinohrady, Žižkov.
Prague 6 Western Bubeneč, Dejvice, Vokovice, Střešovice, Břevnov, Veleslavín, Liboc, Ruzyně, Řepy, Nebušice, Lysolaje, Sedlec, Suchdol.
Prague 7 Holešovice, Letná.

THE BEST OF PRAGUE IN 1 DAY

In order to digest enough of Prague's wonders, do what visiting kings and potentates do on a 1-day visit: Walk the Royal Route (or at least part of it). From the top of the castle hill in Hradčany, tour Prague Castle in the morning. After lunch, begin your slow descent through the odd hill-bound architecture of Lesser Town (Malá Strana).

Then stroll across Charles Bridge, on the way to the winding alleys of Old Town (Staré Město). You can happily get lost finding Old Town Square (Staroměstské nám.), stopping at private galleries and cafes along the way. From Old Town Square, take Celetná Street to Ovocný trh, and you'll reach Mozart's Prague venue, the Estates' Theater. Dinner and your evening entertainment are all probably within a 10-minute walk from anywhere in this area. *Start: Tram no. 22 or take a taxi ride up the castle hill.* **Note:** *You can easily walk this route in reverse, starting at the Náměstí Republiky metro stop (Line B).*

1 Prague Castle ★★★

Since the 9th century, the castle has been the seat of the central state and church. It witnessed the first central unifying power, the Přemyslids, and the reigns of the Luxembourg and the Jagiellos, as well as the Habsburg dynasty. The castle is now the official seat of the Czech president. See p. 94.

2 St. Vitus Cathedral ★★★

King John of Luxembourg and his even more famous son Charles IV laid the foundation stone in 1344 in the place of the original Romanesque rotunda. The first Gothic building period was led by Matyas of Arras, and then Petr Parléř and his sons continued through 1399. The construction of this impressive architectural piece was not completed until 1929. See p. 98.

3 The Royal Palace ★★★

The oldest part of the palace dates from 1135. Famous Czech kings Přemyslid Otakar II, Charles IV, Wenceslas IV, and Vladislav Jagiello then initiated additional reconstructions. The central part, the late Gothic Vladislav Hall, with its ribbed-star-vaulting ceiling, was the largest secular hall in medieval Prague. Still today, every 5 years, the presidential elections take place here. See p. 98.

4 St. George's Basilica ★★

This is the oldest preserved church building of the castle. The originally Romanesque structure gained its baroque facade in the 17th century. Now, as a part of the National Gallery, this venue houses a permanent exhibition of 19th-century Czech art. See p. 101.

5 Golden Lane ★

This bizarre conglomeration of mini town houses within the castle complex was once briefly home to writer Franz Kafka (no. 22). See p. 101.

6 Lobkowicz Palace ★★

This splendid palace, owned by the noble Lobkowicz family, houses the "Princely Collections," the family's valuable holdings of European art, original music scores, rare books, and other fascinating objects.

7 Lobkowicz Palace Café & Restaurant 🍴

Even if you don't decide to tour the palace, be sure to take your midday meal or a coffee here, easily the best restaurant in the entire castle complex.

Start making your way back through the castle's courtyards to Hradčanské náměstí, from which you'll be able to see Prague in its panoramic beauty (if it's not foggy that day). Then as you walk down Nerudova, the road leading to the Lesser Town, you'll find small shops and galleries tucked into every narrow nook.

8 Church of St. Nicholas ★★

The big blue-green dome of the Church of St. Nicholas, with its gilded baroque interior, dominates the view from Lesser Town Square (Malostranské nám.). Organ concerts are held here throughout the year. Note that the interior is not heated in winter. See p. 103.

9 Charles Bridge ★★★

Early on, this pedestrian path became one of the centers of town life. Now it's a promenade best known for its open-air gallery of sculptures, and, of course, the magic views of Prague Castle and Lesser Town. See p. 101.

10 Old Town Square ★★★

Following Karlova Street from the bridge brings you eventually to Old Town Square, the center of life in the Old Town. The square is constantly crowded in high season, but definitely one of the "must-dos." See p. 117.

11 Old Town Hall & Astronomical Clock ★★

In Old Town Square, you can watch a performance of the astronomical clock at the top of each hour. If you aren't tired by now, climb to the top of the Old Town Hall tower for a panoramic view (or take the elevator). See p. 104.

Suggested Itineraries: The Best of Prague

DAY ONE ●🍵
1. Prague Castle
2. St. Vitus Cathedral
3. The Royal Palace
4. St. George's Basilica
5. Golden Lane
6. Lobkowicz Palace
7. Lobkowicz Café
8. Church of St. Nicholas
9. Charles Bridge
10. Old Town Square
11. Old Town Hall and Astronomical Clock
12. The Estates' Theater
13. Kogo Restaurant
14. Celetná and the Powder Tower
15. Municipal House
16. Kavárna Obecní Dům

DAY TWO ●🍵
1. Jewish Museum
2. Melantrichova Street
3. Wenceslas Square
4. National Museum
5. Alfons Mucha Museum
6. Restaurant U Vejvodů
7. Charles Bridge
8. Kampa Island
9. Restaurant Kampa Park

DAY THREE ●🍵
1. Petřín Tower
2. Labyrinth
3. Nebozízek
4. Vrtbovská Zahrada
5. Cruising the Vltava

🍵 Take a Break

12 Estates' Theater ★

If you still have the time and you like opera, try to catch a performance here in the theater that first staged Mozart's *Don Giovanni* in October 1787. Mozart himself was on hand that night to conduct the world premiere of his masterpiece. *Don Giovanni* is still occasionally performed here (usually during the summer for tourists), but there's almost always something interesting on hand. Buy tickets at the National Theater box office (p. 178) or at Ticketpro outlets (p. 178).

13 Kogo ★ ☕

Whether you make it here before the theater or for a late-night, after-opera dinner, you'll not be disappointed by the well-prepared and well-presented Italian food. Havelská 27. ☎ 224-214-543. See p. 85.

14 Celetná and the Powder Tower ★

Continue down the Royal Route with a stroll along Celetná Street, once home to the city's bakers and now given over to a pleasing jumble of bookstores, restaurants, and, naturally, glass shops. The landmark Powder Tower (actually in Czech it's Powder *Gate,* but everyone calls it Powder Tower), once used to store gunpowder, marks the end of the formal coronation route. The tower was once one of the main portals into the Old Town, but these days it's just another set of stairs to climb to get a vantage point out over the Old Town (p. 115).

15 Municipal House ★★

Prague's Art Nouveau jewel! This beautiful corner building just beside the Powder Gate was built on the site of the former Royal Court. It houses the Prague Symphony Orchestra and offers numerous concerts in its Smetana Hall throughout the year. See p. 112.

16 Kavárna Obecní Dům (at the Municipal House) ☕

This is a good time to have coffee or even a little snack. Stop here and take in the unique interior and atmosphere of the Art Nouveau era. Náměstí Republiky 5. ☎ 222-002-763. See chapter 7, "Exploring Prague," p. 91.

THE BEST OF PRAGUE IN 2 DAYS

On your second day, explore the varied sights of the Jewish Quarter, Old Town, and New Town—what you didn't have time for the day before. Just wander and browse. Throughout Old Town, you'll find numerous shops and galleries offering the finest Bohemian crystal, porcelain, and modern artwork, as well as top fashion boutiques, cafes, and restaurants. While the shops aren't that much different from those in other European cities, the setting is.

From Old Town, it's just a short walk across Charles Bridge to the Lesser Town, so you can easily combine this itinerary with a more thorough exploration of Malá Strana. This was once the neighborhood for diplomats, merchants, and those who served the castle, with narrow houses squeezed between palaces and embassies. **Start:** *Metro A, Staroměstská.*

1 Jewish Museum ★★★

From the Staroměstská metro station, follow Kaprová Street toward the Old Town Square before turning left on Maislová to enter the heart of the city's former Jewish quarter of Josefov. Buy a combined entry ticket to the sites of the Jewish Museum (not one building, but an ensemble of several synagogues and the evocative Old Jewish Cemetery). Alternatively, you can forego the expensive ticket and simply walk around the quarter (though you won't be allowed to see the cemetery or any of the interiors). The Pinkas Synagogue displays heart-wrenching sketches by the children held at the Terezín concentration camp during World War II. See p. 105.

2 Melantrichova Street ★

Return to the Old Town Square and pass by the Old Town Hall to find this tiny curving lane that eventually brings you to Můstek metro stop and Wenceslas Square. There are many shops here, as well as little lanes that branch out in all directions.

3 Wenceslas Square ★★

Můstek puts you at the bottom of Wenceslas Square, looking up to the grand building of the National Museum at the other end. This is Prague's liveliest square and the commercial focal point of the city since at least the 18th century, when it was a horse market. It was also the site of some of the most dramatic moments of the Velvet Revolution in 1989. By day, you'll find excellent shopping and dining opportunities. By night, most of the legitimate businesses close down, and the square becomes a haunt for touts pushing strip clubs and "cabarets." See "Historic Squares" in chapter 6.

4 National Museum

This iconic hulk of a building is a good example of the neoclassical and neo-Renaissance architecture of the second half of the 19th century. Its hall of fame is devoted to the memory of outstanding Czech personalities throughout history. Expansive collections of minerals and various zoological and paleontological displays are part of the permanent exhibition here. *Note:* The National Museum closed in 2011 for renovations and is not expected to reopen until 2015. See p. 110.

5 Alfons Mucha Museum ★

This is a pleasant oasis in a busy neighborhood. You can slow down here and relax by stepping into a world of this famous turn-of-the-20th-century artist and his archetypical Art Nouveau designs. See p. 110.

Depending on where you end up, walk along the pedestrian zone of Na Příkopě to Můstek and then continue along Street 28 října. This is prime shopping territory, so feel free to pop in at any stores that catch your eye. Turn right onto Perlová Street and you'll get to a little square, Uhelný trh. Skořepka Street will lead you from there to Jilská. If you get lost around these Old Town winding streets, I'm sure you'll stumble upon a pub or restaurant. This is one in which you'll nearly always be able to find a seat:

6 U Vejvodů ☕

One of the original restaurants of the Pilsner brewery, this spot serves an authentic goulash for 149Kč, and even though you probably won't meet many locals here anymore, you'll still have a good Czech pub experience. Jilská 4. ✆ 224-219-999. See p. 184.

Make your way down Jilská, which eventually takes you to winding Karlova Street. Make a left here and follow the crowds to the Charles Bridge.

7 Charles Bridge ★★★

Try to pace your walk toward Charles Bridge so you stroll across in the evening and witness the unforgettable, panoramic view of Prague at twilight. See p. 101.

8 Kampa Island ★★

Kampa Island runs along the Lesser Town embankment of the Vltava, with a series of quaint shops and restaurants. You can reach it by taking the stairs down from Charles Bridge (on the left side, before you exit the bridge itself). From here, the views out over the river are breathtaking, and if you keep on walking you'll eventually reach a small park. See "Parks & Gardens" in chapter 6.

9 Kampa Park ☕

There are several choice spots around here for an evening meal. If money is no object, splurge for a riverside table at elegant Na Kampě 8b; ✆ 296-826-112. A slightly cheaper option, though the view is just as good, is at nearby Hergetova Cihelna ★★, at Cihelná 2b; ✆ 296-826-103. Back across the river on the Old Town side, try Grosseto Marina ★★ at the foot of Manes Bridge; ✆ 605-454-020. See p. 78 and 84.

THE BEST OF PRAGUE IN 3 DAYS

On your third day, after visiting the most important Prague sights, go for a day's excursion to Karlštejn Castle or one of several other worthwhile day trips. See p. 189 for details.

Alternatively, if you're staying in Prague, on a warm, sunny day, pack yourself a picnic and stroll over to Petřín Hill, the leafy park where kids will enjoy the tower view and mirrored labyrinth. Before you leave Lesser Town, visit its well-hidden secret, the Vrtbovská garden. Try to work in a cruise on the Vltava or pilot your own rowboat ride in the late afternoon or evening. ***Start:*** *Tram no. 12, 20, or 22 to Újezd.*

Begin by walking up the Petřín Hill, or take the funicular from Újezd halfway up to Nebozízek, or all the way up. See p. 123.

1 Petřín Tower ★

In the morning, you'll probably be rested enough to climb the 299 steps up to the top platform of this reduced copy of the Eiffel Tower built in 1891. When the weather cooperates, the bird's-eye view of Prague is worth the hike. There is an elevator, but only seniors 70 and over and people with disabilities may use it. See p. 116.

2 Labyrinth

This funhouse was originally built as a pavilion for the Prague Exhibition in 1891 and later transferred to Petřín. It was fitted with mirrors and made into a maze. See p. 125.

After you find your way out, start looking for a picnic spot. You can have a walk around on the top of the hill or begin your slow descent to the town. There are plenty of benches along the way down.

If you are not ready for a picnic or a walk, use the funicular and go to the midway stop:

3 Nebozízek ☕

This restaurant has a great hillside location, and you probably will forget what you're eating (a pity because the food is actually pretty good) since your attention will be drawn to the view. Petřínské sady 411. ℂ 257-315-329. See p. 80.

Continue walking back down to street level and take tram no. 12, 20, or 22 or walk 10 minutes from Újezd to the Hellichova stop.

4 Vrtbovská Zahrada ★

The entrance to this baroque terraced garden is not well marked, and you won't quite imagine what kind of "backyard" is hidden behind the door at no. 25 on Karmelitská. *Note:* It is closed in winter. See p. 124.

5 Cruising the Vltava

Cruising upstream and enjoying the sights of Prague as dusk descends is a memorable experience. You'll see it all from a low angle surrounded by reflections on the water, providing a new perspective on the city. Choose the 3-hour cruise, which departs from a port under Čechův Bridge at 7pm. Buffet dinner, aperitif, and live music are included in the price. You can also rent your own pedal- or paddle boat and splash around to your heart's content. See p. 129.

THE BEST OF THE CZECH REPUBLIC IN 1 WEEK

The Czech lands offer many historic and cultural monuments. Castles and châteaux dominating the picturesque natural landscape represent the most important part of Czech attractions. For those travelers with more time to discover Bohemia and even Moravia, see chapters 10, 11, and 12 to learn about visits to other Czech towns. Below I suggest just one example out of many possible itineraries.

Days 1–2: Arrive in Prague

Spend the first 2 days as recommended above in "The Best of Prague in 2 Days." Then rent a car from one of the rental agencies recommended on p. 281. Keep in mind that the speed limit is 90kmph (56 mph) on two-lane highways and 50kmph (31 mph) in villages, and that you must keep your headlights switched on while driving. Before setting out, review the other Czech rules for driving on p. 283. *Note:* This trip can also be covered by buses and trains, but you may need an extra day, depending on timetables.

Day 3: Český Krumlov ★★★

Leave for this romantic destination in southern Bohemia early in the morning to give yourself plenty of time to walk around once you get there. Take Hwy. D1 and then E55. The trip takes about 3 hours. Once there, visit the castle first, then just wander, and finally relax in a local restaurant. Spend the night in one

Suggested Itineraries: The Best of the Czech Republic

of the recommended hotels or pensions. But book early, as Krumlov is the most popular Czech destination after Prague. See details in chapter 11.

Day 4: České Budějovice, Castle Hluboká nad Vltavou ★

On this day, start heading for Plzeň via České Buděovice, the home of Budvar beer. Upon arrival at České Buděovice, have a quick stroll and look around one of central Europe's largest squares, where you can also have lunch. In the early afternoon, take Hwy. E49 and then Hwy. 105 north for 30 minutes (this includes parking time) to the tiny town Hluboká nad Vltavou, where you'll see a castle fashioned after the Windsor Castle in England towering above the green meadows. For more information, see p. 236 in chapter 11.

Next, take Hwy. E49 to Plzeň. You'll get there in about 2 hours. Spend the night there. See p. 227.

Day 4: Plzeň ★

Explore Plzeň's center in the morning, when it is the least crowded. If you're interested in the beer-making process, visit the Pilsner Breweries in the early afternoon (but note if you're driving, you'll have to forego the glass of beer at the end of the tour). Just outside the factory is a restaurant that serves traditional Czech food. See chapter 11 for more details.

After your break, hit the road again. Hwy. E49 will take you to the most popular Czech spa town, Karlovy Vary, in about 1 hour. Spend the night there.

Day 6: Karlovy Vary ★★

This town was built for relaxation, which makes it the perfect place to end your Bohemian week.

Start slowly with a stroll around the city's historic center. Then, get your "cup" and taste the mineral waters that make this destination so famous. Find out more about Karlovy Vary in chapter 11.

Day 7: Karlovy Vary to Prague

It's time to return to Prague. Take Hwy. E48. You should reach the capital in 2 hours. Be warned that this two-lane highway is one of the busiest and most accident-prone in the country.

WHERE TO STAY
IN PRAGUE

Not so long ago, Prague used to have a shortage of hotel rooms, and if you arrived in town without reservations there was a good chance you would be without a place to stay. That's no longer the case (though it always pays to reserve in advance if you find a good place at a good price). Hotel construction became a boom industry during the past decade, and if anything, the city now has too many beds, not too few.

4

Ironically, the global economic slowdown of the past few years has had a positive effect for visitors. Faced with the double whammy of too many beds and with tourists tightening their wallets, hotel owners have responded by offering deep discounts, usually advertised over the hotel's website. Indeed, in the summer of 2011, depending on the night, it was possible to snag a good place in the city center for under US$100. It's not clear what the future will bring, but it always pays to shop around. Bargains are out there.

Prague's hotels are spread out all over the four central districts of Hradčany, Malá Strana, Staré Město, and Nové Město, plus outlying areas like Vinohrady, Smíchov, and Dejvice. Each of these areas offers advantages and disadvantages. (See the individual neighborhoods below for more information on where to stay.) In general, the highest demand and highest prices are for properties in Malá Strana and Staré Město. They offer the closest proximity to the main sites and the possibility of a castle or river view out your window. Nové Město, the city's commercial heart, is also a popular lodging choice. A hotel here will probably offer the same walk-to proximity to the major sights, but may lack some of the innate charm of Malá Strana or Staré Město. The leafy inner suburb of Vinohrady has increasingly evolved into an alternative lodging locale. This is an upscale and highly desirable area, but requires a metro or tram ride to get to the center. For other outlying districts, look at the map carefully before booking your room. Try to get as close to a metro or tramline as possible, or you'll spend too much time trying to figure out your transit routes and not enough time enjoying the sights.

Hotels Prague offers everything from five stars on down to modest mom-and-pops perched on the side of the road. Most hotels in the center fall in the three- to four-star range, where rooms are normally clean and secure with attached bathrooms and modern conveniences like TVs, telephones, and occasionally (but not usually) air-conditioning. Nearly all

In most hotels and B&Bs, the room rate includes breakfast—usually heavy bread or rolls *(rohlíky)*, jam, butter, cheese spreads, and sometimes liver pâté, plus yogurt, cereal, juice, milk, and coffee or tea. Occasionally, slices of Prague ham or smoked pork *(debrecínka)*, hard-boiled eggs, local cheeses, and fresh fruit will join the buffet. The better places will also offer bacon and eggs cooked to order. Don't expect, however, to get drinkable coffee. It's invariably of the black-sludge variety. Better to eat your breakfast and grab a coffee somewhere after you leave the hotel.

hotels will offer some form of in-room Internet (whether Wi-Fi or LAN connection). This may or may not be free (always ask before booking).

Many hotels now are smoke-free or at a minimum offer smoke-free rooms (be sure to make your request known upfront). If you're driving, keep in mind that most hotels in the main central areas won't have on-site parking, and street parking is severely restricted. Instead, you'll likely have to use a pay garage or lot nearby. Figure on shelling out an additional 500Kč a day or more for parking. Below, I mark the properties that offer their own on-site parking.

Wheelchair access remains a problem and most older or smaller hotels are not likely to be accessible for persons with disabilities. The best bets are chains and larger hotels built or remodeled in the past couple of years. Contact the hotel directly for up-to-date information on accessibility. See chapter 13, "Planning Your Trip to Prague," for more information on traveling with disabilities, p. 284.

Most of the big international hotel chains, including Hilton, Marriott, Sheraton, and several others, have properties in Prague. A complete list is included in chapter 13.

Pensions　　These are typically guesthouses, often family-owned, which offer fewer services than hotels but tend to be cheaper. In practice, there is little difference between a pension and a two- or three-star hotel.

Short-Term Apartment Rentals　　An increasingly popular option is to pass up high-priced hotel rooms and opt instead for private apartments. Several agencies now offer short-term rentals for what are surprisingly nice places in high-demand areas like Malá Strana, Staré Město, and Nové Město. These often can accommodate up to four people (usually more) and have modest kitchens. Services, however, are limited to things like pickup and drop-off at the airport. You will usually have to arrange a time in advance to pick up the keys, since there's no reception.

Prague-Stay.com at Na Perštýně 2, Prague 1 (www.prague-stay.com; ℃ 222-311-084) offers luxurious short-term rentals starting at about 1,500Kč a night for properties in the center. **Apartments in Prague** at Vlašská 8, Prague (www. apartments-in-prague.org; ℃ 775-588-508) has some beautiful properties in Malá Strana and elsewhere also starting at around 1,500Kč a night during the off season and up to 4,000Kč and higher for New Year's Eve. Check both companies' websites for apartment photos.

Room-Finding Agencies　　Prague has several agencies that can assist in helping to find a room in a hotel or pension, or even book a short-term apartment rental or a private room in someone's house. These agencies normally offer a wide selection of properties and allow for online selection and payment. One of the market leaders is Prague-based **E-Travel.cz** (www.travel.cz). Its office is near the National Theater at Divadelní 24 (☎ **224-990-990;** fax 224-990-999). **Mary's Travel & Tourism** at Italská 31, Prague 2 (www.marys.cz; ☎ **222-254-007**) has an excellent range of hotels from two to five stars and a well-organized website. Simply choose how many stars you want and what district you want to stay in, then type in the data and you're set.

best HOTEL BETS

- **Best Panoramic Views:** The **Corinthia Hotel Prague** (☎ 261-191-111) is a bit out of the center and the high-rise architecture won't appeal to everyone, but each north-facing room provides a gorgeous wide-angle view stretching to Prague Castle and beyond. See p. 67.
- **Best Malá Strana Views:** The terrace at the hotel **U Zlaté studně** (☎ 257-011-213), the Golden Well, offer some of the best old-world views over Malá Strana's red rooftops. See p. 53.
- **Best Bohemian Country Setting:** The **Romantik Hotel U raka** (☎ 220-511-100), in a secret ravine minutes from the castle in Hradčany, has cozy rustic rooms and a tastefully folksy atmosphere. See p. 56.
- **Best Hotel Closest to Prague Castle:** The **U Krále Karla** (☎ 257-531-211), on the main castle-bound thoroughfare Nerudova, tries hard to provide a stay to match its Renaissance motif. It's a few steps above the main turn to the castle, avoiding much of the tourist commotion below. See p. 57.
- **Best for Business Travelers:** Just off Náměstí Republiky near the imposing Czech National Bank, the **Prague Marriott Hotel** (☎ 222-888-888) comfortably fits the bill for those who need to get in, cut a deal, and then get out to see the city (especially if the firm is paying the bill). The **Kempinski Hotel** (☎ 226-226-111) in Nové Město is bolder, brasher, and has a better restaurant. See p. 65 and 65.
- **Best for Stressed-Out Business Travelers:** The **Buddha Bar** (☎ 221-776-300), in Staré Město, is all about lifestyle and finding that right balance between work and spirit. So after you've amassed your fortune, spend it here to decompress. See p. 59.
- **Best Romantic Pension:** Although the **Pension Větrník** (☎ 220-612-404) is well outside the city center, this family-run B&B is a very friendly and romantic place, easily accessible by tram or taxi. It's built into an antique windmill amid lush gardens, and you can't beat it for charm and price. See p. 68.
- **Best Throwback to Prague's First Republic:** The restored Art Nouveau **Hotel Paříž** (☎ 222-195-195) recalls 1920s Prague, one of the wealthiest cities on earth at the time. The hotel's beauty oozes with period elegance. It's across from

another remodeled gem, the Municipal House (Obecní dům). **The K+K Central** (✆ **225-022-000**) has an even more impressive Art Nouveau exterior and the rooms convey a Functionalist 1920s and 1930s feel. See p. 61 and 65.

○ **Best for Families:** Consider a **private apartment** from an agency (see "Short-Term Apartment Rentals," above). Larger and cheaper than hotel rooms, these apartments come with kitchens so you can fix your own meals. (For more options, see "Family-Friendly Accommodations," later in the chapter.)

○ **Best Health Clubs:** The **Hotel InterContinental Prague** (✆ **296-631-111**) has a fully equipped gym with modern machines and free weights and is home to a variety of workout and aerobics classes. There's also a smallish pool on hand and a hot tub. The gym is primarily for hotel guests, but it's possible to buy day passes, as well as short- and long-term memberships. See p. 60.

HRADČANY

Smart Hradčany, the Castle District, just beyond Prague Castle, is far from the madding crowd. It's clean, exclusive, and filled with historic properties, many with pitch-perfect views out over the Petřín valley.

Best For: Couples looking for something quiet and romantic but who don't mind walking, particularly uphill.

Drawbacks: The area is rich with embassies, ministry buildings, and museums, but short on restaurants, clubs, shops, and parking spots.

Very Expensive

Hotel Savoy ★ One of Prague's finest hotels, the Savoy occupies a quiet spot behind the Foreign Ministry and Černín Palace, and is just a few blocks from the castle. The guest rooms are richly decorated and boast every amenity as well as spacious marble bathrooms. The beds are huge, which contrasts with the customary central European style of two twin beds shoved together. The pleasant staff provides an attention to detail that's a cut above that at most hotels in Prague. The Hradčany restaurant is excellent.

Keplerova 6, Prague 1. www.savoyhotel.cz. ✆ **224-302-430.** Fax 224-302-128. 61 units. From 4,500Kč double; from 8,000Kč suite. Rates include breakfast. AE, DC, MC, V. Tram: 22 to Pohořelec. Parking. **Amenities:** Restaurant; bar; concierge; exercise room; health club & spa; room service; sauna; whirlpool; Wi-Fi (free in lobby). *In room:* A/C, TV, DVD player, hair dryer, Internet, minibar.

U Zlaté studně ★★★ The "Golden Well" is a reconstructed Renaissance town house that occupies a perch high above Malá Strana and just below Prague Castle. Many of the rooms afford stunning views out over the river and the Old Town in the distance. The guest rooms are traditional in style and outfitted with antiques and reproductions. The overall effect is of a high-quality guesthouse. Rumors were swirling in April 2009 during U.S. President Barack Obama's visit to Prague that he and First Lady Michelle Obama were going to dine on the restaurant's terrace. He ended up staying (and eating) at the Hilton, but this would have been a more presidential choice. The restaurant is worth a visit even if you are not staying here.

U zlaté studně 4, Prague 1. www.goldenwell.cz. ✆ **257-011-213.** 19 units. From 4,500Kč double. Rates include breakfast. AE, DC, MC, V. Tram: 12, 20, or 22 to Malostranské nám., plus a steep hike. **Amenities:** Restaurant; bar; concierge; room service; Wi-Fi (free in lobby). *In room:* TV, DVD player, hair dryer, minibar, Wi-Fi.

Prague Hotels

Andante **38**
Best Western Hotel
Kampa **14**
Betlem Club **31**
Buddha-Bar Hotel **22**
Casa Marcello **18**
Corinthia Prague Hotel **39**
Czech Inn **43**
Dům U krále Jiřího **29**
Four Seasons Hotel **28**
Hilton Old Town **24**
Hilton Prague **21**
Hotel Absolutum **15**
Hotel Ametyst **41**
Hotel Aria **11**
Hotel Cloister Inn **32**
Hotel Diplomat **2**
Hotel Evropa **34**
Hotel Hoffmeister **4**
Hotel InterContinental
Praha **17**
Hotel Jalta **36**
Hotel Josef **20**
Hotel Meran **35**
Hotel Neruda **8**
Hotel Orion **42**
Hotel Paříž **23**
Hotel Praha **1**
Hotel Savoy **6**
Hotel U páva **10**
Hotel U Prince **30**
K+K Central **26**
Kampa Garden **13**
Kempinski Hotel
Prague **27**
Le Palais Prague **40**
Mandarin Oriental **12**
Palace Hotel **33**
Pension Museum **37**
Pension Větrník **3**
Prague Marriott Hotel **25**
Romantik Hotel U raka **5**
Sir Toby's **16**
Travellers' Hostel-
Pension Dlouhá **19**
U Krále Karla **7**
U Zlaté Studně **9**

4

WHERE TO STAY IN PRAGUE | Hradčany

The best way to save money on a hotel room is to book as far in advance as possible and make use of the local room-finding services (listed above) or big hotel aggregators, like Expedia.com. Their customer-finding clout gives them leverage to extract discounts from hotel owners, part of which they can pass on to you. In addition, always **check out the hotel's own website.** This is where hotels post their special offers as well as last-minute and seasonal discounts. Rates can be shockingly low as hotels, seemingly, will stoop to any level to fill beds. So much the better for you.

Czech hotel receptionists have little interest in haggling over room rates, but sometimes you can still get a deal by simply asking at the end: "Is this the best price you can offer me?" Hotels are under increasing pressure from the competition, and last-minute rate cuts have become the norm and not the exception. Your bargaining position is stronger if you're planning a longer stay.

4

Hradčany

WHERE TO STAY IN PRAGUE

Expensive

Hotel Neruda ★★ Another great writer/philosopher who left his mark on Prague was Jan Neruda, but the street that bears his name—Nerudova—is hardly remembered as the scene of his 19th-century literary greatness. Instead, it is a cozy alley of stores and pubs leading up to the castle. Squeezed into the long row of curiosity shops is a strong contender for the best boutique hotel in Malá Strana—the Hotel Neruda. This refurbished 42-room villa has combined a high level of modern elegance with the original accents of its 14th-century shell. Most of the fixtures—from the fresh new bathrooms to the beds and dining tables—suggest a bold sense of Prague's promising future, but enveloped within its Renaissance past. With the recent summers setting new records for heat, you will appreciate the air-conditioning. Check the website for last-minute discounts.

Nerudova 44, Prague 1. www.hotelneruda-praha.cz. © **257-535-557.** Fax 257-531-492. 42 units. From 4,200Kč double. Rates include breakfast. AE, DC, MC, V. Tram: 12, 20, or 22 to Malostranské nám. **Amenities:** Restaurant; bar; room service. *In room:* A/C, TV, hair dryer, minibar, Wi-Fi (paid).

Romantik Hotel U raka ★ Hidden among the stucco houses and cobblestone streets of a pristine medieval neighborhood below Prague Castle is this pleasant surprise. The Romantik Hotel U raka (At the Crayfish), in a ravine beneath the Foreign Ministry gardens, has been lovingly reconstructed as an old-world farmhouse. It is the quietest getaway in this tightly packed city. The rustic rooms have heavy wooden furniture, open-beamed ceilings, and stone walls. The much-sought-after suite has a fireplace and adjoins a private manicured garden, making it a favorite with honeymooners. Water trickles through the Japanese garden that surrounds the hotel.

The owners are relaxed but attentive and will help you navigate the phalanx of nearby streets. Prague Castle is a 10-minute walk away, and you can catch a tram into the city center by walking up ancient steps at the side of the hotel. Reservations well in advance are recommended.

Černínská 10, Prague 1. www.romantikhotel-uraka.cz. © **220-511-100.** Fax 233-358-041. 6 units (5 with shower only). From 3,500Kč double; from 7,000Kč suite. Rates include breakfast. AE, MC, V. Tram: 22 to stop Pohořelec. **Amenities:** Restaurant. *In room:* A/C, TV, hair dryer, minibar.

U Krále Karla ★   This castle hill property does so much to drive home its Renaissance roots, King Charles's heirs should be getting royalties. Replete with period prints, open-beamed ceilings, and stained-glass windows, the atmosphere is almost Disneyesque in its pretense, but somehow appropriate for this location near the foot of Prague Castle. The rooms offer plenty of space, heavy period furniture, and bed frames with firm mattresses as well as clean bathrooms with a tub/shower combination or shower only. This is a fun, comfortable choice with colorful angelic accents everywhere.

Nerudova-Úvoz 4, Prague 1. www.romantichotels.cz. ℂ **257-533-594.** 19 units (13 with shower only). From 3,000Kč double; 4,500Kč suite. Rates include breakfast. AE, MC, V. Tram: 12, 20, or 22 to Malostranské nám., and then walk up the hill. **Amenities:** Restaurant; bar; babysitting; room service; solarium. *In room:* TV, hair dryer, kitchenette, minibar, Wi-Fi.

MALÁ STRANA (LESSER TOWN)

Malá Strana, the Lesser Quarter, sandwiched between Prague Castle and the Vltava River, is hands down Prague's most beautiful area. Many of the properties here have been carved out of Renaissance and baroque town houses, mixing an evocative historical setting with either period furnishings or stark contemporary interiors (either way, it works).

Best For: Honeymooners and others who want to experience Prague at its most stunning. In addition to the architecture, this part of town is filled with great restaurants, cafes, clubs, and sights, and is just a short walk across the Charles Bridge to Staré Město (Old Town).

Drawbacks: Room rates here are among the highest in the city. Another potential problem is parking. Getting a car down one of these streets is well nigh impossible.

Very Expensive

Hotel Aria ★★   This music-themed hotel occupies a luxuriously reconstructed town house in the heart of Malá Strana, just around the corner from the St. Nicholas Cathedral. Each of its four floors is tastefully decorated to evoke a different genre of music, famous composer, or musician. The rooms and bathrooms vary in their size and layout, and all are kept to the same exceptionally high standard evident throughout the hotel. There is an impressive library of CDs, DVDs, and books about music off the lobby, and a full-time resident musicologist is available to help you choose a concert in the city. The Aria will delight newlyweds or any romantic soul with its luxurious but cozy atmosphere, and the extensive list of amenities, which includes a roof terrace garden with spectacular views of Malá Strana, a screening room, and music salon.

Tržiště 9, Prague 1. www.aria.cz. ℂ **225-334-111.** Fax 225-334-666. 52 units. From 5,800Kč double; 9,500Kč suite. Rates include breakfast. AE, MC, V. Metro: Malostranská and then tram 12, 20, or 22 to Malostranské nám. **Amenities:** Restaurant; bar; free airport transfers (for suite stays); exercise room; room service; Wi-Fi. *In room:* A/C, CD/DVD player, hair dryer, Internet, minibar, MP3 docking station.

Mandarin Oriental Hotel ★★   The Mandarin offers superior accommodations and service in a converted, former Dominican monastery in Malá Strana. Smart, sleek design underlines the relaxing Far East ambience throughout the building. Large rooms and suites are well equipped and some include impressive views. The hotel boasts a spa in what was a Renaissance chapel, so you can heal your body and soul at the same time, while the Essensia restaurant fuses Eastern and Western cuisines. This booking would be a great choice for a business traveler who can take his or her spouse along (and charge it to the expense account).

Nebovidská 1, Prague 1. www.mandarinoriental.com/prague. ℭ **233-088-888.** Fax 233-088-668. 99 units. 4,400Kč double; from 9,000Kč suite. Rates include breakfast. AE, MC, V. Metro: Malostranská; then take tram 12, 20, or 22 to the Hellichova stop. Parking. **Amenities:** Restaurant; bar; tea lounge; exercise room; health club & spa; room service. *In room:* A/C, TV, CD/DVD player, Internet, minibar.

Expensive

Hotel Hoffmeister ★★   Conceived by the son of Adolph Hoffmeister, an artist and former diplomat, the hotel's bold style is striking. Sketches by the father adorn the walls and depict acquaintances of the late artist with celebrities at the time such as Charlie Chaplin, Salvador Dalí, and George Bernard Shaw. The rooms are solid and well equipped. Each has a unique color scheme, with rich fabrics, matching draperies, and even bed canopies. For the ultimate relaxation, visit the wellness center, where massages and other body treatments are on the menu. The in-house restaurant, Ada, is highly recommended and even won a Michelin guide mention for its interior.

Pod Bruskou 9, Prague 1. www.hoffmeister.cz. ℭ **251-017-111.** Fax 251-017-120. 41 units (tub/ shower combo). From 3,600Kč double; from 4,800Kč suite. Rates include breakfast. AE, MC, V. Metro: Malostranská. Parking. **Amenities:** Restaurant; bar; exercise room; health club & spa; room service. *In room:* A/C, TV, hair dryer, minibar, Wi-Fi (free).

Hotel U páva ★   The "Peacock" is a fine B&B in Malá Strana managed by the same group as the U Krále Karla (see "Hradčany" on p. 53). On the narrow street across from the walled Vojanov Gardens, a stone's throw from Charles Bridge, this family-run hotel has the intimacy of a farmhouse and offers room service from its decent kitchen. Original wooden ceilings, antique chairs, and comfortable beds accent the reasonably spacious rooms. The best rooms on the top floor facing the front have a fantastic low-angle view of Prague Castle and a working fireplace. The fully tiled bathrooms of adequate size have tub/shower combinations.

U Lužického semináře 32, Prague 1. www.romantichotels.cz. ℭ **257-533-360.** Fax 257-530-919. 27 units (tub/shower combo). From 3,000Kč double, from 4,500Kč suite. Rates include breakfast. AE, MC, V. Metro: Malostranská. **Amenities:** Restaurant; cafe; bar; babysitting; health club & spa; room service. *In room:* TV, hair dryer, minibar, Wi-Fi (free).

Moderate

Best Western–Hotel Kampa   On the edge of the park where troops once camped along the banks of the Vltava, the Kampa occupies what was a 17th-century armory. It has a choice location on a quiet, winding alley off the park, with easy access to Malá Strana and Charles Bridge. The plain rooms suggest a bit of Communist chintz without much attention to aesthetics, but they're comfortable enough if you don't expect first-class surroundings. Be sure to check the Internet for rates, since the hotel frequently offers big discounts during slow times.

Všehrdova 16, Prague 1. www.praguekampahotel.com. ℭ **257-404-444.** Fax 257-404-333. 84 units (shower only). From 2,500Kč double. Rates include breakfast. AE, DC, MC, V. Metro: Malostranská; then take tram 12, 20, or 22 to the Hellichova stop. **Amenities:** Restaurant w/garden; bar; room service. *In room:* TV, hair dryer, minibar, Wi-Fi (free).

Kampa Garden ★   From the perspective of the rooms, this is just an average hotel, with nondescript furnishings and small but clean bathrooms. Where it gets a star is for the location, alongside the impossibly romantic Čertovka stream that separates Kampa Island from the rest of Malá Strana (complete with watermill right outside your window), and for the helpful and engaged management, which is working hard to make improvements. The price for location cannot be beat.

U Sovových mlýnů 9, Prague 1. www.hotelkampagarden.cz. © **233-920-118.** 35 units (including one double for guests with disabilities). From 2,200Kč double; from 2,800Kč apt. Rates include breakfast. AE, DC, MC, V. Metro: Malostranská, then tram 12, 20, or 22 to the Hellichova stop. *In room:* Minibar, Wi-Fi (free).

STARÉ MĚSTO (OLD TOWN) & JOSEFOV

Staré Město (Old Town) is Prague's downtown, so to speak, with all the goods (and some of the "bads") that it entails.

Best For: Active tourists who want to be close to the best restaurants, cafes, sights, and pubs the city has to offer. If Prague has a vibe, this is where to find it. There are also some beautiful, world-class properties, many occupying sensitively restored Gothic, Renaissance, and baroque town houses.

Drawbacks: The bad side (and I'm not sure there is a *bad* side) might be the crowds. Though most of the hotels are set back from the main tourist thoroughfares, Old Town is the center of the action and can feel overrun at the height of the season.

Very Expensive

Buddha Bar ★★   If you've got the crowns, you can hardly do better than this chic French-Asian–inspired inn in the middle of the Old Town. The rooms are furnished in a style that might be described as tastefully exotic, with warm reds and golds and bright tiles that recall the best of India or the Middle East. The in-house Buddha Bar restaurant features very good Asian-inspired cuisine, including a sushi bar, in a setting that manages to be both hip and high-end at the same time. Stays of 3 nights or more qualify for a 25% discount.

Jakubská 8, Prague 1. www.buddha-bar-hotel.cz. © **221-776-300.** Fax 221-776-310. 39 units. From 9,000Kč double; from 24,000Kč suite. AE, DC, MC, V. Metro: Náměstí Republiky. **Amenities:** Restaurant; cafe, bar; concierge; exercise room; health club & spa. *In room:* A/C, TV, CD, DVD player, hair dryer, minibar, Wi-Fi (free).

Four Seasons Hotel ★★★   Located in an imposing position on the banks of the Vltava River right next to Charles Bridge, the Four Seasons provides an elegant base for exploring Old Town and enjoying the symphonies at the nearby Rudolfinum, while taking in a wonderful panoramic view of Prague Castle across the river.

The property actually melds three historic buildings from the city's most important architectural periods—baroque, Renaissance, and Art Nouveau. The most impressive wing, the 17th-century baroque villa, houses the Presidential Suite with a cozy fireplace, a private dining room, and the privilege of peering into the castle's ornate staterooms across the way. The surrounding executive suites and guest rooms are smaller but still nicely appointed. The best have sweeping views and sunken marble tubs. The Art Nouveau wing is less expensive but the street-side views are less impressive. All rooms are fitted with fine solid wood furniture: some with antique pieces, others with more modern avant-garde accents. The house restaurant, the Allegro, is a Michelin star winner.

Veleslavínova 2a, Prague 1. www.fourseasons.com. ℭ **221-427-000.** Fax 221-426-000. 161 units. From 9,000Kč double; from 20,000Kč suite. AE, DC, MC, V. Metro: Staroměstská. Parking. **Amenities:** Restaurant; bar; executive-level rooms; exercise room; health club & spa; room service. In room: A/C, TV, CD, DVD player, hair dryer, minibar, Wi-Fi (free).

Expensive

Casa Marcello ★★   This is an elegant boutique hotel in a secluded corner of the Old Town, a short walk from Old Town Square and the former Jewish ghetto. The hotel was formed from fusing two town houses dating back to the 13th century and still exudes a feeling of exclusivity and timelessness. The rooms are variously furnished, some in grand period style with big wooden beds, and others in spare contemporary. Ask to see a couple before choosing. There's a relaxing garden restaurant in summer.

Řásnovka 783, Prague 1. www.casa-marcello.cz. ℭ **222-311-230.** Fax 222-313-323. 32 units. From 2,400Kč 1-bedroom suite; from 3,600Kč 2-bedroom suite. Rates include breakfast. AE, MC, V. Metro: Staroměstská. **Amenities:** Restaurant; bar; exercise room; room service. In room: TV, hair dryer, minibar, Wi-Fi.

Hotel InterContinental Prague   The upper suites of this hotel have hosted luminaries, including former U.S. Secretary of State Madeleine Albright, and (legend has it) global terrorist Carlos the Jackal. Secretary Albright came for the comfortably reconstructed rooms; the Jackal apparently came because during the Communist era the hotel was a safe house with decent room and board. The 1970s facade is unappealing, but the interior has been updated with modern rooms, a glittering fitness center, and an atrium restaurant. The standard guest rooms aren't large but are comfortable, with decent but not exceptional upholstered furniture, computer ports, and marble bathrooms. A riverside window might give you a glimpse of the castle or at least the metronome at the top of Letná Park across the river, where a massive statue of Joseph Stalin once stood in the late 1950s and early '60s.

Pařížská 30, Prague 1. www.icprague.com. ℭ **296-631-111.** Fax 224-811-216. 364 units. From 4,161Kč double; from 7,605Kč suite. Rates include buffet breakfast. AE, DC, MC, V. Metro: Staroměstská. Parking. **Amenities:** 2 restaurants; cafe; concierge; executive-level rooms; exercise room; health club & spa; indoor pool; room service. In room: TV, hair dryer, Internet, minibar.

Hotel Josef ★★   The Josef remains the hippest of Prague's hip hotels. British-based Czech architect Eva Jiřičná brings a new study on the interior use of glass to her native land with its own long history of the glazier's craft. Every piece of space breathes with life and light, breaking the stuffy mold of most high-end hotels. She uses modern glass walls, tables, and chairs bathed with the light of modern lighting fixtures to offset funky yellows and greens, and even rust-colored bedspreads are thrown in. There is a daring and dramatic effect in every room. Superior rooms are so bold as to offer transparent bath nooks, shower stalls, and washrooms with a full view of grooming activities for your partner to absorb in the main sleeping chamber. Room no. 801, a penthouse suite with a magnificent vista of the Prague skyline, is highly sought-after for those who want to absorb the Golden City in its full glory.

Rybná 20, Prague 1. www.hoteljosef.com. ℭ **221-700-111.** Fax 221-700-999. 109 units. From 3,400Kč double. AE, DC, MC, V. Metro: Nám. Republiky. Parking. **Amenities:** Restaurant; bar; babysitting; exercise room; health club; room service. In room: A/C, TV, DVD, CD player, hair dryer, minibar, Wi-Fi (free).

PRAGUE'S best HOSTELS

Hostels aren't what they used to be, at least not in Prague. These days, backpackers with a little spare cash are demanding more style for their money, and hotel owners have responded with a new breed of "flashpacker" hostels, combining the stripped-down basics of a hostel (like dorm beds and shared bathrooms) with services and style you might associate more with a boutique hotel.

In Prague, two names to look out for include the **Czech Inn ★★** at Francouzská 76, Prague 10 (www.czech-inn. com; ℰ **267-267-600**), and **Sir Toby's ★** at Dělnická 24, Prague 7 (www.sirtobys. com; ℰ **246-032-610**). Both offer beds in shared dorm rooms for around 390Kč per person, and private doubles from around 1,200Kč—in other words, excellent value for what's available. Prices include a hearty breakfast, and there are thoughtful touches like big banks of computers for checking e-mail and modern efficiency kitchens. Though both are situated outside the center, they are close enough to public transportation that this is not an issue.

Travellers' Hostel-Pension Dlouhá ★ (Dlouhá 33, Prague 1; www.travellers.cz; ℰ **224-826-662;** fax 224-826-665) is one of the best hostels in the city center. This flagship in the local Travellers' group of hostels is open year-round, just a few blocks off Old Town Square and a few floors above one of the better music clubs in town, Roxy. The hostel offers shared accommodations in dorm rooms or private singles and doubles, and attracts a mix of backpackers and veteran tourists taking advantage of the clean, affordable setting. Travellers' offers other hostels at dormitories throughout town during the high season. Check the website for more info. Rates including breakfast are 790Kč per person in a double room.

Hotel Paříž ★★   At the edge of Náměstí Republiky and across from the Municipal House, the 100-year-old Paříž provides a rare chance to put yourself back in the gilded First Republic. Each light fixture, etching, and curve at this Art Nouveau landmark recalls the days when Prague was one of the world's richest cities. The sinuous banister leading past the reception area is an intricate piece of ironwork, and the lobby is tastefully furnished in the Art Nouveau style known here as the *secese* motif. The high-ceilinged guest rooms are done in a purplish theme; they aren't plush but are comfortable and adequately equipped, with more modern furnishings than the lobby would suggest. It's the ground floor that really maintains an authentic period elegance. Stays of 3 nights or more qualify for a 20% discount.

U Obecního domu 1, Prague 1. www.hotel-pariz.cz. ℰ **222-195-195.** Fax 222-195-907. 86 units (most with tub/shower combination). 4,200Kč double; 8,000Kč suite. AE, DC, MC, V. Metro: Nám. Republiky. **Amenities:** Restaurant; cafe; babysitting; exercise room; health club & spa; room service. *In room:* A/C, TV, hair dryer, Internet, minibar.

Hotel U Prince ★★   Sometimes with a location this good, a hotel will fall short of expectations, but the Hotel U Prince has reformed itself into a worthy choice for its price range. Directly across from the Astronomical Clock in Old Town Square, a complete reconstruction of the 12th-century building has given its once ragged rooms and salons a new lease on life. They are spacious and equipped with heavy period furniture, including beds with soft mattresses. The double-glazed windows lock out most of the constant buzz from the square below. Rooms in the back are even more

family-friendly ACCOMMODATIONS

Private apartments where you can fix your own meals are the most convenient option for families (p. 51), but if you would prefer more hotel-like services and settings, try:

Corinthia Hotel (p. 67)   This is one of the few hotels anywhere to offer its own Western-style bowling alley complete with automatic scoring. Vyšehrad Park, with playgrounds and beautiful views for picnicking, is a short walk away.

Orion (p. 66)   This affordable apartment-style hotel in Vinohrady has plenty of space for kids as well as kitchens for meals the way you want them.

Pension Větrník (p. 68)   This country inn has plenty of fresh air and forests for the kids to run around. Mom and Dad will like the price and made-to-order meals.

secluded. However, the showstopper of this property is the roof terrace bar and restaurant, which offers exceptional views for dining in Prague during the high season.

Staroměstské nám. 29, Prague 1. www.hoteluprince.com. ⓒ/fax **224-213-807.** 24 units. 3,000Kč double; from 4,800Kč suite. Rates include breakfast. AE, MC, V. Metro: Staroměstská. **Amenities:** 2 restaurants, including 1 rooftop restaurant open year-round; bar; room service; summer garden. *In room:* A/C, TV, minibar, Wi-Fi (free).

Moderate

Betlem Club ◢   Protestant firebrand Jan Hus launched his reformation drive at the reconstructed chapel across the street, but other than the vaulted medieval cellar where breakfast is served, little about the Betlem Club recalls those heady 15th-century days. Still, this small hotel has a great location on a cobblestone square. The rooms are unimaginatively decorated with bland modern pieces but are comfortable and fairly priced. The bathrooms are small but clean.

Betlémské nám. 9, Prague 1. www.betlemclub.cz. ⓒ **222-221-574.** Fax 222-220-580. 22 units (tub/shower combination). From 2,700Kč double; from 3,125Kč suite. Rates include breakfast. AE, MC, V. Metro: Národní třída. **Amenities:** Babysitting; Internet. *In room:* TV, hair dryer, minibar.

Dům U krále Jiřího   The "King George" perches above a pub and a jazz club on a narrow side street. The rooms are pretty bare but have a bit more charm than they used to. The ceilings are high, and the dark wooden furniture is another improvement. Charles Bridge is a few dozen steps away and a swing to the left from the pension, but this narrow alley has become more like Bourbon Street than the Royal Route. Ask for a room in back if you want to deaden the clamor of the pubs below. Breakfast is served in the wine cellar, which lacks character despite a remodeling.

Liliová 10, Prague 1. www.hotelkinggeorge.com. ⓒ **221-466-100.** Fax 221-466-166. 11 units. From 2,500Kč double or suite. Rates include breakfast. AE, MC, V. Metro: Staroměstská. *In room:* TV, Internet, minibar.

Hotel Cloister Inn ★★ ◢   Between Old Town Square and the National Theater, this property has been renovated into a good-value, midrange hotel. The original rooms of this unique spot were developed from holding cells used by the Communist secret police, the StB; the cells themselves were converted from a convent. It sounds ominous, but the Cloister Inn rooms are actually very inviting. A new proprietor has taken over management from the secret police and has refurbished and expanded the hotel with smart colors and comfortable Nordic furniture. The rooms offer enough space, beds with firm mattresses, and reasonably sized bathrooms with showers only. All is maintained to a high standard. It is just a short walk from both Charles Bridge and Old Town Square.

Konviktská 14, Prague 1. www.cloister-inn.cz. 𝄐 **224-211-020.** Fax 224-210-800. 73 units (showers only). From 2,400Kč double. Rates include breakfast. AE, DC, MC, V. Metro: Národní třída. *In room:* A/C (some), TV, hair dryer, minibar, Wi-Fi (free).

NOVÉ MĚSTO (NEW TOWN)

Nové Město occupies a large area to the south and east of the Old Town. Though the district was laid out as far back as the 14th century, many of the old buildings were ripped down in the 19th century, giving the area a less intimate feel.

Best For: Business travelers, thanks to the proximity of several large four- and five-star properties (many operated by international chains), and drivers, since most of the properties are accessible by car (though parking still remains tight). Budget travelers will also find rates cheaper here than in other central areas.

Drawbacks: Nové Město has admittedly less charm and more grit than either the Old Town or the Lesser Town. That said, it's within easy walking distance of both areas and filled with restaurants and clubs.

Near Wenceslas Square

EXPENSIVE

Hotel Jalta   The Jalta is arguably the nicest hotel directly on the square. It was reconstructed a few years ago, giving the lobby, public areas, and rooms a much-needed makeover. The decor ranges from a stripped down midcentury modern, in keeping with the hotel's 1950s facade, to a more colorful contemporary. The rooms facing the square have balconies, allowing a broad view of the busy square and a chance to imagine the scene on those historic, revolutionary nights from 1989. The hotel offers free Wi-Fi and you can book online.

Václavské nám. 45, Prague 1. www.hoteljalta.com. 𝄐 **222-822-111.** Fax 222-822-833. 94 units. From 4,500Kč double; 5,500Kč suite. Rates include breakfast. AE, DC, MC, V. Metro: Muzeum. **Amenities:** 2 restaurants; concierge; exercise room; room service. *In room:* A/C, TV, hair dryer, minibar, Wi-Fi (paid).

Palace Hotel ★   The Palace is a landmark hotel dating from the first decade of the 20th century. The exterior is a fine example of Secession style, a restrained version of Art Nouveau, though a thorough renovation (maybe too thorough) in the 1990s left the rooms a little on the sterile side. Still, the central location, just a block from Václavské náměsti and about a 10-minute walk to the Old Town, is ideal, and the hotel is renowned for excellent service. Several rooms offer views to the castle or to the opera, though these are more expensive. Book over the Net for big savings over the rack rate.

Panská 12, Prague 1. www.palacehotel.cz. 𝄐 **224-093-111.** Fax 224-221-240. 114 units. From 4,200Kč double; 5,200Kč suite. Rates include breakfast. AE, DC, MC, V. Metro: Můstek. **Amenities:** Restaurant; concierge; exercise room; room service. *In room:* A/C, TV, hair dryer, minibar, Wi-Fi (free in suites, paid elsewhere).

MODERATE

Andante ✿   This best-value choice near Wenceslas Square is tucked away on a dark side street, about 2 blocks off the top of the square. Despite the unappealing neighborhood, this is the most comfortable property at this price. With modern beds and good firm mattresses, as well as high-grade Scandinavian furniture and colorful decorations, the rooms are extremely comfortable. They offer plenty of space and white, well-kept bathrooms with tub/shower combinations, some with shower only.

Ve Smečkách 4, Prague 1. www.andante.cz. ℂ **222-210-021.** Fax 222-210-591. 32 units (some with shower only, some with tub only). From 2,400Kč double; 3,600Kč suite. Rates include breakfast. AE, MC, V. Metro: Muzeum. **Amenities:** Restaurant; room service. *In room:* TV, hair dryer, Internet, minibar.

Hotel Meran   This used to be part of the Hotel Evropa next door (see below), but the Meran is a bit brighter and more inviting than its bigger Art Nouveau neighbor, which draws so much attention to its gilded facade. The Meran has had a face-lift to make it a fair but not spectacular midrange choice on Wenceslas Square, a walkable distance to the main train station. The lobby interior has retained some original Art Nouveau accents, although the rooms have few. They are unimaginatively decorated and seem cramped. The tiny bathrooms have tub/shower combinations or shower only. Like the Hotel Jalta (see above), front windows overlook the place where hundreds of thousands demonstrated until the Communist government fell in a peaceful coup in 1989.

Václavské nám. 27, Prague 1. www.hotelmeran.cz. ℂ **224-238-440.** Fax 224-230-411. 20 units with bathroom (tub or shower). From 2,700Kč double. Rates include breakfast. AE, DC, MC, V. Metro: Muzeum or Můstek. *In room:* TV, Internet, minibar.

INEXPENSIVE

Hotel Evropa   Established in 1889 as the Hotel Archduke Stephan, the Evropa was recast in the early 1900s as a gleaming Art Nouveau hotel. However, this is yet another classic that has seen much better days. Though the statue-studded exterior, still one of the most striking landmarks on Wenceslas Square, has recently been polished, the rooms are aging; most don't have bathrooms and some are just plain shabby. The best choice is a room facing the square with a balcony. The hotel's famous cafe, a wood-encased former masterpiece that no longer glows, furthers the theme. Still, this is an affordable way to stay in one of Wenceslas Square's once grand addresses.

Václavské nám. 25, Prague 1. www.evropahotel.cz. ℂ **224-215-387.** 90 units, 20 with bathroom (tub only). 1,400Kč double without bathroom; 2,000Kč double with bathroom. Rates include continental breakfast. AE, MC, V. Metro: Můstek or Muzeum. **Amenities:** Restaurant; cafe.

Pension Museum ★ ✿   This is yet another example of a successful renovation of a 19th-century building in the very center of the city. Located just across the National Museum, the pension offers clean and comfortable rooms with modern furniture. Do not be put off by the busy road in front, however. There are actually only two rooms facing it, and their new double-glazed windows block the noise very well. The private cozy courtyard garden serves as an oasis for relaxation, which is otherwise hard to find around Václavské náměstí, the city's liveliest shopping area.

Mezibranská 15, Prague 1. www.pension-museum.cz. ℂ **296-325-186.** Fax 296-325-188. 12 units with bathroom (shower only). From 2,200Kč double; 2,700Kč suite. Rates include breakfast. AE, MC, V. Metro: Muzeum. **Amenities:** Atrium garden; concierge; Internet; luggage storage. *In room:* A/C, TV, fridge, hair dryer.

Near Náměstí Republiky
VERY EXPENSIVE

Kempinski Hotel Prague ★★   The Kempinski is a relatively recent entry into Prague's high-end accommodations market. The setting is a jaw-dropping refurbished 17th-century town house. The public areas are all polished stone and glass. The rooms feature a stylish contemporary interior with retro hints, and all the modern conveniences you'd expect at this price. The bathrooms are huge with the de rigueur see-through shower glass (it seems no one wants privacy anymore when showering). The restaurant's Le Grill restaurant is easily one of the best in the city.

Hybernská 12, Prague 1. www.kempinski-prague.com. © **226-226-111.** Fax 226-226-123. 74 units. From 4,700Kč double; 8,125Kč suite. Rates include breakfast. AE, DC, MC, V. Metro: Nám. Republiky. Parking. **Amenities:** 2 restaurants; cafe; exercise room; health club & spa; room service. *In room:* A/C, TV, hair dryer, minibar, MP3 docking station, Wi-Fi.

EXPENSIVE

Hilton Old Town ★   Like the Marriott across the street, this is a top-level business hotel and caters primarily to the expense-account crowd. It's good for what it is, but for the same amount of money, you could stay somewhere with a lot more character. For example, each room is strategically lit, with warm woods and contemporary earth tones, but without any of the period accents found at the Old Town's Art Nouveau hotels. The rooms include comfortable modern beds, flat-panel TVs, and clean, fully tiled bathrooms. There's a very good in-house restaurant.

V Celnici 7, Prague 1. www1.hilton.com. © **221-822-100.** Fax 221-822-200. 305 units. From 3,900Kč double; from 8,000Kč suite. Rates for suites and executive rooms include breakfast. AE, DC, MC, V. Metro: Nám. Republiky. Parking. **Amenities:** 2 restaurants; bar; ballroom; concierge; small exercise room; pool (indoor); room service; sauna; meeting rooms; whirlpool. *In room:* A/C, TV, hair dryer, Internet, minibar.

K+K Hotel Central ★★ 🗲   It wasn't that long ago that Hybernská Street, which runs beside the Masaryk train station, was a forgotten corner of the city and slightly derelict at night. Now it's one of the hottest properties for upscale hotels, including the Kempinski (reviewed above), and this ornate Art Nouveau palace that may even be the better of the two. Fans of early-20th-century architecture will love the highly stylized exterior and public areas. The rooms are on the small side, but done up in a kind of low-slung Functionalist style that recalls the 1920s. The dining and breakfast areas are opulent in the extreme, a series of archways carved into the wall and festooned with 1920s period lighting. Check the website for discounts; the hotel frequently offers rooms that would put this in the moderate category. In other words: a steal.

Hybernská 10, Prague 1. www.kkhotels.com. © **225-022-000.** Fax 225-022-999. 127 units. From 3,400Kč double; from 6,800Kč suite. Rates include breakfast. AE, DC, MC, V. Metro: Nám. Republiky. Parking. **Amenities:** Restaurant; bar; cafe/lounge; babysitting; executive-level rooms; exercise room; room service; sauna. *In room:* TV, hair dryer, Internet, minibar.

Prague Marriott Hotel ★   A major addition to the thin ranks of full-service business hotels, the Marriott provides just what you would expect—a high standard. The large rooms have bright colors, tasteful (if homogenized) furniture, and comfortable beds, as well as phones, faxes, laptop connections, and other services. The bathrooms are spacious and immaculately maintained. In an effort to attract families, the Marriott offers Sunday family brunches in the in-house restaurant, where kids are welcome and PC games are available. The hotel steeply discounts rates on weekends.

V Celnici 8, Prague 1. www.marriott.com. © **222-888-888.** Fax 222-888-889. 328 units. 4,500Kč double; 6,500Kč executive-level double. Rates for executive rooms include breakfast. AE, DC, MC, V. Metro: Nám. Republiky. Parking. **Amenities:** Restaurant; cafe; bar; exercise room; health club & spa; pool (indoor); room service; sauna. *In room:* A/C, TV, hair dryer, Internet, minibar.

VINOHRADY

Vinohrady is an attractive residential district, situated immediately behind the National Museum at the top of Wenceslas Square. Transportation connections are excellent to the center and there are many restaurants and clubs in the area to keep you occupied.

Best For: Couples looking for something quieter than the center, for returning travelers who don't need to be right downtown, and for budget travelers, since rates here are a bit lower than the center.

Drawbacks: The area is removed from the center, so this is not the neighborhood to choose if you want Prague Castle outside your doorstep. It's also not the best choice for mobility-impaired travelers because of the need to take trams and metros everywhere.

Very Expensive

Le Palais Prague ★★   This hotel occupies a tastefully remodeled 19th-century town house in a secluded setting in one of the city's prime residential neighborhoods. It will appeal to people looking to get away from the center and wanting something a little smaller and more personalized than the larger places downtown. There are some nice touches, like a fireplace in the common room, lots of nooks and crannies to get lost in, a very good in-house restaurant, and one of the city's nicest spas, with a full menu of relaxation and massage options. There's paid parking on-site. Book online for big discounts.

U Zvonařky 1, Prague 2. www.palaishotel.cz. © **234-634-111.** Fax 234-634-635. 72 units. From 4,200Kč double; 5,600Kč suite. Rates include breakfast. AE, MC, V. Metro: I.P. Pavlova and then tram 6 or 11 to Bruselska. Parking. **Amenities:** Restaurant; bar; concierge; exercise room; health club & spa; room service. *In room:* A/C, hair dryer, minibar, Wi-Fi.

Moderate

Hotel Ametyst   On a quiet backstreet about 5 blocks from náměstí Míru, the Hotel Ametyst is spotless and decorated in a warm contemporary style. The top-floor rooms are especially bright and cheery, with pitched ceilings and balconies overlooking the peaceful residential neighborhood. The rooms are smartly decorated in contemporary style, with big beds, flatscreen TVs, and wooden floors.

Jana Masaryka 11, Prague 2. www.hotelametyst.cz. © **222-921-946.** Fax 222-921-999. 84 units (some with tub only, some with shower only). From 3,200Kč double. Rates include breakfast. AE, DC, MC, V. Metro: Nám. Míru. Parking. **Amenities:** Restaurant; bar; small exercise room; sauna. *In room:* TV, hair dryer, minibar, Wi-Fi (free).

Inexpensive

Orion ★ ☺   The best family value close to the city center, the Orion is an apartment hotel with each unit sporting a well-equipped kitchen. All accommodations have either one bedroom (sleeps two) or two bedrooms (sleeps up to six). The spacious guest rooms are comfortable but not very imaginative, bordered in pale blue with leather armchairs and dark wooden bed frames without much on the walls. The beds vary in the firmness of their mattresses. The bathrooms are small, basic white, and modern, as are the kitchens. In this friendly neighborhood, fruit and vegetable shops and corner grocery stores can be found around náměstí Míru, just up the street.

Americká 9, Prague 2. www.okhotels.cz/en/hotel-orion. © **222-521-706.** Fax 222-521-707. 26 apts with bathroom (tub/shower combination). From 1,600Kč 1 bedroom; 2,400Kč 2 bedrooms. Breakfast 160Kč. AE, MC, V. Metro: Nám. Míru. Parking. **Amenities:** Room service; sauna. In room: TV, kitchen, Wi-Fi (free).

ELSEWHERE IN PRAGUE

Very Expensive

Corinthia Hotel Prague ★ ☺ Opened in the mid-1980s, this hotel was one of the last "achievements" of Communist central planners. Reserved occasionally for delegates attending Party Congress meetings at the Palace of Culture next door (now the Congress Center), the hotel juts up from a hill with a gorgeous panorama of the city. The medium-size rooms have undergone a recent renovation and are fitted out with solid furniture and firm mattresses on the beds. One of the more unusual amenities is a pub with a bowling alley in the basement, and the top-floor pool has a panoramic city view. Though the city center isn't within walking distance, the Vyšehrad metro station is just below the hotel entrance.

Kongresová 1, Prague 4. www.corinthia.com. © **261-191-111.** Fax 261-225-011. 583 units. 4,000Kč double; from 6,000Kč suite. Rates include breakfast. AE, DC, MC, V. Metro: Vyšehrad. Parking. **Amenities:** 2 restaurants; cafe; babysitting; concierge; well-equipped fitness center w/pool, sauna, and exercise machines; room service; bowling alley. In room: A/C, TV, minibar, Wi-Fi (paid).

Hilton Prague With its jarring 1980s galleria style, the Hilton looks like a huge ice cube outside and a greenhouse inside. The guest rooms are relatively cushy and functional, somewhat like those in an upscale U.S. motel. The building is packed with amenities that include a tennis club, pool, fitness center, and arguably the city's most elegant cocktail bar, the Cloud 9 Sky Bar and Lounge. The 700 plus rooms make this place a natural choice for the largest conferences and conventions; it's also the hotel of choice for visiting U.S. presidents, including Bill Clinton, George W. Bush, and in 2009, Barack Obama and his wife, Michelle. The location just outside the city center isn't ideal, but it's just a short walk to the Florenc metro station.

Pobřežní 1, Prague 8. www.hilton.com. © **224-841-111.** Fax 224-842-378. 788 units (tub/shower combination). From 5,200Kč double; from 7,200Kč suite. AE, DC, MC, V. Metro: Florenc. Parking. **Amenities:** Cafe/restaurant; exercise room; health club & spa; pool (indoor); putting greens; room service; sauna; tennis club. In room: A/C, TV, hair dryer, Internet, minibar.

Moderate

Hotel Absolutum ★★ ◀ This is a sleek, modern hotel, with designer-style rooms at reasonable prices. The rack rates aren't particularly great, but the reception desk will usually offer decent discounts on slow nights (be sure to ask). The location, across the street from the Holešovice train and metro station, won't win any beauty contests, but it is convenient for getting to the center or for checking out Holešovice, one of Prague's up-and-coming neighborhoods. The house restaurant is the best around, and a good place to get a bite if you're stuck waiting on a train at Holešovice nádraží. It's one of the few Prague hotels to offer free parking.

Jablonského 476, Prague 7. www.absolutumhotel.cz. ✆ **222-541-406.** Fax 222-541-407. 34 units (some with tub/shower combination). 2,800Kč double. Rates include breakfast. MC. Metro: Nádraží Holešovice. Parking. **Amenities:** Cafe/restaurant; exercise room; health club & spa (next door); limited room service. *In room:* A/C, TV, hair dryer, minibar, Wi-Fi (free).

Inexpensive

Pension Větrník ★ 🗲 ☺ A mostly scenic half-hour tram ride (or metro-tram combo) from the city center takes you to this romantic country hideaway. After getting off the tram, walk back behind a bunch of large concrete dorms to find a painstakingly restored 18th-century white windmill house. Once you buzz at the metal gate (be careful to avoid the buzzer for the door to the family residence), the owner will greet you. Lush gardens and a tennis court lead to a quaint guesthouse with a stone staircase and spacious rooms with big beds, open-beamed ceilings, and modern amenities. If you opt for dinner at the pension, the owner will whip up a traditional Czech country meal (for around 200Kč) and serve it in a small medieval stone cellar with a fire. There's a patio for drinks outside during pleasant weather.

U Větrníku 40, Prague 6. www.vetrnik1722.cz. ✆ **220-612-404.** Fax 220-513-390. 6 units (4 shower only, 2 tub/shower combo). 1,800Kč double; 2,300Kč suite. Rates include breakfast. MC. Metro: Line A to Hradčanská station, then tram 1 or 18 to Větrník. Parking. **Amenities:** Restaurant; tennis court. *In room:* TV, hair dryer, Internet.

NEAR THE AIRPORT

Prague Airport is located in the extreme western part of the city. Crossing the city to get to the airport can take as long as an hour or more during rush hour. The two properties listed below are not actually in the immediate area of the airport, but close to the main access road. If you'd like to stay at the airport, **Marriott** (www.marriott.com) and **Holiday Inn** (www.holidayinn.com) both manage properties just outside the main arrivals terminals.

Very Expensive

Hotel Praha ★ The Praha is a former luxury hotel for high-ranking Communist party members and is kind of a kitsch choice if you want to know how the other half once lived. Everything is oversized, and the retro-futuristic cocktail bar has to be seen to be believed. The hotel is built into the hillside in a wealthy suburb on the city's western end. It has all the brass, chrome, and marble veneer that Brezhnev and Castro ever could have wanted, but before you dismiss it as a relic, you might be interested to know that Tom Cruise, Johnny Depp, and other celebrities have stayed here. The draws are the fortresslike setting, private balconies, magnificent views, and proximity to the airport. Rooms are spacious but plain compared with the lavish public areas.

Sušická 20, Prague 6. www.htlpraha.cz. ✆ **224-341-111.** Fax 224-311-218. 124 units (tub/shower combination). From 5,000Kč double; from 7,500Kč suite. Rates include breakfast. AE, DC, MC, V. Metro: Dejvická plus tram 2, 20, or 26. Parking. **Amenities:** 2 restaurants; babysitting; exercise room; health club & spa; pool (indoor); room service; sauna; 2 tennis courts. *In room:* A/C, TV, hair dryer, Internet, minibar.

Expensive

Hotel Diplomat The clean and functional Diplomat is a good choice if access to the airport is important. While it's not next to the airport, it does lie next to the main trunk road about 15 minutes away. It's also convenient for getting into town, situated just next to the Dejvická metro station, about 10 minutes by metro to the center. While it won't win any design awards, the Diplomat achieves what it sets out to do: provide an array of business services and spacious rooms with comfortable beds. The colorful decorations and furnishings give the rooms a warm atmosphere.

Evropská 15, Prague 6. www.diplomathotel.cz. © **296-559-111.** Fax 296-559-215. 398 units (tub/ shower combination). 3,600Kč double; 5,200Kč suite. Rates include breakfast. AE, DC, MC, V. Metro: Dejvická. Parking. **Amenities:** 2 restaurants; cafe/bar; executive-level rooms; exercise room; health club & spa. *In room:* A/C, TV, hair dryer, Internet, minibar.

WHERE TO EAT IN PRAGUE

Prague still has a long way to go before people travel here just for the food, but the quality and variety of restaurants have improved tremendously in the past decade. Not that long ago, dining out meant choosing between a pizza covered in ketchup, listless pub grub, or a handful of overpriced "luxury" restaurants—the kind where stiff waiters wheel around tired appetizers on a little cart.

Today, thanks to a massive influx of tourist dollars as well as rising incomes of ordinary Czechs, Prague now supports many very good restaurants, with traditional Czech places supplemented by French, Italian, Japanese, Chinese, and a growing number of Indian restaurants. The most recent craze is for locally sourced and organic foods, all to the benefit of the dining public.

But that doesn't mean every place is good. For every decent restaurant that has opened its doors in the past couple of years, it seems at least two inferior restaurants—tourist traps aimed squarely at unwitting visitors—have popped up. More than ever, it pays to be careful. Avoid places in the heavily touristy areas of town around Old Town Square and Karlova Street. These are pallid imitations of real Czech restaurants that are meant to empty your wallet, not satisfy your palate. Many of the best places are located outside of the city center, so be prepared to hit the metro or grab a taxi if serious food is on the agenda.

The list below includes some of the city's best restaurants. To supplement my picks and see what Prague's expats are saying, check out two English-language restaurant blogs: "Čau Down" (www.praguepost.com/blogs/food) by the food critics at *The Prague Post,* and "Czech Please" (www.czechoutchannel.blogspot.com), by an enigmatic American expat known only as "Brewsta."

Reservations It's usually best to play it safe and book a table in advance in all but the simplest restaurants. You'll get better treatment by the staff if you book, and you'll avoid the disappointment of traveling to a far-flung part of Prague just to hear that there are no more tables for the evening. Most restaurants should be able to handle a reservation request in English. Alternatively, ask your hotel reception desk to make the call.

Service While the quality of the food in Prague's restaurants keeps getting better every year, service still seems stuck in the past. Restaurant owners appear unwilling to commit the necessary resources to proper

5

Decoder: How to Eat Like a Local

Service in Prague restaurants generally still leaves a lot to be desired. But in my experience, at least part of the problem has to do with differing expectations from diners on the one side and servers on the other. Prague, like any other city, has its restaurant quirks. Here are some of my suggestions for understanding some of the unwritten rules and bridging the culture gap.

○**Watch out for touts.** Unlike in southern Europe, for example, Prague has no tradition of restaurant owners hailing prospective diners from the street and pulling them in for a meal. If you find a menu being pushed in your face as you walk down the street, politely decline and move on. It's a tourist trap.

○**Take a good look at the menu before you sit down.** Most reputable places will post a menu on the door outside for you to peruse. If you don't see a menu, it's perfectly fine to ask for one before taking a seat.

○**Greet the staff as you walk in.** A polite *Dobrý den* (good day) is both good manners and lets everyone know you're there.

○**Understand the ordering system.** Czech servers are likely to visit your table in two rounds: The first, almost the moment you arrive, is to take a drinks order and the second is for food. Don't wave the waiter away on the first round or you may never see him or her again (especially if it's a crowded place). Even if you don't know what you want to drink, order water—at least that ensures the waiter is coming back.

○**Don't expect an especially knowledgeable server.** Unless you're in a fancy place, Czech waiters won't likely be able to answer technical cooking questions like what specific ingredients are used in a dish or even how a dish is prepared. Use your waiter, instead, for more basic suggestions, such as which side dish or Czech wine to pair with an entree.

○**Order salads and side dishes separately.** Unlike in the U.S., for example, meals are not usually served as packages, with salads and sides included. If you want a salad to start, order it as an appetizer (but specify you want a small salad). Side dishes (*přílohy*) present added complications and have their own internal rules for pairing with main courses. You'll never see schnitzel served with dumplings, for example (it's just not done). In general, pair dumplings with entrees served in gravy, and potatoes for just about everything else. When in doubt, consult the server.

○**Finally, be prepared for the occasional mix-up.** You ordered mashed potatoes, but got boiled—that kind of thing. Miscommunications are common across languages, and kitchens just screw things up from time to time. Unless it's a crucial mistake (like chunks of ham floating in your vegetarian soup), it's best to go with the flow. I once sent a pizza back that was slightly undercooked and waited 45 minutes for a new one. At some point, it's not worth the hassle.

training, and the result is often impossibly slow service, messed up orders, unfriendly staff, and long waits to pay your bill. The good news is that you're on vacation and time won't usually be a main concern. Just be sure to check your expectations at the door. See the box "Decoder: How to Eat Like a Local," below, for a few tips on how to have a better eating-out experience.

Tipping & Tax   A tip of 10% of the bill is considered standard for good service in a tablecloth restaurant, but don't feel obliged to go the full amount if service was poor. Most Czechs tip considerably less and simply round up the bill to the next logical point. For example, on a 480Kč check, they might hand the waiter a 500Kč bill and tell him to keep the change. Tips are usually handed directly to the waiter or left discreetly in the little pouch or wallet that the bill is delivered in.

Some restaurants have begun the irritating practice of adding the tip—usually 10% but sometimes more for groups—directly to the bill. It's a good idea to look over the tab carefully to make sure you understand all the charges.

Dining Customs   Traditional Czech custom is simply to find whatever seats are available without the assistance of a hostess or maitre d', but newer restaurants have started to employ staff to seat you. Barring this, just point at the table you want and nod at a nearby waiter to make sure it's available. Don't be afraid to sit in open seats at large tables where others are already seated, as is the case in many pubs and casual restaurants. However, it's customary to ask *"Je tu volno?"* ("Is this spot free?") before joining a large table. Likewise, don't be surprised if others ask to sit at your table. Just nod or say *"Ano, je"* ("Yes, it's free"), and make some new friends.

best DINING BETS

o   **Best Splurge:** This is a tough call, but if you're into Michelin stars, give **Allegro** (© **221-427-000**) in the Four Seasons Hotel a try. **La Degustation** (© **222-311-234**) is another natural splurge choice. It's the consensus pick among local critics as the country's best overall restaurant, but expect the bill for two to creep into five-figure territory (10,000Kč or more) with wine. At **Sansho** (© **222-317-425**), the head chef did a stint at Michelin-starred Nobu in London before coming to Prague. See p. 81, p. 82, and p. 87.

o   **Best Expensive Czech Cooking:** In an intricate flower-embellished setting, **U modré kachničky** (© **257-320-308**) brings delicacy to Czech fare, including savvy spins on heavy sauces and wild game. Be sure to try to book upstairs. See p. 79.

o   **Best Affordable Czech Cooking:** I like **Lokál** (© **222-316-265**) on Dlouhá in Staré Město for great food, even better beer, and prices that still let me feel relatively well off. See p. 87.

o   **Best Fancy Italian:** There are lots of great Italian restaurants in town, but for my money, the best overall is still **Aromi** (© **222-713-222**) in Vinohrady. Come for dinner or for a remarkably good-value lunch special. See p. 89.

o   **Best Home-Cooked Italian:** Another tough choice since there are so many possibilities, but if you can get in at tiny **Ichnusa Botega & Bistro** (© **605-525-748**) in Malá Strana, you'll have a meal to remember. See p. 78.

o   **Best Meal With a View:** Several top restaurants offer unparalleled views of the river, the castle, the bridge, and the towers, but for the money you simply can't beat the on-deck location of **Grosseto Marina** (© **605-454-020**), on the Old Town embankment. See p. 84. For cheap eats, it's hard to beat the terrace at **A Divadlo Pokračuje** (© **733-483-900**) in Hradčany for the view. See p. 75.

o   **Best All-You-Can-Eat Buffet:** I don't know how they make any money on this, but the antipasto buffet at **Pizza Nuova** (© **221-803-308**), next to Kotva, is filled with mouthwatering grilled vegetables, meats, cheeses, and fish. Add all the fresh bread and salad you can eat for just 285Kč. See p. 84.

- **Best Bar Food:** It's loud and crude and filled with a boisterous mix of traveling Americans and Czechs bingeing after work, but **Jáma** (© 224-222-383) in Nové Město has, hands down, Prague's best bacon cheeseburger. See p. 88.

- **Best Sushi:** The appropriately named **Sushi Bar** (© 603-244-882) at the southern edge of Malá Strana consistently offers the freshest sushi in a town in the grips of a sushi craze. **Yami** (© 222-312-756) in Staré Město is a close second and a better choice if you're watching your wallet. See p. 78 and 86.

- **Best Bagels: Bohemia Bagel** (© 257-218-192) at Lázeňská in Malá Strana and on Masná Street in Staré Město (© 224-812-560) has filled what was a curious vacuum. See p. 81.

- **Best Hot Dog:** *Párek v rohlíku* (hot dog in a roll) is a popular street food, and arguably the best in town can be found at the little stand on **Náměstí Míru** square. When strolling around Vinohrady, take a break here. There are plenty of benches. See p. 85.

- **Best for Kids/Best Pizza:** You can please the kids and satisfy your own cravings at **Pizzeria Rugantino** (© 222-318-172), a friendly and energetic Staré Město room run by an Italian family that loves kids. See p. 87.

- **Best for Vegetarians:** Relative newcomer **Maitrea** (© 222-316-265) stands head and shoulders above the competition, not just for inventive and delicious dishes, but for its relaxed and elegant setting. See p. 87.

RESTAURANTS BY CUISINE

AMERICAN
Bakeshop ★★ (Staré Město, $, p. 86)
Culinaria ★ (Staré Město, $, p. 85)
Jáma ★ (Nové Město,'$, p. 88)

ASIAN
Sansho ★★★ (Nové Město, $$$$, p. 87)

BAGELS/SANDWICHES
Bohemia Bagel (Malá Strana or Staré Město, $, p. 81)

CAFES/TEAROOMS
Blatouch ★ (Vinohrady, $, p. 92)
Café de Paris ★ (Malá Strana, $$, p. 80)
Café Evropa (Nové Město, $, p. 91)
Café Imperial ★ (Nové Město, $$, p. 91)
Café Louvre (Nové Město, $, p. 92)
Dobrá čajovna ★ (Nové Město, $, p. 92)
The Globe Bookstore and Café ★★ (Nové Město, $, p. 92)

Grand Café (Staré Město, $, p. 91)
Grand Café Orient ★★ (Staré Město, $, p. 91)
Kavárna Obecní dům ★★ (Staré Město, $, p. 91)
Kavárna Slavia ★ (Staré Město, $, p. 91)
Velryba (Nové Město, $, p. 92)

CONTINENTAL
Café de Paris ★ (Malá Strana, $$, p. 80)
Café Savoy ★★ (Malá Strana, $$, p. 80)
Corso (Nové Město, $$, p. 88)
Kampa Park ★ (Malá Strana, $$$$, p. 78)
La Degustation ★★★ (Staré Město, $$$$, p. 82)
Monarch ★ (Staré Město, $$, p. 86)
Nebozízek (Malá Strana, $$, p. 80)
Pálffy Palác ★★ (Malá Strana, $$$, p. 79)
Sansho ★★★ (Nové Město, $$$$, p. 87)

KEY TO ABBREVIATIONS:
$$$$** = Very Expensive   **$$$** = Expensive   **$$** = Moderate   **$ = Inexpensive

U Medvídků ★★ (Staré Město, $,
p. 93)

U Vejvodů ★ (Staré Město, $, p. 93)

Villa Richter ★ (Hradčany, $$$$,
p. 75)

CZECH

A Divadlo Pokračuje ★ (Hradčany, $,
p. 75)

Café Louvre (Nové Město, $, p. 92)

Café Savoy ★★ (Malá Strana, $$,
p. 80)

Corso (Nové Město, $$, p. 88)

Hergetova Cihelna ★ (Malá Strana,
$$$, p. 78)

Klub Architektů (Staré Město, $, p. 86)

La Degustation ★★★ (Staré Město,
$$$$, p. 82)

Lokál ★ (Staré Město, $, p. 87)

Monarch ★ (Staré Město, $$, p. 86)

Nebozízek (Malá Strana, $$, p. 80)

Pivovarský dům ★★ (Nové Město, $,
p. 88)

U Medvídků ★★ (Staré Město, $,
p. 93)

U modré kachničky ★★ (Malá Strana
or Staré Město, $$$, p. 79)

U Vejvodů ★ (Staré Město, $, p. 93)

Vikarka ★ (Hradčany, $$, p. 75)

Villa Richter ★ (Hradčany, $$$$,
p. 75)

DELI

Bakeshop ★★ (Staré Město, $, p. 86)

Culinaria ★ (Staré Město, $, p. 85)

Lahůdky Zlatý Kříž (Nové Město, $,
p. 85)

FRENCH

Café de Paris ★ (Malá Strana, $$,
p. 80)

Chez Marcel (Staré Město, $, p. 86)

Les Moules ★ (Staré Město, $$,
p. 86)

GEORGIAN

Guga ★ (Staré Město, $$, p. 84)

GREEK

Taverna Olympos ★ (Vinohrady, $$,
p. 89)

INDIAN

Masala ★ (Vinohrady, $$, p. 89)

The Pind ★★ (Vinohrady, $$, p. 89)

INTERNATIONAL

A Divadlo Pokračuje ★ (Hradčany, $,
p. 75)

Allegro ★★ (Staré Město, $$$$,
p. 81)

Bellevue ★★ (Staré Město, $$$$,
p. 82)

Café Louvre (Nové Město, $, p. 92)

Corso (Nové Město, $$, p. 88)

Cukrkávalimonáda ★★ (Malá Strana,
$, p. 81)

Grosseto Marina ★★ (Staré Město,
$$$, p. 84)

Hergetova Cihelna ★ (Malá Strana,
$$$, p. 78)

Klub Architektů (Staré Město, $,
p. 86)

Mlýnec ★★ (Staré Město, $$$$, p. 82)

Monarch ★ (Staré Meěsto), $$, p. 86.

Sansho ★★★ (Nové Město, $$$$,
p. 87)

Vinárna V zátiší (Staré Město, $$$$,
p. 82)

INTERNET CAFES

Bohemia Bagel (Staré Město, $, p. 81)

The Globe Bookstore and Café ★★
(Nové Město, $, p. 92)

Spika (Nové Město, $, p. 93)

ITALIAN

Allegro ★★ (Staré Město, $$$$, p. 81)

Aromi ★★ (Vinohrady, $$$$, p. 89)

Grosseto ★ (Dejvice, $$, p. 90)

Grosseto Marina ★★ (Staré Město,
$$$, p. 84)

Ichnusa Botega & Bistro ★★ (Malá
Strana, $$$, p. 78)

Kogo ★ (Staré Město, $$, p. 85)

KEY TO ABBREVIATIONS:
$$$$** = Very Expensive   **$$$** = Expensive   **$$** = Moderate   **$ = Inexpensive

Mirellie ★ (Dejvice, $$, p. 90)
Pizza Nuova ★ (Staré Město, $$, p. 84)

JAPANESE
Sushi Bar ★★ (Malá Strana, $$$$, p. 78)
Yami ★★ (Staré Město, $$, p. 86)

KOSHER
King Solomon Restaurant ★ (Staré Město, $$$, p. 84)

PIZZA
Grosseto ★ (Dejvice, $$, p. 90)
Pizza Nuova ★ (Staré Město, $$, p. 84)

Pizzeria Rugantino ★★ (Staré Město, $, p. 87)

SEAFOOD
Čestr ★★ (Nové Město, $$$, p. 88)
Rybí trh (Staré Město, $$$$, p. 82)

STEAKHOUSE
Čestr ★★ (Nové Město, $$$, p. 88)

VEGETARIAN
Country Life (Staré Město, $, p. 85)
Maitrea ★ (Staré Město, $, p. 87)
Radost FX Café (Vinohrady, $, p. 89)

HRADČANY

Very Expensive

Villa Richter ★ CONTINENTAL/CZECH   A relatively recent entry into Prague's top echelon is this luxury restaurant in a hilltop vineyard just as you exit the Prague Castle complex on the eastern end. There are actually three restaurants here, including an inexpensive option that serves sandwiches and has wine tastings for 45Kč a glass, but the big culinary draw is the "Piano Nobile," a gourmet restaurant offering the best of Czech and international cooking and a wine vault with some 2,000 bottles. There's a five-course tasting menu for 1,690Kč. In winter, dress up for the fancy dining room; in summer, it's more relaxed, with dining on the terrace overlooking Malá Strana to your right and the Old Town across the river.

Staré zámecké schody 6, Prague 1. ℂ **257-219-079.** www.villarichter.cz. Reservations recommended. Main courses 610Kč–690Kč, 1,690 Kč (five-course tasting menu). AE, DC, MC, V. Daily 11am–1am. Metro: Malostranská plus a walk up the stairs.

Moderate

Vikárka ★ ☺ CZECH   Decent places to eat in Hradčany are rare. This wonderfully restored Romanesque and Gothic cellar restaurant within the castle walls not only offers good Czech and international dishes at decent prices, but you also get to eat amid more than 600 years of history. The staff gets into the mood with period costumes, but this is no tourist trap. For a real Czech treat, try the pork knee baked on dark beer served in the traditional style with slices of brown bread, horseradish, and mustard.

Vikářská 39, inside the Prague Castle complex, Prague 1. ℂ **233-311-962.** www.vikarka.cz. Main courses 180Kč–250Kč. AE, DC, MC, V. Daily 11am–9pm. Tram: 22 to Prague Castle.

Inexpensive

A Divadlo Pokračuje ★ 📷 CZECH/INTERNATIONAL   This is a cute coffee shop and pancake house that's recommendable chiefly for its great terrace overlooking the valley, location close to the castle, and exceedingly reasonable prices for sweet

Prague Restaurants

A Divadlo Pokračuje **3**
Aromi **22**
Blatouch **25**
Bohemia Bagel **7**
Café de Paris **10**
Café Savoy **16**
Čestr **19**
Cukrkávalimonáda **8**
The Globe Bookstore
  & Cafe **17**
Grosseto **1**
Hergetova Cihelna **9**
Ichnusa Botega
  and Bistro **14**
Kampa Park **12**
Masala **20**
Mirellie **2**
Nebozizek **13**
Pálffy Palác **6**
Pivovarský dům **18**
Radost FX Café **23**
Sushi Bar **15**
Taverna Olympos **21**
The Pind **24**
U modré kachničky **11**
Vikárka **4**
Villa Richter **5**

and savory pancakes that are both delicious and filling. The main drawback is the slow service, but scout out a seat on the terrace, settle in, and enjoy the afternoon.

Loretánská 13, Prague 1. ℂ **733-483-900.** www.adivadlopokracuje.com. Reservations not necessary. Main courses 80Kč–150Kč. No credit cards. Daily 10am–10pm. Tram: 22 one stop beyond Prague Castle.

MALÁ STRANA (LESSER TOWN)
Very Expensive

Kampa Park ★ CONTINENTAL   This restaurant is worth the considerable splurge, but only if you can snag one of the highly coveted riverside tables. If you can't, move on and try for the terrace at Pálffy Palác or Hergetova Cihelna (both below). For years, Kampa Park was considered Prague's premier restaurant and lured its fair share of visiting celebs (check out the photos on the wall). These days, there's lots more competition, but the setting on the Vltava is still arguably the best in town. The menu, with items like seared monkfish and roast saddle of lamb, looks relatively tame, but the quality of the food is excellent.

Na Kampě 8b, Prague 1. ℂ **296-826-112.** www.kampagroup.com. Reservations recommended. Main courses 495Kč–895Kč. AE, DC, MC, V. Daily 11:30am–1am. Metro: Malostranská.

Sushi Bar ★★ JAPANESE   Sushi came late to the Czech Republic, but now it's here with a vengeance, and you can find sushi and maki on menus all across the city. If you care about truly good sushi, however, this is one of the best in town (also see "Yami" in Staré Město, below). Conveniently, Sushi Bar is situated next to the city's best fish market, so sourcing is not an issue. Everything is fresh, and the "exclusive" jumbo maki are to die for. The dining area is tiny, so reservations are a must.

Zborovská 49. Prague 5. ℂ **603-244-882.** www.sushi.cz. Reservations recommended. Sushi menu 999Kč, exclusive maki 1,190Kč. AE, MC, V. Daily noon–11:30pm. Metro: Malostranská plus tram no. 6, 9, 12, 20, or 22 to Újezd.

Expensive

Hergetova Cihelna ★ INTERNATIONAL/CZECH   The main draw here is the riverside terrace with an unparalleled view of the Charles Bridge—plus the very good food (from the same people who run the more expensive Kampa Park). The building, dating from the 18th century, once served as a brick factory (*cihelna*) before it was renovated into this stylish modern restaurant around a decade ago. The first dining concept here was burgers and pizza, which the owners quickly ditched for more expensive items like rib-eye steaks with maple-glazed carrots (525Kč). Still, it's possible to eat cheaply if you stick to the Czech specialties and pasta dishes. Reserve several days in advance for the terrace.

Cihelná 2b, Prague 1. ℂ **296-826-103.** www.kampagroup.com. Reservations recommended. Main courses 215Kč–695Kč. AE, MC, V. Daily 11:30am–1am. Metro: Malostranská.

Ichnusa Botega & Bistro ★★ ITALIAN   This small, family-owned Sardinian restaurant is a real treat. There's no menu, no staff, and practically no tables to speak of (which makes reserving in advance a necessity). Instead, it's like you're welcomed into the kitchen of a talented Italian friend. The chef doubles as the waiter and there are only usually a couple of entrees available. Start with a family platter of appetizers, including Italian sausages, vegetables, and cheeses, and then dip into an exquisitely

MONEY-SAVING tips

Restaurant prices in Prague have risen dramatically in recent years, and the unfavorable exchange rates for both the dollar and the pound add to the pain. These days, if you're not careful, it's easy to drop US$50 a person on a meal that's only average. Here are some tried and true techniques for keeping the tab manageable. For very cheap meals, try the places covered in "Inexpensive Meals on the Run" (p. 85).

○ **Avoid the area around Old Town Square.** Sadly, the highest prices for meals (and lowest quality) are to be found in the tourist joints that ring Old Town Square, so try to be as far away as possible from the tourist throngs at mealtimes. Eating at restaurants outside the immediate center can cut as much 50% off the tab.

○ **Consider taking some meals in Czech pubs.** These cater largely to local crowds and are priced accordingly. The best deals are offered at lunchtime, when many pubs (and other restaurants as well) offer two- and three-course lunch menus for as little as 100Kč to 150Kč.

○ **Skip the pricey appetizers and aperitifs.** Once you've found a restaurant, remember to politely refuse the waiter's initial offers of an aperitif or an appetizer to start. Czech portions are pretty big and there's often no need to order an appetizer.

○ **Stick to beer (or local wine).** Cocktails and expensive bottles of imported wine can juice the bill very fast. A glass of beer is a perfectly acceptable beverage choice, even in the fanciest places, and rarely costs more than 60Kč a glass. For wines, go for Czech. The quality is nearly as good and the price will be around half of what you'd pay for an imported bottle.

prepared main dish that could be anything from linguini pasta to calamari to tripe. Rest assured, it's all good. Dinners only.

Plaská 5, Prague 5. ✆ **605-525-748.** Reservations essential. Antipasto platter 200Kč, main courses 195Kč–300Kč. AE, DC, MC, V. Daily 7pm–10pm. Tram: 6, 9, 12, 20, 22, stop Újezd.

Pálffy Palác ★★ CONTINENTAL   This restaurant is a good choice, rain or shine. In bad weather, eat in the 17th-century baroque dining room, complete with candles, crystal chandeliers, and impossibly beautiful place settings—it's like having dinner with a wealthy count. In summer, sit on the terrace just below the lights of Prague Castle. Either way, you can't lose. The mostly high-end international dishes, built around standards like lamb and steak, are very good but miss the heights of truly haute cuisine.

Valdštejnská 14, Prague 1. ✆ **257-530-522.** www.palffy.cz. Reservations recommended. Main courses 490Kč–690Kč. AE, DC, MC, V. Daily 11am–11pm. Metro: Malostranská.

U modré kachničky ★★ CZECH   The "Blue Duckling," on a narrow Malá Strana street, comes close to refining standard Czech dishes into true Bohemian haute cuisine. This series of small dining rooms with vaulted ceilings and playfully frescoed walls is packed with antique furniture and pastel-flowered linen upholstery.

☺ family-friendly RESTAURANTS

Bohemia Bagel (p. 81)   The one on Masná Street has a tiny garden with outside seating and a playroom for children, which makes family dining more pleasant and relaxed. Bagels and sandwiches are on the menu together with selections for small children.

Pizza Nuova (p. 84)   The pizzas are great, the menu offers all-you-can eat specials for hungry teens, and there's a small supervised play area in the corner for younger kids.

Pizzeria Rugantino (p. 87)   A long list of crispy individual pizzas and salads, a large nonsmoking section, and child-proof tables make this noisy Old Town stop a staple for families.

Request a table upstairs in a romantic nook not far from the piano. The menu is loaded with wild game and quirky spins on Czech favorites. Starters include lightly spiced venison pâté and duck liver on toast. You can choose from six different duck main courses. Finally, the ubiquitous *palačinky* crepes are thin and tender and filled with fruit, nuts, and chocolate. There is an even more popular sister to the first "kachnička," at Michalská 16, Prague 1 (📞 **224-213-418**), with a similar menu and prices. Reservations are recommended (daily 11:30am–11:30pm; metro: Můstek).

Nebovidská 6, Prague 1. 📞 **257-320-308**. www.umodrekachnicky.cz. Reservations recommended for lunch, required for dinner. Main courses 290Kč–690Kč. AE, MC, V. Daily noon–4pm and 6:30pm–midnight. Metro: Malostranská.

Moderate

Café de Paris ★ CAFE/FRENCH/CONTINENTAL   This delightful French bistro perched on pretty Maltézské náměstí is a perfect addition to a beautiful part of Prague. The menu is tiny with just a few items, though there are daily specials marked on the board outside. The specialty is grilled steak, entrecôte, served with salad, homemade fries, and a secret sauce known as "Café de Paris" sauce. The service is informal but attentive and the wine list is extensive and a good value. An ideal spot for a long lunch or unfussy but good dinner.

Maltézské nám. 4, Prague 1. 📞 **603-160-718**. www.cafedeparis.cz. Reservations recommended. Main courses 250Kč–350Kč. AE, MC, V. Daily noon–midnight. Metro: Malostranská plus tram no. 12, 20, or 22 to Malostranské nám.

Café Savoy ★★ CZECH/CONTINENTAL   This lovingly restored 19th-century cafe recalls Prague's coffeehouse heyday under the Austro-Hungarian Empire. Inside, the kitchen means business, serving a mix of international specialties and well-priced "Czech" entrees like Viennese-style goulash and Wiener schnitzel (made here from chicken breast or pork). It's run by the locally owned Ambiente chain. The cafe is open early for breakfast, with some rather creative menu items such as an "American-style" breakfast served with grilled chicken (which tastes better than it sounds).

Vítězná 5, Prague 5. 📞 **257-311-562**. www.ambi.cz. Reservations recommended. Main courses 150Kč–340Kč. AE, MC, V. Daily 11am–11pm. Metro: Malostranská plus tram no. 12, 20, or 22 to Újezd.

Nebozízek CZECH/CONTINENTAL   The rap on Nebozízek is that it relies too much on its unique location to draw crowds and not enough on the food. You can see their point. The restaurant's hillside setting looking east over Prague is one of the very best vantage points for a city panorama. Nevertheless, the chef is trying to make amends with a menu featuring well-done Continental standards and an exciting mix of Czech dishes like rabbit, shoulder of venison, and duck liver (served with spinach and balsamic vinegar). You get to this white Victorian house midway up Petřín Hill by taking the funicular to the interim stop. Call in advance to reserve a table with a view.

Petřínské sady 411, Prague 1. ℰ **257-315-329.** www.nebozizek.cz. Reservations recommended. Main courses 150Kč–560Kč. AE, MC, V. Daily 11am–11pm. Tram: 12, 20, or 22 to Újezd, then take funicular up the hill.

Inexpensive

Bohemia Bagel ☺ BAGELS/SANDWICHES   The local Bohemia Bagel chain is a solid choice for breakfast or lunch, with several outlets scattered around town. Breakfast offerings include the standard bagel with cream cheese as well as more items like bacon and eggs. The lunch menu is filled with soups and fresh sandwiches, served on a bagel or French bread. Another branch is located just off Old Town Square at Masná 2 (Staré Město; ℰ 224-812-560; Mon–Fri 7am–midnight, Sat–Sun 8am–midnight; metro: Staroměstská), which includes an Internet cafe with 10 terminals, a small garden with outside seating, and a playroom for children.

Lázeňská 19, Prague 1 (Malá Strana). ℰ **257-218-192.** www.bohemiabagel.cz. Bagels and sandwiches 60Kč–175Kč. No credit cards. Daily 7:30am–11pm. Metro: Malostranská plus tram no. 12, 20, or 22 to Malostranské nám.

Cukrkávalimonáda ★★ INTERNATIONAL   This cozy spot serves simple but excellent salads, sandwiches, and pasta dishes. The warm atmosphere is accentuated by exposed beams in the ceiling. It's perfect for a quick and easy lunch, and also ideal for coffee on the go or for killer hot chocolate on a cold day.

Lázeňská 7, Prague 1.(ℰ **257-530-628.** Main dishes 140Kč–200Kč. No credit cards. Daily 9am–11pm. Metro: Malostranská plus tram no. 12, 20, or 22 to Malostranské nám.

STARÉ MĚSTO (OLD TOWN)

Staré Město has Prague's largest concentration of restaurants, but be sure to choose wisely. Be especially careful around Old Town Square, where a dozen different restaurants set out tables in warm weather to take advantage of the incredible views. The problem is these are mostly undistinguished kitchens and prices are high. If you're only here for the views and don't mind the food, then by all means sit back and enjoy. If you're looking for an excellent meal, however, have a beer on the square and choose one of the places below.

Very Expensive

Allegro ★★ ITALIAN/INTERNATIONAL   The house restaurant of the Four Seasons hotel has been at the forefront of Prague dining since opening its doors a few years ago. It was the first recipient of a Michelin star in central Europe and has now grabbed the prize 2 years running. The cooking mixes northern Italian influences with international trends and even a few local influences. Dinners can be prohibitively expensive for anyone not traveling on the company's dime, though the daily prix-fixe lunch specials, 750Kč for two courses and 950Kč for three courses, help bring the food within reach of mere mortals.

Veleslavínova 2a, Prague 1. ℂ **221-427-000.** www.fourseasons.com. Reservations recommended. Main courses 750Kč–1,250Kč. AE, DC, MC, V. Daily 11:30am–5pm and 5:30–10:30pm; Sun brunch 11:30am–3pm. Metro: Staroměstská.

Bellevue ★★ INTERNATIONAL   With its excellent views of Prague Castle, the Bellevue is a perennial top choice. The ambitious owners have put all their energy into the intelligent menu: beef, nouvelle sauces, well-dressed fish and duck, delicate pastas, and artistic desserts. For a tamer but extraordinary treat, try the roasted veal cheek with potato puree. Desserts feature a vanilla-bean crème brûlée. Reserve in advance to snag a coveted table with a castle view.

Smetanovo nábřeží 18, Prague 1. ℂ **222-221-443.** www.bellevuerestaurant.cz. Reservations recommended. Set meals (2-course) from 990Kč to (5-course) 1,390Kč, excluding wine. AE, DC, MC, V. Daily noon–3pm and 5:30–11pm; Sun brunch 11am–3pm. Metro: Staroměstská.

La Degustation ★★★ CONTINENTAL/CZECH   Without a doubt, this is one of the city's best dining spots. It is housed in an Old Town corner building and has a minimalist interior. Two different prix-fixe, seven-course menus are served, as diners are invited to sample a wide array of food and wine. The *Bohême Bourgeois* menu finds inspiration in old Czech cookbooks and raises by miles the level of Czech cuisine usually served in restaurants here. The *Chef's Menu* adds more exotic items such as Kobe beef. Each dish is accompanied by an excellent selection of wines served by experienced sommeliers. Figure on around 10,000Kč for dinner for two, including the wines.

Haštalská 18, Prague 1. ℂ **222-311-234.** www.ladegustation.cz. Reservations essential. Fixed-price menu 2,250Kč–2,750Kč, fixed-price wines 1,390Kč–1,890Kč. AE, MC, V. Mon–Sat 6pm–midnight; Tues–Thurs noon–2:30pm. Metro: Staroměstská.

Mlýnec ★★ INTERNATIONAL   Head chef Marek Purkart has pulled the "Mill's" menu closer to its Czech roots, with mains like Wiener schnitzel, baked duck, and farm-fed chicken breast. This place is owned by the V zátiší group, which is also responsible for Bellevue and V zátiší, but is slightly more casual and fun, with a comfortable, clubby setting and a fantastic side-angle view of Charles Bridge.

Novotného lávka 9, Prague 1. ℂ **277-000-777.** www.mlynec.cz. Main dishes 395Kč–745Kč. AE, MC, V. Daily noon–3pm and 5:30–11pm. Tram: 17 or 18. Metro: Staroměstská.

Rybí trh SEAFOOD   The "Fish Market" has carved out a niche for itself as home to some of the freshest and most expensive seafood in the city, with items like an appetizer of scallops au gratin for 590Kč. But skipping the starters and choosing the delicious and relatively good value mains like crispy pike perch in creamed spinach sauce and mashed potatoes, also 590Kč, can help keep prices at least civilized. Service is attentive and the location, in the secluded Týn courtyard, is ideal.

Týnský Dvůr 5, Prague 1. ℂ **224-895-447.** www.rybitrh.cz. Reservations recommended. Main courses 590Kč–1,190Kč. AE, MC, V. Daily 11am–midnight. Metro: Staroměstská.

Vinárna V zátiší ★ INTERNATIONAL   This is a safe choice for an excellent meal, at a price, in a sophisticated yet still inviting environment. The menu and prices are similar to this restaurant's sister establishments, Mlýnec and Bellevue (also reviewed here), with items such as sea bass, lamb chops, and roasted farm chicken. Two- and three-course set menus help keep the tab relatively reasonable for the quality of the food.

Liliová 1, Prague 1. ℂ **222-221-155.** www.vzatisi.cz. Reservations recommended. Main courses 495Kč–795Kč, 3-course set menu 990Kč, excluding wine. AE, DC, MC, V. Daily noon–3pm and 5:30–11pm. Metro: Národní třída.

5

Staré Město (Old Town) — WHERE TO EAT IN PRAGUE

Old Town Restaurants

Allegro **20**
Bakeshop **6**
Bellevue **22**
Bohemia Bagel **12**
Café Evropa **41**
Cafe Imperial **16**
Café Louvre **36**
Čaez Marcel **8**
Carso **18**
Country Life **33**
Ceam & Dream **23**
Dobrá Čajovna **39**
Grand Café **24**
Grand Café Orient **26**
Grosseto Marina **2**
Guga **28**
Juma **42**
Kevárna Obecní dům **19**
Kevárna Slavia **34**
King Solomon Restaurant **4**
Klub architektů **30**
Ixgo **25, 27**
La Degustation **9**
Lahúdky Zlatý Kříž **38**
Le Café Colonial **3**
Les Moules **1**
Lkál **10**
Maitrea **13**
Mlýnec **21**
Monarch **5**
Pizza Nuova **15**
Pizzeria Rugantino **7**
Rybí trh **14**
Sansho **17**
Spika **40**
U medvídkú **37**
U modré kachničky **32**
U Vejvodů **31**
Velryba **35**
Vinárna V zátiší **29**
Yami **11**

Expensive

Grosseto Marina ★★ 📷 ITALIAN/INTERNATIONAL   This popular Italian restaurant occupies a large boat anchored off the Old Town side of the Vltava River, just near the Mánes Bridge. As you might expect, the views out over Malá Strana and Prague Castle are to die for, and if you're traveling in summer and get good weather, by all means plan a dinner here. The food, mostly pastas and pizzas, is actually very good and reasonably priced for the view, but let's be clear: This place is all about location. Try to reserve on the small deck at the front of the boat. If you can't get a table there, then anywhere on the upper deck away from the light and noise of the kitchen.

Alšovo nábřeží (just under the Mánes Bridge in front of the Rudolfinum), Prague 1. ℂ **605-454-020.** www.grosseto.cz. Reservations essential. Main courses 250Kč–500Kč. AE, MC, V. Daily 11:30am–midnight. Metro: Staroměstská.

King Solomon Restaurant ★ KOSHER   Under the supervision of the Orthodox Council of Kashrut, the King Solomon has brought to Prague a truly kosher restaurant, across from the Pinkas Synagogue. The restaurant's dozen booths are camped under an industrial-looking atrium. During dining hours, which strictly adhere to the Sabbath, you can choose from a variety of fresh vegetable and meat dishes following kosher dietary rules. The broad menu ranges from a vegetable béchamel to a stuffed roast quail. Selections of Israeli, American, and Moravian kosher wine include the restaurant's pride: a Frankovka red from the Baron Aaron Günsberger Moravian cellars.

Široká 8, Prague 1. ℂ **224-818-752.** www.kosher.cz. Reservations recommended. Main courses 250Kč–1,600Kč. AE, MC, V. Sun–Thurs noon–11pm; Fri dinner and Sat lunch by arrangement only. Metro: Staroměstská.

Moderate

Guga ★ GEORGIAN   I'd be the first to admit I'm no expert on Georgian (the country, not the state) food, but I love spending an evening here in this cozy piece of the Caucasus in Prague. First impressions might not be favorable. Guga is a small room, without much in the way of atmosphere or even music. But sit back, relax, and let the waitress choose the food. Meals are built around a series of appetizer plates shared family-style across the table. Some items, like stuffed grape leaves, eggplant, and red beans, are familiar. Others, like Russian steamed dumplings, *pelmene,* and stuffed Georgian bread, *lavash,* may be new sensations. There're just a few tables here, so reservations are essential. Dinner only.

Karolíny Světlé 33, Prague 1. ℂ **775-565-025.** www.uirmy.cz. Reservations essential. Appetizer plates 119Kč–169Kč. AE, DC, MC, V. Daily 3–11pm. Metro: Narodní třída.

Pizza Nuova ★ ☺ ITALIAN/PIZZA   Ambiente Restaurants Group has brought the concept of "tasting restaurant" to Prague. Here you pay a set price and then eat what you can. You can choose from the exquisite antipasto salad bar with a wide selection of meats, cheeses and fish, or the Pasta & Pizza "dégustation"—basically unlimited servings of pizza and pasta brought to your table until you burst. The restaurant is on the first floor of the corner building next to the Kotva department store. For smaller kids, there is a play corner with toys and activities, so you will have a better chance to fully enjoy the tasting.

Revoluční 1, Prague 1. ℂ **221-803-308.** www.ambi.cz. "Eat what you can" cold buffet 285Kč, main courses 265Kč. AE, MC, V. Daily 11:30am–11:30pm. Metro: Náměstí Republiky.

INEXPENSIVE MEALS on the run

The Czech-style delicatessen **Lahůdky Zlatý Kříž,** Jungmannovo nám. 19 (entrance from Jungmannova 34), Prague 1 (℃ **221-191-801**), offers the typical Czech snack food *chlebíčky*—a slice of white bread with ham or salami and cheese or potato salad. You have to eat standing up, but prices are pure Czech. Or take it with you and go eat in the cozy garden behind the corner of this building (enter from the square). It's open Monday to Friday from 6:30am to 7pm and Saturday from 9am to 3pm. No credit cards are accepted.

Culinaria, at Skořepka 9 (℃ **224-231-017**), not far from Lahůdky Zlatý Kříž within the Old Town, is another good value choice, particularly for a quick lunch. It's a high-quality deli counter, with items like curried chicken, roast beef, and other delicacies that you select at the counter and then eat off a paper plate at a small dining area by the window. Maybe the best value for money in the city center.

Vegetarians will like **Country Life,** Melantrichova 15, Prague 1 (℃ **224-213-373**), a health-food store run by the Seventh-Day Adventists; it offers strictly meatless meals in a self-serve cafeteria setting. You'll find tofu, tomato, cucumber, and shredded cabbage salads; zesty wheat-bread pizzas topped with red pepper, garlic, and onions; and vegetable burgers on multigrain buns with garlic-yogurt dressing. Selections are 30Kč to 90Kč. It's open Monday to Thursday from 9am to 8:30pm, Friday 9am to 6pm, and Sunday 11am to 8:30pm. No credit cards are accepted.

At Old Town's **Cream & Dream,** Husova 12, Prague 1 (℃ **224-211-035**), you will definitely revive your mind and body after a tiring tour of the city, or just please your sweet tooth. The gelato here is not particularly cheap, but it's world-class quality, and you will not get better ice cream in Prague, or perhaps even in Italy. This creamery, cafe, and chocolate shop is open daily 9am until midnight.

If you are visiting Prague's Vinohrady quarter, you can't avoid its main square, Náměsti Míru, with St. Ludmila's Church. On the right side of the church, when facing it, near the metro entrance, there is usually a stand with possibly the **best hot dog** in Prague. The dog is topped with ketchup or two kinds of tasty Czech mustard and served on a fresh white roll. It costs 20Kč and it is available Monday to Friday from 9:30am until the supply for that day runs out.

Kogo ★ ITALIAN   This modern, upscale trattoria for years has been a local favorite for brokers and bankers who work nearby. Tucked away on a side street just opposite the Havel Market, Kogo manages to combine the warmth and boisterousness of a family restaurant with a high culinary standard in its pastas, meaty entrees, and desserts. Try the fresh, zesty mussels in white wine and garlic (*cozze al vino bianco e aglio*) or the tangy grilled salmon. The wine list is extensive, and the tiramisu is light and sweet without being soggy.

Kogo has a second, even more popular, location in the atrium of the Slovanský Dům shopping center at Na Příkopě 22 (℃ **221-451-259**). The prices are higher here but the location makes it a logical choice for a pre- or post-film repast when taking in a movie at the multiplex cinema.

Havelská 27, Prague 1. ℃ **224-214-543.** www.kogo.cz. Reservations recommended. Main courses 210Kč–480Kč. AE, MC, V. Daily 9am–midnight. Metro: Můstek.

5

Staré Město (Old Town)

Les Moules ★ FRENCH   Here's a little piece of Belgium tossed into the center of Prague, which includes a range of that country's very good beer (not that I need any more beer, but if you're looking for a little variety . . .). The mussels are the specialty (hence the name), but all the French-inspired bistro food is very good. It's a great spot to plop down after a long day spent walking through the Jewish Museum.

Pařížská 19, Prague 1. ℂ **222-315-022.** www.lesmoules.cz. Reservations recommended. Main courses 300Kč–500Kč. AE, MC, V. 11:30am–midnight. Metro: Staroměstská.

Monarch ★ CZECH/CONTINENTAL/INTERNATIONAL   This is a handsome wine bar and restaurant with a lovely traditional interior, excellent Continental and international dishes, and an extensive and good-value wine list. To splurge, have the Aberdeen Angus steak in a chanterelle mushroom or Hennessy (cognac) sauce. There are a few sidewalk tables available in nice weather.

V kolkovně 7, Prague 1. ℂ **222-315-545.** www.monarch.cz. Reservations recommended. Main courses 180Kč–480Kč. AE, MC, V. Mon–Sat 11:30am–midnight; Sun 5pm–midnight. Metro: Staroměstská.

Yami ★★ JAPANESE   This small restaurant not far from Old Town Square serves excellent sushi and Japanese food at prices that don't break the bank. Start with the soul-healing *wakame* (seaweed soup) and then jump straight to the jumbo fusion rolls. My favorite is the "rainbow roll," with eel, salmon, tuna, red snapper, and avocado. Individual nigiri sushi here is not such a great deal, but the sushi sets are large and satisfying. Unlike many sushi restaurants, the atmosphere here is relaxed and casual.

Masná 3, Prague 1. ℂ **222-312-756.** www.iyami.cz. Reservations recommended. Soups 45Kč, appetizers 90Kč–120Kč, sushi rolls 190Kč–290Kč, sushi sets 470Kč–720Kč. AE, DC, MC, V. Daily 11am–11pm. Metro: Staroměstská.

Inexpensive

Bakeshop ★★ AMERICAN/DELI   Prague's lucky enough to have an American-style bakery and sandwich shop that would be the envy of many an American town or city. Bakeshop is simply the best bakery for miles. Come here for soups, salads, ready-made sandwiches, yogurt cups, and, naturally, bread, cakes, brownies, and cookies. It's one-stop shopping for the perfect picnic lunch. You can eat in at the counter or get it to go.

Kozí 1, Prague 1. ℂ **222-316-823.** www.bakeshop.cz. Sandwiches 90Kč–145Kč. AE, MC, V. Daily 7am–7pm. Metro: Staroměstská.

Chez Marcel FRENCH   Alas, this is no longer the classic French bistro, dripping with Gallic charm, that it once was, but it's still a nice place for a quick glass of house wine or relatively inexpensive meal, like rabbit leg in mustard sauce or chicken and mashed potatoes. The crème brûlée (120Kč) is as good as ever.

Haštalské nám. 12, Prague 1. ℂ **222-315-676.** www.chezmarcel.cz. Main courses 120Kč–240Kč. No credit cards. Daily 11:30am–1am. Metro: Staroměstská.

Klub Architektů CZECH/INTERNATIONAL   Tucked into the alcoves of a 12th-century cellar across the courtyard from Jan Hus's Bethlehem Chapel, this eclectic clubhouse for the city's progressive architects' society is the best nonpub deal in Old Town. Among the exposed air ducts and industrial swag lights hovering above the tables in the stone dungeon, you can choose from baked chicken, pork steaks, pasta, stir-fried chicken, and even vegetarian burritos. It's not really spectacular, but the large portions and variety will satisfy a range of tastes. The wicker seating in the courtyard makes a summer night among the torches enjoyable, though the alfresco menu is limited.

Betlémské nám. 5a, Prague 1. ✆ **224-401-214.** Reservations recommended. Main courses 110Kč–160Kč. AE, MC, V. Daily 11:30am–midnight. Metro: Národní třída.

Lokál ★ CZECH   A more authentic alternative to the "Czech" restaurants on Old Town Square is this popular pub/restaurant about 10 minutes' walk from the square. The decor is a tongue-in-cheek take on a Czech pub in the 1970s. Kitschy ads for tractors line the walls in the restrooms, for example. But the food is much, much better than anything you would have found back then. Goulash, pork cutlets, schnitzels, and *svíčkova* prepared by the same management team that runs the city's best restaurant, La Degustation, at a fraction of the price. The Pilsner Urquell beer is trucked in daily direct from the brewery in Plzeň. Reservations are essential.

Dlouhá 33, Prague 1. ✆ **222-316-265.** www.ambi.cz. Reservations essential. Main courses lunch 80Kč–150Kč, dinner 120Kč–240Kč. AE, DC, MC, V. Daily 11am–11pm. Metro: Staroměstská.

Maitrea ★ VEGETARIAN   Wildly popular vegetarian restaurant with a loyal local following that comes for the traditional couscous and rice dishes as well as concoctions like "meatless" chicken and sushi. The main dining rooms are refined and relatively formal for a vegetarian place, making this a great option for a big meatless night out. Týnská ulička is a little hard to find. From Old Town Square, head east on Dlouhá, making a right at the first small lane, opposite Dušní Street.

Týnská ulička 6, Prague 1. ✆ **222-316-265.** www.restaurace-maitrea.cz. Reservations recommended. Main courses 120Kč–240Kč. AE, DC, MC, V. Mon–Fri 11:30am–11:30pm; Sat–Sun noon–11:30pm. Metro: Staroměstská.

Pizzeria Rugantino ★★ ☺ PIZZA   Pizzeria Rugantino serves generous salads and the best selection of individual pizzas in Prague. Wood-fired stoves and handmade dough result in a crisp and delicate crust. The pizza "Calabrese," with hot chili peppers and spicy pepperoni, is as close as you'll find to American-style pepperoni pizza in this part of Europe. A more spacious Rugantino II is located at Klimentská 40, Prague 1 (✆ **224-815-192;** metro: Florenc or Náměstí Republiky), with a children's corner and plasma TV. The constant buzz, nonsmoking area, heavy childproof wooden tables, and lots of baby chairs make this a family favorite.

Dušní 4, Prague 1. ✆ **222-318-172.** Individual pizzas 120Kč–220Kč. AE, MC, V. Mon–Sat 11am–11pm; Sun noon–11pm. Metro: Staroměstská.

NOVÉ MĚSTO (NEW TOWN)
Very Expensive

Sansho ★★★ ASIAN/CONTINENTAL/INTERNATIONAL   2011 was a great year for restaurant openings in town, and none made a bigger splash than this minimalist Asian-fusion place in the northern part of Nové Město, in a quiet neighborhood behind the Bílá Labut' department store. Head chef Paul Day cut his culinary teeth at London's award-winning Nobu and brought with him a philosophy of mixing the best of East and West in an understated setting that puts the focus squarely on the food. Highlights from the menu include an Indonesian beef rendang, Chinese pork belly, chicken satay and soft-shell crab. Seating is communal at large picnic-style tables. There's only room for about 40 diners, so reservations are a must.

Petrská 25, Prague 1. ☏ **222-317-425.** www.sansho.cz. Reservations essential. Three-course set menu about 750Kč. AE, DC, MC, V. Mon–Fri 11:30am–2:45pm, 6–10:30pm; Sat 6–11pm. Tram: 3, 8, 24 to Bílá Labut'.

Expensive

Čestr ★★ STEAKHOUSE   One of the most exciting new additions to the Prague restaurant scene is this contemporary steakhouse at the top of Wenceslas Square in the same spot the old Zahrada v Opeře used to occupy. This is run by the same Ambiente outfit that brought us both La Degustation and Lokál, and like those two places, Čestr is packed most nights (so best to reserve in advance). The concept is built around high-end steaks and other meats, served in a casual atmosphere, with good beer, French fries, and a great range of desserts.

Legerova 75, Prague 1. ☏ **222-727-851.** www.ambi.cz. Reservations essential. Main courses lunch 80Kč–150Kč, dinner 120Kč–240Kč. AE, DC, MC, V. Daily noon–11pm. Metro: Muzeum.

Moderate

Corso ★ CZECH/INTERNATIONAL   This cozy cafe, just off of Náměstí Republiky, is an ideal choice for lunch or a light dinner, particularly in nice weather when you can dine on the small terrace out front. The lunch menu is built around a daily special, usually something Czech, and supplemented by a regular menu of very good salads, pastas, and light meat entrees. During the evenings, it's just the normal menu. The Caesar salad (168Kč) is authentic and may just be the best in Prague. Good coffees and cakes and a reliable and free Wi-Fi connection.

V Celnici 4, Prague 1. ☏ **224-281-137.** www.corsocafe.cz. Reservations recommended. Main courses: Lunch specials 100Kč, dinner 120Kč–200Kč. AE, DC, MC, V. Daily 11am–11pm. Metro: Náměstí Republiky.

Inexpensive

Jáma ★ AMERICAN   Jáma gets its share of abuse from longtime residents for being a kind of American-style college bar in Prague, but there's no denying it is a fun place to grab a beer, and the burgers and bar food items are some of the best around. Tuesdays are "burger day," when the gourmet cheddar-bacon burger shares menu space with exotics like a Cajun burger, a Cowboy Jack burger (made with Jack Daniel's), and a Black Pepper burger. Lunchtime brings a selection of classic Czech dishes at very good prices.

V Jámě 7, Prague 2. ☏ **224-222-383.** www.jamapub.cz. Reservations not necessary. Burgers and main courses 175Kč–250Kč. AE, MC, V. Daily 11am–1am. Metro: Můstek.

Pivovarský dům ★★ CZECH   Good Czech beer is not made only by the big brewers. This very popular microbrewery produces its own excellent lager as well as harder-to-find varieties like dark beer and wheat beer. The "Brewery House" also dabbles in borderline-blasphemous (but still pretty good) concoctions such as coffee-, cherry-, and banana-flavored beer. Sharing the spotlight with the beer is excellent traditional Czech food, including pork, dumplings, rabbit, goulash, and schnitzel, served in an upscale publike setting. The dining areas are all nonsmoking. You'll need reservations to walk in the door—it's that popular.

Lípová 15 (corner of Ječná), Prague 2. ☏ **296-216-666.** www.gastroinfo.cz/pivodum. Reservations recommended. Main courses 135Kč–275Kč. AE, MC, V. Daily 11am–11:30pm. Metro: I. P. Pavlova plus tram no. 4, 6, 10, or 22 one stop to Štěpánská.

VINOHRADY

Very Expensive

Aromi ★★ ITALIAN Definitely worth the splurge and trip out to residential Vinohrady for possibly the best Italian cooking and seafood in Prague. The swank interior manages to be both fancy and inviting at the same time, lending any meal the feeling of an occasion. The waitstaff is professional yet surprisingly unpretentious for a restaurant of this caliber. My favorite is the homemade ravioli stuffed with potatoes and sea bass, but everything is delicious. Sticking to the pastas can keep the bill manageable. The daily lunch special is a steal at around 200Kč per person.

Mánesova 78, Prague 2. ⓒ **222-713-222.** www.aromi.cz. Reservations recommended. Pastas and main courses 345Kč–600Kč. AE, MC, V. Daily noon–11pm. Metro: Jiřího z Poděbrad or Muzeum plus tram no. 11.

Moderate

Masala ★ INDIAN This Indian mom-and-pop place is just what the doctor ordered if you have a taste for a well-made curry. Be sure to reserve, especially on a Friday or Saturday night, since there's only a handful of tables and they fill up quickly. The engaging staff will ask you how much spice you want—go for broke, since even "very spicy" would only qualify as "medium" in the U.S. or England, let alone back home in India. All the classics are offered, including crispy nan bread and flavored yogurt drinks to start.

Mánesova 13, Prague 2 (behind the National Museum). ⓒ **222-251-601.** www.masala.cz. Reservations recommended. Main courses 175Kč–395Kč. AE, MC, V. Mon–Fri 11:30am–10:30pm; Sat–Sun 12:30–10:30pm. Metro: Muzeum.

The Pind ★★ INDIAN Another 2011 opening that went straight to the top of most "must try" lists, the Pind takes Prague's Indian cooking to a new level. Anyone familiar with Indian restaurants around the world will recognize highlights like chicken tikka masala or lamb roganjosh, which is a little spicier here than other places around town. The ground floor offers informal seating around a bar area, while downstairs is a more formal, and nicer, dining room. The setting works equally well for a casual lunch or a celebratory dinner.

Korunní 67, Prague 2. ⓒ **222-516-085.** www.thepind.cz. Reservations recommended. Main courses 180Kč–265Kč. AE, DC, MC, V. Mon–Thurs 11am–11pm; Fri–Sat noon–11:30pm; Sun 1–10pm Metro: Jiřího z Poděbrad.

Taverna Olympos ★ GREEK This convivial Greek restaurant in Žižkov, just on the Vinohrady line, always feels festive. In summer, sit out in the garden; in winter, bask in the enclosed winter garden. The highlights here are the appetizers like *tzatziki* and baked cheese in foil. The calamari is fresh; my favorite is the baked calamari stuffed with cheese and red pepper. House wine flows from carafes, and the staff is cheerful, if occasionally forgetful.

Kubelíkova 9, Prague 3. ⓒ **222-722-239.** www.taverna-olympos.eu. Reservations recommended. Main courses 180Kč–290Kč. AE, DC, MC, V. Daily 11:30am–11pm. Metro: Jiřího z Poděbrad.

Inexpensive

Radost FX VEGETARIAN Radost has been coasting for years on a menu that was considered daring when it was introduced in 1993, but it's still one of the few—and best—vegetarian options in Prague. The veggie burger served on a grain bun is well seasoned and substantial, and the soups, like lentil and onion, are light and full of flavor. Sautéed vegetable dishes, tofu, and huge Greek salads round out the health-conscious menu. The hipster interior draws a stylish clientele, but the offhand waitstaff lends an impression they are a little too cool to work hard. The bill already includes an obligatory 10% tip, so no need to leave any extra money on the table.

Bělehradská 120, Prague 2. ℂ **603-181-500.** www.radostfx.cz. Main courses 80Kč–285Kč. AE, MC, V. Daily 11:30am–5am. Metro: I. P. Pavlova.

ELSEWHERE IN PRAGUE
Moderate

Grosseto ★ ITALIAN/PIZZA   Grosseto—the same owners as Grosseto Marina, above—is a very popular (reservations a must) pizzeria and Italian-style restaurant in the neighborhood around the Dejvická metro station. This is one of Prague's most desirable areas, yet inexplicably it's short on quality places to eat (hence the huge crowds here). The pizzas, cooked in an oven brought in from Italy, are some of the best in town. The pastas are usually very good. The main dining area is nonsmoking, with a smaller smoking section in the back. The only drawback, a minor one, is the often slow and error-prone service.

Jugoslávských partyzánů 8, Prague 6. ℂ **233-342-694.** Reservations recommended. Main courses 130Kč–250Kč. AE, DC, MC, V. Daily 11:30am–11pm. Metro: Dejvická.

Mirellie ★ ITALIAN   If you like Kogo (p. 85), you'll love Mirellie. It has the same great Yugo-inspired pizzas, seafood, and grilled meats, but at little more than half the price. Try the spicy pappardelle with lamb ragout or the seafood risotto if you're starting to tire of pork and dumplings. The interior is sleekly modern but cozy enough to feel intimate. The only problem is the name—I simply cannot keep it in my head.

V.P. Čkalova 14, Prague 6. ℂ **222-959-999.** www.mirellie.cz. Reservations recommended. Main courses 180Kč–280Kč. AE, MC, V. Daily 11am–11pm. Metro: Hradčanská or Dejvická.

CAFE SOCIETY

In their heyday in the late 19th and early 20th centuries, Prague's elegant *kavárny* (cafes) rivaled Vienna's as places to be seen and perhaps have a carefree afternoon chat. The Bohemian intellectuals, much as their Viennese counterparts, laid claim to many of the local cafes, turning them into smoky parlors for pondering and debating the anxieties of the day.

Today, most of Prague's cafes have lost the indigenous charm of the Jazz Age or, strangely enough, the Communist era. During the Cold War, the venerable **Café Slavia,** across from the National Theater, became a de facto clubhouse in which dissidents passed the time, often within listening range of the not-so-secret police. It's here that Václav Havel and the arts community often gathered to keep a flicker of the Civic Society alive. The Slavia is still thriving today, though the tables, more than likely, will be filled with tourists pouring through maps and guidebooks, rather than monocled dandies or angst-ridden intellectuals bent over the latest *feuilleton.*

That doesn't mean that cafes don't have a role to play. Old standbys like the **Café Louvre** are more popular than ever, and a great spot to relax or have a coffee and a light meal. Many of the gems have been newly spruced up, and a visit to gorgeous **Kavárna Obecní dům, the Grand Café Orient,** or the **Café Imperial** is worth it simply for the wow factor.

Staré Město (Old Town)

Grand Café CAFE FARE   The biggest draw of this quaint cafe, the former Café Milena, is a great view of the Orloj, an astronomical clock with an hourly parade of saints on the side of Old Town Square's city hall. With a new management came wider selection of main courses as well as higher prices. Make sure you get a table at the window.

Staroměstské nám. 22, Prague 1 (1st floor). ℂ **221-632-522.** www.grandcafe.cz. Cappuccino 70Kč; sandwiches 110Kč–140Kč. AE, MC, V. Daily 7am–10pm. Metro: Staroměstská.

Grand Café Orient ★★ CAFE FARE   Round off your visit to the cubist House of the Black Madonna with a pit stop at this lovingly restored 1920s gem on the building's second floor. A 2005 restoration remained faithful to the cafe's original layout, and as you climb the stairs your eyes will glaze over in sepia tones at a picture perfect shot from a bygone era. Good coffee and cakes round out the charms.

Ovocný trh 19, Prague 1. ℂ **224-224-220.** www.grandcafeorient.cz. Cakes and coffees 50Kč–80Kč. AE, MC, V. Daily 10am–10pm. Metro: Náměstí Republiky.

Kavárna Obecní dům ★★ CAFE FARE   An afternoon here feels like a trip back to the time when Art Nouveau was all the rage. The refurbishment of the entire Municipal House in the late 1990s was a treat for those who love this style of architecture, and the *kavárna* might be its most spectacular public room. Witness the lofty ceilings, marble wall accents and tables, altarlike mantle at the far end, and huge windows and period chandeliers. Coffee, tea, and other drinks come with pastries and light sandwiches.

In the Municipal House, Náměstí Republiky 5, Prague 1. ℂ **222-002-763.** www.vysehrad2000.cz. Cakes and coffees 55Kč–135Kč. AE, MC, V. Daily 7:30am–11pm. Metro: Náměstí Republiky.

Kavárna Slavia ★ CAFE FARE   You'll most certainly walk by this Prague landmark across from the National Theater, so why not stop in? The restored crisp Art Deco room recalls the Slavia's 100 years as a meeting place for the city's cultural and intellectual corps. The cafe still has a relatively affordable menu accompanying the gorgeous riverfront panoramic views of Prague Castle.

Národní at Smetanovo nábřeží, Prague 1. ℂ **224-218-493.** www.cafeslavia.cz. Coffees and pastries 40Kč–60Kč; salad bar and light menu items 129Kč–180Kč. AE, MC, V. Daily 8am–midnight. Metro: Národní třída.

Nové Město (New Town)

Café Evropa CAFE FARE   This Art Nouveau gem was once the *grande dame* of cafes on Wenceslas Square. Inexplicably, the owners have allowed the Evropa to fall into disrepair, but it's still worth a look at its etched-glass grandeur.

Václavské nám. 25, Prague 1. ℂ **224-228-215.** Coffee 70Kč; pastries 80Kč. AE, MC, V. Daily 10am–11:30pm; Sat–Sun 9am–11:30pm. Metro: Můstek.

Café Imperial ★ CAFE FARE   One of Prague's many Art Nouveau gems that was left neglected for years, it now has been reopened in its full beauty. You'll be immediately stunned by high ceilings completely covered with original ceramic tiles and

Cafe Society

mosaics. Enjoy morning coffee or afternoon tea and feel the regained First Republic atmosphere. The food has greatly improved in the past couple of years and is easily worth a lunch or dinner stop.

Na Poříčí 15, Prague 1. ℂ **246-011-440.** www.hotel-imperial.cz. Cappuccino 60Kč; English breakfast 200Kč; snacks, sandwiches 150Kč–245Kč. AE, MC, V. Daily 9am–11pm. Metro: Náměstí Republiky.

Café Louvre CZECH/INTERNATIONAL/CAFE FARE A big, breezy upstairs hall, Café Louvre is great for breakfast, coffee, an inexpensive pre-theater meal, or an upscale game of pool. A fabulous Art Nouveau interior, with huge original chandeliers, buzzes with the noise of local coffee talk, the shopping crowd, business lunches, and students. Starters include smoked salmon or Greek *tzatziki* (yogurt and cucumber). Main dishes range from grilled steak of salmon to lamb filets with rosemary. In the snazzy billiards parlor in back, you can enjoy drinks and light meals.

Národní 22, Prague 1. ℂ **224-930-949.** www.cafelouvre.cz. Reservations accepted. Main courses 79Kč–259Kč. AE, DC, MC, V. Daily 8am–11:30pm. Metro: Národní třída.

Dobrá Čajovna ★ CAFE FARE On the walk toward the National Museum on the right side of Wenceslas Square, there is an island of serenity in the courtyard at no. 14. Inside the Dobrá Čajovna (Good Tearoom), a pungent bouquet of herb teas, throw pillows, and sitar music welcomes visitors to this very understated Bohemian corner. The extensive tea menu includes Japanese green tea for 60Kč a cup.

Václavské nám. 14, Prague 1. ℂ **224-231-480.** 40Kč–120Kč for a pot of tea. No credit cards. Mon–Fri 10am–9:30pm; Sat–Sun 2–9:30pm. Metro: Můstek.

The Globe Bookstore and Café ★★ CAFE FARE The Globe remains a popular mainstay for English-speaking expats and a great place for coffee, light food, and books. The front end of the store is a big bookstore on two levels, while the cavernous back room serves coffee, cakes, great sandwiches, and light hot meals. The 89Kč lunch special is excellent value.

Pštrossova 6, Prague 1. ℂ **224-934-203.** www.globebookstore.cz. Salads, sandwiches, pastas, and desserts 60Kč–195Kč. AE, MC, V. Daily 9:30am–1am. Metro: Národní třída.

Velryba CAFE FARE If you're looking for a place where people still occasionally meet to discuss ideas, this smoky haunt on a back street off Národní třída might fit the bill. Though the cafe's vogue has waned in the face of stiff competition, it still draws a mix of intellectuals, journalists, and actors. The kitchen serves good light meals including pastas and salads.

Opatovická 24, Prague 1. ℂ **224-931-444.** www.kavarnavelryba.cz. Light meals 75Kč–135Kč. No credit cards. Daily 11am–midnight. Metro: Národní třída.

Vinohrady

Blatouch ★ CAFE FARE This is a comfortable, laid-back student cafe on one of Vinohrady's nicest residential streets. Come here for an excellent espresso or a glass of wine. The food offerings are meager, but most people come to relax, hang out, and chat. It also does double duty as a gallery and small Czech bookstore.

Americká 17, Prague 2. ℂ **222-328-643.** Cappuccino 40Kč; snacks and sandwiches 80Kč–180Kč. AE, MC, V. Daily 11am–midnight. Metro: Náměstí Míru.

Internet Cafes

The **Globe Bookstore and Café** at Pstrossova 6, Prague 1, Nové Město (© **224-934-203;** www.globebookstore.cz) is one of the better deals in town; it's both a free Wi-Fi hotspot and offers surfing on its own computers for 1Kč per minute. **Bohemia Bagel,** at Masná 2, Prague 1, Staré Město (© **224-812-560;** www.bohemiabagel. cz), charges 2Kč per minute for surfing, and also offers low-cost phone calls. **Spika,** at Dlážděná 4, Prague 1, Nové Město (© **224-211-521**), is open Monday to Friday 8am to midnight and Saturday and Sunday 10am to 11pm, charges 20Kč for 15 minutes, and offers Internet-based cheap international phone calls.

THE PICK OF THE PUBS

Besides being the center of extracurricular activity, *hospody* are the best places for a fulfilling, inexpensive meal and a true Czech experience—not to mention the beer. Food selections are typically the same: braised beef in cream sauce (*svíčková*), goulash (*guláš*), minute steak (*roštěná na roštu*), or breaded fried hermelín cheese (*smažený sýr*). Reservations aren't usually accepted, though, so you'll just have to show up and hope for an empty seat.

Below, I list two top Old Town pub choices based on atmosphere, authenticity, and price. For more pub selections, see chapter 9, "Prague Nightlife," p. 186.

U Medvídků ★★ CZECH/CONTINENTAL   The "House at the Little Bear" is one of the few big Czech pubs in the center where locals and tourists mix happily together, and the mood most evenings is festive. Several varieties of Budvar are on tap as well as the pub's own microbrews. The menu is bigger and better than is usually found in a pub, with several varieties of goulash, Czech standards like pork schnitzel, and more exotic offerings such as venison and boar. In high season, an "oompah" band sometimes plays in the beer wagon in the center of the pub.

Na Perštýně 7, Prague 1. © 224-211-916. www.umedvidku.cz. Main courses 90Kč–250Kč. AE, MC, V. Daily 11:30am–11pm. Metro: Národní třída.

U Vejvodů ★ CZECH/CONTINENTAL   A few years ago, this traditional pub was modernized and supersized and it's lost some of its charm, but the food and service are better, and the size of the place means it's usually possible to snag a table when other places are full. The beer list features the Pilsner Urquell family, including the flagship 12-degree pilsner and Kozel's slightly sweetish dark. A mug of Pilsner Urquell costs 31Kč and can be enjoyed with goulash or goose, and even trout or salmon.

Jilská 4, Prague 1. © 224-219-999. www.restauraceuvejvodu.cz. Main courses 139Kč–349Kč. AE, MC, V. Sun–Thurs 10am–2am; Fri–Sat 10am–4am. Metro: Národní třída.

The Pick of the Pubs

EXPLORING PRAGUE

M ost of Prague's main attractions are grouped in the city's core neighborhoods of Staré Město, Malá Strana, Hradčany, and Nové Město and are within comfortable walking distance of each other. For those that aren't, there are trams and the metro, which can usually get you to within a 5- to 10-minute walk from where you want to go.

As with any historic urban destination, the main sights are made up primarily of museums, churches, parks, and public squares. Most of the city center has been protected as a UNESCO World Heritage site and it's no stretch to say that among European capitals, at least, Prague has the continent's best-preserved stock of buildings from the 13th to the 18th centuries.

You'll find exquisite examples from the history of European architecture—from Romanesque to Renaissance, from baroque to Art Nouveau to cubist—crammed side-by-side on twisting narrow streets. Seen from Charles Bridge, this jumble of architecture thrusts from the hills and hugs the riverbanks, with little of the 20th century's own excesses obscuring the grandeur of the past millennium.

But Prague is more than simply great architecture. The spires and pillars and columns and cherubs festooned onto nearly every building create a festive mood, regardless of the season. A good part of enjoyment is simply strolling around with no particular destination in mind and enjoying the carnival-like atmosphere. The thousands of other visitors who are here for the same reason, while occasionally a distraction, help to reinforce the feeling that something special is going on.

Once you are done drinking in the atmosphere, you are never far from a pub or club for drinking of another sort. Beer lovers will feel especially honored. Czech beer is arguably the best—and cheapest—in the world and no one will look askance if you pair a beer or two with a fine dinner, or indeed have one for breakfast.

PRAGUE CASTLE & CHARLES BRIDGE

The huge hilltop complex known collectively as **Prague Castle (Pražský hrad)** ★★★, on Hradčanské náměstí, encompasses dozens of houses, towers, churches, courtyards, and monuments. It's described in detail in

saving money ON ENTRANCE FEES

Prague's museums, especially the Jewish Museum, the Castle complex, and the holdings of the National Gallery, are becoming more and more expensive every year. Be sure to take advantage of discounted senior or student admission fees if you qualify. Seniors are usually defined as 70 and over (65 and over at some museums); while children (6–15) normally pay a reduced fee (5 and under usually free). Students can be 25 and under holding a valid ISIC card or university ID. Also, many museums offer a discounted "family" rate that normally covers two adults and at least one or two children. Another option, if you think you might be visiting a lot of museums,

is to pre-purchase a **Prague Card.** This pass is valid for 2, 3, or 4 days, and allows you free entry to around 50 attractions in the city, including Prague Castle (but unfortunately not the sites within the Jewish Museum complex), as well as discounts to many others. A 2-day pass costs around 820Kč for adults (1,030Kč including access to public transportation) and 550Kč for students 25 and under (770Kč with transport). You can buy it at the PIS/Prague Welcome information centers at the Old Town Hall at Staroměstské nám. 1 or at Rytířská 31, Prague 1, or online at www.praguecity card.com.

"Walking Tour 2: Prague Castle (Pražský Hrad)" in chapter 7; see also the map on p. 143. A visit to the castle can easily take an entire day, depending on how thoroughly you explore it. Still, you can see the top sights—St. Vitus Cathedral, the Royal Palace, St. George's Basilica, the Powder Tower, and Golden Lane—in the space of a morning or an afternoon.

Although the individual attractions are closed, you can also explore the castle complex at night, as it's generally lit until midnight, or make a return trip to see the fine collection of 19th-century Czech art exhibited in the Convent of St. George (discussed later). The complex is always guarded and is safe to wander at night, but keep to the lighted areas of the courtyards just to be sure.

If you're feeling particularly fit, you can walk up to the castle, or you can take metro line A to Malostranská and then ride tram no. 22 two stops north to "Pražský hrad."

TICKETS & CASTLE INFORMATION You can buy tickets at one of two **Prague Castle Information Centers** on the castle grounds, located in the second and third courtyards after you pass through the main gate from Hradčanské náměstí. The centers also sell useful hand-held audio guides (250Kč) to help you make sense of the sights, and tickets for individual concerts and exhibits. You can also by tickets online through Ticketportal (www.ticketportal.cz). Admission to the grounds is free, but going inside any of the attractions, including St. Vitus Cathedral, requires a combined-entry ticket. A full-price ticket gets you into the following attractions: the cathedral, the Old Royal Palace, a permanent exhibition called "The Story of Prague Castle," St. George's Basilica, the National Gallery at the Convent of St. George, Golden Lane with the Daliborka Tower, the Prague Castle Picture Gallery, and the Powder Tower. It costs 350Kč for adults and 175Kč for students. A cheaper ticket—sufficient for most visitors—covers only the cathedral, the Old Royal Palace, St. George's Basilica, and Golden Lane with Daliborka Tower, and costs 250Kč for adults, 125Kč for students. Tickets are valid for 2 days. The castle is located at

Prague Attractions

ATTRACTIONS
Alfons Mucha Museum **46**
Bedřich Smetana Museum **43**
Bethlehem Chapel **44**
Charles Bridge (Karlův most) **42**
Charles Square
(Karlovo náměstí) **56**
Church of Our Lady Victorious **15**
Church of St. Nicholas
Malá Strana (Lesser Town) **11**
Old Town Square **28**
Dvořák Museum **57**
Estates Theater **40**
Franz Kafka Museum **13**
Havel's Market **41**
House at the Black
Mother of God **39**
Jan Palach Square
(náměstí Jana Palacha) **26**
Kampa **18**
Kampa Gallery-Sovovy
Mlýny **19**
Kinský Palace **30**
Labyrinth **17**
Lennon Wall **16**
Letná Park **21**
Loreto Palace **1**
Maisel Synagogue **27**
Malá Strana Town Hall **12**
Municipal House **31**
Museum of the City
of Prague **32**
Můstek Metro Station **47**
Národní Memorial **48**
National Memorial
on Vítkov Hill **33**
National Museum **53**
National Technical Museum **22**
National Theater **49**
New Jewish Cemetery **54**
Old Jewish Cemetery **24**
Old-New Synagogue **24**
Old Town Hall and
Astronomical Clock **29**
Old Town Square
(Staroměstské náměstí) **37**
Olšanské Cemeteries **54**
Petřín Tower and Petřín Hill **17**
Pinkas Synagogue **25**
Powder Tower **36**
Prague Castle (Pražský Hrad) **6**
Rašín Embankment Building
(Dancing Building) **55**
Royal Garden **5**
Royal Palace **8**
St. Agnes Convent **23**
St. George's Convent **9**
St. Vitus Cathedral **7**
Schwarzenberg Palace **2**
State Jewish Museum **24**
Štefánik Observatory **17**
Šternberk Palace Art Museum **4**
Strahov Monastery and Library **3**
Týn Church **38**

Veletržní Palác **20**
Vrtbovská Garden **14**
Vyšehrad **58**
Waldstein Gardens **10**
Wenceslas Square
(Václavské náměstí) **50**

INFORMATION
Castle Information Office **6**
Čedok Office **45**
Prague Welcome Office **29**

TRANSPORTATION/MAIL
Florenc Bus Station **34**
Main Post Office **51**
Main Train Station **52**
Masaryk Station **35**

Hradčanské náměstí, Hradčany, Prague 1 (© **224-372-423,** second courtyard information office, © 224-372-434, third courtyard information office; www.hrad.cz). The castle is open daily 9am to 6pm (to 4pm Nov–Mar). Metro: Malostranská, then take tram no. 22 up the hill two stops.

Touring St. Vitus Cathedral (Chrám sv. Víta) ★★★

St. Vitus Cathedral (Chrám sv. Víta), named for a wealthy 4th-century Sicilian martyr, isn't just the dominant part of the castle—it's the most important section historically. In 1997, the late Pope John Paul II visited the cathedral and conferred the name of the 10th century Slavic evangelist St. Vojtěch on it, but officially the Czech state still calls it just St. Vitus.

Built over various phases beginning in A.D. 926 as the court church of the Přemyslid princes, the cathedral has long been the center of Prague's religious and political life. The key part of its Gothic construction took place in the 14th century under the direction of Mathias of Arras and Petr Parléř of Gmünd. In the 18th and 19th centuries, subsequent baroque and neo-Gothic additions were made. The **Golden Portal** entrance from the third courtyard is no longer used; however, take a look above the arch. The 1370 mosaic *The Last Judgment* has been painstakingly restored with the help of computer-aided imagery provided by American art researchers.

As you enter the cathedral through the back entrance into the main aisle, the colored light streaming through the intricate **stained-glass windows** that rise to the Gothic ceiling above the high altar may dazzle you. Stained-glass windows painted by the Czech Republic's Art Nouveau master, Alfons Mucha, adorn the windows to your left above the third chapel from the entrance. The center windows, restored in the years after World War II, depict the Holy Trinity, with the Virgin Mary to the left and St. Wenceslas kneeling to the right.

Of the massive Gothic cathedral's 21 chapels, the **St. Wenceslas Chapel (Svatováclavská kaple) ★★** stands out as one of Prague's few must-see, indoor sights. Midway toward the high altar on the right, it's encrusted with hundreds of pieces of jasper and amethyst and decorated with paintings from the 14th to the 16th centuries. The chapel sits atop the gravesite of Bohemia's patron saint, St. Wenceslas.

Just beyond this, the **Chapel of the Holy Rood (Kaple sv. Kříže)** leads to an underground **royal crypt.** In the early 1900s, the crypt was reconstructed, and the remains of the kings and their relatives were replaced in new sarcophagi. The center sarcophagus is the final resting place of Charles IV, the former emperor who died in 1378 and is the namesake of much of Prague. Charles's four wives are also buried here in one sarcophagus, and in front of them is George of Poděbrady, the last Bohemian king, who died in 1471.

Continuing Through the Castle Complex

For more than 700 years, beginning in the 9th century, Bohemian kings and princes resided in the **Old Royal Palace (Starý královský palác) ★★,** located in the third courtyard of the castle grounds. Vaulted **Vladislav Hall (Vladislavský sál),** the interior's centerpiece, hosted coronations and is still used for special occasions of state such as inaugurations of presidents. The adjacent Diet was where kings and queens met with their advisers and where the Supreme Court was held. From a window in the Ludwig Wing, where the Bohemia Chancellery met, the Second Defenestration took place (see "Beware of Open Windows: The Czech Tradition of

1 Sigismund Chapel
2 Old Sacristy
3 St. Anne Chapel
4 St. Agatha Chapel
5 Chapel of St. Anthony the Hermit
6 Chapel of the Holy Trinity
7 Chapel of Sts. Adalbert and Drothea

8 Chapel of Sts. Erhard and Ottilie
9 Mary Magdalene Chapel
10 Royal Oratory
11 Simon Jude Chapel
12 St. Andrew Chapel
13 St. Wenceslas Chapel
14 Hasenburg Chapel

15 Thun Chapel
16 Holy Sepulchre Chapel
17 St. Ludmila Chapel
18 Chapel of St. Agnes of Bohemia
19 Schwarzenberg Chapel
20 Hora Chapel
21 New Sacristy

Enter   Exit

beware of open windows: THE CZECH TRADITION OF DEFENESTRATION

About 600 years before Prague's popular uprising brought down Communism, the Czech people began a long tradition of what might be considered a unique form of political protest—tossing people out of the window!

In 1402, Jan Hus, a lecturer from Prague University, became the leading voice in a growing condemnation of the Catholic Church. From a pulpit in Old Town's Bethlehem Chapel (later destroyed but reconstructed in the 1950s), Hus gained popular support for his claims that the omnipotent power of the mostly German-dominated clergy had to be contained. In 1414, he was invited to the Catholic ecclesiastical Council of Konstanz to explain his beliefs. Though the emperor had promised Hus safe conduct, on arriving he was promptly arrested, and a year later he was burned at the stake. The Protestant Hussite supporters declared him a martyr and rallied their calls for change around his death.

On July 30, 1419, a group of radical Hussites stormed the New Town Hall on Charles Square and demanded the release of other arrested pro-reform Hussites. After town councilors rejected the demand, the Hussites tossed them out of third-story windows, killing several. This became known as the First Defenestration, from the Latin for "out of the window." The incident sparked a 15-year battle known as the Hussite Wars, which ended in the defeat of the radical Protestants in 1434.

By the 17th century, the Habsburg Catholics who came to power in Prague tolerated little dissent, but as the Protestant Czechs became ever more wealthy, they began criticizing the Habsburg monarchy. This bubbled over on May 23, 1618, when a group of Protestant nobles entered Prague Castle, seized two pro-Habsburg Czechs and their secretary, and tossed them out of the eastern window of the rear room of the Chancellery—the Second Defenestration. In the Garden on the Ramparts below the Ludwig Wing, two obelisks mark where they landed. This act led in part to the Europewide conflict known as the Thirty Years' War, which ended in victory in 1648 for the Catholics. The Habsburgs remained in power for another 270 years, ruling over Prague as a provincial capital until the democratic Czechoslovak state was born at the end of World War I.

A possible third defenestration occurred in 1948, with the tragic death of then-Foreign Minister Jan Masaryk in the wake of the Communist coup d'état that year. Masaryk, the son of the country's first president, either fell to his death or was pushed from a high window at the Foreign Ministry's Černín Palace (not far from Prague Castle). The mystery has never been cleared up, though Masaryk was fervently anti-Communist and most of the general public firmly believes the second scenario.

Though Prague's 1989 overthrow of the totalitarian Communist regime gained the name the Velvet Revolution for its nonviolent nature, scattered calls for another defenestration (some serious, some joking) were heard. Contemporary Czech politicians surely know to keep away from open windows.

Defenestration," below). Access to the Old Royal Palace is included in both the full-price and reduced-price entry tickets.

A permanent exhibition called **"The Story of Prague Castle,"** included in the full-price combined-entry ticket, occupies part of the Old Royal Palace and shows the transformation of the castle from the prehistoric period up to the present.

St. George's Basilica (Bazilika sv. Jiří) ★, adjacent to the Old Royal Palace, is Prague's oldest Romanesque structure, dating from the 10th century. Inside the sparse and eerie basilica you will find relics of the castle's history along with a genealogy of those who have passed through it. If you look carefully at the outer towers, you'll notice that they're slightly different from each other: They have an Adam-and-Eve motif. The wider south tower represents Adam, while the narrower north tower is Eve. Access to the Basilica is included in both the full-price and reduced-price entry tickets.

St. George's Convent (Klášter sv. Jiří na Pražském hradě) ★, just to the left of the basilica entrance, no longer serves a religious function and houses a fascinating collection of 19th-century Czech paintings (see "Museums & Galleries," later in this chapter). Admission is included in the full-price ticket or you can buy a separate ticket.

Golden Lane (Zlatá ulička) and Daliborka Tower is a picturesque street of tiny 16th-century houses built into the castle fortifications. Once home to castle sharpshooters, the lane got a fresh makeover in 2011 to restore its 17th-century appearance. In 1917, Franz Kafka is said to have lived briefly at no. 22; however, the debate continues as to whether Kafka actually took up residence or just worked in a small office there. Access to Golden Lane is included in both the full-price and reduced-price tickets.

The Prague Castle Picture Gallery (Obrazárna Pražského hradu) displays European and Bohemian masterpieces, but few are from the original imperial collection, which was virtually destroyed during the Thirty Years' War. Of the works that have survived from the days of Emperors Rudolf II and Ferdinand III, the most celebrated is Hans von Aachen's *Portrait of a Girl* (1605–10), depicting the artist's daughter.

The **Powder Tower** (**Prašná věž,** aka **Mihulka**) forms part of the northern bastion of the castle complex just off the Golden Lane. Originally a gunpowder storehouse and a cannon tower, it was turned into a laboratory for the 17th-century alchemists serving the court of Emperor Rudolf II.

Crossing the Vltava: Charles Bridge

Dating from the 14th century, **Charles Bridge (Karlův most)** ★★★, Prague's most celebrated statue-studded structure, links Staré Město and Malá Strana. For most of its 650 years, the 510m-long (1,673-ft.) span has been a pedestrian promenade, though for centuries walkers had to share the concourse with horse-drawn vehicles and trolleys. These days, the bridge is filled to brimming with tourists, souvenir

💬 A Bridge Tale

Why has Charles Bridge stood for so long? One great yarn through the ages has it that when stones for the bridge were being laid, the master builders mixed eggs into the mortar to strengthen the bond. At the time of the bridge's construction, one village allegedly tried to impress Emperor Charles IV by sending him carts filled with hard-boiled eggs. The gift may have been a welcome snack for the builders, but likely did little to strengthen the mortar hawkers, portraitists, and the occasional busking musician in what feels like a 24/7 Mardi Gras celebration.

The best times to stroll across the bridge are early morning and around sunset, when the crowds have thinned and the shadows are more mysterious. The 30 statues lining the bridge are explained in detail in "Walking Tour 1: Charles Bridge & Malá Strana (Lesser Town)," in chapter 7.

OTHER TOP SIGHTS

Hradčany

Loreto Palace (Loreta) ★   Loreto Palace was named after the town of Loreto, Italy, where the dwelling of the Virgin Mary was said to have been brought by angels from Palestine in the 13th century. After the Roman Catholics defeated the Protestant Bohemians in 1620, the Loreto faction was chosen to lead the re-Catholicization of Bohemia. The Loreto legend holds that a cottage in which the Virgin Mary lived had been miraculously transferred from Nazareth to Loreto, an Italian city near Ancona. The Loreto Palace is an imitation of this cottage, and more than 50 copies have been constructed throughout the Czech lands.

The Loreto's facade is decorated with 18th-century statues of the writers of the Gospel—Matthew, Mark, Luke, and John—along with a lone female, St. Anne, mother of the Virgin Mary. Inside the **Church of the Nativity** are fully clothed remains of two Spanish saints, St. Felicissimus and St. Marcia. The wax masks on the skeletons' faces are particularly macabre.

Inside the **Chapel of Our Lady of Sorrows** is a painting of a bearded woman hanging on a cross. This is St. Starosta, or Vilgefortis, who, after taking a vow of virginity, was forced to marry the king of Sicily. It's said that God, taking pity on the woman, gave her facial hair to make her undesirable, after which her pagan father had her crucified. Thus, Starosta went into history as the saint of unhappily married women. The painting was created in the 1700s. Also on display is a portrait of St. Apolena (or Apollonia), a 3rd-century deacon who had her teeth knocked out as part of a torture for refusing to renounce Christianity. She's often represented in art by a gold tooth or pincer. As the patron saint of dentists, Apolena is sometimes referred to as the "saint of toothaches."

Loretánské nám. 7, Prague 1. ℂ **220-516-740.** www.loreta.cz. Admission 110Kč adults, 90Kč students, free for children 5 and under. Daily Apr–Oct 9am–12:15pm and 1–5pm; Nov–Mar to 4pm. Tram: 22 from Malostranská.

Strahov Monastery and Library (Strahovský klášter) ★★   The second-oldest monastery in Prague, Strahov was founded high above Malá Strana in 1143 by Vladislav II. It's still home to Premonstratensian monks, a scholarly order closely related to the Jesuits, and their dormitories and refectory are off-limits. What draws visitors are the monastery's ornate libraries, holding more than 125,000 volumes. Over the centuries, the monks have assembled one of the world's best collections of philosophical and theological texts, including illuminated (decorated with colored designs) manuscripts and first editions.

The ceiling of the 1679 **Theological Hall** is a stunning example of baroque opulence, with intricate leaf blanketing the walls and framing the 18th-century ceiling frescoes. The rich wood-accented **Philosophical Library's** 14m-high (46-ft.) ceiling is decorated with a 1794 fresco entitled *The Struggle of Mankind to Know Real*

Wisdom, by A. F. Maulbertsch, a Viennese master of rococo. Intricate woodwork frames the immense collection of books. Ancient printing presses downstairs are also worth visiting, as are several altars and the remains of St. Norbert, a 10th-century, German-born saint who founded the Premonstratensian order. His bones were brought here in 1627, when he became one of Bohemia's ten patron saints.

The little square in front of the monastery is a festive place, with a couple of fun pubs to have a break. Paths leading through the monastery grounds take you to a breathtaking overlook of the city.

Strahovské nádvoří 1, Prague 1. © **233-107-718.** www.strahovskyklaster.cz. Admission 80Kč adults, 50Kč students. Daily 9am–noon and 1–5pm. Tram: 22 from Malostranská metro station.

Malá Strana (Lesser Town)

Church of St. Nicholas (Chrám sv. Mikuláše) ★★ ◙ This church is one of the best examples of high baroque north of the Alps. However, K. I. Dientzenhofer's 1711 design didn't have the massive green dome that now dominates the Lesser Town skyline below Prague Castle. Dientzenhofer's son, Kryštof, added the 78m-high (256-ft.) dome during additional work completed in 1752. Even if you're not a fan of baroque, you'll have to admit the interior is stunning. Gold-capped marble-veneered columns frame altars packed with statuary and frescoes. A giant statue of the church's namesake looks down from the high altar. After you visit, climb the tower for views out over the Old Town in the distance.

Malostranské nám. 1, Prague 1. © **257-534-215.** www.psalterium.cz (church and concerts), www.prazskeveze.cz (tower). Admission to the church 70Kč adults, 35Kč students, free for children 9 and under; concerts around 500Kč; tower 70Kč adults, 50Kč students, 20Kč for children 5 and under. Daily 9am–5pm (4pm in winter); concerts are usually held at 6pm. Metro: Line A to Malostranská.

Staré Město (Old Town)

Estates' Theater (Stavovské divadlo) Completed in 1783 by wealthy Count F. A. Nostitz Rieneck, the neoclassical theater became an early symbol of the emerging high Czech culture with the Greek theme *Patriae et Musis* (the Fatherland and Music) etched above its front columns. In 1799, the wealthy land barons who formed fiefdoms known as The Estates gave the theater its current name.

Wolfgang Amadeus Mozart staged the premier of *Don Giovanni* here in 1787 because he said that Vienna's conservative patrons didn't appreciate him or his passionate and sometimes shocking work. They also wanted mostly German opera, but Praguers were happy to stage the performance in Italian. "My Praguers understand me," Mozart was quoted as saying.

In 1834, Czech playwright J. K. Tyl staged a comedy called *Fidlovačka,* in which the patriotic song "Kde domov můj?" ("Where Is My Home?") was a standout. It later became the Czech national anthem. In the heady days at the end of World War II, in 1945, the Estates' Theater was renamed Tyl Theater but when a total reconstruction of the building was completed in 1991 its previous name was reinstated.

Czech director Miloš Forman returned to his native country to film his Oscar-winning *Amadeus* (1984), shooting the scenes of Mozart in Prague with perfect authenticity at the Estates' Theater.

The theater doesn't offer daily tours, so it's not easy to get a look inside. One possibility is to attend a performance here. Normally, the theater hosts dramatic works performed in Czech, but occasionally you'll find opera—particularly baroque opera—that's more accessible to all languages. Purchase tickets for performances at the box office for the National Theater (discussed later). Tour events are occasionally scheduled, and individual tours for this and other major monuments can sometimes be arranged through **Prague Welcome** (☎ 221-714-444; www.praguewelcome.cz). Ovocný trh 1, Prague 1. ☎ **224-901-448.** www.narodni-divadlo.cz. Metro: Line A or B to Můstek.

Old Town Hall (Staroměstská radnice) & Astronomical Clock (Orloj) ★★ ☺

Crowds congregate in front of Old Town Hall's Astronomical Clock (*Orloj*) to watch the glockenspiel spectacle that occurs hourly from 8am to 8pm. Built in 1410, the clock has long been an important symbol of Prague. According to legend, after the timepiece was remodeled at the end of the 15th century, clock artist Master Hanuš was blinded by the Municipal Council so that he couldn't repeat his fine work elsewhere. In retribution, Hanuš threw himself into the clock mechanism and promptly died. The clock remained out of kilter for almost a century.

It's not possible to determine the time of day from this timepiece; you have to look at the clock on the very top of Old Town Hall's tower for that. This astronomical clock, with all its hands and markings, is meant to mark the phases of the moon, the equinoxes, the seasons, the days, and numerous Christian holidays.

When the clock strikes the hour, a kind of politically incorrect medieval morality play begins. Two doors slide open and the statues of the Twelve Apostles glide by, while the 15th-century conception of the "evils" of life—a Death skeleton, a preening Vanity, a corrupt Turk, and an acquisitive Jew—shake and dance below. At the end of World War II, the horns and beard were removed from the moneybag-holding Jew, who's now politely referred to as Greed. A cock crows and a trumpet blares to mark the end of the spectacle, all to enthusiastic applause from the crowds below.

A View with a Warning

It's well worth climbing the Old Town Hall's tower for an excellent view over the red rooftops of Staroměstské náměstí and the surrounding area. But be warned: The steps are narrow, steep, and quite physically demanding, so the less courageous should take the elevator.

Staroměstské nám. 1/3, Prague 1. ☎ **724-911-556.** www.praguewelcome.cz (halls), www.prazs keveze.cz (tower). Admission to tower 100Kč adults, 50Kč students, 20Kč children 5 and under. Mon 11am–6pm (halls), to 10pm (tower); Tues–Sun 9am–6pm (halls), to 10pm (tower). Metro: Line A to Staroměstská.

Josefov

Within Josefov (the former Jewish Quarter), you'll find the remnants of a once-vibrant community that for centuries was forced to fend for itself. Josefov served as the center of Jewish life in Prague from the 14th century to the end of the 19th century, when city authorities cleared the quarter to make way for new blocks of luxury apartment buildings (that are still standing). By that time, most of Prague's Jews had moved to other parts of town and Josefov had become a slum.

The Nazi occupation during World War II brought a violent end to much of Jewish life in Prague and around the Czech Republic. Of the more than 118,000 Jews living in the Czech lands of Bohemia and Moravia in 1939, only 30,000 survived to see the end of the war. Today, the Jewish community in the entire country comprises about 3,000 people, most of whom live in Prague.

It should be noted that the former Jewish ghetto is not a Holocaust site *per se*. By the time Nazis got here, most of the city's Jews had relocated to other, more affluent (at the time) parts of Prague. Nevertheless, Josefov's synagogues can be seen as monuments to the survival of Judaism in central Europe, and the Old Jewish Cemetery, with generations buried upon one another, as an enduring symbol of the cohesion of Prague's ghetto. Prague's Jewish Quarter is described in detail in "Walking Tour 4: Josefov (Jewish Quarter)" in chapter 7.

The **Jewish Museum in Prague** (✆ 222-749-211; www.jewishmuseum.cz) doesn't refer to one building, but rather the organization that manages the main sites of the former Jewish Quarter. These include the **Old Jewish Cemetery,** the **Pinkas Synagogue,** the **Klaus Synagogue,** the **Maisel Synagogue,** the **Ceremonial Hall,** and the **Spanish Synagogue.** Each synagogue features a different exhibition on various aspects of Jewish customs and history. It's not possible to pay for the sites individually; instead, you have to purchase a combined-entry ticket that allows access to all the main buildings. You'll find ticket counters selling the tickets inside the synagogues and at ticket windows around the quarter. Admission is 300Kč for adults, 200Kč for students, and free for children 5 and under. The museum's sites are open from April to October Sunday to Friday 9am to 6pm; and November to March Sunday to Friday 9am to 4:30pm. Note the museum is closed on Saturdays and Jewish holidays. Another synagogue, the **Old-New Synagogue** (see below), is considered separate from the Jewish Museum's main holdings and requires an additional admission ticket.

Old Jewish Cemetery (Starý židovský hřbitov) ★★ Just 1 block from the Old-New Synagogue, this is one of Europe's oldest Jewish burial grounds, dating from the mid–15th century. Because the local government of the time didn't allow Jews to bury their dead elsewhere, graves were dug deep enough to hold 12 bodies vertically, with each tombstone placed in front of the last. The result is one of the world's most crowded cemeteries: a 1-block area filled with tens of thousands of graves. Among the most famous persons buried here are the celebrated Rabbi Loew (Löw; 1520–1609), who created the legend of Golem (a giant clay "monster" to protect Prague's Jews); and banker Markus Mordechai Maisel (1528–1601), then the richest man in Prague and protector of the city's Jewish community during the reign of Rudolf II.

U Starého hřbitova; the entrance is from Široká 3. ✆ 221-711-511. www.jewishmuseum.cz. Admission (combined entry to all Jewish Museum sites) 300Kč adults, 200Kč students, free for children 5 and under. Apr–Oct Sun–Fri 9am–6pm; Nov–Mar Sun–Fri 9am–4:30pm. Closed Sat and Jewish holidays. Metro: Line A to Staroměstská.

Old-New Synagogue (Staronová synagóga) ★ First called the New Synagogue to distinguish it from an even older one that no longer exists, the Old-New Synagogue, built around 1270, is Europe's oldest remaining Jewish house of worship. The faithful have prayed here continuously for more than 700 years, carrying on even after a massive 1389 pogrom in Josefov that killed more than 3,000 Jews. Its use as a house of worship was interrupted only between 1941 and 1945 because of the Nazi occupation. The synagogue is also one of Prague's great Gothic buildings, built with vaulted ceilings and retro-fitted with Renaissance-era columns. It is not part of the Jewish Museum and requires a separate admission ticket that you can buy at the entrance to the synagogue.

Červená 2. ✆ 224-800-812. www.synagogue.cz. Admission 200Kč adults, 140Kč students. (If part of the package for Jewish Museum, 490Kč adults, 330Kč students.) Free for children 6 and under. Jan–Mar Sun–Thurs 9:30am–4:30pm, Fri 9am–2pm; Apr–Oct Sun–Fri 9:30am–6pm; Nov–Dec Sun–Thurs 9:30am–5pm, Fri 9am–2pm. Closed Sat and Jewish holidays. Metro: Line A to Staroměstská.

Elsewhere in Prague

Vyšehrad ★ This sprawling rocky hilltop complex is the cradle of the Bohemian state. From this spot, legend has it, Princess Libuše looked out over the Vltava valley toward present-day Prague Castle and predicted the founding of a great kingdom and capital city. Ancient Vyšehrad Castle, still standing, was the first seat of the first Czech kings in the Přemyslid dynasty before the dawn of the 10th century.

This was also the first Royal Route. Before the kings could take their seat at the more modern Prague Castle, they first had to pay homage to their predecessors at Vyšehrad and then follow the route to Hradčany for the coronation.

PURELY PERSONAL LIST OF five can't-miss sights IN PRAGUE

Everyone has his or her own list of favorite things to see and do in Prague. After living here for more than a decade, I include some of mine below. To avoid repetition, I'll assume that Old Town Square, Charles Bridge, Prague Castle, and the Jewish Museum are givens and there's no need to re-list them here. Contact and transport info for these can be found in the appropriate section of this chapter.

o **Veletržní palác.** The National Gallery's collection of 20th- and 21st-century art is a jaw-dropper. Forget the Klimts, Schieles, Picassos, and Rodins for a moment and head straight for the gallery of constructivist, functionalist, surrealist Czech art from 1900 to 1930. This was an especially fruitful period for Czech art, when it was at the vanguard of modern movements.

o **St. Agnes Convent.** I never would have guessed I had an interest in Gothic art, but this museum in a former convent is full of surprises. The 13th and 14th century paintings are filled with wit and humor and easily could have come off a post-Modern easel somewhere last week. The sculpture and statuary are ample evidence of Prague's preeminence in Europe in the Middle Ages.

o **Gardens Below Prague Castle (Zahrady pod Pražským hradem).** This series of four sculpted baroque gardens on the hill below Prague Castle is simply special, filled with hidden corners and lovely views. They're accessible from Valdštejnská Street below or from Prague Castle above.

o **Vyšehrad cemetery.** I am sucker for celebrities, even dead ones. Dvořák, Smetana, Mucha, and the rest of the Czech pantheon are all laid to rest here in Prague's own version of Paris's Père-Lachaise. It's fun to poke around and look for familiar names, and the hilltop Vyšehrad setting is stunning.

o **Stromovka park.** This seemingly limitless preserve of walks and trails is perfect for cycling, rollerblading, or just strolling among the trees. This park is situated miles from the tourist throng, but it's within easy walking distance of the river promenade and the zoo. Grab a pack lunch, a blanket, and a good book and take the afternoon off (as I like to do as often as I can).

—*Mark Baker*

Today, the fortifications remain on the rocky cliffs, blocking out the increasing noise and confusion below. Within the confines of the citadel, lush lawns and gardens are crisscrossed by dozens of paths leading to historic buildings and cemeteries. In addition to the **Vyšehrad Cemetery** (described below), check out the former **Casements** and castle fortification systems, which were built by the French in the 18th century (when rival French, Prussian, and Austrian armies competed for influence in this part of the world), and include some spooky underground passages and even a couple of original statues from the Charles Bridge that are just standing here in repose.

> ## Impressions
>
> *Upon my word, if fate drove me to the furthest corner of the Earth, I could not otherwise but wander back after a while to ancient Vyšehrad and refresh my mind with the view.*
>
> —Karel Hynek Mácha, Czech poet (1810–36), buried at Vyšehrad Cemetery

Vyšehrad Cemetery (Vyšehradský hřbitov) ★★ is the national cemetery within the ancient citadel on the east side of the Vltava River. It's the final resting place of some 600 honored Czechs, including composers Antonín Dvořák and Bedřich Smetana and Art Nouveau painter Alfons Mucha. The complex of churches and gardens is a pleasant getaway from the city crush.

The casemates and cemetery are just a short walk away from each other on Soběslavova, Prague 2 (𝄎 241-410-348; www.praha-vysehrad.cz). The cemetery is free to enter; the casements cost 50Kč for adults and 30Kč for students and seniors. Vyšehrad sites are open daily November to March from 9:30am to 5pm, and to 6pm from April through October. To get here, take tram no. 3, 7, 16, or 17 to Výtoň south of New Town and walk uphill or take metro line C (red) to Vyšehrad station and walk about 15 minutes.

MUSEUMS & GALLERIES

Many fine private art galleries showing contemporary work by Czech and other artists are in central Prague, within walking distance of Staroměstské náměstí. Although their primary interest is sales, most welcome browsing. See "Art Galleries" in chapter 8 for information on the city's top art galleries.

As for public museums and galleries, note that many museums are closed on Monday.

National Gallery Sites

The national collection of fine art is grouped for display in a series of venues known collectively as the **National Gallery (Národní Galerie).** Remember that this term refers to several locations, not just one gallery.

The National Gallery's holdings are eclectic and range from classic European masters at the **Šternberský palác** across from the main gate at Prague Castle to modern Czech and European works from the 20th and 21st centuries at the **Veletržní palác** in the neighborhood of Holešovice, in Prague 7. Other important museums include a collection of 19th-century Czech art at **St. George's Convent** in the Prague Castle complex and the extensive holdings of medieval and Gothic art at **St. Agnes Convent** near the river in Old Town.

The key Prague sites within the National Gallery system are listed below.

STARÉ MĚSTO (OLD TOWN)

St. Agnes Convent (Klášter sv. Anežky České) ★★ A complex of early Gothic buildings and churches dating from the 13th century, the convent, tucked in a quiet corner of Staré Město, began exhibiting much of the National Gallery's collection of medieval art in 2000. Once home to the Order of the Poor Clares, it was established in 1234 by St. Agnes of Bohemia, sister of Wenceslas I. The Blessed Agnes became St. Agnes when Pope John Paul II paid his first visit to Prague in 1990 for her canonization.

The most famous among the unique collection of Czech Gothic panel paintings are those by the Master of the Hohenfurth Altarpiece and the Master Theodoricus. The convent is at the end of Anežka, off Haštalské náměstí.

U Milosrdných 17, Prague 1. ℭ **224-810-628.** www.ngprague.cz. Admission 150Kč adults, 80Kč students, free for children 5 and under. Tues–Sun 10am–6pm. Metro: Line A to Staroměstská.

HRADČANY

St. George's Convent at Prague Castle (Klášter sv. Jiří na Pražském hradě) ★ The former convent at St. George's houses a fascinating collection of 19th-century Czech painting and sculpture that is especially strong on landscapes and pieces from the Czech national revival period. The collection shows the progression of the Czech lands from a largely agrarian province at the start of the century to a highly developed cultural and industrial space by the end.

Jiřské nám. 33. ℭ **257-531-644.** www.ngprague.cz. Admission 150Kč adults, 80Kč students, free for children 5 and under. Daily 10am–6pm. Metro: Line A to Malostranská plus tram 22.

Šternberk Palace (Šternberský palác) ★★ The jewel in the National Gallery crown, the gallery at Šternberk Palace, adjacent to the main gate of Prague Castle, displays a wide menu of European art throughout the ages. It features 5 centuries of everything from Orthodox icons to Renaissance oils by Dutch masters. Pieces by Rembrandt, El Greco, Goya, and van Dyck are mixed among numerous pieces from Austrian imperial court painters. Exhibits such as Italian Renaissance bronzes rotate throughout the seasons.

Hradčanské nám. 15, Prague 1. ℭ**233-090-570.** www.ngprague.cz. Admission 150Kč adults, 80Kč students, free for children 5 and under. Tues–Sun 10am–6pm. Metro: Line A to Malostranská plus tram 22.

OUTSIDE OF THE CENTER

Veletržní palác (Museum of 20th- and 21st-Century Art) ★★ This 1928 Functionalist (Bauhaus-style) palace, built for trade fairs, was remodeled and reopened in 1995 to hold the bulk of the National Gallery's collection of 20th- and 21st-century works by Czech and other European artists. The highlights on three floors of exhibition space include paintings by Klimt, Munch, Schiele, and Picasso, among other modern European masters, as well as a riveting display of Czech constructivist and surrealist works from the 1920s and '30s. The first floor features temporary exhibits from traveling shows. There's also a good gift shop on the ground floor.

Veletržní at Dukelských hrdinů 47, Prague 7. ℭ**224-301-122.** www.ngprague.cz. Admission 250Kč adults, 120Kč students. Free for children 5 and under. Tues–Sun 10am–6pm. Metro: Line C to Vltavská. Tram: 12, 14, or 17 to Strossmayerovo nám.

DID YOU know?

- Charles University, central Europe's first postsecondary school, opened in Prague in 1348.
- Albert Einstein was a professor of physics in Prague from 1911 to 1912.
- The word *robot* was coined by Czech writer Karel Čapek and comes from a Slavic root meaning "to work."
- Contact lenses were invented by a Czech scientist.
- Baroness Bertha von Suttner, the first female recipient of the Nobel Peace Prize, in 1905, was born in Prague and lived in the Kinský Palace on Old Town Square.

- Prague was a hotbed of early astronomy. The Danish astronomer Tycho Brahe and the German Johannes Kepler (who first discovered the laws of planetary motion) both worked on the court of Rudolf II. Christian Doppler, of "Doppler Effect" fame, taught in Prague and lived in a house not far from Old Town Square (not open to the public).
- The word *dollar* came from the Tolar coins used during the Austrian empire; the coins were minted in the western Bohemian town of Jáchymov from silver mined nearby.

Other Museums & Galleries
MALÁ STRANA

Franz Kafka Museum   A long-term exhibition here presents first editions of Kafka's work, his letters, diaries, and manuscripts. This unique project, which was originally introduced in Barcelona in 1999, has been brought to the writer's birthplace and the city where he had strong ties. The exhibit is divided into two sections: The first, Existential Space, explains the huge influence of the city on Kafka's life and his writing. The second uses 3-D installations as well as good audiovisual technology to depict the author's "Imaginary Topography of Prague." Interesting, but best left for true Kafka fans.

Hergetova Cihelna, Cihelná 2b, Prague 1. ℂ **257-535-373.** www.kafkamuseum.cz. Admission 180Kč adults, 120Kč students. Daily 10am–6pm. Metro: Malostranská.

Museum Kampa–Sovovy mlýny ★   This building on Kampa Island served for most of its history, due to the location, as a mill. Throughout the centuries it was struck by floods, fires, and destructive wars. The premises underwent several transformations and reconstructions. In 2003, the Sovovy mlýny was opened as a museum of modern art by Czech-born American Meda Mládková and her foundation. She has been collecting works of Czech and central European artists since the 1950s. Her dream reached its pinnacle when she presented the permanent exhibition of František Kupka's drawings and Otto Gutfreund's sculptures.

U Sovových mlýnů 503/2, Prague 1. ℂ **257-286-147.** www.museumkampa.cz. Admission 180Kč adults, 90Kč students, free for children 5 and under. Daily 10am–6pm. Metro: Malostranská.

STARÉ MĚSTO (OLD TOWN)
Bedřich Smetana Museum (Muzeum B. Smetany)   Opened in 1936 (in what was the former Old Town waterworks) and jutting into the Vltava next to Charles

Bridge, this museum pays tribute to the deepest traditions of Czech classical music and its most patriotic composer, Bedřich Smetana. The exhibits show scores, diaries, manuscripts, and gifts presented to the composer while he was the preeminent man of Prague music in the mid–19th century. This museum is closed on Tuesdays.

Novotného lávka 1, Prague 1. ✆ **222-220-082.** www.nm.cz. Admission 50Kč adults, 25Kč students and children. Wed–Mon 10am–5pm. Metro: Staroměstská. Tram: 17 or 18.

NOVÉ MĚSTO (NEW TOWN)

Alfons Mucha Museum (Muzeum A. Muchy) ★ This museum opened in early 1998 near Wenceslas Square to honor the high priest of Art Nouveau, Alphonse (Alfons in Czech) Mucha. Though the Moravian-born, turn-of-the-20th-century master spent most of his creative years in Paris drawing luminaries like actress Sarah Bernhardt, Mucha's influence can still be seen throughout his home country. The new museum, around the corner from the Palace Hotel, combines examples of his graphic works, posters, and paintings, and highlights his influence in jewelry, fashion, and advertising. Those who remember the 1960s and 1970s will flash back to one of Mucha's most famous works, the sinuous goddess of Job rolling papers.

Panská 7, Prague 1. ✆ **221-451-333.** www.mucha.cz. Admission 180Kč adults, 120Kč students. Daily 10am–6pm. Metro: Můstek.

Dvořák Museum (Muzeum A. Dvořáka) The country's best-known 19th-century Czech composer, Antonín Dvořák, lived here during his golden years. Built in 1712, the two-story rococo building, tucked away on a Nové Město side street, was Dvořák's home for 24 years until his death in 1901. In the 18th century when the building was erected, this part of Prague was frontier land. Czechs willing to open businesses so far from the center were called "Americans" for their pioneer spirit. This building came to be known as "America." Opened in 1932, the museum displays an extensive collection, including the composer's piano, spectacles, Cambridge cap and gown, photographs, and sculptures. Several rooms are furnished as they were around 1900. Upstairs, a small recital hall hosts chamber-music performances in high season.

Ke Karlovu 20, Prague 2. ✆ **224-918-013.** www.nm.cz. Admission 50Kč adults, 25Kč students, free for children 5 and under. Apr–Sept Tues–Sun 10am–1:30pm and 2–5pm (Thurs till 7pm); Oct–Mar Tues–Sun 10am–1:30pm and 2–5pm. Metro: Line C to I. P. Pavlova.

National Museum (Národní muzeum) The National Museum, dominating upper Wenceslas Square (Václavské nám.), looks so much like an important government building that it even fooled the Soviet soldiers, who fired on it during their 1968 invasion, thinking it was the seat of government. If you look closely at the columns you can still see bullet marks. This grandiose statement of nationalist purpose opened in 1893, as the national revival gained momentum. The exterior is rimmed with names of the great and good of the homeland (albeit with several foreign residents, such as astronomer Johannes Kepler). Inside, the museum is a fairly routine natural science museum, with rocks, meteorites, bones, and stuffed animals. In 2011, the museum closed its doors till 2015 to allow for a thorough housecleaning, and is not open to the public. You'll find more info on the museum website.

Václavské nám. 68, Prague 1. www.nm.cz. Closed until 2015 for renovations. Metro: Line A or C to Muzeum station.

ELSEWHERE IN PRAGUE

National Memorial on Vítkov Hill ★ The National Memorial at Vítkov Hill in Žižkov is visible from nearly anywhere in the city; just look for the big hill with a huge equestrian statue on top (said by some to be the world's biggest horse statue). The building was originally designed in the 1920s as a memorial to the Czechoslovak heroes of World War I, but was never finished (the Nazis put a stop to it in 1939). After the war, it was seconded by the Communists and used as a mausoleum to display the mummified corpse (Lenin-style) of the country's first Communist leader, Klement Gottwald. After 1989, it fell into disuse, and in 2009, the National Museum opened a museum of modern Czech history. It's a fascinating place on many levels, with riveting displays of 1948 (the Communist coup), 1968 (the Soviet-led Warsaw Pact invasion), and 1989 (Velvet Revolution). After you're done learning about Czech history, you can take a look at some of the rooms and equipment used to keep Gottwald's body intact.

U Památníku 1900, Prague 3. ℭ **222-781-676.** www.nm.cz. Admission 110Kč adults, 60Kč students, free for children 5 and under. Wed–Sun 10am–6pm. Metro: Line B or C to Florenc, then bus 175 or 133 to Tachovské nám. station, then walk.

Museum of the City of Prague (Muzeum hlavního města Prahy) ★ Not just another warehouse of history where unearthed artifacts unwanted by others are chronologically stashed, this delightfully upbeat museum covers Prague's illustrious past with pleasant brevity. Sure, the museum holds the expected displays of medieval weaponry and shop signs, but the best exhibit in the neo-Renaissance building is an intricate miniature model of 18th-century Prague. It's fascinating to see Staré Město as it used to be and the Jewish Quarter before its late-19th-century face-lift. A reproduction of the original calendar face of the Old Town Hall astrological clock is also on display, as are a number of documents relating to Prague's Nazi occupation and the assassination of Nazi commander Reinhard Heydrich. The museum is 1 block north of the Florenc metro station.

Na Poříčí 52, Prague 8. ℭ **224-816-772.** www.muzeumprahy.cz. Admission 120Kč adults, 50Kč students, free for children 5 and under. Tues–Sun 9am–6pm (to 8pm 1st Thurs each month). Metro: Line B or C to Florenc.

National Technical Museum (Národní technické muzeum) ★★ ☺ The National Technical Museum reopened in 2010 after a 4-year-long renovation that has updated and modernized the holdings. The interactive displays are divided into transportation (impressive holdings of historic trains, planes, and automobiles), astronomy, printing, and architecture, and are sure to enthrall kids and kids at heart from 8 to 85 years of age.

Kostelní 42, Letná, Prague 7. ℭ **220-399-111.** www.ntm.cz. Admission 170Kč adults, 90Kč students, free for children 5 and under. Tues–Sun 10am–6pm (to 8pm 1st Thurs each month). Tram: 1, 8, 25, or 26 from Hradčanská metro to Letenské nám.

CHURCHES & CEMETERIES

Churches

STARÉ MĚSTO (OLD TOWN)

Bethlehem Chapel (Betlémská kaple) This is the site where, in the early 15th century, the firebrand Czech Protestant theologian Jan Hus raised the ire of the Catholic hierarchy with sermons critical of the establishment. He was burned at the stake as a heretic in 1415 at Konstanz in present-day Germany and became a martyr for the Czech Protestant and later nationalist causes. A memorial to Hus dominates the center of Old Town Square. The chapel was completed in 1394 and reconstructed

THE ART OF PRAGUE'S architecture

Prague's long history, combined with its good fortune in having avoided heavy war damage during World War II, makes it wonderful for architecture lovers. Along with the standard must-see castles and palaces comes a bountiful mixture of styles and periods. Buildings and monuments from the Middle Ages to the present are interspersed with one another throughout the city. For more on Prague's architecture, see chapter 2, "Prague & the Czech Republic in Depth," p. 11.

The best examples of Romanesque architecture are parts of **Prague Castle,** including St. George's Basilica. In Staré Město, you'll see the best examples of the Gothic period from the 13th to the 15th centuries: the **Convent of St. Agnes,** Na Františku; the **Old-New Synagogue,** Pařížská třída; **Old Town Hall** and the **Astronomical Clock,** Staroměstské náměstí; **Powder Tower,** Celetná ulice; and **Charles Bridge.** A few Renaissance buildings from the 16th and early 17th centuries still stand, including **Golden Lane, Malá Strana Town Hall,** and **Pinkas Synagogue** (Široká ulice) in Staré Město.

Many of Prague's best-known structures are pure baroque and rococo, enduring styles that reigned in the 17th to the early 19th centuries, and are associated in Praguers' minds with the Habsburg conquest of 1620 and the years spent converting the Czechs to Catholicism. Buildings on Staroměstské náměstí and Nerudova Street date from this period, as does **St. Nicholas Church,** Malostranské náměstí, in Malá Strana, and the **Loreto Palace,** Loretánské náměstí, in Hradčany.

Renaissance styles made a comeback in the late 19th century, when architecture seemed to run out of ideas and architects started replicating historic styles. Two neo-Renaissance buildings in particular—the **National Theater,** Národní třída, and the **National Museum,** Václavské náměstí, both in Prague 1, have endured and are among Prague's most identifiable landmarks.

An exciting addition to the architectural lineup is the painstakingly refurbished 1911 Art Nouveau **Municipal House (Obecní dům)** ★★ at Náměstí Republiky, Prague 1. Every opulent ceiling, sinuous light fixture, curling banister, etched-glass window, and inlaid ceramic wall creates the astonishing atmosphere of hope and accomplishment from the turn of the 20th century. This is Prague's outstanding monument to itself. The music salon, Smetana Hall (home to the Prague Symphony), has a gorgeous atrium roof with stained-glass windows.

---

in the early 1950s. In the main hall you can still see the original stone floors and the pulpit from where Hus preached; it's now used as a ceremonial hall for Czech national events.

Betlémské nám. 4, Prague 1. ℃ **224-248-595.** Admission 50Kč adults, 30Kč students, free for children 5 and under. Apr–Oct daily 10am–6:30pm; Nov–Mar daily 10am–5:30pm. Metro: Line B to Národní třída.

Church of St. Nicholas (Kostel sv. Mikuláše) At the site of a former Gothic church built by German merchants, this St. Nicholas church was designed in 1735 by the principal architect of Czech baroque, K. I. Dientzenhofer. He's the same Dientzenhofer who designed Prague's other St. Nicholas Church, in Malá Strana (p. 103). This church isn't nearly as ornate, but has a more tumultuous history. The Catholic monastery was closed in 1787, and the church was handed over for use as

After World War I, with independence won, the democratic Czechoslovak Republic was declared here by the first National Council (parliament) in 1918. Daily guided tours are offered in the afternoons; see the information center inside for details and tickets.

Other excellent examples of whimsical Art Nouveau architecture are the **Hotel Evropa,** on Václavské náměstí, and the older section of the main train station, **Hlavní nádraží,** on Wilsonova třída, both in Prague 1.

Prague's finest cubist design, the **House at the Black Mother of God (Dům U Černé Matky boží),** at Celetná and Ovocný trh in Old Town, is worth a look. The building is named for the statuette of the Virgin Mary on its well-restored exterior. It now houses a small Museum of Cubism. You'll also find a full cubist neighborhood of buildings directly under Vyšehrad Park near the right bank (Old Town side) of the Vltava.

Arguably, the city's most unappealing structures—though still interesting from a historical standpoint—are the socialist and Brutalist designs built from the mid-1960s until the end of Communism. Examples are the entrance and departure halls of **Hlavní nádraží,** Wilsonova třída, Prague 1; the **Máj department store** (now a Tesco), Národní třída 26,

Prague 1; and the **Kotva department store,** náměstí Republiky, Prague 1.

However, the absolute worst are the prefabricated apartment buildings (paneláky) reached by taking metro line C to Chodov or Háje. Built in the 1970s, when buildings grew really huge and dense, each is eight or more stories tall. Today, half of Prague's residents live in paneláky, which rim the city.

One post-revolutionary development—the **Rašín Embankment Building** ★, Rašínovo nábřeží at Resslova, Prague 2—continues to fuel the debate about blending traditional architecture with progressive design. Known as the **Dancing Building** (or even sometimes "Fred and Ginger," from Fred Astaire and Ginger Rogers), it opened in 1996. Co-designed by Canadian-born Frank Gehry, who planned Paris's controversial American Center and the Guggenheim Bilbao, the building's method of twisting concrete and steel together had never before been tried in Europe or elsewhere. The building is made out of prefabricated concrete, proving that the Communist panelák apartment houses could have been made more imaginatively. The late ex-president Havel used to live next door in a modest apartment in the neoclassical building built and owned by his family.

a concert hall in 1865. The city's Russian Orthodox community began using it in 1871, but in 1920 management was handed to the Protestant Hussites. One notable piece inside is the 19th-century crystal chandelier with glass brought from the town of Harrachov. Concerts are still frequently held here; for details, see "Classical Music," in chapter 9.

Old Town Sq. at Pařížská, Prague 1. ℂ **224-190-994.** Free admission, except for concerts. Daily 10am–4pm; Sun Mass at 10:30am, noon, and 3pm. Metro: Line A to Staroměstská.

Týn Church or the Church of Our Lady Before Týn (Kostel paní Marie před Týnem) ★

Huge, double square towers with multiple black steeples make this church Old Town Square's most distinctive landmark. The "Týn" was the fence marking the border of the central marketplace in the 13th century. The church's present configuration was completed mostly in the 1380s, and it became the main church of the Protestant Hussite movement in the 15th century (though the smaller Bethlehem Chapel, where Hus actually preached, is the cradle of the Czech Protestant reformation). The original main entrance to the church is blocked from view when you look from Old Town Square because the Habsburg-backed patricians built in front of it with impunity.

Aside from the church's omnipresent lurch over the square and the peculiar way buildings were erected in front of it, it's well known as the final resting place of Danish astronomer Tycho Brahe, who died in 1601 while serving in the court of Austrian Emperor Rudolf II. Brahe's tombstone bearing his effigy as an explorer of many worlds is behind the church's main pulpit. The brilliant floodlights washing over the front of the church at night cast a mystical glow over the whole of Old Town Square.

Staroměstské nám. 14, Prague 1, entrance from Old Town Sq. below the red address marker 604. © **222-318-186.** Tues–Sat 10am–1pm and 3–5pm. Mass Wed–Fri 6pm; Sat 8am; Sun 9:30am and 9pm. Metro: Line A to Staroměstská.

MALÁ STRANA (LESSER TOWN)

Church of Our Lady Victorious—Holy Child of Prague (Klášter Pražského jezulátka) This 1613 early baroque church of the Carmelite order is famous throughout Italy and other predominantly Catholic countries for the wax statue of infant Jesus displayed on an altar in the right wing of the church. The Holy Child of Prague was presented to the Carmelites by the Habsburg patron Polyxena of Lobkowicz in 1628 and is revered as a valuable Catholic relic from Spain. Copies of the "Bambino" are sold at the little museum in the church as well as on the Lesser Town streets, angering some of the faithful.

Karmelitská 9, Prague 1. Museum of the Holy Child of Prague. © **257-533-646.** Free admission. Mon–Sat 8:30am–6:30pm; Sun 9:30am–8pm. Metro: Line A to Malostranská.

Cemeteries

New Jewish Cemetery (Nový židovský hřbitov) Though it's neither as visually captivating nor as historically important as Prague's Old Jewish Cemetery (p. 105), the ivy-enveloped New Jewish Cemetery is popular because writer Franz Kafka is buried here. To find his grave, after emerging from Želivského metro station, enter the cemetery and turn immediately to your right. Go along the wall about 90m (295 ft.) and look down in the first row of graves. There you'll find Kafka's final resting place. If you don't have a yarmulke (skullcap), you must borrow one from the man in the small building at the entrance. He's quite happy to lend one, but don't forget to return it. If you only come to see Kafka, you may find yourself staying longer; the cemetery is a soothing and fascinating place.

Izraelská 1, Prague 3. © **272-241-893.** Apr–Sept Sun–Thurs 9am–5pm, Fri 9am–1pm; Oct–Mar Sun–Thurs 9am–4pm, Fri 9am–1pm. Metro: Line A to Želivského.

Olšanské Cemeteries (Olšanské hřbitovy) Olšanské hřbitovy is the burial ground of some of the city's most prominent former residents, including the first Communist president, Klement Gottwald, and Jan Palach, who set fire to himself in protest of the 1968 Soviet invasion. Olšanské hřbitovy is just on the other side of Jana Želivského Street from the New Jewish Cemetery.

Vinohradská St., Prague 3. Daily dawn–dusk. Metro: Line A to Flora or Želivského.

HISTORIC BUILDINGS & MONUMENTS

EXPLORING PRAGUE

Historic Buildings & Monuments

Education has always occupied an important place in Czech life. Professors at **Charles University**—the city's most prestigious and oldest university, founded in 1348—have been in the political and cultural vanguard, strongly influencing the everyday life of all citizens. During the last 50 years, the university has expanded into some of the city center's largest riverfront buildings, many of which are between Charles Bridge (Karlův most) and Čech's Bridge (Čechův most).

Staré Město (Old Town)

Powder Tower (Prašná brána)   Once part of Staré Město's system of fortifications, the Old Town Powder Tower (as opposed to the Powder Tower in Prague Castle) was built in 1475 as one of the walled city's major gateways. The 42m-tall (138-ft.) tower marks the beginning of the Royal Route, the traditional route along which medieval Bohemian monarchs paraded on their way to being crowned at Prague Castle. It also was the east gate to the Old Town on the road to Kutná Hora. The tower was severely damaged during the Prussian invasion of Prague in 1737.

The present-day name comes from the 18th century, when the development of Nové Město rendered this protective tower obsolete, and it began to serve as a gunpowder storehouse. Early in the 20th century, the tower was the daily meeting place of Franz Kafka and his writer friend Max Brod. On the tower's west side, facing Old Town, you'll see a statue of King Přemysl Otakar II, under which is a bawdy relief depicting a young woman slapping a man who's reaching under her skirt. The remains of the original construction are visible on the first floor above the ground.

Náměstí Republiky, gate to Celetná St., Prague 1. www.prazskeveze.cz. Admission 70Kč adults, 50Kč students, 20Kč children 5 and under. Nov–Feb daily 10am–6pm; Mar, Oct to 8pm; Apr–Sept to 10pm. Metro: Line B to Nám. Republiky.

Nové Město (New Town)

Můstek Metro Station   It's not the metro station itself, which is only about 30 years old, that warrants an entry here. But inside the station (on the Můstek end), you'll see the illuminated stone remains of what was once a bridge that connected the fortifications of Prague's Old and New Towns. In Czech, *můstek* means "little bridge," but the ancient span isn't the only medieval remains that modern excavators discovered. Metro workers had to be inoculated when they uncovered viable tuberculosis bacteria, which had lain here dormant, encased in horse excrement, since the Middle Ages.

Na Příkopě, the pedestrian street above Můstek metro station, literally translates as "on the moat," a reminder that the street was built on top of a protective moat that separated the walls of Staré Město and Nové Město. In 1760, it was filled in. The street follows the line of the old fortifications all the way down to the Gothic Powder Tower at náměstí Republiky (see above).

Václavské nám. Prague 1. Metro: Line A.

National Theater (Národní divadlo) ★★   Lavishly constructed in the late Renaissance style of northern Italy, the gold-crowned National Theater, overlooking

115

the Vltava, is one of Prague's most recognizable landmarks. Completed in 1881, the theater was built to nurture the Czech National Revival Movement—a drive to replace the dominant German culture with homegrown Czech works. To finance construction, small collection boxes with signs promoting the prosperity of a dignified national theater were installed in public places.

Almost immediately upon completion, the building was wrecked by fire and rebuilt, reopening in 1883 with the premiere of Bedřich Smetana's opera *Libuše*. The magnificent interior contains an allegorical sculpture about music and busts of Czech theatrical personalities created by some of the country's best-known artists. The motto *"Národ sobě"* ("A Nation to Itself") is written above the stage. Smetana conducted the theater's orchestra here until 1874, when deafness forced him to relinquish his post.

The theater offers guided tours by prior arrangement; tickets for performances are often available (see chapter 9) on the day of the show.

Národní třída 2, Prague 1. (C) **224-901-448.** Box office daily 10am–6pm. www.narodni-divadlo.cz. Metro: Line B to Národní třída.

Elsewhere in Prague

Petřín Tower (Rozhledna)   A one-third-scale copy of Paris's Eiffel Tower, Petřín Tower was constructed out of recycled railway track for the 1891 Prague Exhibition. It functioned as the city's primary telecommunications tower until the space-age Žižkovská věž (tower) opened across town. Those who climb the 59m (194 ft.) to the top are treated to striking views, particularly at night.

Petřínské sady, atop Petřín Hill, Prague 1. (C) **257-320-112.** www.prazskeveze.cz. Admission 100Kč adults, 50Kč students, 20Kč for children 5 and under. Nov–Feb daily 10am–6pm; Mar, Oct to 8pm; Apr–Sept to 10pm. Tram: 12, 20, or 22 to Újezd, then ride the funicular to the top.

Modern Memorials

One of the city's most photographed attractions is the colorful graffiti-filled **Lennon Wall,** on Velkopřevorské náměstí. This quiet side street in Malá Strana's Kampa neighborhood near Charles Bridge is across from the French Embassy on the path leading from Kampa Park.

The wall is named after singer John Lennon, whose huge image was once spray-painted on the wall's center (now it's a mash-mish of whatever anyone wants to paint, but occasionally the Fab Four still make it onto the wall). Following his 1980 death, Lennon became a hero of freedom, pacifism, and counterculture throughout eastern Europe, and this monument was born. During Communist rule, the wall's prodemocracy and other slogans were regularly whitewashed, only to be repainted by the faithful. When the new democratically elected government was installed in 1989, it's said that the French ambassador, whose stately offices are directly across from the wall, phoned Prague's mayor and asked that the city refrain from interfering with the monument. Today, young locals and visitors continue to flock here, paying homage with flowers and candles, and they continue to paint whatever they want.

The 1989 revolution against Communism is modestly remembered at the **Národní Memorial,** Národní 16, under the arches, midway between Václavské náměstí and the National Theater. A small bronze monument of peace-sign hands marks the spot where hundreds of protesting college students were beaten by riot police on the brutal, icy night of November 17, 1989.

HISTORIC SQUARES

The most celebrated square in the city, **Old Town Square (Staroměstské nám.) ★★★**, is surrounded by baroque buildings and packed with colorful craftspeople, cafes, and entertainers. In ancient days, the site was a major crossroads on central European merchant routes. In its center stands a memorial to Jan Hus, the 15th-century religious martyr who crusaded against what he saw as corrupt influences from Rome. The statue was unveiled in 1915, on the 500th anniversary of Hus's execution. The monument's most compelling features are the dark asymmetry and fluidity of the figures. Take metro line A to Staroměstská. The square and Staré Město are described in more detail in "Walking Tour 3" in chapter 7.

Officially dedicated in 1990, **Jan Palach Square (nám. Jana Palacha)**, formerly known as Red Army Square, is named for a 21-year-old philosophy student who set himself on fire on the National Museum steps to protest the 1968 Communist invasion. An estimated 800,000 Praguers attended his funeral march from Staroměstské náměstí to Olšanské Cemeteries (p. 114). To get to the square, take metro line A to Staroměstská at the Old Town foot of Mánesův Bridge. There is now a pleasant riverside park with benches. Charles University's philosophy department building is on this square; on the lower-left corner of the facade is a memorial to the martyred student: a replica of Palach's death mask.

One of the city's most historic squares, **Wenceslas Square (Václavské nám.) ★★**, was formerly the horse market (Koňský trh). The once muddy swath between the buildings played host to the country's equine auctioneers. The top of the square, where the National Museum now stands, was the outer wall of the New Town fortifications, bordering the Royal Vineyards. Unfortunately, the city's busiest highway now cuts the museum off from the rest of the square it dominates. Trolleys streamed up and down the square until the early 1980s. Today, the 1km-long (½-mile) boulevard is lined with cinemas, shops, hotels, restaurants, and casinos.

The square was given its present name in 1848. The giant equestrian statue of St. Wenceslas on horseback surrounded by four other saints, including his grandmother, St. Ludmila, and St. Adalbert, the 10th-century bishop of Prague, was completed in 1912 by prominent city planner J. V. Myslbek, for whom the Myslbek shopping center on Na Příkopě was named. The statues' pedestal has become a popular platform for speakers. Actually, the square has thrice been the site of riots and revolutions—in 1848, 1968, and 1989. At the height of the Velvet Revolution, 250,000 to 300,000 Czechs filled the square during one demonstration. Take metro line A or B to Můstek.

Built by Charles IV in 1348, **Charles Square (Karlovo nám.)** once functioned as Prague's primary cattle market. New Town's Town Hall (Novoměstská radnice), which stands on the eastern side, was the site of Prague's First Defenestration—a violent protest sparking the Hussite Wars in the 15th century (see "Beware of Open Windows: The Czech Tradition of Defenestration," earlier in this chapter). Today, Charles Square is a peaceful park in the center of the city, crisscrossed by tramlines and surrounded by buildings and shops. It is the largest square in town. To reach it, take metro line B to Karlovo náměstí.

VÁCLAV HAVEL'S PRAGUE

The extraordinary life of former Czech president Václav Havel, who died in December 2011, still acts as a magnet, drawing to Prague those who are interested in understanding one of the most dominant factors of recent history—the Cold War.

While it is easy to ascribe Havel's valiant struggle to pure altruism and a desperate desire to end totalitarian rule in his homeland, many believe a more intimate force was at work—his inextricable relationship to a beautiful, complex character—not his first wife, Olga (to whom he addressed his famous letters from prison), but the city of Prague itself.

To begin to understand Havel (and even close friends say they can't grasp the full depth of his character), you must first try to see Prague in all its complex ironies. Even during the darkest days of Communist rule, Havel remained faithful to the city of his birth, although it would have been much easier to run away—as did many other dissidents and artists—to fame and fortune in the West.

Havel's family roots run deeply in Prague. He was reared in the city's grand palaces and dingy theaters, and received his political education in Prague's smoky cafes and closely observed living rooms.

Described below (and on the accompanying map on p. 120) are some of Havel's most notable haunts both before and after 1989. Luckily for those who want to track his footsteps, Havel's Prague is now somewhat more accessible (albeit heavily reconstructed from the pre-revolutionary days)—and you won't have to worry about any StB (Communist-era secret agents) watching over your shoulder.

The Havel Family

Havel's father and namesake, a wealthy real estate developer and patron of Prague's newly liberated, post–Habsburg Jazz Age, built the **Lucerna Palace** ★ (entry from Štěpánská 61 or Vodičkova 36, Prague 1; metro: Můstek), in the 1920s. This fully enclosed complex of arcades, theaters, cinemas, nightclubs, restaurants, and ballrooms became a popular spot for the city's nouveau riche to congregate. The young Havel spent his earliest years on the Lucerna's polished marble floors until the Communists expropriated his family's holdings after the 1948 putsch. Soon thereafter, the glitter wore off this monument to early Czech capitalism and the Lucerna lost its soul to party-sanctioned singalongs and propaganda films.

After the fall of Communism and the mass return of nationalized property, the new government gave the Lucerna back to the Havel estate. Unfortunately, this led to an ugly family feud over the division of shares in the palace. Eventually the then-president and his second wife worked out a settlement with younger brother Ivan and his wife, but only after the battle became a daily feature in the tabloid press.

Today, the Lucerna is trying hard to regain its original grandeur. It's home to at least two excellent cafes, a trendy music club, a glittering ballroom, and a vintage cinema that still shows first-run movies. There's also a wacky statue descending from the ceiling by Czech artist David Černý depicting St. Wenceslas astride an upside-down horse—an ironic take on the country's obsession with its more glorious past.

To get to **Barrandov Terrace,** you'll need to take one of the tourist boats from the center of Prague and head south on the Vltava (see details of boat tours later in this chapter). After about half an hour, you will pass under the bridge of the superhighway at the southern edge of the city. About a mile farther, look to your right. You will see a creaking remnant of a once spectacular Art Deco resort tucked into the cliff. This is Barrandov Terrace, another heart-wrenching example of the elder Havel's grandiose plans destroyed by Communist-era squalor. The flowing white balconies of the Barrandov Terrace were Prague's answer to 1920s Hollywood. Havel's uncle, Miloš Havel, commissioned Jazz Age architect Max Urban to build his dream—a top-notch riverside restaurant and cafe. It was meant to capture the glamour of the films produced at nearby Barrandov Studios, whose productions at the time rivaled Hollywood films in style and panache. Sadly, much of this splendor is still awaiting renovation.

Theater & Politics

Divadlo ABC   Havel's first theater job was as a stagehand here in the late 1950s. This is one of the many intimate theaters in Prague where excitement was found in the spoken word rather than expensive visuals. Czech musicals and dry comedies are still performed here.

Vodičkova 28, Prague 1. ℭ **224-215-943.** Tickets 90Kč–300Kč. Metro: Můstek.

Divadlo Na zábradlí   Havel became the resident playwright here in the early 1960s. It was on this stage that his play *The Garden Party* launched 25 years of subtly subversive dramas, which were to become the subtext of many dissident struggles during the Cold War. At present, dramas (for example, Chekhov's *Ivanov*) are on the program here every evening at 7pm. Performances are in Czech.

Anenské nám. 5, Prague 1. ℭ **222-868-868.** Tickets 90Kč–250Kč. Metro: Staroměstská. Tram: 17 or 18.

Činoherní klub   After the early days of the revolution when Laterna Magika played a major role, the first attempts at forming a true political movement were made in this tiny club theater on a back street near Wenceslas Square. It is here that the Civic Forum (Občanské Fórum) movement took shape under Havel's understated leadership. This small theater, founded in the 1960s by a group of young and progressive actors and directors, has always been popular for its nonconventional performances. Talented Czech actors perform here nightly at 7:30pm.

Ve Smečkách 26, Prague 1. ℭ **296-222-123.** Tickets 30Kč (standing) or 320Kč. Metro: Muzeum.

StB Holding Cells   Housed in a former convent, the StB Holding Cells were used by the StB (Communist secret police) to interrogate and hold political prisoners. Havel stayed in room P6 during one of his frequent visits between 1977 and 1989. After the revolution, the holding cells became a spartan but popular hostel with months-long waiting lists of tourists who wanted to stay in Havel's hovel. It's now a hotel.

Bartolomějská 9, Prague 1. Metro: Národní třída.

Laterna Magika Stage (Divadlo bez Zábradlí)   This became Havel's "War Room," where he and a hearty band of artists and intellectuals plotted the peaceful overthrow of the government in late 1989. From this platform, Havel chaired 10 nights of debates among striking actors and artists on how best to rally the masses to their democratic cause. The resignation of the Politburo at the end of November 1989 set off rapturous celebrations in the theater. The remodeled place no longer reeks of cigarettes and stale beer nor, unfortunately, the aura of those heady November revolutionary days. Performances in Czech (mostly comedies by Czech and foreign playwrights) take place here every evening at 7pm.

Jungmannova 31, Prague 1. ℭ **224-946-436.** Tickets up to 300Kč. Metro: Můstek or Národní třída.

Apartment Block **13**
Barrandov Terrace **3**
Činoherní klub **11**
Divadlo ABC **8**
Divadlo Na zábradlí **4**
Kavárna Slavia **6**
Laterna Magika Stage
   (Divadlo bez Zábradlí) **7**
Lucerna Palace **9**
Melantrich **10**
Na rybárně **14**
President's Office **2**
Private Villa **1**
StB Holding Cells **5**
Vltava Water Tower
   & Mánes Gallery **12**

Milady Horákové

Korunovační

Čechova

Veletržní

Milady Horákové

Heřmanova

Nad Štolou

Jirečkova

Ovenecká

Letohradská

Kostelní

Veverkova

Františka Křížka

Janovského

Antonínská

Vltavská

Letenský Tunnel

Stefánikův most

nábřeží Kpt. Jaroše

LETNÁ

LETENSKÉ SADY

HOLEŠOVICE

ostrov
Štvanice

Hlávkův most

nábřeží Edvarda Beneše

Těšnovský Tunnel

Rohanské nábřeží

Kosárkovo nábřeží

Vltava

Čechův most

Dvořákovo nábřeží

nábřeží Ludvíka Svobody

Lannova

Klimentská

Klimentská

KARLIN

nám. Curieových

St. Agnes Convent

zeď

Dušní

Bílkova

Haštalská

Revoluční

Soukenická

Hradební

Petrská

těšnov

Ke Štvanici

Wilsonova

Florenc

JOSEFOV

Dlouhá

Truhlářská

Zlatnické

Na Poříčí

Biskupská

Na Florenci

Rudolfinum

Jewish Cemetery

17. listopadu

Vězeňská

Kozí

Masná

Rybná

Náměstí Republiky

Na Poříčí

Havlíčkova

Na Florenci

Florenc

Máneův most

nám. Jana Palacha

Široká

Dušní

Dušní

Pařížská

Tynská

V Celnici

Masarykovo Station

Florenc Bus Station

Staroměstská

St. Nicholas Church

Kaprova

Staroměstské náměstí (Old Town Square)

Tyn Church

Štupartská

Celetná

Municipal House

Hybernská

Hybernská

Husitská

Platnéřská

Malé náměstí

Old Town Hall

Powder Tower

Senovážná

Řehořova

Karlův most (Charles Bridge)

Karlova

Husova

STARÉ MĚSTO

Estates Theater

Senovážné náměstí

Opletalova

Bolzanova

Seifertova

Anenské nám.

Anenská

Zlatá

Michalská

Na příkopě

Panská

Jindřišská

Jeruzalémská

Vrchlického sady

nám. W. Churchilla

Náprstkova

Liliová

Uhelný trh

Rytířská

Perlová

28. října

Václavské náměstí (Wenceslas Square)

Opletalova

Politických vězňů

Růžová

Hlavní nádraží

Italská

Betlémská

Konviktská

Bartolomějská

Skořepka

Můstek

Hlavní nádraží (Main Train Station)

Krocinova

Národní

Spálená

Národní Třída

Vodičkova

Washingtonova

Wilsonova

Legerova

Vozová

National Theater

V jirchářích

Voršilská

Ostrovní

Jungmannova

V jámě

Štěpánská

Muzeum

Španělská

Riegrovy sady

Slovanský ostrov

Masarykovo nábřeží

Opatovická

Černá

Křemencova

Lazarská

Navrátilova

Řeznická

NOVÉ MĚSTO

Ve Smečkách

Krakovská

Mezibranská

National Museum

Čelakovského sady

Vinohradská

Balbínova

Polská

VINOHRADY

Mánesova

Pštrossova

Myslíkova

Žitná

Školská

Zítná

V Tůních

Sokolská

Anglická

Římská

Resslova

Karlovo nám.

Štěpánská

Lípová

Karlovo Náměstí

Ječná

nám. I.P. Pavlova

I.P. Pavlova

Jugoslávská

nám. Míru

Náměstí Míru

Korunní

Jiráskův most

Dittrichova

Karlovo Náměstí

Na Moráni

U Nemocnice

Kateřinská

Ke Karlovu

Tyršova

Tylovo nám.

Rumunská

Londýnská

Lublaňská

Ječná

Belgická

Bruselská

Uruguayská

Americká

Varšavská

Sázavská

Francouzská

Palackého most

Palackého nám.

Zítkovy sady

Vyšehradská

To Vyšehrad

Lumírova

Botanical Garden

Apolinářská

Fügnerovo nám.

Koubkova

Záhřebská

Jana Masaryka

Máchova

0   1/4 mi
0   1/4 km

4

5

6

7

8

9

10

11

12

13

14

Melantrich   Midway up the right side of Wenceslas Square at no. 36 (now the British Marks & Spencer store), you will see a balcony jutting from the Melantrich publishing house. This is where, in late November 1989, Havel made his first appearances in front of the hundreds of thousands who were clamoring for his leadership in a peaceful coup d'état. His mumbling yet stoically defiant speeches solidified his position as the popular choice to guide Czechoslovakia out of the dark days. Soon, Alexander Dubček—leader of 1968's failed attempt to deliver "Socialism with a Human Face," which led to his banishment after the Warsaw Pact invasion—joined Havel along with blacklisted singers and artists to mark the beginning of the end of 4 decades of totalitarian rule.

Václavské nám. 36, Prague 1. Metro: Můstek.

Kavárna Slavia   Of all the Prague pubs, restaurants, and cafes that Havel patronized, this was his most recognized haunt (p. 91). Its reputation as the hangout of choice for Prague's dissidents and secret police became a staple in Western media accounts of life on this side of the iron curtain. These days, unfortunately, it's a popular tourist haunt, with nary an intellectual to be found.

Smetanovo nábřeží 2, Prague 1. © **224-218-493.** Metro: Národní třída.

Vltava Water Tower & Mánes Gallery   Jutting from the quay on the right (east) bank of the Vltava next to Jiráskův Bridge stands this brooding, dark, defunct water tower with a bulbous dome. Inside the dome, secret police agents spent days peering into Havel's meager top-floor flat on the opposite street corner. Havel spoke often of the ways he used to taunt his hunters during his effective house arrests, and of the suffocation of knowing they were almost always there, watching his comings and goings and those of his guests.

Just below the tower stands an unspectacular building of white boxes, the art gallery and meeting hall **Mánes.** Havel called this his favorite building in Prague. In a BBC documentary filmed several years after he became president, Havel described his love for this place of art right under his wardens' noses. The Mánes now shows many avant-garde artists who were taboo before the revolution.

Masarykovo nábřeží 250, Prague 1. © **224-932-938.** www.galeriemanes.cz. Tues–Sun 10am–6pm. Tram: 17 or 21.

Apartment Block   While standing on the river side of the street from Jiráskův Bridge, look past the Frank Gehry–inspired Dancing Building. Next door you will find a discreet apartment block with a small tilted globe on its roof. The top-floor windows were the focus of secret agents' binoculars from the water tower across the way. This was Havel's base, his small, Bohemian bunker, from where he wrote his subversive essays and plotted his peaceful putsches. Until 1995, he and his first wife, Olga, lived as president and first lady in this relatively tiny place, refusing to accept the accommodations of state at Prague Castle. Later the couple bought a stylish villa in the high-rent district on the west side of town (financed by Havel's royalties and property). They chose to live in one of the castle's residences until the villa was reconstructed.

Rašínovo nábřeží 78, Prague 2. Metro: Karlovo nám. Tram: 17 or 21.

Na rybárně   At this fishmonger around the corner from his dissident-era apartment, Havel spent hours debating politics over a plate of trout and a bottle of tart Czech Frankovka wine. After the revolution, the back room became a shrine to visiting dignitaries and rock stars, who were treated to a down-market "state dinner" and then signed the wall in a bizarre piece of presidential protocol. It's still open and still a decent place to get a fish dinner. Among the famous autographs on the wall is Mick Jagger's, one of Havel's favorite rockers.

Gorazdova 17, Prague 2. Metro: Karlovo nám. Tram: 17 or 21.

The Presidential Years

From the baroque balcony at the **President's Office** in Prague Castle (tram no. 22) that hovers over the courtyard opposite St. Vitus Cathedral in Prague Castle, Havel delivered a stirring inauguration speech following his first investiture on December 29, 1989. To a world transfixed by his unlikely journey from prison to presidential palace, he proclaimed the rebirth of "a humane republic that serves the individual and that therefore holds the hope that the individual will serve it in turn."

Havel's common-man image was largely destroyed when he moved out of his modest riverside flat and into a **Private Villa** (Dělostřelecká 1, Prague 6; metro: Hradčanská, then tram no. 1, 8, or 18 to U Brusnice stop) in 1995. With this move, Havel returned to the tightly knit circle of wealthy Prague homeowners. Unfortunately, the high walls surrounding the villa made it nearly impossible to have the brief encounters with Havel frequently experienced by visitors to his old home.

PARKS & GARDENS

Hradčany

The **Royal Garden (Královská zahrada)** ★ at Prague Castle, Prague 1, once the site of the sovereigns' vineyards, was founded in 1534. Dotted with lemon trees and surrounded by 16th-, 17th-, and 18th-century buildings, the park is consciously and conservatively laid out with abundant shrubbery and fountains. Entered from U Prašného mostu Street, north of the castle complex, it's open daily from 10am to 6pm in the summer season.

The castle's **Garden on the Ramparts (Zahrada na Valech)** ★ is on the cityside hill and runs alongside the castle complex. Beyond beautifully groomed lawns and sparse shrubbery is a tranquil low-angle view of the castle above and the city below. Enter the garden from the south side of the castle complex, below Hradčanské náměstí. The garden is open daily from 10am to 6pm in the summer season.

In 2000, Prince Charles himself was present when the **Gardens Below Prague Castle (Zahrady pod Pražským hradem)** ★★, just under the castle toward Malá Strana, were reopened after years of cleaning and reconstruction. The **Ledeburská, Malá** and **Velká Pálffyovská, Kolowratská,** and **Malá Fürstenberská** gardens are accessible from Valdštejnské nám. 3 (Ledeburský palác), or from Valdštejnská Street no. 12, or from the Garden on the Ramparts (© **724-823-719;** www.palacove-zahrady.cz). Admission is 80Kč for adults, 50Kč for children. Open April and October daily 10am to 6pm, May and September to 7pm, August to 8pm, and June and July to 9pm.

Malá Strana

Looming over Malá Strana, adjacent to Prague Castle, lush green **Petřín Hill (Petřínské sady)** is easily recognizable by the miniature replica of the Eiffel Tower that tops it (p. 116). Gardens and orchards bloom in spring and summer. Throughout the myriad monuments and churches are a mirror maze and an observatory (p. 125).

The Hunger Wall, a decaying 6m-high (20-ft.) stone wall that runs up through Petřín to the grounds of Prague Castle, was commissioned by Charles IV in the 1360s as a medieval welfare project designed to provide jobs for Prague's starving poor. Take tram no. 12, 20, or 22 to Újezd and ride the funicular or start climbing.

Just below Petřín's steep slope, not far from Malostranské náměstí, you'll find a lovely baroque garden, the **Vrtbovská zahrada** ★. Its entrance is through Karmelitská 25, Prague 1 (© **272-088-350;** www.vrtbovska.cz). This is sometimes referred to as the most beautiful terraced garden north of the Alps. It was built in the 18th century's baroque style by architect Kaňka, and Matyas Braun provided some of his sculptures. This very special site was totally neglected during the old regime (it partially served as a playground for a local nursery). The garden is open daily April to October from 10am to 6pm. Admission is 55Kč adults, 35Kč students. Take tram no. 12, 20, or 22 to Malostranské náměstí.

Near the foot of Charles Bridge in Malá Strana, **Kampa Park (Na Kampě)** ★ was named by Spanish soldiers who set up camp here after the Roman Catholics won the Battle of White Mountain in 1620. The park as it is today wasn't formed until the Nazi occupation, when the private gardens of three noble families were joined. It's a fine place for an inner-city picnic, though the lawns are packed in high season.

Part of the excitement of **Waldstein (Wallenstein) Gardens (Valdštejnská zahrada)** ★ at Letenská, Prague 1 (© **257-072-759**) is its location, behind a 9m (30-ft.) wall on the back streets of Malá Strana. Inside, elegant gravel paths dotted with classical bronze statues and gurgling fountains fan out in every direction. Laid out in the 17th century, the baroque park was the garden of Gen. Albrecht Waldstein (or Wallenstein; 1581–1634), commander of the Roman Catholic armies during the Thirty Years' War. These gardens are the backyards of Waldstein's Palace—Prague's largest—which replaced 23 houses, three gardens, and the municipal brick kiln. It's now home to the Czech Senate. The gardens are free to enter and are open March to October daily from 10am to 6pm.

Elsewhere in Prague

The plain on the hilltop across the Vltava north of Old Town is a densely tree-covered swath, maintained as a park since 1858. **Letná Park (Letenské sady)** ★★ is easy to spot from Pařížská Street in Old Town; just look north to see a giant metronome atop a hill. This spot once held the world's largest statue of Soviet dictator Josef Stalin, which was pulled down with much difficulty in 1962. Today, the park is a great spot for strolling and jogging, and the far eastern stretch holds arguably the city's nicest beer garden, with a drop-dead-gorgeous view of Old Town below. The garden is connected to two restaurants in a recently renewed, 19th-century, neo-Renaissance château (Letenský zámeček), where you can get either a beer and a pizza (at one place) or formal dinner (next door). Take tram no. 1, 8, 25, or 26 to Letenské náměstí from Hradčanská metro station (and a short walk), or walk across the bridge at Čechův Most from Old Town (at the end of Pařížská St.) and up a steep flight of steps.

Farther to the north of Letná is the former royal hunting ground and now a nature reserve, **Stromovka** ★★ (tram no. 1, 8, 25, or 26 to Letenské nám. and short walk down leafy Čechova St.). Acres of densely tree-lined paths, mostly flat and paved, comprise a shaded set of corridors for long strolls, jogging, and even in-line skating.

Another favorite getaway is **Vyšehrad Park** ★ above the Vltava south of the city center. This 1,000-year-old citadel encloses a peaceful set of gardens, playgrounds, footpaths, and the national cemetery next to the twin-towered Church of Sts. Peter and Paul, reconstructed from 1885 to 1887. The park provides a fantastic wide-angle view of the whole city. Take metro line C to Vyšehrad or tram no. 3 or 16 to Výtoň. The park is open at all times.

If you have the time and want to spend the whole day relaxing in a natural setting, take tram no. 26 or bus no. 119 from Dejvická metro stop toward the airport to **Divoká Šárka** natural park ★★ in Prague 6. In just 30 minutes, you will find yourself in a forest full of paths, creeks, rocks, and waterfalls. Whether you like to just wander, jog, hike, or swim, you will enjoy visiting this natural wonder, far off the tourist radar.

PRAGUE WITH KIDS

Traveling with children can be an exhausting experience if you don't plan ahead. Prague offers many options, including museums, theaters, cinemas, and parks with playgrounds. If your brood gets tired of walking, take a tram ride. The kids will quickly forget about sore legs. Also, the Vltava River offers the possibility of exploring the city from yet another angle. Below are some places to take your family to make visiting Prague more enjoyable.

On Hradčany

The Toy Museum (Muzeum hraček; ✆ 224-372-294), situated within the complex of Prague Castle, at Jiřská 6, is a place to come with your family to see and feel the nostalgia of the past. This is the world's second-largest exposition of toys, where you can find everything from pieces dating back to ancient Greece up to a collection of the most popular toys of our time. It is open daily from 9:30am to 5:30pm. Admission is 60Kč adults, 30Kč students (children 6–15), free for children 5 and under.

On Petřín Hill

Kids will enjoy the funicular ride to the top of Petřín Hill, capped by the **Petřín Tower,** a miniature replica of the Eiffel Tower. Once there, look for the **Labyrinth (Bludiště; ✆ 257-315-212;** www.prazskeveze.cz), a mirror maze that you walk through. Like the tower replica, the Labyrinth was built for the 1891 Prague Exhibition, an expo that highlighted the beauty and accomplishments of Bohemia and Moravia.

Inside the Labyrinth is a gigantic painting/installation depicting the battle between Praguers and Swedes on the Charles Bridge in 1648, a commemoration of the fighting that ended the Thirty Years' War. In 1892, the building's other historic exhibits were replaced with mirrors, turning the Labyrinth into the fun house it is today. It's open April daily from 10am to 7pm; May to September daily from 10am to 10pm; October daily from 10am to 6pm; and November to March Saturday and Sunday from 10am to 5pm. Admission is 70Kč for adults, 50Kč for children aged 6 to 15 years, and 20Kč for children 5 and under.

Also in the park is the **Štefánik Observatory (✆ 257-320-540;** www. observatory.cz), built in 1930 expressly for public stargazing through a very big telescope. It is open April to August Tuesday to Friday from 2 to 7pm and 9 to 11pm, and Saturday and Sunday from 10am to noon, 2 to 7pm, and 9 to 11pm; September Tuesday to Friday 2 to 6pm and 8 to 10pm, Saturday and Sunday 10am to noon, 2 to 6pm, and 8 to 10pm; March and October Tuesday to Friday 7 to 9pm, Saturday and Sunday 10am to noon, 2 to 6pm, and 7 to 9pm; January, February, November, and

ATTRACTIONS ●

Astronomical
  Clock (orloj) **15**
Golden Lane
  (Zlatá ulička) **2**
Krizík's Fountain
  (Křižíkova fontána) **10**
National Museum
  (Národní muzeum) **18**
National Technical
  Museum
  (Národní technické
  muzeum) **8**
Petřín Tower, Labyrinth
  and Observatory **7**
Planetárium **9**
Prague Zoo **11**
Sea World
  (Mořský svét) **10**
The Toy Museum **3**

HOTELS ■

*See chapter 4 for
hotel listings*
Corinthia Hotel Prague **19**
Hotel Orion **20**
Pension Větrník **1**

RESTAURANTS ◆

*See chapter 5 for
restaurant listings*
Bohemia Bagel **6, 13**
Cream & Dream **16**
Pizza Nuova **14**
Pizzeria Rugantino **12**

SHOPPING ●

*See chapter 8 for
shopping listings*
Obchod loutkami **5**
Rocking Horse
  Toy Shop **4**
Sparky's **17**

December Tuesday to Friday 6 to 8pm, Saturday and Sunday 10am to noon and 2 to 8pm. Admission is 65Kč for adults and 45Kč for children. The funicular departs from a small house in the park just above the middle of Újezd in Malá Strana; tram no. 12, 20 or 22 will take you to Újezd.

Elsewhere in Prague

Budding astronomers can try to catch the stars at the **Planetárium** in Stromovka Park, Královská obora, Prague 7 (✆ **220-999-001;** www.planetarium.cz). Most of the shows are in Czech, but headphones with commentary in English are available (be sure to show up 15 min. before showtime), and some shows are presented in English only (check the website for showtimes). To reach the planetarium, take tram no. 12, 14, 15, or 17 to Výstaviště and walk through the park to your left about 200m (600 ft.). Admission is from 80Kč to 200Kč. It's open Monday to Thursday from 8:30am to noon and from 1 until the end of the last program at 8pm (Monday's last show ends at 6pm). Saturday and Sunday hours are from 9:30am to noon and from 1 until the end of the evening program (6pm).

In the somewhat dilapidated **Výstaviště** fairgrounds adjacent to Stromovka Park is **Křižík's Fountain (Křižíkova fontána).** A massive system of water spigots spout tall and delicate streams of color-lit water in a spectacular light show set to recorded classical and popular music. Small children are especially fascinated. There's also a small amusement park on the fairgrounds. The water/music program (✆ **723-665-694;** www.krizikovafontana.cz) runs from April to October with shows on the hour from 7 to 11pm, and in the summer it's 8 to 11pm. Admission is 200Kč, free for children 5 and under. Take tram no. 12, 14, 15, or 17 to Výstaviště.

In the same complex—the Výstaviště fairgrounds—is located an attraction called **Sea World (Mořský svět;** ✆ **220-103-275;** www.morsky-svet.cz). This permanent exhibition of sea fish and animals as well as simulations of the underwater world appeals to children and adults. Sea World is open daily 10am to 7pm and tickets cost 280Kč adults, 180Kč children. Take tram no. 12, 14, 15, or 17 to Výstaviště.

If you are visiting Prague with kids, leaving the city center for a short trip makes for a good break. Try a trip to the **Prague Zoo,** which is situated in Prague 7–Trója, U Trojského zámku 120 (✆ **296-112-230;** www.zoopraha.cz). Take bus no. 112 from Nádraží Holešovice on the C line all the way to the zoo park. It is open April, May, September, and October daily 9am to 6pm; June to August 9am to 7pm; March 9am to 5pm; January, February, November, and December 9am to 4pm. On weekends, the place is packed with Praguers; it's better to plan the trip on a weekday. Tickets cost 150Kč adults, 100Kč children. A family ticket for 1 day costs 450Kč for two adults and two children.

SIGHTSEEING OPTIONS

Bus Tours

Prague streets can often become gridlocked, making any tour by car or bus frustrating. But if you want to take a guided English-language bus tour, among the best are those given by **Prague Sightseeing Tours,** Klimentská 52, Prague 1 (✆ **222-314-655;** www.pstours.cz). Its 3½-hour Grand City Tour leaves April to October, daily at 9:30am and 2pm (only 9:30am during winter), from the company's bus stop at náměstí Republiky. The tour costs 690Kč adults, 630Kč students, 380Kč children.

Martin Tours, Štěpánská 61, Prague 1 (© **224-212-473;** www.martintour.cz) is a similar outfit and offers a corresponding number of tours at comparable prices.

Better for the kids is the green, open-air, electric **Ekoexpres** (an electric bus in the shape of a train; © **602-317-784;** www.ekoexpres.cz) that usually leaves every 30 minutes from behind the Jan Hus monument on Old Town Square. An hour's drive around the tourist areas of Old Town and up the hill to Prague Castle with a recorded narration in several languages costs 250Kč for adults and teenagers. Children 11 and under travel free with their parents.

Cruise-Ship Tours

Tourist cruise ships are the only commercial vessels allowed to pass through the city. This is an enjoyable, relaxing way to see Prague.

Evropská vodní doprava (© **224-810-030;** www.evd.cz), with a four-ship fleet, offers the most interesting sightseeing excursions. From April to October, several tours, including some serving decent inexpensive meals, disembark from Čechův, most at the northern turn of the Vltava, and sail past all the key riverside sights. A daily lunch tour with a smorgasbord and traditional Czech music leaves at noon, travels to the south end of the city, and returns by 2pm. The price, including meal, is 690Kč. A 1-hour tour, without meal, sails to Charles Bridge and back, leaving every hour from 10am to 6pm. It costs 220Kč. A 2-hour tour, without meal, leaves at 3pm and costs 350Kč. A dinner cruise to the south end of town leaves at 7 and returns by 10pm. The price, including meal, is 790Kč for adults, 500Kč for children.

A competing service, **Jazzboat** (© **731-183-180;** www.jazzboat.cz), offers a similar nighttime dinner cruise along the river, but features a rotating menu of jazz music, including traditional, swing, blues, and Latin, on different nights of the week. The tours begin at 8pm nightly at pier no. 5 next to Čechův most (in front of the Inter-Continental Hotel) and last about 3 hours. The trip costs 690Kč adults, and around 1,000Kč including dinner.

Renting a Rowboat

Many people rent rowboats or paddle boats on the Vltava, which can be a remarkably romantic way to see the city. You'll find a couple of boat rental outlets on Slovanský ostrov (Slavic Island). Walk onto the island by crossing a small bridge just along the side of the National Theater. Both rowboats and paddleboats are on offer, and rates run about 250Kč per hour.

Walking Tours

Sylvia Wittmann's tour company, **Wittmann Tours,** Novotného lávka 5, Prague 1 (© **222-252-472;** www.wittmann-tours.com), offers daily walks around Prague's compact Jewish Quarter. A thousand years of history are discussed during the 3-hour stroll. From May to October, tours led by an English-speaking guide depart Sunday to Friday from Pařížská 28 at 10:30am and 2pm. From March 15 to April 30, and from November to December, tours depart at 10:30am. The tour's cost, including entrance fees to sights, is 880Kč for adults and 700Kč for students, free for children 5 and under.

Prague Private Guides (© **222-518-259;** www.guidingprague.com) is run by an American expat living in Prague. This company offers both private guides for hire for half- and full-day walking tours of Prague, as well thematic group trips. **Prague**

🔘 AN old-fashioned TRAM RIDE

Prague has had a system of tramlines since horses pulled the cars in the mid–19th century. The Communist-era tram cars aren't very attractive, and the new futuristic designs are built for efficiency rather than charm. You have to go back in time to have fun in a Prague tram, and you can, thanks to the Prague Transport Authority's (www.dpp.cz) **Historic Tram no. 91.**

On weekends from March until November, the old-timer tram no. 91 clanks along a special circuit around town that takes it through major stops at Malostranské náměstí, Národní třída, Václavské náměstí, and many others. You are free to jump aboard and exit the tram at any stop you choose. Buy the ticket from the onboard conductor. Tickets cost 35Kč for adults and 20Kč for children 9 and under.

Walking Tours (✆ **222-873-307;** www.prague-walkingtours.com) offers mixed walking and bus tours of Prague highlights in their Prague Tour and more advanced Prague Tour All Inclusive.

It's not exactly a "walking tour," but tours on a Segway personal transporter have become increasingly popular in recent years. **Segway Tours** at Mostecká 4 (✆ **731-238-264;** www.segwayfun.eu) offers a series of guided Segway "walks" starting at around 1,500Kč per person for a tour of about 3 hours.

By Horse-Drawn Carriage

Each day, dozens of *fiakry,* **horse-drawn carriages,** line up along the western side of Old Town Square to take visitors on a jaunt around the Old Town. It can be quite romantic, especially in the fall in the late afternoon or early evening, when there's a nip in the air and the coachman throws you a blanket to keep warm. Carriage rides don't come cheap, however. Negotiate the fare individually with the driver, but expect to pay around 1,000Kč for a 20- to 30-minute ride. It's customary to toss in a 10% tip for a personable driver.

By Vintage Automobile

Old-fashioned jalopies have become a familiar sight on the streets of Prague's Old Town and Malá Strana as more and more operators offer these popular antique car tours around town. You'll find most of the cars parked in and around Malé naměstí, near Old Town Square. **Prague Vintage Cars** (✆ **776-829-897;** www.historytrip.cz) is a reliable operator and offers several types of tours starting at 1,100Kč per person for a ride around Old Town and a walking tour of Prague Castle.

By Plane

AeroPrague (✆ **775-365-320;** www.aeroprague.com) organizes sightseeing airplane and helicopter flights over the city as well as popular plane outings over Karlštejn Castle, taking off from a small airport in the outlying district of Letňany. Check the website for current prices, but the 40-minute flight over Karlštejn costs about 6,200 Kč for three people. Helicopter flights are more expensive. A 30-minute flight over Prague will cost about 8,000Kč per person. Licensed pilots can also rent planes. See the website for details.

To get to Letňany airport, take metro line C to the final stop: Letňany. It's a short walk from there.

By Balloon

Ballooning.cz, Na Vrcholu 7, Prague 3 (© **739-318-121;** www.ballooning.cz) offers an hour-long ride in a hot-air balloon for around 4,000Kč Monday to Friday or 4,500Kč on weekends. The takeoff is usually from Konopiště, about 40km (25 miles) south of Prague, so your trip there can be easily combined with a visit to Konopiště Castle. Buy your ticket online or at the reception desk of the Hotel Amedia Teatrino at Bořivojova 53 in Žižkov, Prague 3.

STAYING ACTIVE

Activities

BIKING   Prague has a growing number of specially marked bike lanes, including a long and popular run that follows the Vltava River south of the center from the National Theater and another that starts around the Prague Zoo and follows the Vltava northward toward Germany. Two companies in central Prague specialize in rentals (and also give organized bike tours): **Praha Bike,** Dlouhá 24, Prague 1 (© **732-388-880;** www.prahabike.cz); and **City Bike Prague,** Králodvorská 5, Prague 1 (© **776-180-284;** www.citybike-prague.com).

GOLF   Czechs are rediscovering golf on a tournament-caliber course with a world-class view at the **Prague Karlštejn Golf Club,** 30 minutes southwest of Prague. You can rent clubs and carts on the premises, but it'll likely be more expensive than you are used to back home. For details and directions, see chapter 10.

HEALTH & FITNESS CLUBS   On the 25th floor of the Corinthia Hotel Prague, Kongresová 1, Prague 4, the **Apollo Day Spa** (© **261-191-111**) provides weight machines, free weights, exercise bikes, step machines, a small pool (surrounded by glass with an expansive view of the city), a sauna, and a solarium. The modern facility also offers tanning beds, a whirlpool, and massages. A 1-day pass is 500Kč. The club is open Monday to Friday from 6:30am to 10pm and Saturday and Sunday from 7am to 10pm. Take metro line C to Vyšehrad.

World Class gym at Václavské nám. 22 (© **234-699-100**) is a large health club in the city center, where you can try classes including aerobics, spinning, and yoga, or work out in the gym for around 500Kč a day. It is open Monday to Friday 6am to 10:30pm, Saturday 7am to 10pm, Sunday 9am to 10pm.

JOGGING   There are several nice runs near the center. One of the best is to head to **Letná** park, atop the hill across the Vltava from the InterContinental hotel. Here you'll find a peaceful loop that measures around 2km (1.2 miles). Probably the best no-traffic, long-distance run, within easy commute by public transportation, is at **Stromovka** park (p. 124). There's a small map close to the entrance to the park, just to the left of the entrance to the Výstaviště, that plots out three courses, according to distance.

If you want to run through central Prague, use the traffic-restricted walking zones as often as you can. For an approximately 2.5km (1.5-mile) circuit, start at Můstek at the end of Wenceslas Square, run down Na Příkopě through the Powder Tower (Prašná brána) to Celetná Street all the way to Old Town Square, run around the Hus monument, run back to Železná Street past the Estates' Theater on to Rytířská Street, and run back to Můstek. This route is virtually free of cars, and your feet will be pounding the bricks. Try running in early morning or late evening when the streets aren't packed with crowds.

SWIMMING   Summer doesn't last long in Prague, and when it arrives, many city dwellers are only too happy to cool off in one of the city's many pools. In addition to the hotel pools listed in chapter 4, there's the **Džbán Reservoir,** in the Divoká Šárka nature reserve, Prague 6. Džbán is fronted by a grassy "beach" that can—and often does—accommodate hundreds of bathers. There's a special section for nude swimming and sunbathing. To reach Šárka, take tram no. 26 from the Dejvická metro station. If you prefer a swimming pool or the weather doesn't cooperate, visit one of Prague's best aqua centers. The **Letňany Lagoon,** Tupolevova 665, Prague 9– Letňany (✆ **283-921-799;** www.letnanylagoon.cz), has a full-length pool as well as Jacuzzi and toboggan, which is good fun for the whole family. You can also get a little refreshment and a drink while around the pool. The Lagoon is open daily from June to September from 9am to 9pm. Out of season, the hours are Monday, Wednesday, and Friday 6 to 9am and noon to 10pm; Tuesday 7 to 9am and 4 to 10pm; Thursday 7 to 9am and noon to 10pm; Saturday and Sunday 9am to 10pm. Admission is 140Kč adults, 100Kč students. To get there, take bus no. 140, 186, or 195 from metro line C Letňany station to the Tupolevova stop.

TENNIS   At the **Olšanská Tennis Center** at Chelčického 4 in Žižkov (✆ **606-810-852;** www.tenisolsanska.cz) offers covered courts you can rent by the hour, as well as the possibility to rent rackets and buy balls. The court rental rate ranges from 300Kč to 700Kč, depending on the hour (earlier times are generally cheaper).

YOGA   Yoga's popularity has been growing rapidly in Prague, and yoga classes are now on the menu at most fitness centers. One standout is **Hatha Yoga,** on Jana Masaryka 6, Prague 2 (✆ **774-139-596;** www.satoriya.eu), which offers classes in English for 180Kč for 90 minutes.

Spectator Sports

For information on games, tickets, and times for hockey and soccer games, check *The Prague Post* sports section (www.praguepost.com). Buy tickets at stadium box offices or over team websites. The Ticket Portal website (www.ticketportal.cz) usually has a good selection of sports tickets, including booking for the Sparta Praha ice hockey team. To see the hockey team HC Slavia play, go to the website of Sazka arena (www.sazkaticket.cz), where the team plays its home matches.

ICE HOCKEY   The main Czech professional hockey league, the 02 Extraliga, is one of the best in the world, and Czech stars are regularly drafted from here to play in the North American National Hockey League. Hockey season runs from mid-September until April, and taking in a match can be a real treat, especially for kids.

Prague has two professional teams that traditionally battle it out for national hockey supremacy. **HC Sparta Praha** plays its home matches at **Tesla Arena,** Za Elektrárnou 419, Prague 7 (✆ **266-727-443;** www.hcsparta.cz). Tickets are available from the stadium box office, open Monday to Friday 1 to 5:30pm, or over the Internet at www.ticketportal.cz. Tickets run from 110Kč to 190Kč. The stadium is part of the Výstaviště exhibition grounds. To find it, take metro line C to Holešovice, and then tram no. 5, 14, 15, or 17 one stop to Výstaviště.

The second Prague-based team, **HC Slavia,** plays its home games at glamorous
Sazka Arena, Ocelářská 460, Prague 9 (✆ **266-121-122;** www.hc-slavia.cz), the
country's biggest and most modern indoor sports facility. In addition to hosting hockey
matches, Sazka is a regular venue for rock concerts, wrestling matches, and rodeos,
as well as other cultural and sporting events. Buy tickets at the Sazka box office starting from 10am on the day of the event or in advance over the Internet at www.
sazkaticket.cz. Tickets run from 130Kč to 220Kč. To find the arena, take metro line
B to the stop Českomoravská, and it's a short walk from there.

SOCCER   Soccer, or *fotbal* as it's called locally, is only slightly less popular than ice
hockey. The Czechs traditionally rank among the world's best national teams. The
main soccer league, the Gambrinus Liga, plays its games from late summer through
November.

AC Sparta Praha, the top local soccer team, has a fanatical following, and games
draw rowdy crowds to **Generali Arena** (or simply "Sparta Stadium"), Milady
Horákové 98, Prague 7 (✆ **296-111-400;** www.sparta.cz). Tickets for big matches
often sell out before game time, but seats are usually available up to the last moment
for lesser matches. Buy the tickets at the stadium customer service center (*Záka-
znické centrum*), situated near entrance no. 1. It's open Monday to Friday 9am to
noon, 1 to 5pm, or on game days 3 hours before kickoff. Tickets range from 100Kč
to 360Kč for a domestic league game, higher for an international match. Take metro
line A to Hradčanská, and then take tram no. 1, 8, 25, or 26 to the Sparta stop.

STROLLING AROUND PRAGUE

7

Forget bus tours and taxis—walking is really the only way to explore Prague. Most of the oldest areas are walking zones with limited motor traffic. It's best to wear very comfortable, preferably flat, shoes. The crevices between the bricks in the street have been known to eat high heels. You might want to get in shape for all this walking before you leave home.

Below are some recommended routes, but don't worry about following the maps too closely—getting lost among the twisting narrow streets is also a wonderful way to discover Prague. Let the turns take you where they may; they usually lead to something memorable.

WALKING TOUR 1: CHARLES BRIDGE & MALÁ STRANA (LESSER TOWN)

START: **Old Town Bridge Tower (Staroměstská mostecká věž).**

FINISH: **Church of St. Nicholas (Kostel sv. Mikuláše).**

TIME: **About 3 to 4 hours.**

BEST TIMES: **Early morning or around sunset, when crowds are thinner and the shadows most mysterious.**

WORST TIME: **Midafternoon, when the bridge is packed.**

Dating from the mid-14th century, Charles Bridge is Prague's most celebrated structure. As the primary link between Staré Město and the castle, it has always figured prominently in the city's commercial and military history. For most of its 650 years, the 510m-long (1,673-ft.) span has been a pedestrian promenade, as it is today.

The first sculpture, St. John of Nepomuk, was placed upon the bridge in 1683. It was such a hit that the church commissioned another 21 statues, which were created between 1698 and 1713. Since then, the number has increased to 30. The locations of each statue are shown on the accompanying map.

Before approaching the bridge, it's worth pondering for a moment the question of why put statues on a bridge at all. After all, not many bridges around the world are lined with statues. The short answer is the statues played an important propaganda role in helping the rulers at the time in

Walking Tour 1: Charles Bridge

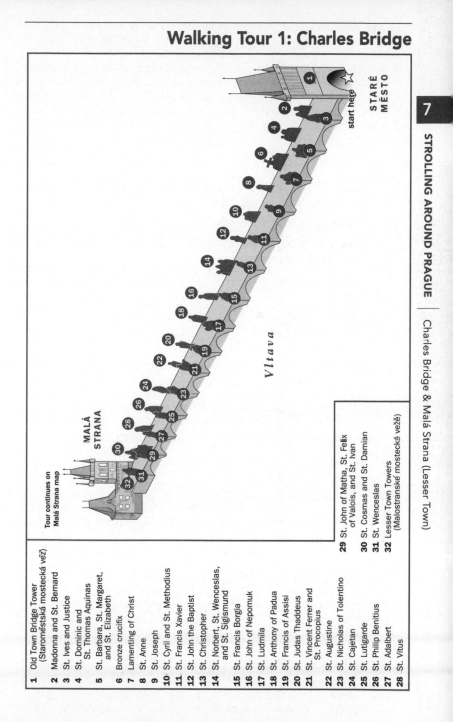

STARÉ MĚSTO

start here

Vltava

MALÁ STRANA

Tour continues on
Malá Strana map

1 Old Town Bridge Tower
    (Staroměstská mostecká věž)
2 Madonna and St. Bernard
3 St. Ives and Justice
4 St. Dominic and
    St. Thomas Aquinas
5 St. Barbara, St. Margaret,
    and St. Elizabeth
6 Bronze crucifix
7 Lamenting of Christ
8 St. Anne
9 St. Joseph
10 St. Cyril and St. Methodius
11 St. Francis Xavier
12 St. John the Baptist
13 St. Christopher
14 St. Norbert, St. Wenceslas,
    and St. Sigismund
15 St. Francis Borgia
16 St. John of Nepomuk
17 St. Ludmila
18 St. Anthony of Padua
19 St. Francis of Assisi
20 St. Judas Thaddeus
21 St. Vincent Ferrer and
    St. Procopius
22 St. Augustine
23 St. Nicholas of Tolentino
24 St. Cajetan
25 St. Lutgarde
26 St. Philip Benitius
27 St. Adalbert
28 St. Vitus
29 St. John of Matha, St. Felix
    of Valois, and St. Ivan
30 St. Cosmas and St. Damian
31 St. Wenceslas
32 Lesser Town Towers
    (Malostranské mostecké věže)

the Czech lands, the staunchly Catholic Habsburg monarchy in Vienna, to introduce Catholicism more widely among the Protestant Czech masses. The reasoning went something like: "We'll dazzle them with art and they'll convert."

It worked. Over the generations, the Czechs gradually converted to Catholicism and the statues became such a fixture on the bridge that it's impossible to imagine the bridge without them. Even hard-core Czech patriots, who still bristle—4 centuries later—at the mention of the Austrian occupation, will admit to the pleasing artistic effect created by the play of curvaceous baroque statuary atop a stern Gothic bridge.

As you stand in the shadow of the tower on the Old Town side of the bridge, first turn to your right, where you'll find an 1848 statue in tribute to Charles IV, who commissioned the bridge's construction between Prague's oldest quarters. Now walk toward the bridge entrance straight ahead, but first look up at the:

1 Old Town Bridge Tower (Staroměstská mostecká věž)

This richly ornate 1357 design was made for Charles IV by Petr Parléř, the architect who drafted the Gothic plans for St. Vitus Cathedral. The original east side of the tower (facing the Old Town side) remains pristine, with coats of arms of the Bohemian king and Holy Roman Empire. Shields also depict each territory under the auspices of the Bohemian crown at that time.

Above the east-side arch, seated to the right of the standing statue of St. Vitus, is Charles himself, and on the left is a statue of his ill-fated son, Wenceslas IV (Václav IV), who lost the crown of the empire.

The tower's western side was severely damaged in a battle against invading Swedish troops in 1648. The Swedes were never able to penetrate the gate and sack the Old Town, and in memory of that struggle, this side of the tower has never been repaired.

Climb to the top of the observation tower for postcard views of the bridge below.

As you pass through the archway, the first statue on the right is of the:

2 Madonna

She is attending to a kneeling **St. Bernard,** flanked by cherubs. Like most of the statues on the bridge, this is a copy; the originals were removed to protect them from weather-related deterioration.

Organized Walking Tours

Prague Private Guides (☎ 222-518-259; www.guidingprague.com) is run by an American expat living in Prague. This company offers both private guides for hire for half- and full-day walking tours of Prague, as well thematic group trips. **Prague Walking Tours** (☎ 222-873-307;

www.prague-walkingtours.com) offers mixed walking and bus tours of Prague highlights in their Prague Tour and more advanced Prague Tour All Inclusive. For a complete discussion of all Prague touring options, see p. 128.

Walking Tour 1: Malá Strana (Lesser Town)

33 V lázních (In the Baths)
34 U zlatého jednorožce
   (At the Golden Unicorn)
35 Cukrkávalimonáda ☕
36 Church of Our Lady Below the Chain
   (Kostel Panny Marie pod řetězem)
37 Lennon Peace Wall

38 Maltézské náměstí (Maltese Square)
39 Konírna ☕
40 Nostitz Palace (Nostický palác)
41 Church of Our Lady Victorious
42 Vrtba Palace (Vrtbovský palác)
43 Church of St. Nicholas
   (Kostel sv. Mikuláše)

With your back to the Madonna statue, directly across the bridge is a statue of:

3 St. Ives

He is the patron saint of lawyers and is depicted as promising to help a person who petitioned him. **Justice,** with a sword on his right, is also portrayed. If you see his outstretched hand holding a glass of beer, you'll know that Prague's law students have just completed their finals.

Cross back again and continue to do so after you view each statue.

4 St. Dominic & St. Thomas Aquinas

These two figures are shown receiving a rosary from the hands of the Madonna. Below the Madonna are a cloud-enshrouded globe and a dog with a torch in its jaws, the symbol of the Dominican order.

5 St. Barbara, St. Margaret & St. Elizabeth

These statues were sculpted by two brothers who worked under the watchful eye of their father, Jan Brokoff, who signed the work as a whole. Franz Kafka has written about the finely sculpted hands of St. Barbara, the patron saint of miners, situated in the center of the monument. To art experts, however, the sculpture of St. Elizabeth (on the left) is the most artistically valuable figure in this group.

6 The Bronze Crucifix

Produced in Dresden, Germany, it was bought by the Prague magistrate and placed on Charles Bridge in 1657. The statue's gilded Hebrew inscription, which translates as "holy, holy, holy God," is believed to have been paid for with money extorted from an unknown Jew who had mocked a wooden crucifix that formerly stood on this site.

7 The Lamenting of Christ

This sculpture depicts Jesus lying in the Virgin Mary's lap, with St. John in the center and Mary Magdalene on the right. Executions were regularly held on this site during the Middle Ages.

8 St. Anne

The Virgin Mary's mother holds the baby Jesus as the child embraces the globe in this statue from 1707.

9 St. Joseph

This statue of Joseph with Jesus dates from 1854 and was put here to replace another that was destroyed by gunfire 6 years earlier by anti-Habsburg rioters.

10 St. Cyril & St. Methodius

These Catholic missionaries are credited with introducing Christianity to the Slavs.

11 St. Francis Xavier

One of the cofounders of the Jesuit order, he is depicted carrying four pagan princes on his shoulders—an Indian, a Tartar, a Chinese, and a Moor—symbolizing the cultures targeted for proselytizing. This is widely regarded as one of the most outstanding Czech baroque sculptural works.

12 St. John the Baptist

The saint is depicted here with a cross and a shell, symbols of baptism.

13 St. Christopher

The patron saint of raftsmen is shown carrying baby Jesus on his shoulder. The statue stands on the site of the original bridge watch-house, which collapsed into the river along with several soldiers during the Great Flood of 1784.

14 St. Norbert, St. Wenceslas & St. Sigismund

All three are patron saints of the Czech lands.

15 St. Francis Borgia

He was a Jesuit general and is depicted with two angels holding a painting of the Madonna. Look on the lower part of the sculpture's pedestal, where you'll see the three symbols of the saint's life: a helmet, a ducal crown, and a cardinal's hat.

16 St. John of Nepomuk

He was thrown to his death in chains from this bridge, and this, the oldest sculpture on the span, was placed here to commemorate him. The bronze figure, sporting a gold-leaf halo, was completed in 1683. The bridge's sole bronze statue, St. John is now green with age and worn from years of being touched for good luck. **Note:** To find the exact spot from which John was thrown, walk back in the direction of the Old Town, just past the statue of St. Norbert, St. Wenceslas & St. Sigismund, to see a cross and a wrought-iron memorial. You're supposed to touch this for good luck as well, placing the five fingers of your left hand on the stars around his head, while placing your right foot on a small knob in the ground. (I confess I haven't done this every time I've crossed the bridge, but it certainly can't hurt!)

17 St. Ludmila

She points to a Bible from which St. Wenceslas is learning to read. In her left hand, St. Ludmila holds the veil with which she was suffocated. The statue's relief depicts the murder of St. Wenceslas.

18 St. Anthony of Padua

Dedicated in 1707, this statue depicts the preacher with baby Jesus and a lily. The relief is designed around a motif inspired by the saint's life.

19 St. Francis of Assisi

The first Roman Catholic martyr to be incorporated into the Bohemian liturgy, the contemplative saint is shown here between two angels.

20 St. Judas Thaddeus

He is depicted holding both the Gospel and the club with which he was fatally beaten.

21 St. Vincent Ferrer

He is shown boasting to **St. Procopius** of his many conversions: 8,000 Muslims and 25,000 Jews.

22 St. Augustine

Holding a burning heart and walking on "heretical" books, this statue of St. Augustine is a 1974 copy of a 1708 work. On the pedestal is the emblem of the Augustinians.

23 St. Nicholas of Tolentino

He is depicted as handing out bread to the poor. Behind him is a house with a Madonna, a mangle, and a lantern on its top-floor balcony. Walk quickly. Legend holds that if the lantern goes out while you pass by the statue, you'll die within the year.

24 St. Cajetan

The saint stands here in front of a column of cherubs while holding a sacred heart. Behind the statue, a triangle symbolizes the Holy Trinity.

25 St. Lutigarde

This figure was created in 1710 by 26-year-old M. B. Braun, and it is widely considered to be the most valuable sculpture on Charles Bridge. St. Lutigarde, a blind nun, is depicted here as able to see Christ on the cross, in order that she might kiss his wounds.

26 St. Philip Benitius

He was the general of the Servite order and is the only marble statue on the bridge. He's portrayed with a cross, a twig, and a book. The papal tiara lying at his feet is a symbol of the saint's refusal to assume the pope's throne in 1268 on the death of Pope Clement IV.

27 St. Adalbert (1709)

The first bishop of Bohemia is blessing the Czech lands after returning from Rome.

28 St. Vitus

Attired as a Roman legionary, he stands on a rock between the lions to which he fell victim.

29 St. John of Matha, St. Felix of Valois & St. Ivan

This statue was commissioned for the Trinitarian order, which rescued Christians from Turkish captivity. In the huge rock is a prison, in front of which there's a dog and a Turk with a cat-o'-nine-tails guarding the imprisoned Christians. With money for their freedom, St. John is standing on the summit of the rock. St. Ivan is seated on the left, and St. Felix is loosening the bonds of the prisoners.

30 St. Cosmas & St. Damian

They are the patron saints of physicians and were known for dispensing free medical services to the poor. The statues, which were commissioned by Prague's medical faculty, are attired in gowns and hold containers of medicines. **Note:** In 2011, this pedestal was empty as Cosmas and Damian got a long-overdue cleaning. It's not clear at this writing whether they will be ready by 2012.

31 St. Wenceslas

This statue was commissioned in 1858 by Prague's Klar Institute for the Blind.

Follow the brick path toward the archway at the end of the bridge, but on your way, look up at the:

32 Lesser Town Towers (Malostranské mostecké věže)

The small tower on the left was built in the 12th century before Charles ever began construction on the bridge. It was a plain Romanesque structure, but Renaissance accents were added in the 16th century. The taller tower was built in the 15th century and completed the connection of the archway with the smaller tower built in the early 1400s.

After passing through the tower, you'll enter Mostecká Street. Take the first left to Lázeňská Street. At no. 6, on the left, you'll find a former hotel and bathhouse that now houses a small cafe:

33 V Lázních (In the Baths)

This was a well-known stop for visitors to Prague in the 1800s. The pub and baths, which once hosted writer François-Rene de Chateaubriand, were in operation on this spot from the earliest periods of Lesser Town's existence.

Just up Lázeňská at no. 11, on the right side, is the former hotel:

34 U Zlatého Jednorožce (At the Golden Unicorn)

This was another favored stop for honored guests, including Beethoven. A plaque on the front bears the composer's face. The hotel was originally built into the heavy walls that once ringed Malá Strana.

35 Take a Break ☕

To the left of the Golden Unicorn, you'll find a welcome respite from the tourist horde and the perfect spot for coffee or light lunch of salad or pasta. **Cukrkávalimonáda** (literally "sugarcoffeelemonade") at Lázeňská 7 has a comfy and countrified feel with wooden floorboards and a blackboard menu. The impossibly thick hot chocolate, perfect on a cold rainy day, is so rich it should be illegal. One cup is plenty for two. Main dishes run between 120Kč and 280Kč, coffee around 50Kč (p. 81).

On the other side of the street, at the curve of Lázeňská, you come to the:

36 Church of Our Lady Below the Chain (Kostel Panny Marie Pod Řetězem)

One of the best Romanesque designs in Prague, this church was built for the Order of the Maltese Knights, replacing the oldest church in Malá Strana after it burned in 1420. You can see remnants of the original inside the church courtyard.

After exiting the church back onto the street, follow Velkopřevorské náměstí around the corner a few meters to find the French embassy on one side and a long graffiti-covered wall on the other:

37 The Lennon Peace Wall

Czechs have gotten pretty tired of graffiti in the past 20 years, but during the grim days of Communism, the scrawl on this wall was seen as outlet of free expression. The "Peace Wall" got its start with the tragic death of Beatle musician John Lennon in New York in 1980 (the Lennon/Lenin irony made it all the more potent). It's still a popular place to scribble graffiti if you're so inclined, and even now you'll still find lots of writing about Lennon and The Beatles. For more information, see chapter 6, "Exploring Prague," p. 94.

Return to the Church of Our Lady Below the Chain, but this time make a left on Lázeňská and follow it a few steps to enter Maltese Square (marked by the statue in the middle):

38 Maltese Square (Maltézské Náměstí)

On the first corner of the square is one of the city's most posh French restaurants packed into a former pub, U Malířů or "At the Painter's."

39 Take a Break ☕

If Cukrkávalimonáda (see above) was full or you're in the mood for something more traditionally Czech, **Konírna** at no. 10 hits the spot. You can sit out front on the terrace and order coffee and dessert or a meal from a full Czech-style menu. Main dishes cost between 180Kč and 600Kč, though daily lunch specials cut the cost substantially.

At one end of Maltézské náměstí you'll find the large:

40 Nostitz Palace (Nostický Palác)

This palace represents a grand, 17th-century, early baroque design attributed to Francesco Caratti. A Prague family that strongly supported the arts used to own it. Its ornate halls once housed a famed private art collection. The building now houses the Ministry of Culture, though you can still occasionally hear chamber concerts through its windows.

Facing Nostitz Palace, walk to the right and across Maltese Square (past the Mandarin Oriental Hotel) to find narrow Harantova Street (which was not signposted at the time of writing). Follow this a short way to Karmelitská Street. After crossing Karmelitská and walking to the right another 50m (150 ft.), you'll come to the:

41 Church of Our Lady Victorious (Kostel Panny Marie Vítězné)

This is the home of the famed wax statue of the baby Jesus, the **Bambino di Praga,** seen as an important religious relic in Italy and other predominantly Catholic countries. For more information, see chapter 6, "Exploring Prague," p. 94.

From the church entrance, continue up Karmelitská Street to see a complex of houses on the left side at no. 25, collectively known as:

42 Vrtba Palace (Vrtbovský Palác)

In 1631, Sezima of Vrtba seized a pair of Renaissance houses and connected them to create his palace among the vineyards at the bottom of Petřín Hill. The lush, terraced gardens (Vrtbovská zahrada), which you can enter for a fee, surrounding this complex add to its beauty. See chapter 6 under "Parks & Gardens," p. 123.

Proceed up Karmelitská, where you'll come finally to Malostranské náměstí. To the left, around the uphill side of the square, is the imposing dome of the:

43 Church of St. Nicholas (Kostel sv. Mikuláše)

This high-baroque gem was designed by K. I. Dientzenhofer and completed by his son in 1752. Relax among the statues and take in the marble-and-gilt interior (entry by paid admission only). The church often hosts excellent if expensive afternoon concerts. Buy tickets at the western entrance (on the side of the church facing Prague Castle). You can also climb the tower for views over Malá Strana and the Old Town in the distance. For more information, see chapter 6, "Exploring Prague," p. 94.

WALKING TOUR 2: PRAGUE CASTLE (PRAŽSKÝ HRAD)

START:	**The castle's front entrance, at Hradčanské náměstí.**
FINISH:	**Daliborka Tower.**
TIME:	**Allow approximately 2½ hours, not including rest stops.**
BEST TIMES:	**Weekdays from 9am to 5pm (to 4pm Nov–Mar).**
WORST TIMES:	**Weekends, when the crowds are thickest.**

Walking Tour 2: Prague Castle

Church ✝
Post Office ⊠
Information 𝑖
"Take-a-Break" 🍴

300 ft
91 m

Belvedere

finish here ☆ 24

Staré zámecké schody

23
21
20
19
22

Jiřská

18

17
15 16
14
13

Královská Zahrada (Royal Garden)

Míčovna

Jelení Příkop

9
12
8
11
7
5
6
10

Vikářská

U Prašného mostu

Jízdárna Art Gallery

Šternberk Palace

Archbishop's Palace

Third Courtyard

Second Courtyard

3
2
4
First Courtyard

start here ☆

Hradčanské náměstí

Zámecké schody

Říšská dvorská rada

1 First Castle Courtyard (První hradní nádvoří)
2 Matthias Gateway (Matyášova brána)
3 Holy Rood Chapel (Kaple sv. Kříže)
4 Spanish Hall (Španělský sál)
5 Rudolf Gallery (Rudolfova galerie)
6 Picture Gallery of Prague Castle (Obrazárna Pražského hradu)
7 St. Vitus Cathedral (Chrám sv. Víta)
8 Chapel of St. Wenceslas (Svatováclavská kaple)
9 Royal Crypt (Královská krypta)
10 Monolith (Monolit)
11 Golden Gate (Zlatá brána)
12 Royal Palace (Královský palác)
13 Vladislav Hall (Vladislavský sál)
14 Ludwig Wing (Ludvíkovo křídlo)
15 Chamber of the Imperial Court Council (Říšská dvorská rada)
16 Old Diet (Stará sněmovna)
17 Cafeteria U Kanovíku 🍴
18 St. George's Basilica (Bazilika sv. Jiří) and the Convent of St. George (Klášter sv. Jiří)
19 Lobkowicz Palace (Lobkovický palác)
20 Palace meal 🍴
21 Burgrave's Palace (Nejvyšší purkrabství)
22 Golden Lane (Zlatá ulička)
23 Daliborka Tower (Daliborka)
24 Toy Museum

The history and development of Prague Castle and the city of Prague are inextricably entwined; it's impossible to envision one without the other. Popularly known as the "Hrad," Prague Castle dates to the second half of the 9th century, when the first Czech royal family, the Přemyslids, moved their seat of government here. Settlements on both sides of the Vltava River developed under the protection of the fortified castle. Keep in mind as you are touring the castle that to enter most of the sites, including St. Vitus Cathedral, now requires a combined-entry ticket that you can buy at one of two information centers in the castle courtyards. It's possible to buy a reduced-price ticket if you're only interested in hitting the main attractions. For more detailed information on visiting Prague Castle, see chapter 6, "Exploring Prague," p. 94. The Lobkowicz Palace's "Princely Collections," unfortunately, requires a separate entry ticket.

Begin your tour from the castle's front entrance at Hradčanské náměstí. Walk through the imposing rococo gateway, topped by the colossal Battling Giants statues (1911 copies of 18th-c. granite works), to the:

1 First Castle Courtyard (První hradní Nádvoří)

An informal changing of the guard occurs here daily on the hour, with the grandest spectacle at noon. The guards wore rather drab khaki outfits until 1989, when Václav Havel asked costume designer Theodor Pištěk, who costumed the actors in the film *Amadeus*, to redress them. Their smart blue outfits are reminiscent of those worn during the First Republic.

Directly ahead is the:

2 Matthias Gateway (Matyášova Brána)

Built in 1614 as a freestanding gate, it was later incorporated into the castle itself. The gateway bears the coats of arms of the various lands ruled by Emperor Matthias. Once you pass through it, you'll see a stairway on the right leading to the staterooms of the president of the republic. They're closed to the public.

The gateway leads into the Second Castle Courtyard (Druhé hradní nádvoří). Ahead, on the eastern side of the square, is the:

3 Holy Rood Chapel (Kaple sv. Kříže)

Originally constructed in 1763, this chapel was redesigned in 1856. The chapel is noted for its high-altar sculpture and ceiling frescoes.

On the western side of the courtyard is the opulent:

4 Spanish Hall (Španělský Sál)

This hall was built in the late 16th century. During 1993 restorations, officials at the castle discovered a series of 18th-century *trompe l'oeil* murals that lay hidden behind the mirrors lining the hall's walls.

Adjoining the Spanish Hall is the:

5 Rudolf Gallery (Rudolfova Galerie)

This official reception hall once housed the art collections of Rudolf II. The last remodeling of this space—rococo-style stucco decorations—occurred in 1868.

light it up: THE ROLLING STONES GIVE SATISFACTION

Are the lights flickering in Spanish Hall? If they are, someone might be playing with the remote control that operates the lighting.

In the summer of 1995, during the go-go '90s, the Rolling Stones played to a crowd of more than 100,000 people in their second Prague concert since the Velvet Revolution. After finishing, the Stones gave Václav Havel, then president and a big fan, a bright gift: They paid for a $32,000 overhaul of the lighting in four of the castle's grand halls, including the Spanish Hall and Vladislav Hall. The

director and lighting designer of their record-breaking Voodoo Lounge Tour managed the project.

The result? Well, it's a somewhat more dignified spectacle than the raucous light show that was part of the mythical Voodoo Lounge Tour on stage. Mick Jagger, Keith Richards, Charlie Watts, and Ron Wood presented Havel with a remote control to operate the chandeliers and spotlights that now strategically cast their beams on baroque statues and tapestries.

On the northern side of the square is the:

6 Picture Gallery of Prague Castle (Obrazárna Pražského Hradu)

Containing both European and Bohemian masterpieces, the gallery holds few works from the original imperial collection, which was virtually destroyed during the Thirty Years' War. Of the works that have survived from the days of Emperors Rudolf II and Ferdinand III, the most celebrated is Hans von Aachen's *Portrait of a Girl* (1605–10), depicting the artist's daughter.

A covered passageway leads to the Third Castle Courtyard (Třetí hradní nádvoří), dominated by the splendid:

7 St. Vitus Cathedral (Chrám sv. Víta)

Begun in 1334, under the watchful eye of Charles IV, Prague's most celebrated Gothic cathedral has undergone three serious reconstructions. The tower galleries date from 1562, the baroque onion roof was constructed in 1770, and the entire western part of the cathedral was begun in 1873. The whole thing was only finished in 1929.

Before you enter, notice the facade, decorated with statues of saints. The bronze doors are embellished with reliefs; those on the central door depict the construction history of the cathedral. The door on the left features representations from the lives of St. Adalbert (on the right) and St. Wenceslas (on the left).

Inside the cathedral's busy main body are several chapels, coats of arms of the city of Prague, a memorial to Bohemian casualties of World War I, and a Renaissance-era organ loft with an organ dating from 1757.

According to legend, St. Vitus died in Rome but was then transported by angels to a small town in southern Italy. Since his remains were brought here in 1355, Vitus, the patron saint of Prague, has remained among the most popular saints in the country. Numerous Czech Catholic churches have altars dedicated to him.

8 Chapel of St. Wenceslas (Svatováclavská Kaple)

The chapel is built atop the saint's tomb. A multitude of polished semiprecious stones decorates the chapel's altar and walls. Other spaces are filled in with 14th-century murals depicting Christ's sufferings and the life of St. Wenceslas.

Below the church's main body is the:

9 Royal Crypt (Královská Krypta)

The crypt contains the sarcophagi of kings Václav IV, George of Poděbrady, Rudolf II, and Charles IV and his four wives. The tomb was reconstructed in the early 1900s, and the remains of the royalty were placed in new encasements. Charles's four wives share the same sarcophagus.

Exit the cathedral from the same door you entered and turn left into the courtyard, where you'll approach the:

10 Monolith (Monolit)

The marble obelisk measuring over 11m (36 ft.) tall is a memorial to the victims of World War I. Just behind it is an equestrian statue of St. George, a Gothic work produced in 1373.

Continue walking around the courtyard. In the southern wall of St. Vitus Cathedral, you'll see a ceremonial entrance known as the:

11 Golden Gate (Zlatá Brána)

The tympanum over the doorway is decorated with a 14th-century mosaic, *The Last Judgment*, which has been carefully restored, bit by bit. The doorway's 1950s-era decorative grille is designed with zodiac figures.

An archway in the Third Castle Courtyard connects St. Vitus Cathedral with the:

12 Royal Palace (Královský Palác)

Until the second half of the 16th century, this was the official residence of royalty. Inside, to the left, is the **Green Chamber (Zelená světnice),** where Charles IV presided over minor court sessions. A fresco of the court of Solomon is painted on the ceiling.

The adjacent room is:

13 Vladislav Hall (Vladislavský Sál)

This ceremonial room has held coronation banquets, political assemblies, and knightly tournaments. Since 1934, elections of the president of the republic have taken place here below the exquisite 12m (39-ft.), rib-vaulted ceiling.

At the end of Vladislav Hall is a door giving access to the:

14 Ludwig Wing (Ludvíkova Křídlo)

In this wing, built in 1509, you'll find two rooms of the Chancellery of Bohemia (Česká kancelář), once the administrative body of the Land of the Crown of Bohemia. When the king was absent, Bohemia's nobles summoned assemblies here. On May 23, 1618, two hated governors and their secretary were thrown out of the eastern window of the rear room. This act, known as the Second Defenestration, marked the beginning of the Thirty Years' War (see the box "Beware of Open Windows: The Czech Tradition of Defenestration," on p. 100).

7

STROLLING AROUND PRAGUE — Prague Castle (Pražský Hrad)

15 Chamber of the Imperial Court Council (Říšská Dvorská Rada)

The chamber met here during the reign of Rudolf II. In this room, the 27 rebellious squires and burghers who fomented the defenestration were sentenced to death. Their executions took place on June 21, 1621, in Staroměstské náměstí. All the portraits on the chamber walls are of Habsburgs. The eastern part of Vladislav Hall opens onto a terrace from which there's a lovely view of the castle gardens and the city.

Also located in the palace is the:

16 Old Diet (Stará Sněmovna)

The Provincial Court once assembled here. It's interesting to notice the arrangement of the Diet's furniture, which is all centered on the royal throne. To the sovereign's right is the chair of the archbishop and benches for the prelates. Along the walls are seats for the federal officials; opposite the throne is a bench for the representatives of the Estates. By the window on the right is a gallery for the representatives of the royal towns. Portraits of the Habsburgs adorn the walls.

Stairs lead down to St. George's Square (nám. Svatého Jiří), a courtyard at the eastern end of St. Vitus Cathedral. If the weather is nice, you might want to:

17 Take a Break 🍺

Cafeteria U Kanovníku, in the courtyard between St. Vitus and St. George's (nám. Sv. Jiří 3), has a terrace garden with tables, where you can enjoy light fare and hot Czech food. They offer coffee for 60Kč and decent chicken wraps for 120Kč daily from 10am to 5pm.

This square is dominated by:

18 St. George's Basilica (Bazilika sv. Jiří) & the Convent of St. George (Klášter sv. Jiří)

Benedictine nuns founded the convent in A.D. 973. In 1967, the convent's premises were acquired by the **National Gallery,** which now uses the buildings to display its interesting collection of 19th-century Czech art. See chapter 6 for complete information.

Leave the basilica and continue walking through the castle compound on Jiřská Street, the exit at the southeastern corner of St. George's Square. About 60m (197 ft.) ahead on your right (at no. 3) is the entrance to:

19 Lobkowicz Palace (Lobkovický Palác)

This relatively recently reconstructed 16th-century manor now houses the "Princely Collections Exhibition," a gallery devoted exclusively to the Lobkowicz family collections, including some old masters paintings, original scores by Beethoven, and fine musical instruments. Note that entry to this museum requires a separate ticket and is not included on the combined Prague Castle entrance ticket.

20 Take a Break 🍺

Even if you don't decide to spring for the admission to see the "Princely Collections," be sure to take a meal here inside the palace, which offers easily the best food and best views in the entire castle complex. You can have just a coffee and cake or a full Czech repast. In nice weather, sit in the courtyard or, better, inside on the terrace overlooking Malá Strana. The views are as good as or even better than the food. It's open daily from 9am to 5pm.

Opposite Lobkowicz Palace is:

21 Burgrave's Palace (Nejvyšší Purkrabství)

This 16th-century building, now considered the House of Czech Children, is used for cultural programs and exhibitions aimed toward children.

Walk up the steps to the left of Burgrave's Palace or, if these are closed, head back up in the direction of St. George's and take the first right to find tiny:

22 Golden Lane (Zlatá Ulička)

This picturesque street of 16th-century houses built into the castle fortifications was once home to castle sharpshooters. It was reopened in 2011 after a year's worth of renovations. Franz Kafka supposedly lived at no. 22 for a brief time in 1917.

Turn right on Golden Lane and walk to the end, where you'll see:

23 Daliborka Tower (Daliborka)

This tower formed part of the castle's late Gothic fortifications dating from 1496. The tower's name comes from Squire Dalibor of Kozojedy, who in 1498 became the first unlucky soul to be imprisoned here. One Dalibor legend, immortalized in an opera by Czech composer Bedřich Smetana, has it that Dalibor learned to play the violin in prison and charmed the citizens of Prague who used to stand below the tower and listen to him play.

Turn right at Daliborka Tower, then left, and go through the passageway and down Jiřská Street. Here, at no. 6, you can visit the:

24 Toy Museum

Especially appreciated by children, this museum unsurprisingly holds a permanent exhibition of toys. Wooden and tin toys are on display here along with a collection of Barbie dolls.

Follow the main street downhill and walk through the lower castle gate to see a stunning panorama of Malá Strana and the Old Town across the river. From here you have two choices for reaching the Malostranská station on line A of Prague's metro. Make a right and follow the old castle steps (Staré zámecké schody) or bear slightly to the left for a more scenic journey through some restored vineyards and several more cafes and restaurants.

WALKING TOUR 3: STARÉ MĚSTO (OLD TOWN)

START: **Municipal House (Obecní dům), at Náměstí Republiky.**
FINISH: **Havel's Market (Havelský trh).**
TIME: **Allow approximately 1 hour, not including any breaks or museum visits.**
BEST TIMES: **Sunday to Thursday from 9am to 5pm and Friday from 9am to 2pm, when the museums and market are open.**
WORST TIMES: **Weekend afternoons when the crowds are thickest, Monday when the museums are closed, and after 6pm when the market is closed.**

Staré Město, founded in 1234, was the first of Prague's original five towns. Its establishment was the result of Prague's growing importance along central European trade routes. Staré Město's ancient streets, most meandering haphazardly around Staroměstské náměstí, are lined with many stately buildings, churches, shops, and theaters.

Although this tour is far from exhaustive, it takes you past some of Old Town's most important buildings and monuments. Go to Náměstí Republiky 5, from the metro station of the same name. Begin at the:

1 Municipal House (Obecní Dům)

One of Prague's most photographed cultural and historical monuments, the Municipal House was built between 1906 and 1911 with money raised by Prague citizens. In the spring of 1997, it reopened after a long reconstruction, and historians say that it has been returned faithfully to its original grandeur.

From the beginning, this ornate Art Nouveau building has been an important Czech cultural symbol—the document granting independence to Czechoslovakia was signed here in 1918. The **Prague Symphony** performs in Smetana Hall, the building's most impressive room, with a gorgeous stained-glass ceiling. The detail of every decoration tells a story (see p. 178 for more information).

Inside you'll find a spacious period cafe, a French restaurant, and a Czech pub in the cellar with a fascinating ceramic still-life mural. Guided tours are offered most days (usually two or three times daily in the afternoon); buy tickets at the information center inside.

Facing the Municipal House main entrance, walk around to your left under the arch of the:

2 Powder Tower (Prašná Brána, literally Powder Gate)

Once part of Staré Město's system of fortifications, the Powder Tower was built in 1475 as one of the walled city's major gateways. After New Town was incorporated into the City of Prague, the walls separating it from the new section became obsolete. So did the Powder Tower, which was recommissioned as a gunpowder storehouse. Climb to the top for a better view of where you're going.

The tower marks the beginning of the **Royal Route,** the traditional path along which medieval Bohemian monarchs paraded on their way to being crowned in Prague Castle's St. Vitus Cathedral. For more information, see chapter 6, "Exploring Prague," p. 94.

Continue through the arch down Celetná Street (named after *calt,* a bread baked here in the Middle Ages) to the corner of Ovocný trh, where you'll find the:

3 House at the Black Mother of God (Dům U Černé Matky boží)

At the corner of Celetná 34 and Ovocný trh 19, this building is important for its cubist architectural style. Cubism, an angular artistic movement, was confined to painting and sculpture in France and most of Europe. As an architectural style, cubism is exclusive to Bohemia.

Constructed in 1912, this house features lots of jarring rectangular and triangular shapes that try to re-create in 3-D what cubism did for painting. The house is named for the Virgin Mary emblem on the corner of the building's second floor that was salvaged from the last building to stand on this site. There's also a small cubist museum to the left of the main entrance and around the corner is a sumptuous shop, Kubista, specializing in early Modern reproduction design and home furnishings.

7

STROLLING AROUND PRAGUE | Staré Město (Old Town)

With your back to the House of the Black Mother of God, cross Celetná and bear right to find a small passageway leading into Templová that begins just to the right of Celetná 27. Walk 2 short blocks, and turn left onto Jakubská. At the corner, on your right, you'll see:

4 St. James's Church (Kostel sv. Jakuba)

Prague's second-longest church contains 21 altars. When you enter, look up just inside the church's front door. The object dangling from above is the shriveled arm of a 16th-century thief.

With your back to the entrance of St. James Church, cross the street and turn left to find the small Týn passageway that starts just to the left of Malá Štupartská 5. Walk through the pretty courtyard of the former custom's house, the Ungelt. Keep the Ungelt in mind for a future shopping trip as there are some great stores here. Continuing straight through the second gate and up a small alleyway to the heart of the Old Town, the Old Town Square.

5 Old Town Square (Staroměstské Naměstí)

Surrounded by baroque buildings and packed with colorful cafes, craftspeople, and entertainers, Staroměstské náměstí looks the way an old European square is supposed to look.

This square has long been a focal point of Czech history and politics. Since the city's inception it has served as a meeting place for commerce, from the simple bartering of the Middle Ages to the privatization deals of the 1990s.

Old Town Square has also seen its share of political protest and punishment. Protestant Hussites rioted here in the 1400s. In 1621, the Catholic Habsburg rulers beheaded 27 Protestants here and hung some of the heads in baskets above Charles Bridge. A small white cross has been embedded in the square near the Old Town Hall for each of the beheaded.

In the 20th century, the square witnessed a whirlwind of political change. In 1918, the Czechs celebrated the founding of the new sovereign Republic of Czechoslovakia here. But then in 1939, the Nazis celebrated their occupation of the country on the same site. The Soviets then celebrated kicking the Nazis out of Prague in 1945. But in 1968 the Russians rolled their tanks through Prague again, this time as unwelcome invaders.

In February 1948, Communist party leader Klement Gottwald led a celebration in honor of the Communist seizure of power. No wonder the Czechs chose nearby Wenceslas Square to celebrate the return of their government in 1989.

Start your exploration of the Old Town Square at the Church of Our Lady Before Tý, just to the left as you first enter the square at Staroměstské náměstí 14:

6 Church of Our Lady Before Týn (Kostel Paní Marie Před Týnem)

This is one of the largest and prettiest of Prague's many churches. Famous for its twin spires that loom over nearby Staroměstské náměstí, the church was closely connected to the 14th-century Hussite movement for religious reform. After Roman Catholics crushed the reformers, many of the church's Hussite symbols were removed, including statues, insignia, and the tower bells that were once known by Hussite nicknames. Note the tomb of Danish astronomer Tycho de Brahe (d. 1601), near the high altar. For more information, see chapter 6, "Exploring Prague," p. 94.

Walking Tour 3: Staré Město (Old Town)

1 Municipal House
(Obecní dům)

2 Powder Tower
(Prašná brána)

3 House of the Black
Mother of God
(Dům U černé Matky boží)

4 St. James's Church
(Kostel sv. Jakuba)

5 Old Town Square
(Staroměstské náměstí)

6 Church of our Lady
before Týn
(Týnský chrám)

7 House at the Stone Bell
(Dům U kamenného
zvonu)

8 Kinský Palace
(Palác Kinských)

9 Jan Hus

10 St. Nicholas Church
(Kostel sv. Mikuláše)

11 Old Town Hall
(Staroměstská radnice)
and its Astronomical
Clock

12 Estates' Theater
(Stavovské divadlo)

13 Kogo 🍴

14 Česká spořitelna

15 Havel's Market
(Havelský trh)

151

If it's just before the hour, head straight across the square to the Old Town Hall (no. 11, below) to see the hourly performance of the Astronomical Clock. If not, linger in this part of the square for a few minutes to see some of the other buildings here. Start first at the House of the Stone Bell, at Staroměstské náměstí 13:

7 House at the Stone Bell (Dům U Kamenného Zvonu)

The medieval Gothic tower was built in the 14th century for the father of Charles IV, John of Luxembourg. These days it often hosts high-quality art exhibits.

One door down from the House of the Stone Bell, at Staroměstské náměstí 12, check out the pinkish rococo Kinský Palace. This is arguably the grandest, and certainly gaudiest, town palace on the square:

8 Kinský Palace (Palác Kinských)

From the rococo balcony jutting from the palace's stucco facade, Communist leader Klement Gottwald declared the proletariat takeover of the Czechoslovak government in February 1948. Italian architect Lurago originally designed the building for Count Goltz. It was later taken over by the Habsburg Prince Rudolf Kinský in 1768. Aside from the dubious distinction of providing a balcony for Comrade Gottwald, the Kinský Palace is famous as the site of Franz Kafka's father's haberdashery on the ground floor as well as being the former home of Baroness Bertha von Suttner, a secretary to Alfred Nobel of peace prize fame and herself the first female recipient of the Nobel Peace Prize in 1905.

Now it's time to move into the square to see the statue of who could arguably be called the spiritual father of the Czech people:

9 Jan Hus Statue

Jan Hus was a fiery 15th-century preacher who challenged the Roman Catholic hierarchy and was burned at the stake for it. The statue's pedestal has been used as a soapbox by many a populist politician trying to gain points by associating himself with the ill-fated Protestant, although today you're more likely to find the international youth holding sway.

The struggle between the supporters of Hus, known as Hussites, set the stage for the religious wars that tore Bohemia apart in both the 15th and 17th centuries. The Hussite Church still lives today as the Protestant Czech Brethren, but since Communism its numbers have dwindled. Membership in the Catholic Church has also declined.

From here, turn briefly to the northwest corner of the square to see the white St. Nicholas Church:

10 St. Nicholas Church (Kostel sv. Mikuláše)

This is the 1735 design of Prague's baroque master architect K. I. Dientzenhofer. The three-towered edifice isn't as beautiful or as ornate inside as his St. Nicholas Church in Lesser Town, but the crystal fixtures are worth a look. Like its namesake in Malá Strana, this church hosts expensive but high-quality concerts most afternoons. Tickets are sold at the door on the day of the performance. For more information, see chapter 6, "Exploring Prague," p. 94.

Now it's time to head to the Old Town Hall and Astronomical Clock. As you're walking along the side of the square, notice the crosses on the ground marking spot of the public executions of 27 Czech noblemen in 1621.

11 The Old Town Hall (Staroměstská Radnice) & Astronomical Clock (Orloj)

Try to time your walk so you can pass the hall and its **Astronomical Clock** at the top of the hour. It's a brief but amusing show each hour where a mechanical parade of saints and sinners performs for the crowd watching below. If you have time and your knees are up to it, try making the steep, narrow walk up to the top of the tower for a picturesque view of Old Town's red roofs. You'll also find a very helpful branch of the city's tourist information office here. For more information, see chapter 6, "Exploring Prague," p. 94.

From here, walk about toward the main part of the square and turn right toward the square's south end. Begin walking down Železná. Continue down this car-restricted walking zone about 100m (330 ft.); then, on the left, you'll see the pale green:

12 Estates' Theater (Stavovské Divadlo)

Mozart premiered his opera *Don Giovanni* in this late-18th-century grand hall. More recently, director Miloš Forman filmed many scenes in the story of the composer's life here.

Make sure to walk down Rytířská in front of the theater to get a full view of this beautifully restored building.

From the front of the theater, walk about 10 steps back up Železná and take the first left on Havelská.

13 Take a Break 🍴

At Havelská 27, you can stop for a tasty pasta, lasagna, tiramisu, or thick Italian espresso at **Kogo** (p. 85). There are tightly packed tables inside, but if the weather is nice, you can sit in the more comfortable archway. Hours are daily from 9am to 11pm. Salads and appetizers start at 180Kč, and you won't be disappointed by their homemade pasta (from around 200Kč).

Continue down Havelská. On the left, you'll see:

14 Czech Savings Bank (Česká Spořitelna)

After serving as the museum to late Communist party leader Klement Gottwald, the large neo-Renaissance building with statue inlays is once again a bank. The 1894 building was originally intended to be a bank, but after the 1948 coup it was seized by the government and turned into a repository for Communist propaganda. After the 1989 revolution, the building was returned to the bank, which restored the intricate friezes and frescoes depicting bankers' propaganda of early Czech capitalism. This is the largest Czech savings bank and worth a peek.

Your next destination is the popular street market that overtakes the remainder of Havelská Street. Simply continue on to:

15 Havel's Market (Havelský Trh)

At this popular local meeting place, you'll find vegetables, fruit, drinks, soaps, toiletries, and an assortment of souvenirs. Prices here are generally lower than in most shops. Have fun browsing.

The nearest metro is Můstek, line A or B.

START:	**Lesser Square (Malé náměstí).**
FINISH:	**Restaurant Les Moules.**
TIME:	**Allow approximately 1 hour, not including rest stops or museum visits, 3 hours to take in the Jewish Museum sights.**
BEST TIMES:	**Sunday to Friday from 9am to 5pm, when the cemetery and sights are open.**
WORST TIME:	**Saturday, the Sabbath, and Jewish holidays when everything is closed.**

7

Josefov, Prague's former Jewish ghetto, lies within Staré Město. The wall that once surrounded the ghetto was almost entirely destroyed at the end of the 19th century to make way for luxury apartment buildings (that you still see to this day).

Jews have been here since the end of the 10th century, and despite the occasional pogroms and restrictive laws preventing Jews from moving outside this ghetto until the middle of the 19th century, Prague was traditionally considered one of the centers of Jewish scholarship and learning.

Today, Prague's Jewish community numbers less than 3,000, and while few Jews live here these days, this is still the community's spiritual heart. Note that to enter most of the sites here, you'll need to buy a combined entry ticket (ticket windows and cashiers are located at points throughout the former ghetto). Admission to the Old-New Synagogue is not included and requires a separate (and expensive) ticket. For more information on the Jewish Museum and Josefov, see chapter 6, "Exploring Prague," p. 94.

This tour may seem short, but the sights are highly detailed and provide much to ponder, so budget your time loosely. Start at:

1 Lesser Square (Malé Náměstí)

This square is adjacent to Staroměstské náměstí. Though it can't boast as much history as its larger companion, excavations have proven that Malé náměstí was a prime piece of real estate as far back as the 12th century. Archaeologists turned up bits of pottery, evidence of medieval pathways, and human bones from the late 1100s, when developers committed the medieval equivalent of paving over a cemetery to build a shopping mall. Today, the square is home to Prague's branch of the Hard Rock Cafe chain, which only slightly diminishes the impact.

From Malé náměstí, walk north along the square to find U radnice. One block ahead, in the courtyard across from the Magistrate Building and tucked against St. Nicholas Church, you'll see:

2 Franz Kafka's House

This building, on the site where the famous author was born, now houses a small gallery and shop to re-create the history of his life. But the best way to get a look at Kafka's life is by visiting the Kafka Museum in Hergetova Cihelna (p. 109).

An unflattering cast-iron bust of Kafka, unveiled in 1965, sits just at the corner of Maiselova and U radnice. Walk straight ahead onto:

Walking Tour 4: Josefov (Jewish Quarter)

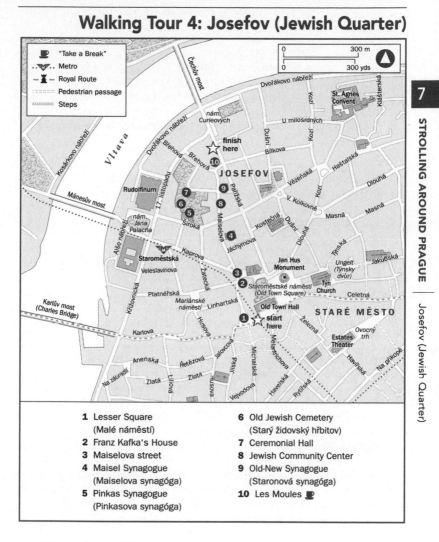

Legend:
- 🍺 "Take a Break"
- Ⓜ️ Metro
- ─🚶─ Royal Route
- ┈┈┈ Pedestrian passage
- ▦▦▦ Steps

0   300 m
0   300 yds

Dvořákovo nábřeží
St. Agnes Convent
nám. Curieových
Čechův most
U milosrdných
Kozí
Klášterská
☆ **finish here** ⑩
Dušní
Bílkova
JOSEFOV
Vězeňská
Haštalská
Dlouhá
Rudolfinum ⑦ ⑨ *Pařížská*
17. listopadu
⑥ ⑧ *V. Kolkovně*
⑤ *Maiselova*
Masná
Masná
nám. Jana Palacha
Široká
Kostečná
Dušní
④ *Jáchymova*
Dlouhá
Alšovo nábřeží
Kaprova
Týnská
Jakubská
Staroměstská Ⓜ️
Veleslavínova
Jan Hus Monument
Ungelt (Týnský dvůr)
Záteská
③
Platnéřská
Mariánské náměstí *Linhartská*
Staroměstské náměstí (Old Town Square)
Týn Church
Celetná
②
Karlův most (Charles Bridge)
Karlova
Husova
Old Town Hall
① ☆ **start here**
STARÉ MĚSTO
Železná
Estates Theater
Ovocný trh
Anenská
Řetězová
Zlatá
Liliová
Husova
Jilská
Michalská
Melantrichova
Jalovcová
Vejvodová
Havelská
Rytířská
Havířská
Na příkopě
Na zábradlí

7

STROLLING AROUND PRAGUE | Josefov (Jewish Quarter)

1. Lesser Square (Malé náměstí)
2. Franz Kafka's House
3. Maiselova street
4. Maisel Synagogue (Maiselova synagóga)
5. Pinkas Synagogue (Pinkasova synagóga)
6. Old Jewish Cemetery (Starý židovský hřbitov)
7. Ceremonial Hall
8. Jewish Community Center
9. Old-New Synagogue (Staronová synagóga)
10. Les Moules 🍺

3 Maiselova Street

This is one of the two main streets of the walled Jewish Quarter, founded in 1254. As elsewhere in Europe, Prague's Jews were forced into ghettos. By the 16th century, Prague's 10,000 isolated Jews comprised 10% of the city's population.

The ban on Jews living outside the ghetto was lifted only in 1848. Eighty percent of the ghetto's Jews moved to other parts of the city, and living conditions on this street and those surrounding it seriously deteriorated. The authorities responded by razing the entire neighborhood, including numerous medieval houses and synagogues. The majority of the buildings here now date from the end of the 19th century; several on this street sport stunning Art Nouveau facades.

About halfway down the street, on your right, is the:

4 Maisel Synagogue (Maiselova Synagóga)

This neo-Gothic temple is built on a plot of land donated by Mordechai Maisel, a wealthy inhabitant of Prague's old Jewish Quarter. The original synagogue was destroyed by fire in 1689 but was rebuilt. During the Nazi occupation of Prague, it was used to store furniture seized from the homes of deported Jews. Today, the building holds no religious services; it's home to the Jewish Museum's collection of silver ceremonial objects, books, and Torah covers confiscated from Bohemian synagogues by the Nazis during World War II. There's also a small but good gift shop.

Continue walking down Maiselova and turn left onto Široká to find the entrance to the Pinkas Synagogue and the Old Jewish Cemetery on the left side:

5 Pinkas Synagogue (Pinkasova Synagóga)

This is Prague's second-oldest Jewish house of worship. After World War II, the walls of the Pinkas Synagogue were painted with the names of more than 77,000 Czech Jews who perished in Nazi concentration camps. The Communist government subsequently erased the names, saying that the memorial was suffering from "moisture due to flooding." After the revolution, funds were raised to restore and maintain the commemoration. Here too is another gripping reminder of the horrors of World War II. Displayed are the sketches by children who were held at the Terezín concentration camp west of Prague (see chapter 11). These drawings, which are simple, honest, and painful in their playful innocence, are of the horrific world where parents and other relatives were packed up and sent to die.

Next to the Pinkas Synagogue, you'll find the entrance to the Old Jewish Cemetery. If you're not up for paying the (admittedly) steep combined entry fee to see the cemetery and the other sites, you can still sneak a peak at the cemetery through a small window off the street. To find the window, follow Široká street to ul. 17 listopadu, turn right and walk about 10m (30 ft.) beyond the entrance to the Museum of Applied Arts (ul. 17 listopadu 2). There you'll find a small opening in the fence on the right side.

6 Old Jewish Cemetery (Starý Židovský Hřbitov)

This is Europe's oldest Jewish burial ground, where the oldest grave dates from 1439. Because the local government of the time didn't allow Jews to bury their dead elsewhere, as many as 12 bodies were placed vertically, with each new tombstone placed in front of the last. Hence, the crowded little cemetery contains tens of thousands of graves.

Like other Jewish cemeteries around the world, many of the tombstones have small rocks and stones placed on them—a tradition said to date from the days when Jews were wandering in the desert. Passersby, it's believed, would add rocks to gravesites so as not to lose the deceased to the shifting sands. Along with stones, visitors often leave small notes of prayer in the cracks between tombstones.

Buried here is Rabbi Löw, who made from the mud of the Vltava River the legendary Golem, a clay "monster" to protect Prague's Jews. Golem was a one-eyed or three-eyed monster, depending on how you look at him. Legend has it that the rabbi would keep Golem around to protect the residents from the danger of mean-spirited Catholics outside the walls of the Jewish ghetto.

Löw's grave, in the most remote corner opposite the Ceremonial Hall, is one of the most popular in the cemetery; you'll see that well-wishers and the devout cram his tombstone with notes. Across the path from the rabbi is the grave of Mordechai Maisel, the 16th-century mayor of Josefov whose name was given to the nearby synagogue built during his term in office.

As you exit the cemetery on the left you'll pass the:

7 Ceremonial Hall

Inside the hall, rites for the dead were once held. Today, it holds a part of the museum's permanent collection of Jewish customs and traditions, mostly relating to sickness and death.

Follow the street U Starého hřbitova back to Maiselova Street. Make a short right to find the Jewish Community Center at no. 18.

8 Jewish Community Center

This is an information and cultural center for local members of the Jewish community and their invited guests. It once was the Jewish Town Hall. Activities of interest to the community are posted here.

On the Community Center wall facing the Old-New Synagogue is a clock with a Hebrew-inscribed face. It turns left, counter to what's considered "clockwise."

Continue walking 1 block along Maiselova to find the small alley called Červená. You're now standing between two synagogues. On the right is the High Synagogue (Vysoká synagóga), closed to visitors. On your left is the:

9 Old-New Synagogue (Staronová Synagóga)

Originally called the New Synagogue to distinguish it from an even older one that no longer exists, the Old-New Synagogue, built around 1270, is the oldest Jewish temple in Europe. The building has been prayed in continuously for more than 700 years, except from 1941 to 1945, during the Nazi occupation in World War II. The synagogue is also one of the largest Gothic buildings in Prague, built with vaulted ceilings and fitted with Renaissance-era columns.

Until a 19th-century planning effort raised the entire area about 3m (10 ft.), much of Josefov and Staré Město used to be flooded regularly by the Vltava. The Old-New Synagogue, however, has preserved its original floor, which you reach by going *down* a short set of stairs.

You can attend services here. Men and women customarily sit separately during services, though that's not always rigorously enforced.

At the end of Maiselova are a couple of decent refreshment options where you can have a meal and ponder the day:

10 Take a Break 🍺

Les Moules, at Pařížská 19, is a fairly authentic Belgian tavern tossed down amid one of the fanciest parts of the Czech capital. There's good beer, mussels (of course), and a nice assortment of French-inspired hot and cold dishes. Mains run from 300Kč to 500Kč, but the daily lunch special offers better value. Around the corner, at Břehova 8, you'll find **Shelanu,** a small kosher deli (if you're more in the mood to keep the Jewish theme going). It's not exactly a deli in the New York sense, but has a refreshing mix of salads and sandwiches as well as pies and blintzes. Sandwiches run about 200Kč each. Open Sunday to Thursday 9am to 10pm, with shorter hours on Fridays and closed Saturdays. The casual atmosphere is better suited to a lunch or snack than an evening out.

Following Pařížská will lead you back to Staroměstské Náměstí.

PRAGUE SHOPPING

Prague has become a fun shopping destination in recent years, spurred by rising wages and the influx of visitors with euros and dollars to spend. This is especially true for women's (and to a lesser extent men's) fashion. If your taste runs to the high-end, look no further than the Old Town's Pařížská Street, where a half-mile stroll takes you past luxury boutiques like Cartier and Prada, though these shops tend to have smaller inventory (and even higher price tags) than their brethren in Paris or New York. Slightly less-expensive but still top-quality Czech fashion designers have opened up shops throughout the Old Town, and Na Příkopě and Václavské Náměstí (Wenceslas Square) are lined with trendy, mid-market European clothing retailers like Zara and Mango (see "Shopping Areas" below).

For those looking to take a little bit of the Czech Republic home with them, popular souvenirs include Bohemian crystal and glass, garnet jewelry, hand-crafted wooden toys and puppets, old books and maps, and, naturally, distinctly Czech liquid refreshments like Moravian wine, beer, and Becherovka. The best advice is simply to walk around and poke your nose in wherever it looks interesting. Throughout the city center, you'll find quaint, obscure shops, some without phones or advertising.

THE SHOPPING SCENE
Shopping Areas
The L-shaped half-mile running down from the middle of **Wenceslas Square** around the corner to the right on **Na Příkopě** and to the **Palladium Shopping Center** on **Náměstí Republiky** has become Prague's principal shopping hub. In this short distance you'll find several multilevel shopping gallerias, with foreign chains like **H&M, Next, Kenvelo, Pierre Cardin, Adidas,** and **Zara.** Between the centers is a wide array of boutiques and antiques shops.

The wide, tree-lined **Pařížská,** from Old Town Square to the river and the Hotel Inter-Continental, has become Prague's answer to L.A.'s Rodeo Drive, filled with top-end luxury names like **Cartier, Hermes, Louis Vuitton, Hugo Boss,** and **Prada.** Along the streets running off of Pařížská, many of the best young Czech designers have set up shop.

In the streets radiating off **Old Town Square,** particularly Celetná and Dlouhá, you'll find many of the city's best outlets for glass, porcelain, and jewelry. Indeed, Celetná has evolved into Prague's "glass alley."

How to Claim Your VAT Refund

If you're planning to fly to a destination outside of the European Union after your visit to Prague and carry a non-E.U. passport, it might be worth looking into getting a VAT refund. While the process is slightly bureaucratic, it's certainly worth the effort to recoup nearly 20% of your money on big purchases. Here's how to do it:

○ When paying for your goods, ask the store for a Global Refund Cheque.

○ Within 90 days of the date of purchase, present the voucher to a Czech Customs official at Prague Airport (Terminal 1) to get a stamp. Note that the official may ask to see the goods,

so have them handy. At the airport, the Customs Stamps official is located before Passport Control.

○ Hand the stamp in after Passport Control to one of the Cash Refund Offices. Their staff will then refund your VAT, free of charge. Alternatively, you can use a direct crediting of a chosen credit card, or have a bank check sent to a chosen address.

○ Be sure to give yourself plenty of time at the airport to handle all the formalities, including finding the offices and standing in line. For more information, go to **www.global-blue. com**.

Karlova, the street that connects the Old Town Square to Charles Bridge, is the place to go for cheap, throwaway souvenirs, like T-shirts, ball caps, and key chains. However, keep in mind that many of the goods on offer here, such as faux "KGB" fur caps, Russian nesting dolls, and those ridiculously overpriced "Prague Drinking Team" sweatshirts, have little genuine relation to the city.

In **Malá Strana,** Nerudova Street, which climbs its way to the castle, is filled with old book shops, art galleries, antique stores, and the usual gaggle of T-shirt and glass outlets.

Hours & Taxes

Prague's centrally located shops rely heavily on the tourist trade to keep afloat and maintain fairly long opening hours. Most are open Monday to Friday from about 9am to 7pm and Saturday from 10am to 3pm, and sometimes much later. Many open on Sunday as well, though usually for a shorter time.

Prices for goods include the government's 20% value-added tax (VAT). All tourists carrying passports from outside the E.U., including Americans, Canadians, and Australians, can recoup much of this tax through VAT refund schemes. To make use of this concession, buy from stores displaying a TAX FREE sign. To qualify, the purchase price must exceed 2,000Kč, including the VAT, in 1 day in one store.

Shipping

For sending letters or postcards, the Czech postal service is perfectly adequate. However, for shipping valuable or fragile items, you might want to consider an international shipping company, where you can track and insure what you send. **DHL** (Prague Airport; ℂ **220-300-111** or 840-103-000; www.dhl.cz) charges around 2,000Kč for a 1-kilogram (2¼-lb.) parcel to the U.K. or the United States. You can use the DHL terminal at Prague Airport (ℂ **840-103-000**), open Monday to Friday 7am to 9pm and Saturday 8am to 6pm, or visit the DHL drop-off point at the Prague City Center at Klimentská 46, Prague 1 (ℂ **840-103-000**), open Monday to Friday 9am to 6pm.

Prague Shopping

LETNÁ

Korunovační

Čechova

Veletržní

Milady Horákové

Jirečkova

Nad Štolou

Overnecká

Heřmanova

Milady Horákové

Veverkova

Františka Křížka

Janovského

Antonínská

Vltavská

Nad Štolou

Letohradská

Letenský Tunnel

Kostelní

HOLEŠOVICE

LETENSKÉ SADY

nábřeží Kpt. Jaroše

Šeřfánkův

most

Hlávkův most

ostrov
Štvanice

nábřeží Edvarda Beneše

Vltava

Kosárkovo nábřeží

Dvořákovo nábřeží

nám.
Curieových

Kozí

Dušní

St. Agnes Convent

Revoluční

Hradební

nábřeží Ludvíka Svobody

Lannova

Těšnovský Tunnel

Rohanské nábřeží

KARLÍN

Mánesův
most

Čechův
most

Haštalská

Klimentská

Klimentská

JOSEFOV

Bílkova

Věženská

Dlouhá

Soukenická

Petrská

Biskupská

Na Poříčí

Florenc

Rudolfinum

17. listopadu

Jewish Cemetery

Pařížská

Dlouhá

Masná

Truhlářská

Zlatnická

Na Poříčí

nám.
Jana Palacha

Široká

Dlouhá

Kozí

Náměstí Republiky

Havlíčkovo

Na Florenci

Florenc Bus Station

Staroměstská

Kaprova

St. Nicholas Church

Tyn Church

Rybná

V Celnici

Na Poříčí

Husitská

Žatecká

Staroměstské náměstí
(Old Town Square)
Old Town Hall

Stupartská

Celetná

Municipal House

Hybernská

Masarykovo Station

Hybernská

Řehořova

**Karlův most
(Charles Bridge)**

Karlova

Husova

Malé
náměstí

**STARÉ
MĚSTO**

**Powder
Tower**

Senovážné
náměstí

Bolzanova

Anenská

Anenské
nám.

Náprstkova

Zlatá

Liliova

Michalská

Havelská

Uhelný

Rytířská

Na příkopě

Nekázanka

Jeruzalémská

Růžová

Vrchlického sady

Seifertova
nám.
W. Churchilla

Smetanovo nábřeží

Betlémská

Konviktská

Bartolomějská

Perlova

Skořepka

28. října

Panská

Politických vězňů

Jindřišská

**Hlavní
nádraží**

Italská

Krocínova

Národní

Voršilská

Ostrovní

Můstek

Vodičkova

Václavské náměstí
(Wenceslas Square)

Opletalova

**Hlavní nádraží
(Main Train Station)**

Vozová

**National
Theater**

V jirchářích

Jungmannova

**Národní
Třída**

V jámě

Štěpánská

Washingtonova

Wilsonova

Španělská

Italská

Riegrovy sady

Slovanský
ostrov

Masarykovo nábřeží

Pštrossova

Opatovická

Černá

Lazarská

Navrátilova

Řeznická

Školská

Ve Smečkách

Krakovská

Mezibranská

Muzeum

**National
Museum**

Celakovského
sady

Legerova

Vinohradská

Baldínova

Polská

NOVÉ MĚSTO

Žitná

Žitná

V Tůních

Sokolská

VINOHRADY

Jiráskův
most

Resslova

Ječná

Lípová

Štěpánská

Kateřinská

I.P. Pavlova

nám.
I.P. Pavlova

Jugoslávská

**nám.
Míru**

Korunní

Mánesova

Římská

Anglická

Budečská

**Karlovo
Náměstí**

Karlovo
nám.

U Nemocnice

Ke Karlovu

Sokolská

Tylovo
nám.

Rumunská

Londýnská

Bělehradská

**Náměstí
Míru**

Palackého
most

Palackého
nám.

Na Moráni

Vyšehradská

Benátská

**Botanical
Garden**

Apolinářská

Fügnerovo
nám.

Tyršova

To Vyšehrad

Zítkovy
sady

Ztracená

Rašínovo nábřeží

Dittrichova

Myslíkova

Karlovo
nám.

Resslova

Viničná

0   1/4 mi
0   1/4 km

Metro

Royal Route

Pedestrian passage

Šteps

161

SHOPPING A TO Z

Antiques

Antikvariát Pařížská ★   This is a musty market with valuable pieces of Czechoslovak history. Pictures, graphics, coins, medals, paper currency, and maps are on offer. Open daily from 10am to 6pm. Pařížská 8, Prague 1. ✆ **222-321-442.** Metro: Staroměstská.

Antique-Andrle Vladimír   A wide selection of antique porcelain and ceramics, jewelry, and clocks distinguishes this shop. There's also a large selection of small antique sculptures and other accessories. Open Monday to Saturday from 10am to 7pm and Sunday from 10am to 6pm. Křížovnická 1, Prague 1. ✆ **222-311-625.** www.antique andrle.cz. Metro: Staroměstská.

Art Deco Galerie ★   This dandy store sells the trappings of Prague's golden age and is filled with colored perfume bottles and clothing from the 1920s and 1930s. Furniture and household items include Art Deco clocks and lamps. Open Monday to Friday from 2 to 7pm. Michalská 21, Prague 1. ✆ **224-223-076.** Metro: Můstek.

Art Galleries

Galerie Art Praha ★   Unlike most of the shops in the vicinity of Old Town Square, this is a serious art gallery that offers innovative works from some of the best Czech and Slovak artists of the 20th century. Open daily from 10:30am to 6pm. Staroměstské nám. 20, Prague 1. ✆ **224-211-087.** www.galerie-art-praha.cz. Metro: Staroměstská.

Galerie Peron ★★   This visual arts and design shop is a bit unusual in that it specializes mostly in Czech modern art from the early to mid–20th century. Prices are on the high side, but the quality of the holdings is unmatched. Open Monday to Friday from 11am to 7pm, Saturday and Sunday from noon to 6pm. U Lužického semináře 12, Prague 1. ✆ **257-533-507.** www.peron.cz. Metro: Malostranská.

Hunt Kastner Artworks ★   This small, private gallery in the neighborhood behind Letná park features contemporary art from the best new Czech artists working in photography, painting, and video. Open Tuesday to Friday from 1 to 6pm and Saturday from 2 to 6pm. Kamenická 22, Prague 1. ✆ **222-969-887.** www.huntkastner.com. Metro: Vltavská plus tram 1 or 25.

Beer, Wine & Spirits

Beer, wine, and spirits like Becherovka are sold in shops all over Prague, but one of the cheapest places to buy them is **Tesco** (see "Department Stores & Shopping Malls" on p. 165). Expect to pay about 300Kč for a medium-sized bottle of Becherovka and 150Kč for six bottles of Budvar.

You can find beer everywhere, but locating specialty beers from smaller brewers around the country can be a problem. **Galerie Piva** at Lázeňská 15, Prague 1, sells beer by the bottle from around the country, including Primátor's hard to find but worth the search 16-degree lager. Open daily 10am to 6pm. Farther afield but worth the trip is the **Pivní Galerie** at U Průhonu 9, Prague 7 (✆ **220-870-613**), in the outlying district of Holešovice. The friendly crew out here stock dozens of small-town and regional brews.

Blood-red **garnets** are the official Czech national gem, and the ones that you can buy here are among the world's finest, as well as one of the country's top exports. Most garnets are mined near Teplice, about 63km (39 miles) northwest of Prague. There are at least five specific kinds. Bohemian garnets are the Pyrope type, an amalgam of calcium and magnesium that's almost always deep red. You can get a small necklace for as little as 700Kč or densely packed brooches or bracelets for more than 30,000Kč, depending on whether they're set in silver or gold. Be warned that fake garnets are common, so purchase your stones from a reputable shop like the ones recommended below.

Fine **crystal** has been produced in the Bohemian countryside since the 14th century. In the 17th and 18th centuries, it became the preferred glass of the world's elite, drawing royals and the rich to Karlovy Vary to buy straight from the source. The king of Siam made a fabled trip to this western Czech spa town in the 1930s just to choose place settings for his palace. Bohemian factories are responsible for artistic advances in gilding, cutting, and coloring. Today, the quality remains high, and you can still purchase contemporary glass for prices that are much lower than those in the West. See below for a list of Prague's most prominent glass retailers.

Antiques and **antiquarian books and prints** are widely available and are distinctive souvenirs, sold by specialist *antikvariáts*. For non-Czech speakers, the books will hold little appeal, but the real treasures here are old postcards, lithographs, and maps. These antiques shops are located throughout the city, but you'll find many in Old Town and Malá Strana.

Since beer is a little heavy to carry home, take home a bottle of **Becherovka,** the nation's popular herbal liqueur from Karlovy Vary. You'll find the distinctive green decanter in shops around the city; it costs about 400 Kč per liter, but smaller sizes are widely available.

Books

Big Ben Bookshop ★   Situated just opposite St. James Church in Old Town, Big Ben is a convivial spot to pick up Czech authors in translation, as well as a decent range of fiction and nonfiction. It also carries English magazines, newspapers, guidebooks, and a good selection of children's books. Open Monday to Friday from 9am to 8pm, Saturday 10am to 8pm, and Sunday from 11am to 6pm. Malá Štupartská 5, Prague 1. ℂ **224-826-565.** www.bigbenbookshop.com. Metro: Staroměstská.

Globe Bookstore and Café ★★   This beautiful bookshop in Nové Město is the current home of Prague's first English-language literary hangout (the original location was in Holešovice in Prague 7). There are lots of goodies on offer, including arguably the city's largest collection of English language literature and nonfiction (new and used). There's an adjacent large cafe, serving excellent espresso drinks and a great menu of soups, sandwiches, and small entrees. There are computers on hand to check e-mail, and the Wi-Fi is free. Open daily from 9:30am to 1am. Pštrossova 6, Prague 1. ℂ **224-934-203.** www.globebookstore.cz. Metro: Národní třída.

Shopping Etiquette

Shopping in the Czech Republic isn't quite the same as shopping at home. Sure, in the big department stores and large international chains, you'll be free to mill around the aisles as you like and pick up and try on items that catch your eye. In smaller stores, however, the clerks are likely to keep a much sharper watch on the merchandise and will look askance if you start unfolding shirts or (in their eyes) disrupting the shelves without a clear intent to buy. While this can be annoying in practice, rest assured it's not personal; it's cultural. To minimize any potential misunderstandings, stick to a few easy-to-follow rules:

o Always greet the shop clerk with a hearty *"dobrý den"* (good day or hello) on entering the store. And say *"Na shledanou"* (goodbye) when leaving.

o If you're just browsing, say *"podívam se"* (I am just looking). If you find something you like, point to it and let the shop clerk unfold it or pull it off the rack. A simple way to say, "Can I try it on?" is *mohu zkusit?*

o Don't expect too much in the way of small talk or even smiles. Naturally there are plenty of outgoing store clerks out there, but local custom dictates more of a formal politeness over casual interaction with the customers.

o Before buying something, make sure you really want it. The local policy on returns is usually far less forgiving than in the U.S. or U.K. You may be able to get your money back (provided you've kept the receipt), but more likely you will be offered store credit in return or even possibly refused altogether.

o Lastly, try to relax and don't be intimidated. After all, you're the customer and they are simply there to help.

Shakespeare & Sons ★★ A veritable oasis of excellent English-language literature and nonfiction, including a wealth of Czech and other central European authors in translation. It's not as tiny as it looks from the outside, and once among the shelves in the back or downstairs, you'll be tempted to browse for hours. The location is convenient, just off of Charles Bridge on the Malá Strana side. The same company operates a second branch in Český Krumlov. Open daily 11am to 7pm. U Lužického semináře 10, Prague 1. © **257-531-894.** www.shakes.cz. Metro: Malostranská.

Crystal & Glass

Artěl ★★ If your interest runs to functional glass and stemware from the early Modern period (1920-'30s), when Czech design led the world, look no further than this upscale gift shop on a quiet square just down from the Hotel Paříž. American expat Karen Feldman pioneered the practice of adapting classic Czech design to make her high-end reproductions. In addition to glass, you'll find funky retro gifts, jewelry, books, and found objects. Open daily 10am to 7pm. Celetná 29 (entry from Rybná), Prague 1. © **224-815-085.** www.artelshop.com. Metro: Náměstí Republiky. Branch at U Lužického semináře 7, Prague 1. © **251-554-008.** Metro: Malostranská.

Celetná Crystal A wide selection of world-renowned Czech crystal, china, arts and crafts, garnets, and jewelry is on display in a spacious three-floor showroom not far from Old Town Square. Open daily 10am to 7pm. Celetná 15, Prague 1. © **222-324-022.** www.czechcrystal.com. Metro: Náměstí Republiky.

Material ★★ Breathtakingly beautiful designer of glass and crystal, including vases, chandeliers, candleholders, and bottles, as well as smaller beaded necklaces and bracelets. The best traditional and modern designs, and all the products are made locally. Open daily 10:30am to 8pm. Týnský dvůr 1, Prague 1. © **608-664-766.** www. i-material.com. Metro: Staroměstská.

Moser ★★ The Moser family began selling Bohemia's finest crystal in central Prague in 1857, drawing customers from around the world. Even the king of Siam made a special trip to the Karlovy Vary factory in the 1930s to pick his place settings. Soon after, the Nazis took over, and the Jewish Mosers fled. Following the war, the Communists seized the company but kept the Moser name. Surprisingly, the quality and reputation suffered little. The dark-wood showroom upstairs is well worth a look in. Open Monday to Friday from 9am to 8pm, Saturday and Sunday from 10am to 7pm. Na Příkopě 12, Prague 1. © **224-211-293.** www.moser-glass.com. Metro: Náměstí Republiky.

Department Stores & Shopping Malls

Koruna Palace A small passage at the bottom of Wenceslas Square, Koruna Palace has an interesting mix of jewelry shops and clothing boutiques, plus the city's biggest music store, **Bontonland Megastore,** in the basement. Open Monday to Saturday from 9am to 8pm and Sunday from 10am to 8pm. Václavské nám. at Na Příkopě 1, Prague 1. © **224-219-526.** www.koruna-palace.cz. Metro: Můstek.

Kotva ★ During Communist times, Kotva was the city's premier shopping address, and it's still fascinating as an architectural curiosity, built in the "Brutalist" style that was all the rage in the 1970s on both sides of the Iron Curtain. It's gotten a makeover in the past year, and a new line of mid- to high-end fashion labels. The kiosks on the ground floor sell everything from wine and knives to watches and ground coffee. Open Monday to Friday from 9am to 8pm, Saturday from 10am to 7pm, and Sunday from 10am to 6pm. Revoluční 1, Prague 1. © **224-801-111.** www.od-kotva.cz. Metro: Náměstí Republiky.

Obchodní Centrum Nový Smíchov This large Western-style shopping mall anchors the redevelopment of the once-derelict neighborhood of Smíchov around the Anděl metro stop. Nice mix of low- and high-end stores, including a larger branch of the Zara chain than you'll find in Old Town. There's a large food court and multiplex cinema on the top floor. Open daily 9am to 9pm (shops), 11am to 11pm (restaurants and entertainment). Plzeňská 8, Prague 5. © **251-511-151.** www.novysmichov.eu. Metro: Anděl.

Palác Flora Similar to Obchodní Centrum Nový Smíchov (see above), this large shopping mall is in Vinohrady, just above the Flora metro station. Inside you will find a wide selection of shops, restaurants, and cafes and an entertainment center that includes Prague's only IMAX cinema. Open Monday to Saturday 9am to 9pm, Sunday 10am to 9pm. Vinohradská 149, Prague 3. © **255-741-712.** www.palacflora.cz. Metro: Flora.

Palác Myslbek Clothing stores such as **H&M** and **Next** are part of this atrium, as well as a number of smaller fashion names and a large sporting goods shop, **Intersport.** They're open Monday to Saturday from 9:30am to 7pm and Sunday from noon to 6pm. Na Příkopě 19–21, Prague 1. © **224-835-000,** www.ngmyslbek.cz. Metro: Můstek.

Palladium ★★   The city's largest and most prestigious shopping mall occupies a monumental historic building on Náměstí Republiky that for centuries served as barracks for the city. Built into the original facade, five floors made of steel and glass entertain regiments of visitors in almost 200 shops and 30 restaurants. Among others, here, you will find brands like Levi's, Marks & Spencer, Benetton, Guess, and Quicksilver. The food court is easily the city's best. Open daily 9am to 10pm (shops), 7am to 10pm (food store), 7am to 3am (restaurants and entertainment). Náměstí Republiky 1, Prague 1. ℂ **225-770-250.** www.palladiumpraha.cz. Metro: Náměstí Republiky.

Slovanský dům ★   An attractive smaller shopping center with a few upscale names like Mexx that's chiefly prized for its handsome open-air courtyard, Kogo restaurant at the back, and multiplex cinema that shows nearly everything, including occasional Czech films in English or with English subtitles. Na Příkopě 22, Prague 1. ℂ **227-202-420.** www.slovanskydum.com. Metro: Náměstí Republiky.

Tesco   U.K. retailer Tesco runs this midrange department store in the center of town, along busy Národní třída. It's a good place to find practical items, like extra socks or an umbrella, that you may have forgotten at home. The grocery store in the basement is arguably the best in the center of town. Open Monday to Friday from 8am to 9pm (food department from 7am), Saturday from 9am to 8pm (food department from 8am), and Sunday from 10am to 8pm (food department from 9am). Národní třída 26, Prague 1. ℂ **222-003-111.** Metro: Národní třída.

Van Graaf ★★   This German retailer on Wenceslas Square is arguably the best department store in the city for fashion, offering top international brands like Joop, Hugo Boss, Ralph Lauren, and many others in a clean, modern space and at affordable prices. Václavské nám. 17, Prague 1. ℂ **296-304-200.** Metro: Můstek.

Fashion

Over the past few years, Prague has evolved into a great place to buy clothing, mostly for women, but some shops also cater to men's fashion. The area around **Wenceslas Square** and **Na Příkopě** features high-end mass market retailers like popular

---

A Trip To The Farmers' Market

The biggest food retail trend in Prague these days is the explosion of **farmers' markets** (www.ceskefarmarsketrhy.cz), in effect open-air food markets that sell high-quality (often organic) fruits and vegetables, meats, cheeses, and dairy products that are fresh off the farm to a population that's been waiting decades to liberate itself from international grocery chains that value profit over freshness and health. Sadly, at this writing there were no farmers' markets in the center of the city, so a visit will require a little advance preparation. Two of the best, though, are only a short ride from the center on metro line A (green). On Saturday morning (8am–2pm), head out to the suburb of Dejvice, Prague 6 (metro stop: Dejvická), for arguably the city's best open-air market. It's a sprawling space right next to the metro station with dozens of vendors selling their wares in a carnival-like atmosphere. On Wednesday and Saturday mornings (8am–2pm), you'll find a similar but smaller market in Vinohrady, Prague 2, at Jiřího z Poděbrad Square (metro stop: Jiřího z Poděbrad). Bring your own bags.

Spanish brand **Zara,** Na Příkopě 15, Prague 1 (© **224-239-860;** www.zara.com; metro: Můstek) and the ubiquitous **H&M** at Václavské nám. 19 (© **234-656-051;** www.hm.com), among others. You'll find the more exclusive names along Pařížská, including **Cartier** (no. 2), **Hugo Boss** (no. 6, no. 19), **Hermes** (no. 12), **Louis Vuitton** (no. 13), and **Prada** (no. 16). Most stores along this stretch are open Monday to Friday from 9am to 7pm and on Saturday and Sunday from 10am to 6pm.

Old Town is also home to the best Czech designers. Try **Boheme** at Dušní 8 (© **224-813-840;** www.boheme.cz) for stylish and well-made women's tops, dresses, and accessories. Boheme is open Monday to Friday from 11am to 7pm and Saturday from 11am to 5pm. **Tatiana** at Dušní 1 (© **224-813-723;** www.tatiana. cz) is less sensible, more elegant, and much more expensive. It's open Monday to Friday from 10am to 7pm and Saturday from 11am to 6pm.

Garnets & Jewelry

Dušák (Watchmaker and Goldsmith) Dušák features Cartier, Gucci, Omega, Rado, and Certina chronographs and does repairs, too. Open Monday to Friday from 10am to 7pm, Saturday from 9am to 6pm, and Sunday from 1 to 6pm. Na Příkopě 17, Prague 1. © **224-213-025.** www.dusak.cz. Metro: Můstek.

Granát ★ Authentic Czech garnets sourced from the original garnet veins in northern Bohemia are offered here. Prices are surprisingly reasonable; the settings, a mix of traditional and modern in both gold and silver. Open Monday to Friday from 10am to 6pm and Saturday from 10am to 1pm. Dlouhá 28, Prague 1. © **222-315-612.** www.granat.eu. Metro: Staroměstská.

Halada ★ Beyond garnets, Halada has one of the best arrays of market-priced gold, silver, platinum, and fine gems in this city, which a little more than 2 decades ago used to ration wedding rings as a subsidized entitlement (no joke). Open Monday to Saturday from 9am to 7pm, Sunday 10am to 6pm. Na Příkopě 16, Prague 1. © **224-218-643.** www.halada.cz. Metro: Můstek. Also at Pařížská 7, Prague 1. © **222-311-868.** Metro: Staroměstská.

Royal Jewelry-Zlatnictví The designs of the pendants and brooches sold here are some of the most unusual in the city. All items are set in 14- or 18-karat gold and range from 500Kč to about 50,000Kč and up. Open Monday to Saturday from 9am to 9pm and Sunday from 11am to 9pm. Václavské nám. 8, Prague 1. © **224-222-404.** Metro: Můstek.

Studio Šperk ★★ This factory store from an exclusive jewelry designer from northern Bohemia features Czech garnets and rarer stones like dark-green moldavite in a mix of traditional and modern settings. Prices range from a few thousand crowns for a heart-shaped garnet pendant set in silver to my favorite, a stunning bracelet of diamonds and moldavite priced at 180,000Kč. Each purchase receives certificate of authenticity. Open Monday to Friday from 10am to 7pm, Saturday 10am to 6pm. Dlouhá 19, Prague 1. © **224-815-161.** www.drahonovsky.cz. Metro: Staroměstská.

Gifts & Souvenirs

Botanicus ★★ 📗 This chain of natural scent, soap, and herb shops is an amazing Anglo-Czech success story. Started by a British botanist and Czech partners on a farm northeast of Prague, Botanicus has found 101 ways to turn a plant into a sensuous gift and a lucrative trade. Open daily from 10am to 8pm. Týnský dvůr 3, Prague 1. ℂ **234-767-446.** www.botanicus.cz. Metro: Staroměstská.

Manufaktura ★ Come here for one-stop shopping for authentic if eclectic Czech souvenirs, including wooden toys, natural soaps, regenerative salts, and ceramic figurines. Open daily from 10am to 8pm. Melantrichova 17, Prague 1. ℂ **221-632-480.** www.manufaktura.biz. Metro: Můstek.

Health & Beauty

Prague has several studios where you can buy the best names in cosmetics as well as schedule an appointment for a facial or pedicure. **Estée Lauder,** Železná 18, Prague 1 (ℂ **224-232-023;** metro: Můstek), is open Monday to Friday from 10am to 7pm and Saturday from 10am to 4pm. **Yves Rocher,** Václavské nám. 47, Prague 1 (ℂ **221-625-570;** www.yvesrocher.cz; metro: Muzeum), is open Monday to Friday from 8:30am to 8pm and Saturday and Sunday from 10am to 6pm. **L'Institut Guerlain,** at Dlouhá 16, Prague 1 (ℂ **227-195-330;** www.linstitut.cz; metro: Staroměstská), is open Monday to Friday 9am to 9pm, Saturday noon to 7pm.

Home Decor & Design

Kubista ★★ Fans of Bauhaus and early Modern design will think they died and went to heaven here. The home furnishings, textiles, glassware, and jewelry mix originals and reproductions, but everything here looks classy. Open daily from 10am to 8pm. Ovocný trh 19, Prague 1. ℂ **224-236-378.** www.kubista.cz. Metro: Náměstí Republiky.

Modernista ★ Similar to Kubista, this little shop tucked away in a courtyard specializes in early and mid-20th century Czech furniture and decorative arts. Most of the merchandise consists of carefully crafted reproductions, but there are a few original pieces, like desk lamps, on hand as well. Good selection of old posters on hand too. Open daily from 11am to 7pm. Celetná 12, Prague 1. ℂ **224-241-300.** www.modernista.cz. Metro: Náměstí Republiky.

Qubus ★ Qubus features funky retro furniture, lighting, and glass and furnishings with a distinctly contemporary feel from some of the best modern Czech designers. Open daily from 10am to 6pm. Rámová 3, Prague 1. ℂ **222-313-151.** www.qubus.cz. Metro: Staroměstská.

Music

Bontonland Megastore This big music store in the basement of the Koruna Palace shopping center has a good collection of the best modern and retro Czech pop as well as a very good collection of jazz and classical CDs. There are also plenty of CDs of the best U.S. and U.K. groups and a good set of DVD movies (though the DVDs sold here play on European, but not American, DVD players). Open Monday to Saturday from 9am to 8pm and Sunday from 10am to 7pm. Václavské nám. at Na Příkopě 1, Prague 1. ℂ **224-473-080.** www.bontonland.cz. Metro: Můstek.

Musical Instruments

Dům hudebních nástrojů ♪ You'll find no fewer than two floors of guitars here: electric makes, including lots of legendary models from the '60s and '70s, in the basement, and classical guitars upstairs, plus the city's best selection of musical instruments of all sorts. Open Monday to Friday from 9am to 6pm, Saturday from 10am to 3pm. Jungmannovo nám. 17, Prague 1. ✆ **224-222-501.** www.guitarpark.cz. Metro: Můstek.

Photography

FotoŠkoda ★★ This is a top-flight retail camera store with a huge array of the latest digital and film cameras from around the world. Also sells lenses, accessories, and tripods, as well as digital camera necessities like batteries, cables, and memory cards. The digital photo lab on the ground floor can make prints from memory cards and thumb drives, as well as plain old film. Open Monday to Friday from 9am to 8pm, Saturday 10am to 6pm. Vodičkova 37, Prague 1. ✆ **222-929-029.** Metro: Můstek.

Jan Pazdera ★ Camera repairs and cheap darkroom equipment make this a Prague photo-snapper's favorite. The bulk of the selection is secondhand cameras, including Pentaxes and Russian Smenas. You can also find old telescopes, Carl Zeiss microscopes, light meters, and enlargers. Open Monday to Friday from 10am to 6pm. Vodičkova 28, pasáž ABC, Prague 1. ✆ **224-216-197.** Metro: Můstek.

Shoes

Bat'a Czechoslovakia's favorite footwear émigré, the late Tomáš Bat'a, made his post-Communist return with a vengeance, taking a sizable chunk of the market long after the Nazis and then the Communists cut the original Moravian family factory to pieces. His huge outlet on the site where his father started selling shoes earlier this century on Wenceslas Square has been remodeled for modern comfort. Bat'a goods include travel bags, leather accessories, sports outfits, and top-line brands of athletic shoes. Open Monday to Friday from 9am to 9pm, Saturday from 9am to 8pm, and Sunday from 10am to 8pm. Václavské nám. 6, Prague 1. ✆ **221-088-472.** www.bata.cz. Metro: Můstek.

Sporting Goods

Intersport With row upon row of clothes and equipment, Intersport is Prague's mega–sporting goods retailer. The prices aren't much better than what you'd find abroad. Still, it's a decent option for picking up camping gear or sports equipment you might have forgotten to pack back home. Open daily from 9:30am to 7pm. Palác Myslbek, Na Příkopě 19, Prague 1. ✆ **221-088-097.** www.intersport.cz. Metro: Můstek.

Toys & Puppets

Obchod loutkami ☺ Although there are no ventriloquist dummies, many kinds of puppets are available here, including hand, glove, rod, and marionettes. Obchod loutkami isn't cheap, but its creations are expertly made and beautifully sculpted. Hundreds of characters from trolls to barmen are available in the store as well as online. Open daily from 10am to 8pm. Nerudova 47, Prague 1. ✆ **257-532-735.** www.marionettes.cz. Metro: Malostranská.

Rocking Horse Toy Shop ★★ ☺ The Rocking Horse (*Houpací Kůň*) has an unmatched selection of traditional Czech wooden and wind-up toys, including the shop's namesake little wooden rocking horse. Younger kids will love the toys, and parents will love the reasonable prices. Open daily from 9:30am to 6:30pm. Loretánské nám. 3, Prague 1. ✆ **603-515-745.** Metro: Malostranská.

Sparky's ☺ This flagship store of a local toy store chain is a welcoming spot for the whole family. The younger ones will find terrific souvenirs of Prague here. Open Monday to Saturday from 10am to 7pm, Sunday to 6pm. Havířská 2 (short street btw. Na Příkopě and the Estates' Theater), Prague 1. ✆ **224-239-309.** www.sparkys.cz. Metro: Můstek.

Truhlář Marionety ★★ ☺ With handmade wooden marionettes from timeless classic designs that date back to the Middle Ages, Truhlář Marionety is not cheap but worth every penny for an authentic souvenir. Open daily from 10am to 8pm. Týnský dvůr 1, Prague 1. ✆ **224-895-437.** www.marionety.com. Metro: Staroměstská.

PRAGUE NIGHTLIFE

For many Czechs, the best way to spend an evening is at the neighborhood pub, enjoying the good beer and some boisterous conversation. These types of evenings are always open to visitors, of course, though the language may occasionally be an issue (at least at the start of the night before the beer kicks in).

If raucous beer nights are not your thing, Prague offers plenty of other diversions. The contemporary music scene is alive and kicking, and clubs all across town offer live acts or DJs playing rock, indie, techno, hip-hop, or whatever is popular at the moment. Prague has also developed into a popular stop for visiting international acts, both large and small. The year 2011 brought to town indie and club acts like Hurts and Underworld, superstar singers like Rihanna, and oldie acts like Uriah Heep, Roxette, Sade, and Ringo Starr, among others. See the ticket agencies listed below for shows that might be in town during your visit.

Jazz, too, has enjoyed a long tradition in the Czech lands from the early decades of the 20th century when American jazzmen were played on gramophones on imported vinyl. You'll find no fewer than five decent jazz clubs in the city center (listed later) and the quality of the playing is high.

Czechs are avid theatergoers and Prague for decades has enjoyed a vibrant drama scene (though with nearly all of the output in Czech, much of this sadly is inaccessible to visitors). Occasionally the National Theater will subtitle in English important works aimed at international audiences, and theaters like Švandovo divadlo in Smíchov and Divadlo Archa in Nové Město sometimes stage English and American productions in their original language.

Opera is more accessible and Prague has at least two premier venues: the State Opera at the top of Wenceslas Square (Václavské nám.) and the National Theater. The former's repertoire is made up largely of Italian classics, while the latter frequently holds performances of works by national composers like Bedřich Smetana and Leoš Janáček. Both theaters are good value and tickets are often available at short notice, though the quality will vary from show to show.

Prague's longest-running entertainment tradition, of course, is classical music. Serious music lovers are best advised to take in a performance of the **Czech Philharmonic** at the Rudolfinum in Staré Město or the **Prague Symphony Orchestra** at the Obecní dům, near Náměstí Republiky. Another option is to see one of the many **chamber concerts** offered at churches and palaces around town. These can be very good, though ticket prices are often higher than for the Philharmonic and the quality may not be nearly as good.

If you're getting tired just reading about all these entertainment possibilities, there's always the option of a good dinner followed by a quiet stroll over the Charles Bridge and through Malá Strana over ancient cobblestones and lit by mellow gas lamps.

Tickets   Cultural events are surprisingly affordable and accessible, and except for a few high-profile performances at the National Theater or the Prague Spring Music Festival, they rarely sell out. To check on schedules and secure tickets before arriving, look over the websites of the various venues you might want to visit. That will at least give you an idea of what's happening while you're here. Many venues now allow you to purchase tickets directly online with a credit card and either print them at your home computer or pick them up at the box office once you get here (be sure to note the order number).

You can also buy tickets ahead of your visit through the websites of major ticketing agencies, all of which have English-language pages and are geared to serve incoming visitors. The major local agencies include **Ticketpro** (www.ticketpro.cz), **Bohemia Ticket** (www.bohemiaticket.cz), **Ticket Stream** (www.ticketstream.cz), and **Ticket Portal** (www.ticketportal.cz). **Sazka Ticket** (www.sazkaticket.cz) handles ticketing for all events at the massive O2 Arena, a frequent venue for international pop stars. These sites have the advantage of aggregating all the events and highlighting the biggest shows that will be on during your visit. Once in town, you can pick up your ticket at the ticket agency office or occasionally, for a fee, have the tickets sent over to your hotel.

Once in town, you have several options for sourcing tickets. The simplest and often cheapest option is to go directly to the venue box office. Most box offices hold normal working hours on weekdays and usually open again an hour or so before performances in the evenings. If you're intimidated by the language issue at the box office, simply write down what you want to see and the dates and number of tickets you need; the person behind the window will sort it out from there.

Another easy way to get tickets once you're in Prague is to visit one of the local ticket agency offices and buy the tickets in person. The man or woman behind the counter is likely to have a good idea of the biggest events happening on that day or in the coming days and provide good advice. Pay in cash or with a credit card. **Ticketpro** has several offices around town, including at **Prague Information Services** (© **221-714-444;** www.pis.cz) offices at the Old Town Hall and at Rytířská 31. Ticketpro also sells tickets at Václavské nám. 38, Prague 1 (© **296-329-999**), and through the helpful **Prague Tourist Center,** near the Můstek metro stop at Rytířská 12, Prague 1 (© **296-333-333**), open daily from 9am to 8pm. **Bohemia Ticket** has offices at Na Příkopě 16, Prague 1 (© **224-215-031;** www.bohemiaticket.cz) and is open Monday to Friday from 10am to 7pm, Saturday from 10am to 5pm, and Sunday from 10am to 3pm.

THE PERFORMING ARTS

Mozart reportedly shocked the Viennese when he once scoffed at his Austrian patrons, claiming that "my Praguers understand me." His trips to Prague, then considered a mere outpost in the Austrian Empire, became the subject of music folklore. His defiant 1787 premiere of *Don Giovanni* is the high watermark in Prague's cultural history—not that there haven't been fine performances since. Czech composers Antonín Dvořák and Bedřich Smetana each moved the resurgent nation to tears in the 19th century, while Bohuslav Martinů and Leoš Janáček ushered in a new industrial-age sound to classical compositions in the first half of the 20th century. You can still hear many works in grand halls throughout Prague; they're worth a visit just to immerse yourself in the grandeur of the setting, let alone the musical accompaniment.

Opera

Prague is a great opera town, though the standards don't quite reach New York, London, or Vienna levels. The good news is that opera here is much more affordable and tickets are usually easier to get. Prices at the State Opera, for example, range from 250Kč up to 1,200Kč for the best seat in the house.

Prague has three main venues for opera. The primary stage is the **Prague State Opera (Státní opera Praha),** at the top of Wenceslas Square, situated in a beautiful neo-Renaissance building blighted only by its unfortunate location across a major highway from the square. To find it, look to the left of the grand National Museum building at the top of the square. The opera house is just beside a modern building that now holds an annex of the National Museum.

The State Opera's repertoire is focused mainly on Italian classics, though a few Czech favorites are included each season. These are highly enjoyably performances, though local critics have been tough on the opera in recent years, calling its staging of Puccini's *Tosca,* for example, solid but staid and without sufficient emotion. Verdi's works like *La Traviata* and *Aïda* have also received mixed reviews.

The **National Theater (Národní divadlo)** is also a prime opera venue. This is home to the **National Opera,** and as you might expect the repertoire leans more toward home-grown productions such as Smetana's peppy *Prodaná nevěsta (The Bartered Bride)* or Janáček's inscrutable but interesting *Kát'a Kabanová.* The choreography is fun for the whole family, and explanations of the plot are provided in English. Once in a while, internationally acclaimed soloists stop by.

A third main venue, the **Estates' Theater (Stavovské divadlo)** ★, is wholly affiliated with the National Theater and as such mostly focuses on dramatic works performed in Czech. During some summers, however, private troupes put on performances of Mozart's *Don Giovanni* aimed primarily at tourists and these are worth looking out for. Other times of year, the theater occasionally stages wonderful and rare works of baroque opera.

9

PRAGUE NIGHTLIFE | The Performing Arts

Prague Nightlife

Agharta Jazz Centrum **21**
Baráčnická Rychta **2**
Blues Sklep **31**
Bugsy's **15**
Chapeau Rouge **23**
Church of St. Nicholas
  (Malá Strana) **1**
Cross Club **9**
Divadlo Archa **27**
Divadlo Ponec **46**
Estates' Theater **22**
Fraktal **8**
Hapu **50**
Iron Curtain **34**
Jáma **43**
James Joyce **18**
JazzDock **6**
Karlovy Lázně **29**
Kino Aero **45**
Kino Světozor **40**
Klementinum **14**
Klub Termix **50**
Kolkovna **17**
Laterna Magika **39**
Lávka **28**
Lucerna Music Bar **41**
Malostranská Beseda **4**
Mecca **10**
Municipal House
  (Smetana Hall) **25**
National Marionette
  Theater **13**
National Theater **38**
Nový Smíchov multiplex **7**
Palác Akropolis **50**
Palác Flóra **50**
Prague Beer Museum **20**
Radost FX **48**
Reduta Jazz Club **37**
Rocky O'Reilly's **44**
Roxy **19**
Rudolfinum **12**
Saints Bar **50**
SaSaZu **11**
Slovanský Dům **24**
State Opera House **47**
Švandovo Divadlo **5**
Theater on the
  Balustrade **30**
Tlustá Koala **26**
Tretter's **16**
U Fleků **42**
U Malého Glena **3**
U medvídků **36**
U Vejvodů **35**
U zlatého tygra **29**
Valentino **50**
Vinohrady Theater **49**

Czechs generally are a casual live-and-let-live people. The late ex-president Václav Havel, who had collected an extensive official wardrobe, is etched in everyone's memory as the dissident playwright wearing old frayed sweaters. Journalists often showed up for news conferences with the then-president or the prime minister in T-shirts. But if you plan on attending the opera or theater, **proper eveningwear is highly recommended.** There may be no worse faux pas in Bohemia than dressing bohemian for a classical performance. For men: a dark suit or at least a coat and tie. For women: a mid-length dress or pants.

See "Landmark Theaters & Concert Halls," below, for contact and ticketing details for the theaters discussed here.

Classical Music

Prague is truly a great city for classical music, and a trip here is a rare chance to hear works by Czech composers such as Antonín Dvořák or Bedřich Smetana and other central Europeans performed in their natural setting.

The capital boasts three full orchestras and a virtual army of smaller chamber groups that perform regularly in churches and palaces around town. On any given day during the season (Sept–May), there may be as many as a dozen classical performances going on.

The high point of the classical music season is the annual **Prague Spring Music Festival** (www.festival.cz), which draws performers and music fans from around the world to Prague for 2 weeks from mid-May until the beginning of June. The main performances are held at the Art Nouveau **Smetana Hall** at the **Municipal House (Obecní dům;** see "Landmark Theaters & Concert Halls," below), though concerts are held at other venues around town. Tickets for festival concerts range from 400Kč to more than 3,000Kč and are available in advance through Ticketpro or in person at Hellichova 18, Prague 1 (✆ **257-310-414;** www.festival.cz).

The country's main orchestra, the **Czech Philharmonic** (www.ceskafilharmonie. cz), has an international reputation and performs at the stunning neo-Renaissance **Rudolfinum** in Staré Město. The Philharmonic has gone through some turbulent years in the recent past; nevertheless, the performances are of a high standard and programs usually include at least one regional composer you're not likely to hear during a visit to your hometown symphony. Tickets range from around 400Kč to 600Kč for the best seats. For more on the venue and ticketing, see "Landmark Theaters & Concert Halls," below.

The Philharmonic's main rival, the **Prague Symphony Orchestra,** known locally by the initials **"FOK"** (www.fok.cz), has positioned itself as a fresher alternative, with a frequently livelier and more daring repertoire, and many more modern composers on the roster. The FOK performs regularly at the **Smetana Hall** of the **Municipal House (Obecní dům),** and this is where you'll find the company's box office and scheduling information.

The **Prague Radio Symphony Orchestra** is primarily a studio band but does make regular concert appearances. The group plays sufficiently good versions of classical and contemporary works in the Rudolfinum or Obecní dům.

Two solo Czech violinists to look out for when booking your tickets: the veteran virtuoso **Josef Suk,** a great-grandson of Dvořák, who still plays with crisp, if not exact, precision; and his flashier heir apparent, **Václav Hudeček,** who attacks every stanza with passion and bleeds through his bow.

Church Concerts

In the years since the Velvet Revolution, Prague has developed a rapidly growing cottage industry of informal church concerts. Initially, these concerts were performed by music students and journeymen musicians as a way of picking up some spare cash. Nowadays, church concerts are big business and wherever you go, you're likely to see posters and flyers advertising the next extravaganza, featuring well-known and popular composers like Bach, Handel, Vivaldi and, naturally, Mozart.

Church concerts can be great when done well and a real treat, combining a lovely baroque setting with music that was composed precisely for that time period. However, like many other things in Prague's tourist world, caveat emptor. Ticket prices for these informal church concerts have crept up so high in recent years, anywhere from 250Kč to 500Kč, that the more expensive concerts now cost as much as or more than a good seat at the Czech Philharmonic, and the quality of the playing is likely to be vastly inferior.

Be wary of touts, often dressed like Mozart and offering a menu of concerts, or aggressive promoters that seem more intent on getting you in the door than delivering a quality performance. The venues listed below can be counted on to hold concerts that provide good value for money.

Because of its extravagant beauty, the **Chapel of Mirrors ★** in the Klementinum, Mariánské nám. 5, Prague 1 (✆ **222-220-879;** www.klementinum.com), is a favorite chamber concert venue. Almost every evening, a classical concert highlights strings, winds, or the organ. Note that the concert hall was closed in 2011 for reconstruction but was expected to open for the 2012 season.

The Church of St. Nicholas (Kostel sv. Mikuláše), Staroměstské náměstí, Prague 1 (✆ **224-190-994),** is one of the city's finest baroque gems. Chamber concerts and organ recitals are popular here, usually starting in the late afternoon, and the acoustics are terrific. There's also a lot to look at: rich stucco decoration, sculptures of saints, and a crown crystal chandelier.

Prague's *other* **Church of St. Nicholas (Chrám sv. Mikuláše),** in Malá Strana, at Malostranské nám. 1 (✆ **257-534-215;** www.psalterium.cz), is another beautiful baroque venue for early evening concerts. The music normally starts at 6pm and runs about 60 minutes. Admission costs 490Kč for adults, and 300Kč for students.

Dance

Of all the musical arts in Prague, dance is the most accessible. From classical ballet to innovative modern dance, there are several options each week that demonstrate an enjoyable mix of grace, beauty, and athleticism. The **National Theater Ballet** at the National Theater focuses mainly on classical dance and ballet. Tickets range from 250Kč to 1,000Kč and are available from the National Theater box office (see below for details).

Divadlo Ponec ★, at Husitská 24a (✆ **222-721-531;** www.divadloponec.cz) in the outlying district of Žižkov, is home to more progressive modern dance and each year in June hosts the city's popular Tanec Praha modern dance festival.

Performances are held most nights of the week and tickets cost around 200Kč. You can buy them through Ticketpro or at the theater box office (Mon–Fri 5–8pm as well as 1 hr. before performances).

Landmark Theaters & Concert Halls

The Czech Philharmonic at Rudolfinum 📷 Named for Habsburg Prince Rudolf, the beautifully restored Rudolfinum has been one of the city's premier concert venues since it opened in the 19th century. The Rudolfinum's Small Hall mostly presents chamber concerts, while the larger, more celebrated Dvořák Hall is home to the Czech Philharmonic. Though the acoustics aren't faultless, the grandeur of the hall makes a concert experience here worthwhile.

Alšovo nábřeží 12, Prague 1. ℂ **227-059-227** (box office Mon–Fri 10am–6pm). www.ceskafilharmonie. cz. Metro: Staroměstská.

Estates' Theater (Stavovské divadlo) ★★ In a city full of spectacularly beautiful theaters, the massive pale-green Estates' still ranks as one of the most awesome. Built in 1783, the Estates' was home to the premiere of Mozart's *Don Giovanni*, which was conducted by the composer himself. The building, an example of the late baroque style, was reopened on the 200th anniversary of Mozart's death in 1991, after nearly 9 years of reconstruction. The theater hosts mainly dramas performed in Czech but occasionally has performances of *Don Giovanni* for tourists and also puts on very worthwhile baroque opera. Buy tickets at the National Theater box office (see below) or try at the theater's own box office 45 minutes before performances start.

Ovocný trh 1, Prague 1. ℂ **224-901-448**. www.narodni-divadlo.cz. Metro: Line A or B to Můstek.

National Theater (Národní divadlo) ★★ This neo-Renaissance building overlooking the Vltava River was completed in 1881. The theater was built to nurture the Czech National Revival—a grassroots movement to replace the dominant German culture with that of native Czechs. To finance it, small collection boxes with signs promoting "the prosperity of a dignified national theater" were installed in public places. Almost immediately upon its completion, the building was wrecked by fire; it was rebuilt and opened in 1883 with the premiere of Bedřich Smetana's opera *Libuše*. The magnificent interior contains an allegorical sculpture about music and busts of Czech theatrical personalities as well as paintings created by Czech artists of the National Theater generation—Myslbek, Aleš, Hynais. Composer Bedřich Smetana conducted the theater's orchestra here until 1874, when deafness forced him to relinquish his post. Today, the theater plays host to a demanding repertoire of drama, opera, and ballet. Buy tickets online, through Bohemia Ticket, or at the theater box office.

Národní 2, Prague 1. ℂ **224-901-448** (box office daily 10am–6pm). www.narodni-divadlo.cz. Metro: Národní třída.

Prague Symphony Orchestra–Smetana Hall (Smetanova síň) ★★ Named for the popular composer and fervent Czech nationalist Bedřich Smetana (1824–84), Smetana Hall is an Art Nouveau gem. Since its reopening after the building's painstaking reconstruction in the 1990s, the ornate and purely exhilarating Smetana Hall has held a series of varied and top-notch musical events, and each May hosts the Prague Spring Music Festival.

In the Municipal House (Obecní dům), Náměstí Republiky 5, Prague 1. ℂ **222-002-336** (box office Mon–Fri 10am–6pm). www.fok.cz. Metro: Náměstí Republiky.

State Opera House (Státní opera) ★ First called the "New German Theater" and then the "Smetana Theater," the State Opera was built in the 1880s for the purpose of staging Germanic music and drama. Based on a Viennese design, the Renaissance-style theater was rebuilt after suffering serious damage during the bombing of Prague in 1945. Over the years, the auditorium has hosted many great names, including Richard Wagner, Richard Strauss, and Gustav Mahler, whose *Seventh Symphony* premiered here. In addition to being home to the State Opera, the house stages other music and dance events. Buy tickets through Bohemia Ticket or at the theater box office.

Wilsonova 4, Prague 2. © **224-227-266** (box office Mon–Fri 10am–5:30pm; Sat–Sun 10am–noon and 1–5:30pm). www.opera.cz. Metro: Muzeum.

Theaters

Drama has a long tradition in Czech life. Its enormous influence was reconfirmed during the revolutionary events of 1989, when theaters became the focal points and strategy rooms for the opposition.

Most of the city's theater offerings are in Czech, but a few English-language expatriate troupes have taken root and stage performances whenever they are ready—or not—at various locations. Check *The Prague Post* (on newsstands or at www.prague post.com) for the latest listings.

Czech productions by local and translated authors are staged almost every night. The most highly respected theaters are the gorgeous **Vinohrady Theater (Divadlo na Vinohradech),** Náměstí Míru 7, Prague 2 (© **224-257-601;** www.dnv-praha. cz), the former workplace of late ex-president Václav Havel's wife, Dagmar, who made a final performance as Queen Kristina soon after becoming first lady. The **Theater on the Balustrade (Divadlo Na Zábradlí),** Anenské nám. 5, Prague 1 (© **222-868-868;** www.nazabradli.cz), is the place where Havel (d. 2011) got his start as a playwright. Tickets, usually costing between 150Kč and 300Kč, should be bought in advance. Simultaneous translation into English is sometimes offered through earphones provided by the theaters, but the translator reads all parts from a script (usually without much dramatic verve). Ask when booking if translation is offered.

Two Prague theaters deserve special mention for their unusual commitment to performing dramatic works in their original language, including occasional English and American plays. They also both regularly schedule engaging concerts, performance-art pieces, and dance, and are worth checking out during your visit. **Divadlo Archa** ★★ is at Na Poříčí 26 in Nové Město, Prague 1 (© **221-716-333;** www. archatheatre.cz). The box office is open Monday to Friday from 10am to 6pm and performances usually start at 8pm.

The second theater, **Švandovo divadlo** ★★, at Štefánikova 57 in Smíchov, Prague 5 (© **257-318-666;** www.svandovodivadlo.cz), focuses on international dramatic works and dance and many performances in the main hall are subtitled in English (ask for a balcony seat for a better view). The box office is open Monday to Friday from 11am to 7pm, Saturday and Sunday 5 to 7pm.

Laterna Magika This performance-art show based in the newer wing of the National Theater stages a range of multimedia productions, from the latest production, *The Legends of Magical Prague,* to *Casanova* and others. These are adult themes combining unique uses of dance, music, film, and light and can be very entertaining and easy to follow for audiences of any language.

Národní třída 4, Prague 1. ☏ **224-931-482.** www.laterna.cz. Box office Mon–Sat from 10am–8pm. Tickets 680Kč; should be bought in advance. Metro: Národní třída.

National Marionette Theater (Národní divadlo marionet) This is the best of Prague's handful of puppet theaters. The company's mainstay for years has been Mozart's *Don Giovanni*. It's entertaining, but you might want to bone up on the opera's storyline beforehand so that you have a better idea of what's going on. Žatecká 1, Prague 1. ☏ **224-819-322.** www.mozart.cz. Tickets 590Kč. Metro: Staroměstská.

THE CLUB & MUSIC SCENE

The 1989 Velvet Revolution had its roots in the underground rock clubs that kept the youth tuned into something more than the monotones of the Communist Party during the gray 1970s and 1980s period known as "normalization." The Communists' persecution of the Czech garage band Plastic People of the Universe, named for a Frank Zappa refrain, motivated playwright Václav Havel and his friends to keep the human rights heat on the Politburo. As president, Havel paid homage to rock's part in the revolution and kept company with the likes of Zappa, Springsteen, Dylan, and the Stones—all of whom paid tribute to him as "the rock-'n'-roll president." (Havel died in December 2011.)

Almost universally, the amps in clubs are turned up to absurd distortion. But while most wannabe bands playing Prague today lack the political edge of the pre-revolution days, some have kept their unique Slavic passion without slavishly copying international trends. Some bands to watch out for include hard rockers Kabát, the trendy folk band Čechomor, or pop acts like Kryštof, Chinaski, and Support Lesbiens.

Rock & Dance Clubs

Cross Club ★★ The reigning king of Prague's alternative, indie, and clubbing scene, Cross Club fuses a funky industrial-age interior—pipes and wires hanging from the ceiling (and lots more)—with DJ-led trance and electronic dance music. Draws a mix of university students, backpackers, and anyone else looking for something that feels a little more authentic than some of the clubs downtown. The location in the nether reaches of Holešovice, Prague 7, keeps the tourists away, though in fact it's only a few minutes' walk from the Nádraží Holešovice metro stop (line C), meaning you can be there from the top of Wenceslas Square in under 20 minutes. Plynární 23 Prague 7. ☏ **775-541-430.** www.crossclub.cz. Admission 100Kč. Metro: Nádraží Holešovice.

Karlovy Lázně This multilevel club has been around for several years and is getting a little long in the tooth, yet it still manages to draw huge lines out front after midnight of mostly high school- and university-age students clamoring to get inside to dance. The building consists of several floors of music, with each level having a different theme, with R&B on one level, disco on another, and so on. You get the idea. The club is open daily 9pm to 5am. Smetanovo nábřeží 198 at Novotného lávka, Prague 1. ☏ **222-220-502.** www.karlovylazne.cz. Cover 150Kč. Metro: Staroměstská.

Klub Lávka This classic late-night meat-market dance club has been around since shortly after the Velvet Revolution. It's actually a lot of fun if you're in the mood

PRAGUE'S mysterious NIGHTS

If you've never been here, Steven Soderbergh's 1991 film *Kafka* (widely available on DVD), starring Jeremy Irons, will give you a fine sense of the dark mystery trapped in the shadows cast over the palace walls and cobblestone streets throughout Old Town and Malá Strana. You'll never forget a slow stroll across Charles Bridge, with its dim lampposts cutting eerie silhouettes from the attendant statues. The artfully lit facades of Prague Castle hover above as if the whole massive complex is floating in the darkness. The domes and spires of the skyline leading up to Hradčany have more varied textures and contours than a Dutch master could ever have dreamed of painting. On warm evenings, students singing with a guitar, or a violinist playing his heart out for a few koruny in his hat, create the bridge's ambient sound.

Evenings are also a fine time to walk through the castle courtyards; as the crowds disperse, a quiet solemnity falls over the city. From high atop the castle hill, you can see Prague sparkling below.

Across the river, the brightly lit belfries of Týn Church cast a spine-tingling glow on the rest of Old Town Square, and the mellow lamps around the Estates' Theater provide light for a memorable walk home after a performance.

for it, and the crowd is a good mix of Czechs and visitors. The setting couldn't be lovelier, on a jetty that extends into the river just south of the Charles Bridge, with castle views to die for. For hard-core partiers, the good news is that Klub Lávka is open late, and the music goes on until 5am.

Novotného lávka 1, Prague 1. ☏ **221-082-299.** www.lavka.cz. Cover 150Kč. Metro: Staroměstská.

Lucerna Music Bar ★   Big and a bit dingy, this Prague landmark in the belly of the downtown palace built by Václav Havel's father provides the best lineup of Czech garage bands, ex-underground acts, and an occasional reggae or blues gig. The drinks are still cheap for the city center. The crowd is mostly local and the biggest draws are the wildly popular '80s- and '90s-themed dance nights on Fridays and Saturdays. Open daily from 8pm to 3am, with live music usually beginning at 9pm.

Vodičkova 36, Prague 1. ☏ **224-217-108.** www.musicbar.cz. Cover 100Kč–200Kč. Metro: Můstek.

Malostranská Beseda ★★   One of the city's leading venues for Czech rock and folk acts, particularly groups and singers from the '80s and '90s. In addition to a music club, there's an art gallery and theater, plus a busy pub, cafe, and restaurant on the ground floor. The box office is open Monday to Saturday from 5 to 10pm, Sunday 3 to 8pm.

Malostranské nám. 21, Prague 1. ☏ **257-409-123** (box office). www.malostranska-beseda.cz. Metro: Malostranská.

Mecca   For those who don't mind trekking into the depths of Prague 7 to be with some of the trendiest people in town, make your way to Mecca. You don't have to pray to the east to get in, but you'd better be one of the beautiful people, dressed well enough to get by the bouncers at the usually packed entrance. This converted warehouse in northeast Prague has been one of the most popular discos in town for several years now and shows no signs of letting up. Open Wednesday to Saturday 11am to 5am.

U Průhonu 3, Prague 7. ☏ **283-870-522.** www.mecca.cz. Cover 190Kč–290Kč, women enter free on Wed. Metro: Vltavská, then tram 1.

Palác Akropolis ★★★ This reconverted cinema in Žižkov is Prague's premier venue for club-level live rock and world music acts. Brings in a surprisingly good roster of bands, including in recent years the Flaming Lips, the Strokes, Jon Spencer Blues Explosion, N.O.H.A., and many more. The main concert hall, the old screening room, is makeshift and still feels kind of edgy after all these years. The back room doubles as a bar and a DJ room, with dancing going on into the wee hours long after the concert's over.

Kubelíkova 27, Prague 3. ⓒ **296-330-911.** www.palacakropolis.cz. Cover 100Kč–250Kč, depending on the show. Metro: Jiřího z Poděbrad.

Radost FX This was one of the first big dance clubs to open up after the Velvet Revolution and, surprisingly, it's still here and still going strong. The ground-floor vegetarian restaurant and cafe are mainstays of the neighborhood dining scene (p. 89), and the trendy downstairs club draws a mixed straight and gay crowd for themed dance nights. Open daily from 10pm to 5am.

Bělehradská 120, Prague 2. ⓒ **224-254-776.** www.radostfx.cz. Cover 150Kč–250Kč. Metro: I. P. Pavlova.

Roxy ★★ Another dance club and live music venue in a reconverted theater, Roxy pushes the boundaries of bizarre in its dark, stark dance hall down Dlouhá Street, near Old Town Square. Acid jazz, funk, techno, salsa, and reggae are among the tunes on the playlist. The list of acts, including the Hives, Asian Dub Foundation, and Franz Ferdinand, among others, is legendary. Bands usually hit the stage early because of noise restrictions, but the party goes on until the wee hours.

Dlouhá 33, Prague 1. ⓒ **224-826-296.** www.roxy.cz. Cover 100Kč–250Kč. Metro: Staroměstská.

SaSaZu ★★ Arguably Prague's most glamorous nightclub is set, ironically, in one of the city's most work-a-day neighborhoods, Holešovice. Most nights DJs and dance tunes rule the floor, but occasionally SaSaZu plays host to a big name international act. In 2011, the British electronic band Underworld played its only Prague gig here. Check the website or ticket agencies to see if anyone big is here during your visit. The cavernous dance club shares a name and space with an excellent Asian restaurant, meaning it's possible to slide right from dinner to the dance floor. Open daily from 11am to 3am.

Bubenské nábřeží 306, Prague 7. ⓒ **284-097-455.** www.sasazu.com. Cover from 150Kč–1,000Kč-plus, depending on the act. Metro: Vltavská, then tram 1 or 25.

Jazz

While Dixieland swing was huge in Prague during the 1920s and '30s, urban jazz really made its mark here during the 1960s, when those testing Communist authority flocked to the smoky caves and wore dark glasses. The chubby Czech songstress Vlasta Průchová grabbed a few hints from Ella Fitzgerald with her throaty voice and set the standard for Czech be-bop wannabes in the postwar period leading up to the Prague Spring. After defecting, Průchová's son Jan Hammer made it big in the United States with his computerized scores, among them the theme for the classic '80s TV hit *Miami Vice.*

Luckily, most of Prague's ensembles follow Vlasta's lead and not Jan's. There are several good venues for a cool evening with a traditional upright bass, piano, sax, and drum group or occasional shots of fusion and acid jazz. Probably the most publicized local gig of all time happened at the Reduta Jazz Club in 1994, when Bill Clinton showed up to play "Summertime" and "My Funny Valentine" for then-President Václav Havel during a state visit.

U Malého Glena, listed under "Pubs," below, also offers jazz, fusion, and sometimes funk on most nights in its cellar. Try to go on a Sunday night, when they have a kind of local open-mic night and you never know who's going to show up. Some nights the best jazzmen in town turn up for an impromptu gig.

AghaRTA Jazz Centrum ★★ Upscale by Czech standards, the AghaRTA regularly features some of the best music in town, from standard acoustic trios and quartets to Dixieland, funk, and fusion. Bands usually begin at 9pm, but try to come much earlier to snag one of the few places to sit. Open daily from 7pm to midnight. Železná 16, Prague 1. ✆ **222-211-275.** www.agharta.cz. Cover 250Kč. Metro: Můstek.

Blues Sklep A relative and welcome newcomer to Prague's jazz scene, the Blue Sklep (Blues Cellar) focuses not surprisingly on the blues, bringing in bands and singers from around central Europe. Open daily from 7pm to 2:30am. Shows start around 9pm. Liliová 10, Prague 1. ✆ **774-277-060.** www.bluessklep.cz. Cover 150Kč. Metro: Národní třída.

Jazz Dock ★★ This riverside jazz club in Smíchov brings together a lineup of some of central Europe's best jazz, blues, and soul singers, along with good food and beautiful views out over the river. The club is big enough to give at least some of the tables good sightlines to the stage (unlike lots of other clubs in Prague); at the same time, it's small enough to be intimate. If you're looking for a romantic night of music and a view, this is your place. Concerts begin around 9pm. Open daily from 11am to 4am. Janáčkovo nábřeží 2, Prague 5. ✆ **774-058-838.** www.jazzdock.cz. Cover 150Kč. Metro: Anděl.

Reduta Jazz Club ★ Reduta has been around since the 1950s and still has a kind of welcoming retro feel, as if Charlie Parker or Miles Davis himself might walk in at some point during the night. The club brings in basically the same mix of performers that the other clubs do, and standards here most nights are pretty high. The music usually starts around 9:30pm. Open daily from 9pm to midnight. Národní 20, Prague 1. ✆ **224-933-487.** www.redutajazzclub.cz. Cover 150Kč. Metro: Národní třída.

PUBS

Good pub brews and conversations are Prague's preferred late-evening entertainment. Unlike British, Irish, or German beer halls, a true Czech pub ignores accoutrements like cushy chairs and warm wooden paneling, and cuts straight to the chase—beer. While some Czech pubs do serve a hearty plate of food alongside the suds, it's the *pivo,* uncommonly cheap at usually less than 40Kč a pint, that keeps people sitting for hours.

Foreign-theme pubs are popping up all over Prague, offering tastes ranging from Irish to Mexican. Still, it feels a bit like trying to sell Indian tea in China. Below are listed the best of the Czech brew stops followed by choices whose inspirations come from abroad.

Czech Pubs

Baráčnická rychta One of the nicest pubs in Malá Strana, the "Small Home-owners Association" (as the name translates) is away from the tourist throng on a small street just above the U.S. Embassy. It serves good food and Czech beer in a kind of old-time atmosphere. Open daily noon until 1am. Tržiště 23, Prague 1. ℂ **257-532-461.** www.baracnickarychta.cz. Metro: Malostranská.

Kolkovna ★ Hard-core pub aficionados will claim this is not a true pub, since it's relatively free of smoke, has clean restrooms, and serves excellent food, including both Czech classics and international dishes. On the other hand, no one will argue with the beer: Pilsner Urquell served from huge tanks brought in directly from the brewery to ensure freshness. It's a great spot to relax after a stroll through Old Town. Open daily from 11am to midnight. V kolkovně 8, Prague 1. ℂ **224-819-701.** www.kolkovna. cz. Metro: Staroměstská.

Prague Beer Museum ★★ Unlike what you might think from the name, this is not a "museum," it's a pub. What makes it stand out, though, is that it eschews the typical pub practice of selling one or two beers from a supporting brewery. Instead, the mission here is to bring in hard-to-find smaller regional and micro-brews. Leaf through the menu and name your poison. Open daily from 11am to 1am. Dlouhá 46, Prague 1. ℂ **732-330-912.** www.praguebeermuseum.com. Metro: Staroměstská.

U Fleků 🖐 It's hard to get too enthusiastic about U Fleků. Granted, the home-made beer, dark and sweetish, is some of the best in town and the place does date from 1459, but on most nights this pub is filled to brimming with tourists newly disgorged from buses waiting outside, and so ironically it's hard to get that feeling you're having an authentic experience. The food is decent but pricey for a pub; some nights there's music and you could be assessed a cover charge. Open daily from 9am to 11pm. Křemencova 11, Prague 2. ℂ **224-934-019.** www.ufleku.cz. Metro: Národní třída.

U medvídků (At the Little Bears) ★ This 5-century-old pub off Národní třída was the first in town to serve the original Budweiser, Budvar, on tap. It now serves its own microbrews, including some incredibly strong beers it calls "X-Beers." It also serves typical Czech pub food, including *cmunda,* potato pancakes topped with sau-erkraut and cured meat. It's smoky inside, but still easier to breathe here than at most local pubs. Open daily from 11:30am to 11pm. Na Perštýně 7, Prague 1. ℂ **224-211-916.** www.umedvidku.cz. Metro: Národní třída.

U Vejvodů In the early years after the 1989 revolution, for many expats, U Vejvodů kept the spirit of a grimy student/workers pub alive in Old Town—dark, smoky, and noisy, with plenty of Pilsner beer flowing for just a couple of crowns. It was only a matter of time until this 15th-century building, "At the Duke's," became the subject of corporate interest for its space, history, and prime location. The brew-ers of Pilsner have moved in with row upon row of well-tended tables and booths among the alcoves and balconies, along with big-screen TVs showing the latest Czech sports triumph, and a wider range of cuisine beyond the pigs' knuckles and pickled eggs of yesteryear. Open Monday to Saturday 10am to 4am and Sunday 11am to 3am. Jilská 4, Prague 1. ℂ **224-219-999.** www.restauraceuvejvodu.cz. Metro: Národní třída.

U zlatého tygra (At the Golden Tiger) One of the most Czech of the central city pubs, this was once the favorite watering hole of the late Václav Havel and one of his mentors, writer Bohumil Hrabal, who died in 1997. Particularly smoky and not especially visitor-friendly, this is a one-stop education in Czech pub culture. Pilsner Urquell is the house brew. Havel and former U.S. president Bill Clinton joined Hra-bal for a traditional Czech pub evening here during Clinton's visit in 1994, much to the chagrin of the regulars. Open daily from 3 to 11pm; try to arrive before 3pm to secure a table. Husova 17, Prague 1. ℂ **222-221-111.** www.uzlatehotygra.cz. Metro: Staroměstská or Můstek.

TO NENÍ PIVO JAKO PIVO: there's no beer like beer

This seemingly absurd local proverb makes sense when you first taste the golden nectar (*pivo*) from its source and realize that you've never really had *beer* before. While Czechs on the whole aren't religious, beer still elicits a piety unseen in many orthodox countries. The golden Pilsner variety that accounts for most of the beer consumed around the world was born here and has inspired some of the country's most popular fiction, films, poetry, and prayers.

For many Czechs, the corner beer hall (*hospoda* or *pivnice*) is a social and cultural center. Regulars in these smoke-encrusted caves drink beer as lifeblood and seem ill at ease when a foreigner takes their favorite table or disrupts their daily routine. For those wanting to sample the rich, aromatic taste of Czech lagers without ingesting waves of nicotine, dozens of more ventilated pubs and restaurants have emerged since the Velvet Revolution. Alas, the suds in these often cost double the price of a standard *hospoda*.

According to brewing industry studies, Czechs drink more beer per capita than any other people. The average Czech downs 320 pints of brew each year; the average American drinks about 190. Of course, a Czech *hospoda* regular will drink the year's average for a family of six. Pub regulars do not wonder why the Czech national anthem is a song that translates as "Where Is My Home?"

Several widely held Czech superstitions are connected with drinking beer. One says that you should never pour a different kind of beer in a mug holding the remnants of another brew. Bad luck is sure to follow. Some believe that the toast—usually *"Na zdraví!"* ("To your health!")—is negated if anyone fails to clink his or her mug with any of the others at your table and then fails to slam the mug on the table before taking the first chug. With beer such a cultural icon, it should come as no surprise that beer bellies, far from scorned or hidden, are actually a point of pride in many pubs. One popular Czech saying has it that "beer makes beautiful bodies" (well, it certainly makes for bigger ones). For more Czech beer lore, see chapter 2, p. 31.

International Pubs

Jáma (The Hollow) ★   This place has been popular for several post-revolutionary years and draws an agreeable mix of Czech professionals as well as expats and visitors. It feels a lot like an American college pub; Czech and international food is served and a welcoming selection of the best Czech regional and microbrews on tap. There are excellent burgers, especially on Tuesdays, Jáma's official "burger day." Open daily from 11am to midnight. V Jámě 7, Prague 1. ✆ **224-222-383.** www.jamapub.cz. Metro: Můstek.

James Joyce ★★   This comfy pub evokes the authentic warmth of an old country inn on a rainy Irish night. The farmhouse atmosphere is loaded with old-fashioned sewing-machine tables, velvet drapes, and a roaring fireplace. There's plenty of boisterous laughter and Guinness on tap. Excellent pub meals are served daily from 11am to 8pm. The hot chicken wings are the best in Prague. Open Sunday to Thursday from 11am to 1am and Friday and Saturday from 11am to 2am. U Obecního dvora 4, Prague 1. ✆ **224-818-851.** www.jamesjoyceprague.cz. Metro: Staroměstská.

Rocky O'Reilly's Rocky's is one of the most popular of several Irish-themed bars around town, drawing in loads of British and Irish tourists on a Prague binge weekend, as well as some locals who enjoy the relaxed atmosphere and mix of Irish, English, and American food like burgers, salads, and sandwiches. Open daily from 10am to 2am. Štěpánská 32, Prague 1. ℰ **222-231-060.** www.rockyoreillys.cz. Metro: Můstek.

Tlustá Koala The "Fat Koala" is a convivial pub that looks as if it might have stepped right out of the British Midlands. It's a great spot for an after-cinema beer or light meal if you've just seen something at the nearby Slovanský dům multiplex. Serves the Staropramen family of beers, which includes Stella Artois and Hoegaarden. There's a stand-up pub in the front room and lots of tables in the back. Open daily from noon to 2am. Senovážná 8, Prague 1. ℰ **222-245-401.** www.tlustakoala.cz. Metro: Náměstí Republiky.

U Malého Glena Guinness is served on tap in this small Malá Strana haunt by the expat American called "Little Glen," who also owns the chain of Bohemia Bagel restaurants around town. This place has developed a firm clientele, with regular jazz nights performed in the microscopic-sized cellar. Sunday nights are open-jam nights; the lineup varies according to who feels like coming out that night, but can include some of the best players in town. Decent food—soups, salads, and burgers—are served until 1am. Open daily from 7:30pm to 3am. Karmelitská 23, Prague 1. ℰ **257-531-717.** www.malyglen.cz. Metro: Malostranská.

Late-Night Bites

Getting something to eat after normal restaurant hours is not that easy in Prague. Kitchen staffs seem to like to shut down early, especially on slow nights, meaning that at most places if you haven't put in a food order by 10pm, you might as well wait until breakfast. Most of the places mentioned above, including U Malého Glena and Rocky O'Reilly's, will serve food until at least midnight. **Radost FX** (p. 89) in Vinohrady is the top late-dining choice, offering its vegetarian dishes, cocktails, and coffee drinks until at least 3am. If you get stuck, you'll find a bunch of late-night fast-food windows selling gyros, pizzas, and snacks throughout the night at the Národní třída tram stop next to Tesco in Nové Město.

THE BAR SCENE

Czechs still largely prefer the more intimate atmosphere of a pub to the colder, more business-like mood of a typical bar, but nevertheless bars of all sorts, including honky-tonks, dives, and cocktail bars, continue to open up all over town. Some of the flashiest cocktail bars are located in Staré Město, near the Old Town Square.

Bugsy's This is similar to Tretter's New York Bar (see below) in that the bartenders are some of the best in town. If there's a difference, it's that this place feels quieter and less status conscious. Come for the great drinks and the chance to actually have a conversation. Open daily 7pm to 2am. Pařížská 10, Prague 1. ℰ **840-284-797.** www.bugsys bar.com. Metro: Staroměstská.

Chapeau Rouge Hidden on a small Old Town back street, this loud and lively expat favorite has bars on several stories and a reckless, no-holds-barred vibe that draws huge crowds until well into the early morning hours. Also books live bands. Not for the fainthearted. Open daily 11am to 3am. Jakubská 2, Prague 1. ℰ **222-316-328.** www. chapeaurouge.cz. Metro: Náměstí Republiky.

Fraktal ★   This expat-friendly neighborhood joint is a good spot to seek out if you're traveling alone and want to pick up some new friends. Pull up a chair at the bar and order a Pilsner, or sit down at a table in the backroom to have one of the better burgers in Prague or a surprisingly good steak. In nice weather you can sit out on the terrace, but be sure to arrive early to snag one of the few coveted tables. Open daily 11am to midnight. Šmeralová 1, Letná, Prague 7. ℂ **777-794-094.** www.fraktalbar.cz. Metro: Hradčanská plus tram 1, 8, 25, or 26 two stops to Letenské nám.

Hapu ★★   This is a cocktail bar with a difference. There's no flash and no attitude at this strictly neighborhood joint in Žižkov. The prices are lower here than at other cocktail places like Tretter's or Bugsy's, but the drinks are every bit as well made. Good for singles, since you can pull up a chair at the bar and chat up a cute barmaid or barman, whatever the case may be. Open daily 11am to 2am. Orlická 8, Žižkov, Prague 3. ℂ **222-720-158.** Metro: Flora.

Iron Curtain (Propaganda Club) ★   This fun, English-friendly pub and club in the center of the Old Town occupies a huge Gothic cellar festooned with all kinds of Communist era bric-a-brac (posters of Lenin and the like). There's live music some nights and always a good crowd on hand. Also serves decent bar food. Open daily 6pm to 4am. Michalska 12, Prague 1. ℂ **242-480-728.** www.propagandapub.cz. Metro: Mustek.

Tretter's New York Bar ★   This popular cocktail bar, situated a couple of blocks from Old Town Square, is modeled loosely on a New York–style club circa 1930. The draws here are the very good cocktails and the flashy new-money crowd. Come early to get a table or try phoning to reserve in advance. On busy nights the guys who control the velvet rope outside enforce a dress code; play it safe and dress up a bit. Open daily 7pm to 2am. V kolkovně 3, Prague 1. ℂ **224-811-165.** www.tretters.cz. Metro: Staroměstská.

Gay & Lesbian Clubs

Prague's gay and lesbian community is small but growing, as are the number of choices of nightclubs and entertainment. See "LGBT Travelers" in Fast Facts, chapter 13, for more information, or www.prague.gayguide.net.

The residential district of Vinohrady (Prague 2) has evolved into Prague's de facto gay district. While it's certainly no match for San Francisco's Castro or New York's West Village, the area does sport a number of clubs, cafes, and discos that are gay or gay-friendly.

Klub Termix   This small basement in Vinohrady is one of the city's most popular gay discos and can get impossibly crowded on weekend evenings. Enter by ringing the buzzer and the doorman will let you in, but be sure to get there early in order to ensure entry. Open Monday to Saturday 8pm to 5am. Třebízského 4a, Prague 2. ℂ **222-710-462.** www.club-termix.cz. Metro: Muzeum, then tram 11 two stops.

Saints Bar ★★   This relaxed bar on a quiet Vinohrady street is the place to go if big, loud discos are not your thing and you're more interested in kicking back and enjoying some friendly conversation. Open daily from 7pm to 4am. Polská 32, Prague 2. ℂ **222-250-326.** Metro: Jiřího z Poděbrad.

Valentino ★   Another popular Vinohrady dance club that anchors a number of gay-friendly businesses, including the adjacent Celebrity Café, in the former Radio Palác building on Vinohradská Street. This cavernous club spreads out on several floors, and the giant dance room can accommodate a big crowd. The clientele is mixed, including lots of straight people who come for the music and the vibe. Open daily from 5pm to 4am. Music starts around 11pm. Vinohradská 40, Prague 2. ⓒ **222-520-630.** www.club-valentino.cz. Metro: Muzeum, then tram 11 two stops.

MOVIE THEATERS

The Czech Republic has an active domestic film industry and Czechs are avid moviegoers. The good news for visitors is that most Czech cinemas don't usually dub foreign films, meaning that American and English films are nearly always shown in their original language. The only exceptions generally are children's movies, where the kids are not expected to be able to read the subtitles.

The best places for first-run Hollywood blockbusters and the like are the multiplex cinemas at shopping centers around town. The best of these is arguably the Palace Cinemas complex at centrally located **Slovanský dům** ★, Na Příkopě 9/11, Prague 1 (ⓒ **840-200-240;** www.cinemacity.cz), where around a dozen screens regularly show the best releases from Hollywood just as those movies are being released in the United States. Other good multiplexes with good transport connections to the center include **Palác Flóra,** Vinohradská 151, Prague 3 (ⓒ **255-741-002;** www.cinema city.cz), near the Flora metro station, which has around 10 screens plus the city's only **IMAX** cinema, and the Palace Cinemas multiplex at the **Nový Smíchov shopping center,** Plzeňská 8, Prague 5 (ⓒ **840-200-240;** www.cinemacity.cz), near the Anděl metro station.

Czech films are more problematic since they're usually screened exclusively in Czech, though some cinemas, including Slovanský dům (see above), occasionally show Czech films with English subtitles. **Kino Světozor** ★★ at Vodičkova 41, Prague 1 (ⓒ **224-946-824;** www.kinosvetozor.cz), across from the Lucerna Shopping Passage, is a classic art-house cinema showing a wide range of independent films from around the world, as well as Czech films subtitled in English. Another cinema gem, **Kino Aero** ★, at Biskupcová 31, Prague 3, in Žižkov (ⓒ **271-771-349;** www. kinoaero.cz), shows a similar collection of golden oldies, indies, and Czech movies, usually with English subtitles.

Prague is also home to a number of very interesting film festivals, including one of the largest urban international film festivals of its kind, **Febiofest** (www.febiofest. cz), in March, and the ever-popular **One World** human rights film festival (www. jedensvet.cz) in March or April, which usually brings dozens of blockbuster documentaries to town. Most years in spring see the arrival of the **Days of European Film** festival (www.eurofilmfest.cz), bringing the continent's best movies from the previous year to the city for a 2-week run. See the festival websites for dates and details.

DAY TRIPS FROM PRAGUE

P rague is undeniably a fascinating city and one could easily spend a week or more taking in the various museums, attractions, and exhibitions. But at some point, you're going to start tiring of the crowds and the cobblestones and want something a little more slow-paced and laid-back. That's when it helps to "Get out of Dodge," if only for the day.

The Czech capital is blessed with several attractive excursion possibilities. High on the list would be a trip to one of the many majestic castles in the area, like **Karlštejn, Český Šternberk,** the hunting lodge of **Konopiště,** or the interior of **Křivoklát.** The castle at **Orlík,** which overlooks a wide expanse of the Vltava River, may be the nicest of them all.

In addition to castles, there are several outings for history buffs, especially to sites oriented around the events of World War II. You can visit the remains of the village of **Lidice,** which was leveled by the Nazis in a reprisal attack during World War II. A little farther on, **Terezín** (*Theresienstadt* in German) served as a "model" Jewish ghetto and concentration camp that was used by the Nazis to dupe the world that its anti-Jewish policy was "humane."

Also worth exploring is the quirky medieval mining town of **Kutná Hora** and especially the macabre "Bone Church" a mile away in Sedlec.

It's always possible to pair a sightseeing trip with an activity like hiking or cycling. Golfers might consider combining a trip to Karlštejn Castle with 9 (or even 18) holes at the nearby championship golf course. If you enjoy wine tasting and don't have time to visit Moravia, by all means head to nearby **Mělník,** where you can taste very good wines at the Lobkowicz Château.

TIPS FOR DAY-TRIPPING

Choosing a destination depends not only on your interests, but also on how much time and energy you've got to spend. While all the destinations described below can be visited in an out-and-back from Prague within a day, not all the trips are equal in terms of the time and preparation needed to get there. That's especially true if you're relying on buses and trains.

If you've only got part of a day, keep it realistic and choose a day trip that's on a direct bus or train line from the city, with frequent out and back departures. That list would include **Karlštejn,** which is just 45 minutes away by frequent train, **Kutná Hora,** which is a little more than an hour by train or bus each way, and **Mělník,** about 40 minutes away by hourly bus (complete transport information for each destination is included below).

If you can afford to blow off the whole day (or even better have a couple of days to kick around), that allows for more possibilities. From the list below, **Český Šternberk, Konopiště, Křivoklát,** and **Orlík** are likely to pose the greatest challenges, not so much because they are far away (they're not), but the paucity of decent bus and train connections will require more advance planning and time spent waiting around.

Several of the destinations are covered by local tour companies (see "Organized Day Tours," below), and while using a tour bus can take some of the adventure out of the trip, it will certainly help save time on transport.

Getting There

BY CAR   Renting a car has the compelling advantage of taking inconvenient train and bus schedules out of the equation and allowing you to pack several destinations into a single day of sightseeing. Like the best car commercials on TV, you can hit the open road (and there are some very pretty country roads to hit) and roam to your heart's content.

That's the positive side, but there are some negatives to consider as well. Renting a car is expensive. In addition to the basic rental costs and insurance, the price of gasoline has crept up to a shocking 35Kč a liter. Visiting any of the destinations below from Prague is likely to eat up 20 liters or more of fuel for a mid-size car. Gas stations are plentiful, though, and you won't have any problem finding a place to tank up.

There's also the hassle factor. Once you're out of Prague, the traffic eases back to normal, but getting in and out of the city, particularly during rush hour, can easily eat up an hour of time all on its own. Czech drivers are notoriously reckless to boot, and the quality of the roads leaves a lot to be desired. At night, stick to the major highways, since smaller roads are likely to be poorly lit and signposted. And don't leave home base without a good auto atlas or GPS navigation system. Rental companies should be able to provide both. Even so, rest assured that at some point, you're going to get lost. For details on car travel and rentals, see chapter 13.

If you experience car trouble on the road, major highways have emergency telephones from which you can call for assistance. There's also the **ÚAMK,** a 24-hour motor assistance club that provides service for a fee. They drive bright-yellow pickups and can be summoned on main highways by using the SOS emergency phones located at the side of the road every kilometer or so. If you are not near one of these phones or are on a road that doesn't have them, you can contact ÚAMK at ✆ **1230.** This is a toll-free call.

BY TRAIN   Trains have the dual advantage of feeling adventurous while at the same time following a reliable timetable. Train travel is also a pretty good deal. A trip of 50km (31 miles) costs just 75Kč in second class and around 100Kč in first class. First class is not usually available, or needed, on shorter trips.

The only problem with train travel is that not all the destinations below are accessible by train and travel times are infrequent on the more lightly traveled routes. The state-run **České dráhy** (Czech Rail; ✆ **840-112-113**) operates an online timetable at www.cd.cz. You can also use the timetable at www.jizdnirady.idnes.cz for both trains and buses (see the box "Finding Train & Bus Connections Online," below).

Most of the trips below depart from the main station, **Hlavní nádraží (Main Station),** Wilsonova 80, Prague 1, at the metro stop of the same name on metro line C

Prague & Environs

(red) in the center, though you might also be able to pick up your train at **Nádraží Holešovice,** Vrbenského ulice, Prague 7, above the Nádraží Holešovice metro stop on line C (red). Some trains for Karlštejn and Beroun (for onward travel to Křivoklát) leave from **Smíchovské nádraží,** Nádražní ulice, Prague 5, on metro line B (yellow).

BY BUS   Buses have the advantage of seemingly going everywhere. Just about every one of the day-trip destinations listed below, except Karlštejn, can be reached by bus. Buses, like trains, are also reliable and cheap. Fares for even the farthest day trips will rarely creep above 100Kč each way.

The downside to traveling by bus is simply figuring out the Czech bus system, which is made up of a confusing mix of private and semi-private operators. And then there are those arcane timetables posted at the bus stops, with confusing lists of departure times, stops, asterisks, and exceptions. I take the bus all the time, but rest assured that I (and no one else for that matter) can make heads or tales out of the timetables either.

Most buses depart from Prague's main bus station, **Florenc,** Křižíkova 5, Prague 8 (© **900-144-444** for bus information; www.florenc.cz), which is above the Florenc metro stop on line C (red). The bus station has done a good job in recent years in improving information, and there's now a big electronic board that notes

10

DAY TRIPS FROM PRAGUE | Tips for Day-Tripping

You'll find a highly useful timetable showing both train and bus connections, as well as times, prices and departure stations, at **www.jizdnirady.idnes.cz** (note that you have to input city and destination names using their Czech spellings; such as "Praha" for Prague).

Czech Rail has its own confusing website in English, German, and Czech at **www.cd.cz**, also showing departure times and stations as well as allowing you to reserve seats and book tickets online.

impending departures. The central information desk here is also helpful, but be sure to get travel times both for the outward and return journeys.

Note that not all buses use the Florenc bus station. You might go to Florenc for information just to be told that your bus leaves from another area, usually a smaller stop above an outlying metro station. In the destinations below, I note cases where buses use other stations. In these cases, buy tickets directly from the driver.

Organized Day Tours

Taking a day tour can be a lifesaver if you're pressed for time or don't have the patience for sorting out train and bus schedules. They also usually provide guided commentary in English (or at least recorded information through headphones), which is useful for sorting out the history (and especially recommended for sites like Terezín, where knowing the history is essential). The downside, of course, is that being crowded onto a tour bus with 20 or 30 other people can dilute your impressions and take away from some of the impact of a sight. Also, many of the better day trips I list here are not covered in the standard tours.

Below is a list of the leading tour companies. The tours usually have a central meeting point, though some will pick you up at your hotel. Many tours also include lunch, but be sure to inquire when you book.

○ **Martin Tour,** Štěpánská 61, Prague 1 (℗ **224-212-473;** www.martintour.cz), offers highly competent tours to Karlštejn, Konopiště, Terezín, and Kutná Hora. The Karlštejn tour takes around 5 hours and is expedient because you don't wait around for the next general tour at the castle. A traditional Czech lunch at a nearby restaurant is included. That tour with lunch costs 950Kč.

○ **Wittmann Tours,** Novotného lávka 5, Prague 1 (℗ **222-252-472;** www.wittmann-tours.com), specializes in Jewish legacy trips and offers a guided bus tour to the Terezín camp that costs 1,250Kč for adults, 1,100Kč for students, free for children 9 and under. The bus leaves from Prague daily at 10am from May to October. March 15 through April, and November through December, the tour is available on Tuesday, Thursday, Saturday, and Sunday only. They also offer combined trips to Terezín and Lidice.

○ **Prague Sightseeing Tours,** Klimentská 52, Prague 1 (℗ **222-314-655;** www.pstours.cz), promises no headphones on their trips, meaning they provide real guides in each of the languages, and the advantage of hotel pickup and drop-off. It offers the usual range of day trips, including to Karlštejn, Terezín, and Kutná Hora, among other destinations.

KARLŠTEJN CASTLE ★★

29km (18 miles) SW of Prague

Karlštejn Castle is the go-to day trip for people with only a few hours to spend. The train whisks you to Karlštejn in under an hour. Though the castle is a bit of a trek uphill from the train station, if you opt out of a castle tour, you can be there and back in less than 4 hours. And it's a fascinating place in its own right. Charles IV built this medieval castle from 1348 to 1357 to safeguard the crown jewels of the Holy Roman Empire. Although the castle had been changed over the years, with such additions as late Gothic staircases and bridges, renovators have removed these additions, restoring the castle to its original medieval state.

As you approach, little can prepare you for your first view: a spectacular Disney-like castle perched on a hill, surrounded by lush forests and vineyards. In its early days, the king's jewels housed within enhanced the castle's importance and reputation. Vandalism having forced several of its finest rooms to close, these days the castle is most spectacular from the outside. Unfortunately, many of the more interesting restored rooms are kept off-limits and open only for special guests.

Essentials

GETTING THERE   Trains leave regularly from either Prague's Main Station (at the Hlavní nádraží metro stop on line C) or from Smíchovské nádraží, metro line B, and take about 40 minutes to reach Karlštejn. The one-way, second-class fare is 50Kč. It's a short, relaxing trip along the Berounka River. On the way, you pass through Řevnice, Martina Navrátilová's birthplace. Keep your eyes open for your first glimpse of the majestic castle. Once you arrive at Karlštejn train station, it's a 20- to 30-minute hike up the road to the castle. While you're at the station, mark down the return times for trains to Prague to better plan your trip back.

A Walk in The Woods from Beroun to Karlštejn ★

Castles in the Czech Republic, it seems, are always surrounded by lovely woods that offer a perfect chance to combine a cultural outing with a little exercise and fresh air. If you've got a full day to spend, why not pair a visit to Karlštejn Castle with a beautiful 15km (10-mile) hike through the forest? The trail passes through the tiny village of **Svatý Jan pod Skalou** (St. John under the Cliff), before taking you along a beautiful little waterfall. To start, take the train from Hlavní nádraží or Smíchovské nádraží to the town of Beroun. Exit Beroun station, walk through a small parking lot, and keep your eyes peeled for a red-marked trail running to the right. The first 10 or 15 minutes of the hike are not that encouraging, passing through a semi-industrialized area, but don't despair. The trail quickly plunges into deep and quiet wood. The hike is of moderate difficulty, with one pretty good uphill climb coming out of Svatý Jan. Be sure to wear good walking shoes (sneakers are fine), and bring along a hiking map and water. After around 3 hours, you'll emerge at the top of Karlštejn village, not far from the restaurant **Pod Dračí skalou** (see p. 196). If you've gotten an early start, you can have a late lunch here before moving on to see the castle. After the castle, saunter downhill through Karlštejn village to the train station to catch a late afternoon train back to Prague.

You can also **drive** along one of two routes, both of which take 30 minutes. Here's the more scenic one: Leave Prague from the southwest along Hwy. 4 in the direction of Strakonice and take the Karlštejn cutoff, following the signs (and traffic!). The second, much less scenic route follows the main highway leading out of Prague from the west as if you were going to Plzeň. About 20 minutes down the road is the well-marked cutoff for Karlštejn. (You can tell you have missed the cutoff if you get to the town of Beroun. If that happens, take any exit and head back the other way; the signs to Karlštejn are also marked heading toward Prague.)

By car, a trip to Karlštejn can easily be combined with a visit to Křivoklát (see below).

VISITOR INFORMATION The ticket/castle information booth (✆ **311-681-370**) can help you, as can any of the restaurants or stores. The castle website at www.hradkarlstejn.cz is easy to navigate and has lots of useful information on the castle's history as well as tours and opening hours. You can also book tour tickets online.

ORGANIZED TOURS All of the tour operators listed in "Organized Day Tours" above offer sightseeing trips to Karlštejn.

Exploring the Castle

Since Karlštejn's beauty lies more in its facade and environs than in the castle itself, the 20- to 30-minute walk up the hill is, along with the view, one of the main features that makes the trip spectacular. It's an excursion well worth making if you can't get farther out of Prague to see some of the other castles. Seeing hordes of visitors coming, locals have discovered the value of fixing up the facades of their homes and opening small businesses (even if they have gone a little overboard on the number of outlets selling crystal). Restaurants have improved tremendously. When you finally do reach the top, take some time to look out over the town and down the Well Tower.

To see the interior of the castle, you can choose from one of two tours. The 50-minute **Tour 1** will take you through the **Imperial Palace, Hall of Knights, Chapel of St. Nicholas, Royal Bedroom,** and **Audience Hall. Tour 2,** which lasts 70 minutes, offers a look at the **Holy Rood Chapel,** famous for the more than 2,000 precious and semiprecious inlaid gems adorning its walls; the **Chapel of St. Catherine,** Charles IV's own private oratory; the **Church of Our Lady;** and the **library.** Note that you need to make a reservation to visit the Holy Rood Chapel on Tour 2 (✆ **274-008-154;** fax 274-008-152; www.hradkarlstejn.cz). You can buy tickets and make reservations online.

> ### ✎ A Castle-Viewing Tip
>
> Karlštejn is probably best seen from a distance, so take time to browse in the stores, enjoy the fresh air, and sit out on one of the restaurant patios or down by the riverside. Buy a bottle of the locally grown Karlštejn wine, a vintage started by King Charles IV, and admire the view.

The shorter Tour 1 costs 270Kč adults, 180Kč students, 20Kč children 5 and under. Tour 2 with the Holy Rood Chapel costs 300Kč adults, 200Kč students, free for children 5 and under. The castle is open Tuesday to Sunday: May, June, and September 9am to noon and 12:30 to 5pm; July and August 9am to noon and 12:30 to 6pm; April and October 9am to noon and 1 to 4pm; November, December, and March 9am to noon and 1 to 3pm; closed January and February.

📷 A romantic GETAWAY

If the air and noise of Prague start to grate on your nerves, or if a quiet, romantic, overnight trip to a castle in the country sounds like the perfect getaway, head for the **Romantic Hotel Mlýn (Mill Hotel)** ★, 267 18 Karlštejn (www. hotelmlynkarlstejn.cz; © **311-744-411;** fax 311-744-444).

On the river's edge on the bank opposite the castle, the Mlýn is exactly what its name says—a mill. Converted into a hotel and recently reconstructed, this reasonably priced country inn takes you away from the hustle and bustle of traveling. Its 28 rooms are a little on the small side, but they're quaint and nicely decorated with rustic furniture. At the outdoor patio bar and very good restaurant, you can relax and enjoy the soothing sounds of the river. Service here is a cut above what it is at the other hotels in the area. If you are here for lunch or dinner when the outdoor grill has been fired up, take advantage of it. Use the hotel also as a base for bike and canoe trips along the river. The staff can help you with local tennis courts and reservations for a round of golf.

Rates average around 2,100Kč for a single and 2,600Kč for a double, though they fluctuate according to the season. Check the website for rates on the day you plan to travel. Credit cards are accepted. To get to the hotel, take the bridge across the river that leads to the train station and turn left at the first street. If you cross the rail tracks, you've gone too far.

Tee Time: Karlštejn's Championship Golf Course

Golfers may want to try their luck at the North American–designed **Prague Karlštejn Golf Club,** a course that hosted its first European PGA tour event 10 years ago. This challenging 27-hole, 10,523-yard course on the hill just across the river from the castle offers some pretty views. At the elevated tee on the second hole, you'll hit toward the castle. It's a breathtaking place to lose a ball. If you want a real challenge, see if you can match former Masters winner German Bernhard Langer's four-round total of 264 (24 under par).

Karlštejn is one of the few courses in the Czech Republic that really challenges a golfer's ability—narrow fairways, long roughs, and lightning-fast greens. Be prepared to walk uphill between holes. The course is open daily from 8am to sundown, and reservations for weekends should be made a couple of days in advance; call © **311-604-999** or go online to www.karlstejn-golf.cz. Be forewarned, however, it's not cheap, especially for visitors who may need to rent clubs and carts: Greens fees are 2,000Kč for 18 holes Monday to Friday (slight discount if you tee off before 11am), and 3,000Kč Saturday, Sunday, and holidays. Motorized cart rentals are 1,300Kč per 18 holes, while a pull cart is 200Kč per round. Club rental is 1,000Kč per round.

To get here by car from Prague, take Hwy. 116 south through the castle town of Karlštejn. Once you cross the river and a set of train tracks, stay on the road, which veers right and goes up a hill. You'll see the golf course on the left and an entrance soon after. If you've taken the train, you can walk to the course through town, but be warned that it's an uphill hike. Take a taxi, which should cost around 150Kč.

Where to Eat

Like any tourist town, Karlštejn is filled with fairly ordinary restaurants that are more interested in moving meals than in pleasing palates. The best advice is simply to cruise the main drag (there's only one street in town) and look for something that catches your eye.

Restaurace U Janů (℃ 311-681-210; www.ujanu.sweb.cz), at the top of the village, is always a good choice. The food is decent (though nothing to write home about). The draws here are a welcoming, shady terrace in the hot summer and a working fireplace on a cold day in winter. The venison specials make a nice change from the usual meat-and-dumpling meals. Main courses are up to 199Kč. It's open daily 9:30am to 10pm.

Farther uphill along the main road, away from town and beyond the castle, you'll find the rustic inn **Pod Dračí skalou** ★ (℃ 311-681-177; www.poddraciskalou. eu). This is a great spot for a traditional pub lunch, including lots of dishes featuring wild game like boar, pheasant, and venison. Main courses are 150Kč to 250Kč. The restaurant is open Monday to Saturday 11am to 11pm, Sunday 11am to 8pm.

KŘIVOKLÁT ★

43km (27 miles) W of Prague

Less crowded and much less touristy than its neighbor upstream at Karlštejn, Křivoklát is the perfect destination for a lazy afternoon of touring. A royal castle mentioned as early as the 11th century, Křivoklát is set in the tranquil Berounka River Valley. The fortress was rebuilt several times over the years but retains its Gothic style. The royal family was among Křivoklát's frequent visitors, and during the Hussite Uprising, King Sigmund of Luxembourg hid his jewels here. The area surrounding the fortress is protected by UNESCO as a biosphere preservation area.

Essentials

GETTING THERE Trains run regularly from Prague's Smíchov station to the town of Beroun, where you must change to go on to Křivoklát. The trip takes 1¾ hours; the one-way, second-class fare is 97Kč. This is one of the nicer train rides in the Czech Republic, even though you have to change trains in Beroun. The train winds its way along the Berounka through some wooded areas near Prague.

If you're **driving,** leave Prague on the E50 expressway, heading west toward Plzeň and exit at the Křivoklát cutoff. From there, follow Hwy. 116 as it snakes along the Berounka and turn left onto Hwy. 201, which eventually winds its way around to Křivoklát. The trip takes 45 minutes.

VISITOR INFORMATION There is a small tourist information office at Náměstí Svatopluka Čecha 82 (no phone), situated away from the castle just behind the Pension U Jelena, though English is spotty here and they don't have too much information. They can book rooms for around 200Kč per person a night and there's a computer on-hand to check e-mail. They are open May to September from Monday to Friday 9am to 5pm, and Saturday and Sunday 10am to 4pm. The castle's official website, www.krivoklat.cz, has a small section in English.

ORGANIZED TOURS At the time of writing, none of the major sightseeing tour operators were offering dedicated tours to Křivoklát.

Exploring the Castle

Often a castle tour fails to live up to expectations (Karlštejn comes to mind), but this is one of the best castle tours; it's almost a reverse of Karlštejn. Outside, Křivoklát pales in comparison to Karlštejn's beauty. But inside, Křivoklát blows its rival out of the water. Take time to study the intricate carvings at the altar in the **Royal Chapel.** They're not exactly angelic, as the angels are actually holding instruments of torture; Křivoklát was a prison for political criminals in the Middle Ages. The **Kings Hall,** a whopping 24m (79 ft.) long, is the second-longest secular hallway in the country after Prague's Vladislav Hall. In the **Knights Hall,** you'll find a collection of fabulous late Gothic art. And the **Furstenberg Picture Gallery** is one of the country's largest castle libraries, with some 53,000 volumes on its shelves. Take that, Karlštejn!

> ### 📎 A Sightseeing Tip
>
> Křivoklát is near Karlštejn, so consider visiting both in 1 day if you drive or take the train. The contrast between the bustling Karlštejn and the sleepy Křivoklát is startling.

Admission to tour the entire castle is 190Kč for adults and 130Kč for children. The castle is open to the public in March and November on Saturday and Sunday from 10am to 3pm. In October, it's open Tuesday to Sunday from 10am to 4pm. In April, May, June, and September, hours are Tuesday to Sunday from 9am to 4pm. In July and August, hours are daily from 9am to 6pm. The tour runs about an hour, and information in English is available.

Where to Stay & Eat

Since Křivoklát is less touristy than Karlštejn, there aren't many restaurants here. Of the few that do exist, **Pension U Jelena,** at the bottom of the hill as you approach the castle, is your best bet. With six rooms, the pension can be used as an overnight stop if you want to spend a leisurely weekend hiking and biking between Křivoklát and Karlštejn. The restaurant specializes in game and main courses run from around 70Kč to 300Kč; American Express, MasterCard, and Visa are accepted.

For reservations at the hotel (you won't need them for the restaurant), call ☎ **313-558-529** (fax 313-558-235; www.u-jelena.cz). Doubles cost 1,000Kč. If you don't want to stop here, you're better off eating down the road in Karlštejn or back in Prague.

KUTNÁ HORA ★

72km (45 miles) E of Prague

A medieval town that grew fantastically rich from the silver deposits beneath it, Kutná Hora is also a popular day trip from Prague. Small enough to be seen in a single day at a brisk pace, the town's ancient heart has decayed, which makes it hard to believe that this was once the second most important city in Bohemia. However, the town center is also mercifully free of the ugly, Communist-era buildings that plague many of the country's small towns. The historic center and Kutná Hora's main draw, **St. Barbara's Cathedral,** have been on the UNESCO list for more than 10 years. Also, the macabre **Bone Church (Kostnice) ★★** (see the box, "The Bone Church in Sedlec," below), in the nearby suburb of Sedlec (about 2km/1.2 miles from the center of Kutná Hora), is definitely worth a visit.

Essentials

GETTING THERE   The 50-minute **drive** from Prague is relatively easy. Take Vinohradská Street, which runs due east from behind the National Museum at the top of Wenceslas Square, straight to Kutná Hora. Once out of the city, the road turns into Hwy. 333.

If you don't have a car, then it's a toss up between the **bus** and the **train,** both of which cover the same ground in pretty much the same amount of time. Buses have the advantage of dropping you closer to Kutná Hora's town center and St. Barbara's, while Kutná Hora's main train station in Sedlec is more convenient to the Bone Church.

Buses normally depart from Prague's Florenc bus station (though some leave from a small bus stop at the Háje metro station at the end of line C). The trip takes about 1½ hours and costs 70Kč.

Trains leave from Prague's Hlavní nádraží station and arrive at Kutná Hora's main station in Sedlec in just over an hour for 97Kč. Once you arrive at the station, you can walk to the Bone Church in about 10 minutes or take a handy **shuttle bus** (© 733-551-011). The bus runs regularly from May through September to the Bone Church and then on to the town center. Tickets cost 35Kč each and are available from the driver.

VISITOR INFORMATION   The **Information Center** (**Informační Středisko;** © 327-512-378; www.kutnahora.info), on Palackého nám. 377, provides the most comprehensive information service in town. Check to see if anything special such as a recital or an exhibition is showing. The office is open daily 9am to 6pm (Apr–Sept); Monday to Friday from 9am to 6pm and Saturday and Sunday from 10am to 4pm (Oct–Mar). The town has also posted very useful signs just about everywhere to help visitors get where they're going.

ORGANIZED TOURS   After Karlštejn, Kutná Hora and the Bone Church are the second most-popular day trips from Prague. At press time, all the leading tour operators were offering out-and-back excursions, usually offering lunch.

Seeing the Sights

The main attraction is the enormous **St. Barbara's Cathedral (Chrám sv. Barbory)** ★★ at the southwestern edge of town. In 1380, Peter Parléř began construction of the cathedral. The task was so great that it took several more Gothic masters, including Matthias Rejsek and Benedikt Rejt, close to 200 years to complete the project. From the outside, the cathedral's soaring arches, dozens of spires, and intricate designs raise expectations that the interior will be just as impressive—and you won't be disappointed.

On entering (you have to enter from the side, not the front), you'll see several richly decorated frescoes full of symbols denoting the town's two main industries of mining and minting. The ceiling vaulting, with floral patterns and coats of arms, has made many a jaw drop. Admission is 50Kč for adults and 30Kč for children. The cathedral is open from May until the end of September from Tuesday to Sunday from 9am to 5:30pm, and Monday from 10am to 4pm. From October until the end of April, it's open Tuesday to Sunday from 10am to 4pm.

When you leave the cathedral, head down statue-lined **Barborská Street,** where you'll pass the early baroque **Jesuit College,** built in the late 17th century by Giovanni Domenico Orsi. Farther down the road is the **Hrádek,** a 15th-century

Kutná Hora

ATTRACTIONS ●
Czech Museum of Silver **3**
Italian Court (Vlašský Dvůr) **5**
Jesuit College **2**
St. Barbara's Cathedral (Chrám Sv. Barbory) **1**
St. James's Church (Kostel Sv. Jakuba) **6**

RESTAURANTS ◆
Organzza Café **7**
Pizza Navona **8**
U Kamenného Domu **4**
U Žlutého kola **9**

castle that now houses the **Czech Museum of Silver (Muzeum stříbra)** ★ (📞 **327-512-159**). If you take the tour of Hrádek, you'll actually tour one of the town's mine shafts. The tour begins in a small room filled with artifacts from the town's mining and minting industries. After a brief speech, it's time to don hard hats and work coats to tour the mine shaft. After a hike of about 270m (886 ft.), you'll descend into a narrow corridor of rock and dampness to spend about 15 minutes in the mines. Children like this part of the tour almost as much as they do the Bone Church. Admission is 120Kč for adults and 80Kč for children. The museum is open Tuesday to Sunday: April and October from 9am to 5pm; May, June, and September from 9am to 6pm; and July and August from 10am to 6pm. It's closed from November until the end of March.

Once you're back aboveground, go down the hill to **St. James's Church (Kostel sv. Jakuba)** and the **Italian Court (Vlašský Dvůr;** 📞 **327-512-873).** Even though the door is usually closed at St. James's, it's worth trying

Two Warnings

The Hrádek mine shaft can be a little claustrophobic (what mine isn't?). Never take your hard hat off (low, jagged ceilings can quickly bring about premature balding).

the bone church IN SEDLEC

A visit to Kutná Hora isn't complete without a trip to the **Bone Church** (signposted as *kostnice* in Czech) ★★ (© **728-125-488;** www.kostnice.cz). It's located about 2km (1.2 miles) down the road in Sedlec (within comfortable walking distance from the train station if you arrive by train). From the town center, walk about 25 minutes or take a taxi or shuttle bus.

From the outside, the kostnice looks like most other small churches. But from the moment you enter the front door, you know that this is no ordinary church—all the decorations are made from human bones. No kidding. František Rint, the church's interior decorator, created crosses of bone, columns of bone, chalices of bone, and even a coat of arms in bone for the Schwarzenberg family, which owned the church.

The obvious questions are: Where did the bones come from, and why were they used for decorations? The first question is easier to answer: The bones came from victims of the 14th-century plague and the 15th-century Hussite wars; both events killed thousands, who were buried in mass graves on the church's site. As the area developed, the bones were uncovered, and the local monks came up with this idea of how to put the bones to use.

Admission is 60Kč for adults and 40Kč for children. From April to September, the Bone Church is open daily from 8am to 6pm; October 9am to noon and 1 to 5pm; November to March 9am to noon and 1 to 4pm.

to open; perhaps you'll be able to glimpse the baroque paintings on the walls. More likely, though, you'll have to admire the church from the outside and then head on to the Italian Court.

Constructed in 1300 as a royal mint (what better way for a town to become rich than to print money?), the Italian Court derives its name from its original occupants, who were brought in from Florence to mint coins. The building houses a museum of coins made here between the 14th and 18th centuries, including the Czech groschen, the currency of choice in the Middle Ages. Another reason to take the tour is to see the ornate chapels, impressive in their details. There's also a separate, rather ghoulish exhibition in the basement called **"Unveiling the Mysterious Face of Kutná Hora"** that focuses on hideous crimes and instruments of torture. Admission to the Italian Court, including the tour, is 100Kč adults and 60Kč for children. It's open daily April to September from 9am to 6pm; October and March from 10am to 5pm; and November to February from 10am to 4pm. The exhibition has the same opening hours and costs 50Kč for adults and 35Kč for students.

Where to Eat

Surprisingly for the number of visitors it attracts, Kutná Hora has very few good restaurants. Still, you'll likely be hungry after a day of traveling and walking around, so here below are some of the best of an admittedly mediocre bunch.

You'll find a lovely garden and above-average Czech food at **U Žlutého Kola** (© **327-512-749**), Havlíčkovo nám. 16 (just off the main square). Main courses like goulash or pork tenderloin cooked with bacon run from 90Kč to 180Kč; no credit cards are accepted. It's open daily from 10:30am to 11pm. They run special grill nights in summer on Fridays and Saturdays after 7pm.

U Kamenného Domu (☎ **327-514-426**), Lierova 147 (2 blocks west of Palackého nám.), is popular with locals and serves hearty Czech specialties at bargain prices. The best bet here is the Czech staple meal of roasted pork, potato dumplings, and cabbage (109Kč), which will fill you up without the heavy cream sauce that seems to come on a lot of the other dishes. Main courses cost 69Kč to 180Kč. Credit cards are not accepted. The restaurant is open daily from 11am to 10pm.

Pizza Navona (☎ **327-512-588**), Palackého nám. 90, has crisp, thin-crust pizzas that could do with just a little more flavor, but it's a relatively quick and cheap option on the main square. No credit cards accepted. The restaurant is open daily from 9am to 10pm.

Organzza Café (☎ **777-635-565**), Palackého nám. 93, also on the main square, has great coffee drinks and a welcoming terrace. There are a few toasted sandwiches on the menu for a light lunch and ice cream. No credit cards are accepted. The cafe is open daily from 9am to 10pm.

KONOPIŠTĚ ★

48km (30 miles) S of Prague

A 17th-century castle-turned-hunting-lodge built by the Habsburgs, Konopiště was the Club Med of its time. Here, the nobility relaxed amid the well-stocked hunting grounds surrounding the castle. In 1887, the castle became the property of Habsburg heir to the throne, Archduke Franz Ferdinand, who was particularly enamored of hunting until that fateful day in Sarajevo when he and his wife, Sophie, became the prey. It was Franz Ferdinand's assassination in 1914, after all, that set off the Europewide conflagration of World War I.

If you're driving, you can see both Konopiště and Český Šternberk in 1 day (see directions on p. 203).

Essentials

GETTING THERE   If you're **driving,** leave Prague on the D1 expressway heading south and exit at the Benešov cutoff. From there, turn right at the signs for Konopiště. *Watch out:* The turn sneaks up on you. The trip takes 45 minutes in average traffic. Note that the parking lot just outside the castle is your best bet, at 50Kč per car. There aren't any closer lots, and police are vigilant about ticketing or booting cars parked at the side of the road. The minimum fine is 1,000Kč.

If you don't have a car, the bus is the next-best option. Several **buses** run daily from a small commuter bus station at the **Roztyly** metro stop on metro line C (red) and let you off not far from the castle (tell the driver where you want to go), or go to nearby Benešov, where you catch another bus or hike the 5km/3 miles to Konopiště. Purchase tickets directly from the driver at the Roztyly bus stop. The 1-hour trip costs around 60Kč.

It's a little trickier to get here by **train** since the closest station is in nearby Benešov. The trip takes 50 minutes and costs 68Kč for a one-way, second-class fare. From Benešov, you'll have to catch a local bus or hike the 5km/3 miles to the castle.

Organized Tours   **Martin Tour** (see "Organized Day Tours," above) offers an out-and-back to Konopiště in summer (May–Sept) on Tuesdays and Thursdays. The trip costs around 1,000Kč per person and includes a beer tasting at the nearby Velké Popovice brewery.

Exploring the Castle & Hunting Grounds

Since hunting on the grounds is no longer an option, Tour 1 at Konopiště will have to suffice. You'll know what I mean as soon as you begin the tour: Hundreds of antlers, bears, wild boars, and birds of prey practically jump off the walls, catching unsuspecting sweaters and dazzling children. The main hall is a testament to the archduke, who reportedly bagged tens of thousands of animals—only an estimated 1% of his total hunting collection is on display, and it still ranks as one of Europe's largest collections. Tour 1 also takes you through the castle's parlors, which have been restored with great attention to detail. Note the handcrafted wooden Italian cabinets with wonderfully detailed inlays and the collection of Meissen porcelain. Tour 1, lasting about 50 minutes, costs 210Kč for adults and 130Kč for children, and includes an English-speaking guide.

Tour 2 (for which you must buy tickets separately) is a little longer at 55 minutes and takes you through the weapons room, the chapel, and the party room, where only men were allowed. This tour is also 210Kč for adults and 130Kč for children, including a guide.

Tour 3 takes you through Ferdinand's private rooms. It lasts only about 10 minutes longer than the other tours and costs 310Kč for adults and 210Kč for children. While the third tour is interesting, unless you're a die-hard castle fan, it's not worth the money.

After exploring the castle's interior, wander around the manicured gardens where quails, pheasants, and peacocks roam freely. Children enjoy the moat, home to two bears who wander in circles for hours at a time. Down below the castle is a large pond where some people go swimming, though the water quality is questionable; I'd advise against it. Several large, open areas beg for a blanket, some sandwiches, and a nice bottle of red Frankovka wine. Picnicking is allowed, but stock up before coming since there's no place to get groceries near the castle.

The castle is open in April from Tuesday to Friday from 9am to noon and 1 to 3pm, Saturday and Sunday 9am to noon and 1 to 4pm; May to August Tuesday to Sunday from 9am to noon and 1 to 5pm; September Tuesday to Friday from 9am to noon and 1 to 4pm, Saturday and Sunday 9am to 5pm; October Tuesday to Friday from 9am to noon and 1 to 3pm, Saturday and Sunday 9am to 4pm; and November Saturday and Sunday from 9am to noon and 1 to 3pm. The castle grounds are open 24 hours year-round. For more information, visit www.zamek-konopiste.cz or call ℂ **317-721-366.**

Where to Stay & Eat

Connections are not that great to Prague and if you have to stay the night, there's a decent motel just a short walk through the woods from the castle. The **Amber Hotel Konopiště** (www.amberhotels.cz; ℂ **739-246-726,** fax 317-722-053) resembles a mountain motor lodge. Rooms are on the small size, but cute with rustic decor and well outfitted. The hotel has a small restaurant inside and a more comfortable, traditional grill restaurant, the **Stodola,** out front. Doubles run 1,600Kč a night. The Stodola restaurant is open daily from 8am to 11pm and accepts American Express, Diners Club, MasterCard, and Visa.

On the castle grounds, the handsome **Stará Myslivna** restaurant ★★ (ℂ **317-700-280;** www.staramyslivna.com) has recently undergone a thorough face-lift and is by far the nicest place to eat within shouting distance. Not surprisingly, given the archduke's proclivities, the menu focuses on game, with several variations of pheasant, venison, and other forest animals, usually served in traditional Czech style with a sauce and dumplings. When the sun is out, sit outside on the terrace; in winter, there's usually a roaring fire in the fireplace. Main courses run from 140Kč to 240Kč; major credit cards are accepted. Open daily 10am to 10pm.

ČESKÝ ŠTERNBERK

48km (30 miles) SE of Prague

About 16km (10 miles) east of Benešov lies the menacing **Český Šternberk** castle, once one of Bohemia's most powerful fortifications. The structure was built in the Gothic style in the first half of the 13th century, during the reign of Wenceslas I. The Habsburgs put in some baroque additions and improved its defenses, leaving few Gothic elements in their wake. The setting feels relatively remote, but the castle's perch on the banks of the Sázava River means you can combine a visit here will a little aquatic fun like kayaking and canoeing.

Essentials

GETTING THERE If you're **driving,** leave Prague on the D1 expressway heading south and exit at the Český Šternberk cutoff. From there, follow Hwy. 111. It's a 45-minute drive. From Konopiště, take Hwy. 112 to Hwy. 111. It's about a 25-minute drive. There's paid parking (40Kč per car) at the base of the castle.

A few **buses** run daily to and from Český Šternberk, but not from Prague's main Florenc station. Instead, you must take metro line C (red) south to the Roztyly stop. You can buy tickets, costing around 70Kč each way, from the bus driver. Depending on the route, the trip takes anywhere from 50 to 90 minutes.

Once in Český Šternberk, the **Samba** tourist agency (℃ **604-904-737;** www. pujcovna-lodi.cz), situated below the castle adjacent to the parking lot, rents kayaks, canoes and even mountain bikes. A full day out-and-back canoe trip from Český Šternberk to the town of Sázava (22km/14 miles) costs 400Kč for a two-person canoe and 500Kč for a three- to four-person boat. You can also rent canoes by the hour (50Kč/person) for just puttering around the river. They are open daily from May through September from 9:30am to 10pm.

ORGANIZED TOURS At the time of writing, none of the major sightseeing tour operators were running regular, dedicated tours to Český Šternberk, though **Prague Sightseeing Tours** does offer Český Šternberk in winter on days that Karlštejn Castle is closed. See "Organized Day Tours," above, for contact details.

Seeing the Fortress

This impressive fortress **castle** stands atop a hill, rising above the Sázava River. The 1-hour tour of Český Šternberk is worth taking. The enormous main hall and several smaller salons, with fine baroque detailing, elaborate chandeliers, and period art, are testaments to the wealth of the Šternberk family. After the tour, enjoy the grounds and relax among the trees and babbling streams that surround the fortress before heading out.

Admission to the castle is 170Kč for adults and 110Kč for children, including a guided tour in English. The fortress is open Tuesday to Sunday: June to August from 9am to 6pm, and May and September from 9am to 5pm. In April and October, it's open only on Saturday and Sunday from 9am to 5pm. The rest of the year, it's closed. For information, call ℃ **317-855-101** or go to www.hradceskysternberk.cz.

Where to Eat

Just below the castle near the parking lot, **Restaurace pod Hradem** (✆ 605-572-200) serves standard meat-and-potatoes meals at prices ranging from 60Kč to 130Kč per main course; no credit cards are accepted. They also serve pretty good Russian-style *pelmene* (steamed dumpling stuffed with meat) and traditional Czech fruit dumplings. There's a restful garden out back.

MĚLNÍK

32km (20 miles) N of Prague

Bohemia isn't known as a winemaking region—this is beer country. Except, that is, for the town of Mělník, where the Vltava and Labe (Elbe) rivers meet. While it's not quite the Loire Valley, Mělník has a decidedly French bent, as the vineyards are stocked with vines that originated in the Burgundy region.

Princess Ludmila began the tradition centuries before Bohemia passed through the hands of the Romans and eventually King Charles IV. The center of Mělník winemaking is the **Renaissance Lobkowicz Château,** owned since 1739 by the family of the same name (except for a 40-year Communist-imposed interruption). The confluence of the rivers provides a stunning backdrop to the château, where another French pastime—sitting on a terrace with a glass of Ludmila, Mělník's finest, as the afternoon sun slowly fades—can be an art.

If you get a chance to visit in mid-September, check out the harvest festival, **Mělnické Vinobraní** (www.melnicke-vinobrani.cz), for the latest vintages. Even if wine isn't your cup of, well, wine, Mělník's historic center is worth a look, with its Gothic church of St. Peter and St. Paul and its tower that provides a beautiful panorama of the area.

Essentials

GETTING THERE   If you're **driving** from the north end of Prague, follow Hwy. 9, which leads straight into Mělník. The trip takes 30 minutes.

Buses leave for Mělník from above the Nádraží Holešovice metro station in Prague every hour or so. The trip takes about 40 minutes and costs 46Kč.

It's also possible if you're lucky to take a **boat** to Mělník down the Vltava River. The **Pražská paroplavební** company runs all-day boat trips in summer (usually one Sun a month) from the company's dock on the Vltava at Rašínovo nábřeží, Prague 1, just in front of the Dancing Building (see chapter 6, p. 113). This romantic and scenic tour takes about 6 hours (one-way); a round-trip ticket costs 490Kč adults, 250Kč students. To find out more, write an e-mail to pps@paroplavba.cz or call ✆ **224-931-013.**

VISITOR INFORMATION   The information center is at Náměstí Míru 11 (✆ **315-627-503;** www.melnik.cz), and is open from May to September daily 9am to 5pm, and October to April Monday to Friday 9am to 5pm.

ORGANIZED TOURS   At the time of writing, none of the major sightseeing tour operators were running dedicated tours to Mělník.

Touring the Château & Tasting the Wine

Mělník's main attraction is the **Renaissance Lobkowicz Château ★** (✆ **315-622-121;** www.lobkowicz-melnik.cz). The château is a mélange of styles, from its

Renaissance balconies and *sgrafitti* (decoration made by cutting away parts of a surface layer—like plaster or clay—to expose a different-colored layer beneath) to its Gothic touches and baroque southern building. The tour showcases the Lobkowicz's fine taste; in the living quarters, you'll see a barrage of baroque furniture and 17th- and 18th-century paintings. A second tour lets you into the 13th-century wine cellar, where wine tastings regularly occur.

Admission to the château is 110Kč for adults and 90Kč for students. The wine cellar tour is 40Kč, and wine tastings run from 90Kč for two wines to as much as 220Kč for 10 tastings. Buy tickets in the gift shop just off the castle courtyard. The château is open daily from 9:30am to 5pm.

Where to Eat

Be sure to time your visit to the château to take a meal at the wonderful **Zámecká Restaurace** ★ (© 315-622-121), with its stunning views out over the valley. In fact, better yet, call in advance to book a window table or a seat out on the terrace in nice weather. The menu has lots of sumptuous choices, including confit of duck breast for 240Kč. The restaurant is open daily from 10am to 10pm.

TEREZÍN (THERESIENSTADT) ★★

48km (30 miles) NW of Prague

Noticing that northwest Bohemia was susceptible to Prussian attacks, Joseph II, the son of Austrian Empress Maria Teresa, in the 18th century decided to build a military compound at Terezín to ward off further offensives. Two fortresses were built, but the Prussian army bypassed the area during the last Austro-Prussian conflict and in 1866 attacked Prague anyway. That spelled the end of Terezín's fortress charter, which was repealed in 1888. More than 50 years later, the fortifications were just what occupying Nazi forces needed.

When people around the world talk of Nazi atrocities during World War II, the name Terezín (*Theresienstadt* in German) rarely comes up. At the so-called Paradise Ghetto, there were no gas chambers, no mass machine-gun executions, and no medical testing rooms. Terezín wasn't used to exterminate the Jews, Gypsies, homosexuals, and political prisoners it held. Rather, the occupying Nazi forces used it as a transit camp. About 140,000 people passed through Terezín's gates; more than half ended up at the death camps of Auschwitz and Treblinka.

Instead, Terezín will live in infamy for the cruel trick that SS chief Heinrich Himmler played on the world within its walls. On June 23, 1944, three foreign observers—two from the Red Cross—came to Terezín to find out if the rumors of Nazi atrocities were true. They left with the impression that all was well, duped by a well-planned "beautification" of the camp.

The Germans had carefully choreographed every detail of the visit. The observers saw children studying at staged schools that didn't exist, and store shelves, which had been specially set up, stocked with goods. So that the observers wouldn't think the camp was overcrowded, the Nazis transported some 7,500 of the camp's sick and elderly prisoners to Auschwitz. Children even ran up to an SS commandant just as the observers passed; the commandant handed the children cans of sardines to shouts of "What? Sardines again?" The trick worked so well that the Nazis made a film of the camp, *The Führer Presents a Town to the Jews,* while it was still "self-governing."

Russian forces liberated Terezín on May 10, 1945, several days after Berlin had fallen to the Allies. Today, the camp stands as a memorial to the dead and a monument to human depravity.

Essentials

GETTING THERE   If you're **driving,** Terezín lies just off the D-8 motorway that leads north out of Prague in the direction of Dresden and Berlin. Watch for the turnoff signs. It's a 45-minute drive. There's a large public parking lot just outside the Large Fortress area (40Kč per car), but it's a long walk to the entrance to the Ghetto Museum. With a car, it's easy to combine a trip here with Mělník (see above), which lies pretty much in the same direction.

Several **buses** leave daily during the week from the small bus station above the **Nádraží Holešovice metro stop** (line C, red). On weekends, this slows down to just a few, so best to plan accordingly. The ride takes about an hour and costs 80Kč.

VISITOR INFORMATION   The Museum of the Ghetto has a gift shop that stocks maps and reading material in several languages. Before heading out, you can read up on the area at the well-organized website www.pamatnik-terezin.cz.

ORGANIZED TOURS   Nearly all the major touring companies offer a guided tour of Terezín (see "Organized Day Tours," above). **Wittmann Tours,** Novotného lávka 5, Prague 1 (② **222-252-472;** www.wittmann-tours.com), specializes in Jewish heritage trips and has dedicated tours both to Terezín and combined trips to Terezín and Lidice (see below).

Seeing the Camp

Terezín is a little hard to grasp at first. There are two main areas: The **Large Fortress** is essentially the town itself, the rectilinear streets laid out according to the best 18th-century military technology. Here was where the majority of ghetto residents lived during the Nazi occupation and the drab houses look remarkably little changed from how they must have looked then. Start your exploration here at the **Museum of the Ghetto** (*Muzeum Ghetta),* which is headquartered in what was once the ghetto's school. The exhibits here chronicle the rise of Nazism and daily life in the camp. Another focal point in the Large Fortress is the **Magdeburg Barracks,** which was formally the seat of the Jewish Council. Today, the barracks holds a replica of a ghetto dormitory to give a feel of how the people lived.

A 10-minute walk from the Large Fortress over the Ohře River brings you to the second main site, the **Small Fortress,** a smaller, more heavily fortified area that the Nazis used as a prison and torture zone for political prisoners. As you enter the main gate, the sign above, ARBEIT MACHT FREI (Work Sets One Free), sets a gloomy tone. You are free to walk through the prison barracks, execution grounds, workshops, and isolation cells. In front of the fortress's main entrance is the **National Cemetery (Národní hřbitov),** where the bodies exhumed from the mass graves were buried.

A combined admission allows entry to the Museum of the Ghetto, Magdeburg Barracks, and Small Fortress, and costs 200Kč for adults and 150Kč for children. Alternatively, you can buy separate admissions to the Ghetto Museum and Small Fortress for 160Kč adults and 130Kč children. The museum complex is open daily: November to March from 9am to 5:30pm and April to October from 9am to 6pm. For more information or reservations for guided tours, call ② **416-782-225** (fax 416-782-300; www.pamatnik-terezin.cz).

Terezín (Theresienstadt)   DAY TRIPS FROM PRAGUE

Where to Eat

It's understandable that there are few places to eat in Terezín. Indeed, you may not want to stay here much longer than you have to. However, inside the Large Fortress and the Museum is a decent inexpensive **buffet** with standard Czech fare. A livelier option is to take a local bus (ask at the Museum of the Ghetto for directions to the bus stop) to the nearby larger town of **Litoměřice,** with a charming vantage point over the river and a nicely restored central square. There are half a dozen good places lining central Mírové náměstí. For simple but decent Czech food, including a crispy pork schnitzel, try **U Zlatého Bažanta** (© 603-522-146) at Mírové nám. 21. Open daily from 11am to 10pm.

LIDICE ★

32km (20 miles) NW of Prague

A common perception of the Czechs' fate during World War II under the Nazi occupation is that they had it relatively easy compared with the Poles, Ukrainians, and Belarusians. That may be the case, but a trip here to the former village of Lidice, just 30 minutes by car or bus from Prague, is a sobering reminder that Czechs too suffered from extreme acts of cruelty committed by the occupying German forces.

Lidice entered the world's collective consciousness in 1942, at the height of the Nazi occupation, when Czech and Slovak paratroopers stationed in Britain were dropped into the country to assassinate the Nazi head of the protectorate, Reinhard Heydrich, the highest-ranking German officer in the Czech lands. The paratroopers managed to blow up Heydrich's limousine in late May 1942, and he died in the hospital a week later. So enraged were the Germans by the assassination that they vowed reprisal killings and selected Lidice as an example. Why Lidice? No one knows for sure, but this town was rumored to have accommodated the paratroopers, and someone had to pay.

On the night of June 9 to June 10, 1942, the Germans razed Lidice to the ground, destroying every house, church, and building in the village. Lidice's men were rounded up and executed at point-blank range in groups of 10. The women and children were separated from each other and sent to concentration camps, where many perished. In all, some 348 of Lidice's 500 residents were killed.

Today, there's a small but fascinating museum explaining the tragedy. You can also walk the grounds of the former village, marked here and there with plaques and crosses.

Essentials

GETTING THERE   If you're **driving,** take Hwy. 7 from the west side of Prague past the airport and head west onto Hwy. 551. It's a 20-minute drive.

Buses marked LIDICE-KLADNO depart for Lidice at the bus stops across the street from the Diplomat Hotel near the Dejvická metro station (last stop on the green A line). Not all the buses to Kladno stop in Lidice, so make sure you're on the right bus by confirming it with the driver. The ride takes about 30 minutes; it costs around 30Kč. Buy tickets from the driver.

Learning About Lidice

The **Lidice Memorial Museum** is a sobering monument to the town's martyred residents. The museum has gotten an update in the past few years with richer video and more interactivity. The exhibition is divided into two segments. The first is a 10-minute film (with an English-language introduction on request) providing the historical backdrop to the tragedy, including Czechoslovakia's independence in 1918, the rise of Nazism in Germany, the German invasion in 1939, and finally Heydrich's assassination by Czech patriots in late May 1942 and the Nazi destruction of Lidice on June 9 and 10 of that year. The second part is an absorbing exhibition (comprised of video and material evidence) of various aspects of the tragedy, including the grisly execution of the town's male population and the separation of the women from the children, who were then transported by train to the Lodz ghetto in Poland, where many were eventually gassed.

Admission is 80Kč adults, 40Kč for students and seniors, and it's open daily: March from 9am to 5pm; April to October from 9am to 6pm; and November to February from 9am to 4pm. Call ✆ **312-253-755** or go to www.lidice-memorial.cz for further information.

After the museum, you're welcome to wander the field where the village once stood. Memorials in the "old" Lidice include a wooden cross marking the spot where the executed men were buried in a mass grave, and Lidice's old and new cemeteries (the old one was desecrated by the Nazis, when looking for gold from the teeth of the dead).

ORLÍK

70km (43 miles) S of Prague

Castles closer to Prague like Karlštejn and Konopiště get all the attention, but it is worthwhile to take the time to visit **Orlík Castle ★**. Set among forests that line the Vltava where it swells from the Orlík Dam, the castle never disappoints. It was built in the 13th century but has burned down several times, only to rise from the ashes with new additions and extensions. Inherited by the Schwarzenberg family in 1719 upon the death of Maria Ernestina, a member of the Habsburg dynasty, the castle was set high up on a hill, overlooking a once-vibrant trade route. It stayed that way until 1962, when water trapped by the Orlík Dam downriver flooded thousands of acres of land, bringing the water level up to the castle's lower walls.

Returned to the Schwarzenberg family in 1992, the castle retains its splendor, while the surrounding area has become one of the most popular lake resorts in the Czech Republic. Orlík is also one of the nicest swimming areas in the country and therefore is a very popular vacation destination for camping.

Essentials

GETTING THERE   By car, this is a fairly easy 1-hour **drive** from Prague. Take Hwy. 4 heading southwest out of the city. Turn right on Hwy. 19, and then right again into Orlík.

By bus, it's a little trickier. Buses headed to **Orlík** leave from the bus stop **Na Knížecí** at the Smíchovské nádraží station. Most buses will require a change, usually in Písek, but be sure to ask the driver. The 2-hour trip will cost around 100Kč each way.

VISITOR INFORMATION   There's no real information center in this tiny town, but if you go to the castle gift shop, you can get some basic information.

ORGANIZED TOURS   At the time of writing, none of the major tour operators were running dedicated trips to Orlík.

Exploring the Castle

Castle tours explain the history of the Schwarzenberg family and take you through a fine collection of artifacts celebrating the victory over Napoleon at the Battle of Leipzig in 1815. Keep an eye out for the hand-carved wooden ceiling that took more than 4 years to complete. Admission, including a guided tour in English, is 160Kč for adults and 90Kč for children. Hours are Tuesday to Sunday: June to August, from 9am to 6pm; May and September, from 9am to 5pm; and April and October, from 9am to 4pm. For more information, call ✆ **382-275-101** or go to www.schwarzenberg.cz/orlik.

Where to Eat

Behind the castle gift shop, the **Restaurace U Toryka ★**, U zámku 116 (✆ **777-766-458;** www.utoryka.cz), has surprisingly high-quality Czech offerings, including a spicy house goulash, though portions could be bigger. Main courses are 100Kč to 240Kč; no credit cards are accepted. It's open daily from 10am to 8pm.

THE BEST OF BOHEMIA

Most people don't realize it, but the word "Bohemia" has two distinct meanings. One is well known, referring to the land of hipsters, free spirits, and, well, "Bohemians." The other meaning is geographic and refers to the westernmost province of the Czech Republic. (Moravia, to the east, is the Czech Republic's other province).

While you won't find many hipsters in the real "Bohemia," the fields, forests, castles, and spa towns certainly encourage a bit of free-spirited wandering.

Bohemia has a long tradition as a united entity stretching back to the Middle Ages, when it was the stomping ground of the earliest Czech kings and then later as a province of Habsburg Austria. In the 14th century, it rose to prominence under Emperor Charles IV and briefly could be said to have ruled the world, or at least the remnants of the Holy Roman Empire, as they existed at that time.

The 15th and 17th centuries brought decades of ruin and destruction in the form of sectarian wars between Protestants and Catholics. Southern Bohemia, in particular, was a hotbed of Hussite radicalism and a sanctuary for those opposed to the Catholics, Habsburgs, and nobility arrayed against them. The action shifted to Western Bohemia in the Thirty Years' War of the 17th century. It was in the town of Cheb, at the far western edge of the province, where fabled Habsburg army commander Albrecht von Wallenstein was assassinated by his own men in 1634 after it was feared he was negotiating a separate peace with the Protestant forces of Sweden and the German city states.

The 18th and 19th centuries were kinder to Bohemia as it evolved into the leading industrial region of the Austria-Hungarian Empire, and the richest noble families of the day, including the Schwarzenbergs and Liechtensteins, decorated the area with villas and castles to show off this wealth. As with the rest of the country, Bohemia declined markedly under Communism, and this history too is on display in the form of sometimes-dilapidated factories, villages, and infrastructure.

For visitors today, Bohemia offers two major types of attractions. Western Bohemia is dominated by its fabled spa towns, particularly **Karlovy Vary** and **Mariánské Lázně,** which in the 19th and early 20th centuries hosted luminaries from around the world and remain as beautiful as ever.

Southern Bohemia offers mainly castles and beautifully preserved towns showing off their Renaissance and baroque architecture, with the

jewel in the crown being **Český Krumlov.** It's also become one of the country's leading regions for cycling and hiking.

EXPLORING BOHEMIA

Though Bohemia was never divided historically, there are clear-cut distinctions in the region's geography that make going from town to town easier if you "divide" it into sections. After exploring Prague and central Bohemia, decide which area you'd like to see first and then plan accordingly.

Western Bohemia

Home to the country's spa towns, Western Bohemia is one of the few places where a full-blown tourist infrastructure was already in place by the time of the Velvet Revolution in 1989. Its main towns—**Karlovy Vary (Carlsbad), Mariánské Lázně (Marienbad),** and **Plzeň**—offer a wide array of accommodations, restaurants, and services to meet every visitor's needs and means.

A relatively inexpensive network of trains and buses covers the region, allowing travel between towns and to and from Prague with a minimum of fuss. Regular trains and buses link Prague to the main industrial city in the region, Plzeň, while buses ply the route to Karlovy Vary hourly from Prague's Florenc bus station. Western Bohemia is generally rougher terrain, so only serious bikers should consider seeing the area on two wheels.

Southern Bohemia

Once the religious hotbed of the country, Southern Bohemia was a focal point of the Hussite wars that eventually ravaged many of its towns and villages. Though the days of war took their toll, the region still features fine examples of architecture from every era. Southern Bohemia is also home to the Czech Republic's second-largest castle at **Český Krumlov,** a UNESCO-protected site that dazzles with its Disney-like qualities no matter how many times you visit.

There are two good approaches for exploring Southern Bohemia. If you're traveling by train or bus from Prague, make **Tábor** your first stop. It's on a main route, so the arrangements are easy. Then continue heading south, hooking up with **Třeboň, České Budějovice,** and **Český Krumlov.** If time is of the essence, you may want to set up camp in the area's main city, České Budějovice, and make several day trips, since nothing is that far away (Tábor, the farthest town, is 60km/37 miles away).

For those who have more time, consider a bike tour. These days, with the possibility of attack from Austria far diminished, Southern Bohemia is a much quieter setting with a less rugged terrain than Western Bohemia. Biking here is much more feasible, and you'll find dozens of quaint towns dotting the countryside. **Central European Adventures,** Jáchymova 4, Prague 1 (✆ **222-328-879;** http://cea51.tripod.com), can arrange superb tours that include bike rentals, guides (English-speaking), transportation, and even canoe trips through Southern Bohemia at a fraction of what it would cost if you arranged the same trip from home. Another organizer, the Czech-based **Greenways Travel Club** (✆ **519-511-572;** www.gtc.cz), organizes several Bohemian bike trips, including along the popular Prague-Vienna trail that runs straight through Southern Bohemia, that include stops in Tábor, Český Krumlov, and Třeboň.

KARLOVY VARY (CARLSBAD) ★★

120km (75 miles) W of Prague

The discovery of Karlovy Vary (Carlsbad) by Charles IV reads like a 14th-century episode of the old hit TV show *The Beverly Hillbillies*. According to local lore, the king was out huntin' for some food when up from the ground came a-bubblin' *water* (though discovered by his dogs and not an errant gunshot). Knowing a good thing when he saw it, Charles immediately set to work building a small castle in the area, naming the town that evolved around it Karlovy Vary, which translates as "Charles's Boiling Place." The first spa buildings were built in 1522, and before long, notables like Albrecht of Wallenstein, Peter the Great, and later Bach, Beethoven, Freud, and even Karl Marx all came to Karlovy Vary for a holiday retreat.

After World War II, Eastern Bloc travelers (following in the footsteps of Marx, no doubt) discovered the town, and Karlovy Vary became a destination for the proletariat. On doctors' orders, most workers would enjoy regular stays of 2 or 3 weeks, letting the mineral waters ranging from 110° to 162°F (43°–(72°C) from the town's 12 springs heal their tired and broken bodies. Even now, a large number of spa guests are here on doctors' orders and many of the "resorts" you see, in fact, are upscale hospitals.

Most of the 40-plus years of Communist neglect have been erased as a barrage of renovations continues to restore the spa's former glory. Gone is the statue of Russian cosmonaut Yuri Gagarin. Gone are almost all the fading, crumbling building facades that used to line both sides of the river. In their places stand restored buildings, cherubs, caryatids, and more.

Today, some 150,000 people, both traditional clientele and newer patrons, travel to the spa resort every year to sip, bathe, and frolic, though most enjoy the "13th spring" (actually a hearty herb-and-mineral liqueur called Becherovka) as much as— if not more than—the 12 nonalcoholic versions. Czechs will tell you that all have medical benefits. In a historical irony, the Russians have rediscovered Karlovy Vary in droves, so don't be surprised to hear Russian on the streets much more frequently than English, German, or Czech.

Essentials

GETTING THERE   Karlovy Vary is one of those destinations that it makes much more sense to take the bus than the **train** from Prague. The train travels a comically circuitous route and can take longer than 4 hours. The train is a more feasible option if you happen to be arriving from Mariánské Lázně or Cheb. Trains from Cheb, for example, depart hourly during the day and take around an hour. The fare is 72Kč second class.

Note that Karlovy Vary has two train stations. Trains from Prague and most other points arrive at Horní nádraží (upper station), while trains from Mariánské Lázně and a few other small towns (as well as all buses) arrive at Dolní nádraží (lower station). This latter station has better services and houses a branch of the local tourist information office. Horní nádraží is connected to the main spa area and town center by bus no. 12 or 13. Dolní nádraží is a 10-minute walk from the spa area or take local bus no. 4.

Traveling to Karlovy Vary by **bus** from Prague is much more convenient. Frequent express buses travel from Prague's Florenc bus station in around 2 hours at a cost of about 150Kč. One of the best bus lines offering the trip is **Student Agency** (© **841-101-101;** www.studentagency.cz), which runs hourly buses to Karlovy Vary from

Florenc bus station, and even shows a film during the trip. For information on train and bus timetables, go to www.jizdnirady.cz.

The nearly 2-hour **drive** from Prague to Karlovy Vary can be very busy and dangerous due to undisciplined Czech drivers. If you're going by car, take Hwy. E48 from the western end of Prague and follow it straight through to Karlovy Vary. This two-lane highway widens in a few spots to let cars pass slow-moving vehicles on hills. The spa area is closed to private vehicles, so you'll have to leave the car in one of several parking lots surrounding the area or use paid street parking (40Kč/hr.).

> ### A Driving Warning
>
> Be warned that drivers on Hwy. E48 between Prague and Karlovy Vary are often reckless. Please take extra care when driving.

VISITOR INFORMATION   Confusingly, Karlovy Vary is one of those towns that changes the location of its tourist information office, the **Infocentrum města Karlovy Vary** (www.karlovyvary.cz), every couple of years or so. Currently, the city has three tourist offices, with branches at the Hotel Thermal, I.P. Pavlova 11 (© 355-321-171), the Vřídelní Kolonáda along the main spa promenade (© 773-291-243), and the Dolní nádraží bus and train station, Západní ul. 2a (© 353-232-838). All the offices are open Monday to Friday from 9am to 5pm and Saturday and Sunday from 10am to 5pm, including an hour break for lunch. These offices can be real lifesavers and can hand out maps, advise on rooms, and help you plan out a day of sightseeing or a spa treatment.

SPECIAL EVENTS   The **Karlovy Vary International Film Festival** is the place to see and be seen. Each summer (in early July), the country's film stars, celebrities, and wealthy folks, supported by a cast of international stars like Sharon Stone, Robert Redford, and Morgan Freeman, can be spotted taking part in one of Europe's biggest film festivals. Nine venues screen more than 300 films during the 10-day festival. If you think you might want to attend, book accommodations well in advance, and note that the prices for rooms and meals are correspondingly higher during the festival. Go to www.iffkv.cz for more information.

Karlovy Vary plays host to several other events, including a **jazz festival** and **beer Olympiad** in May, a **Dvořák singing contest** in June, a **Summer Music Festival** in August, and a **Dvořák Autumn Music Festival** in September and October.

For details on the festivals, contact the information center listed above.

ORIENTATION   Most of the hotels, restaurants, spa colonnades and sights line a long pedestrian promenade that runs on both sides of the tiny Teplá River. The promenade starts at about the Hotel Thermal and ends 3km/2 miles later at the Grandhotel Pupp. The walk takes about an hour at a leisurely pace.

Exploring Karlovy Vary

The town's slow pace and pedestrian promenades, lined with turn-of-the-20th-century Art Nouveau buildings, turn strolling into an art form. Nighttime walks take on an even more mystical feel as the sewers, the river, and the many major cracks in the roads emit steam from the hot springs running underneath.

Avoid Karlovy Vary's "New Town," which happens to be conveniently left off most tourist maps. Its only real attractions are a McDonald's and a couple of ATMs (which you can also find in the historic center).

ATTRACTIONS

Church of St. Mary
Magdalene **14**
Diana Lookout Tower **22**
Hotel Thermal **3**
Jan Becher Museum **1**
Mlýnská Kolonáda **6**
Sadová Kolonáda **4**
Vřídelní Kolonáda **13**

SPA CURES & TREATMENTS

Alžbětiny lázně **2**
The Castle Bath **8**

HOTELS

Grandhotel Pupp **22**
Hotel Astoria **8**
Hotel Central **18**
Hotel Dvořák **19**
Hotel Embassy **22**
Hotel Kolonáda **7**
Hotel Krásná Královna **18**
Hotel Palacký **19**
Hotel Promenáda **13**
Hotel Romance-Puškin **10**
Hotel Thermal **3**
Parkhotel Pupp **20**

RESTAURANTS

Café Elefant **16**
Embassy Restaurant **22**
Grand Restaurant **21**
Hospoda U Švejka **15**
Promenáda **12**
Tandoor **5**

SHOPPING

Moser **11**

If you're traveling here by train or bus, a good place to start your exploration is the **Hotel Thermal,** I. P. Pavlova 11 (© **359-001-111**), at the northern end of the Old Town's center. Built in the 1970s, it exemplifies how obtrusive Communist architecture could be. Nestled between the town's eastern hills and the Ohře River, the glass, steel, and concrete Thermal sticks out like a sore thumb amid the rest of the town's 19th-century architecture. Nonetheless, you'll find three important places at the Thermal: the only centrally located outdoor public pool; an upper terrace boasting a truly spectacular view of the town; and Karlovy Vary's largest theater, which holds many of the film festival's premier events. Take it all in. But since the Hotel Thermal is not that pleasing to the eye, it's best to keep walking so you won't remember too much of it.

As you enter the heart of the town on the river's west side, you'll see the ornate white wrought-iron gazebo named **Sadová Kolonáda** adorning the beautifully manicured park, **Dvořákovy Sady.** Continue to follow the river, and about 100m (328 ft.) later you'll encounter the **Mlýnská Kolonáda ★**. This long, covered walkway houses several Karlovy Vary springs, which you can sample free 24 hours a day. Each spring has a plaque beside it describing its mineral elements and temperature. Bring your own cup or buy one just about anywhere (see the box "Spa Cures & Treatments," below) to sip the waters, since most are too hot to drink from with your hands. When you hit the river bend, you'll see the majestic **Church of St. Mary Magdalene** perched atop a hill, overlooking the **Vřídlo,** the hottest spring. Built in 1736, the church is the work of Kilián Ignác Dientzenhofer, who also created two of Prague's more notable churches—both named St. Nicholas.

Housing Vřídlo, which blasts water some 15m (49 ft.) into the air, is the glass building where a statue of Soviet cosmonaut Yuri Gagarin once stood. (Gagarin's statue has since made a safe landing at the Karlovy Vary Airport, where it greets the waves of Russian visitors who flood the town.) Now called the **Vřídelní Kolonáda ★**, the structure, built in 1974, houses several hot springs that you can sample for free daily from 6am to 7pm. There are also public restrooms, open daily 6am to 6pm and costing 10Kč.

Heading away from the Vřídelní Kolonáda are Stará and Nová Louka streets, which line either side of the river. Along **Stará (Old) Louka** are several fine cafes and glass and crystal shops. **Nová (New) Louka** is lined with many hotels and the historic town's main theater, built in 1886, which houses paintings by notable artists like Klimt and has just finished a major renovation project that has restored the theater to its original splendor.

Both streets lead eventually to the **Grandhotel Pupp ★**, Mírové nám. 2 (© **353-109-111**). Several years ago, the Pupp's main entrance and building underwent extensive renovations that more or less erased the effects of 40 years of state ownership under Communism (under the former regime, the hotel's name was actually "Moskva-Pupp" just to remind everyone who was actually calling the shots). Regardless of capitalism or Communism, the Pupp remains what it always was: the grande dame of hotels in central Europe. Once catering to nobility from all over Europe, the Pupp still houses one of the town's finest restaurants, the Grand (see below), while its grounds are a favorite with the hiking crowd.

If you still have the energy, atop the hill behind the Pupp stands the **Diana Lookout Tower ★** (© 353-222-872). Footpaths lead to the tower through the forests and eventually spit you out at the base of the tower, as if to say, "Ha, the trip is only half over." The five-story climb up the tower tests your stamina, but the view of the town is more than worth it. For those who aren't up to the climb up the hill, a cable car runs up the hill every 15 minutes June to September daily from 9:15am to 6:45pm; February, March, November, and December 9:15am to 4:45pm; April, May, and October 9:15am to 5:45pm; for 40Kč one-way, 70Kč round-trip.

And if you have some time left at the end of your stay, visit the **Jan Becher Museum,** T. G. Masaryka 57 (© **359-578-142;** www.becherovka.cz), to find out about the history of the town's secret: the formula for Becherovka. This herbal liquor is a sought-after souvenir, and you will get to taste it here. The museum is open daily 9am to 5pm; admission is 100Kč adults, 50Kč students.

Shopping

Crystal and porcelain are Karlovy Vary's other claims to fame. Dozens of shops throughout town sell everything from plates to chandeliers.

Ludvík Moser founded his first glassware shop in 1857 and became one of this country's foremost names in glass. You can visit and take a 30-minute tour of the **Moser Factory,** kapitána Jaroše 19 (© **353-416-112;** www.moser-glass.com; bus no. 1 or 22 from the bus stop Tržnice), just west of the town center. Its glass museum is open daily 9am to 5pm, and tours run daily 9am to 3pm. There's also a **Moser Store,** on Tržiště 7 (© **353-235-303**), right in the heart of New Town; it's open daily from 10am to 7pm (Sat–Sun until 6pm). Dozens of other smaller shops also sell the famed glass and are as easy to find in the Old Town as spring water.

If you're looking for something a little cheaper, try a box of *Oplatky,* thin round wafer cookies on sale throughout the spa area. The fillings range from vanilla to chocolate to nut and occasionally coffee—just don't try to wash them down with a mug of spa water!

Where to Stay

Private rooms used to be the best places to stay in Karlovy Vary with regard to quality and price. But this is changing as more and more hotels renovate and raise standards—as well as prices. Private accommodations can still provide better value, but they take a little extra work. If you want to arrange a room, try the **Infocentrum** (see above). Expect to pay about 1,500Kč for a double.

Some of the town's major spa hotels accommodate only those who are paying for complete treatment, unless for some reason their occupancy rates are particularly low. The hotels listed below accept guests for stays of any length.

Parking is a problem for nearly all the hotels, aside from the bigger properties like the Grandhotel Pupp and the Thermal, which have their own paid parking lots. You're best advised to leave your car in one of the paid lots just outside the immediate spa area and walk (or take a taxi) to your hotel.

VERY EXPENSIVE

Grandhotel Pupp ★★   The Pupp, built in 1701, is one of Europe's oldest grand hotels. Its public areas boast the expected splendor and charm, as do the renovated guest rooms. The best ones tend to be those facing the town center and are located on the upper floors; these have good views and sturdy wooden furniture. Some rooms have amenities such as air-conditioning, television, minibar, and safe, though not all do. The Grand has as grand a dining room as you'll find, with the food to match (see "Where to Eat," below). The hotel also has a stylish casino (midnight–4am). The rack rates are high, but check the website for occasional deals.

Mírové nám. 2, 360 91, Karlovy Vary. www.pupp.cz. © **353-109-111.** Fax 353-226-032. 111 units. 6,000Kč double deluxe; from 9,000Kč suite. Rates include breakfast. AE, DC, MC, V. Valet parking. **Amenities:** 4 restaurants; bar; casino; cafe; golf course; health club; pool (indoor); room service; tennis courts. *In room:* TV, hair dryer, minibar, Wi-Fi.

EXPENSIVE

Hotel Central   Located next to the theater, this hotel certainly is central. A recent face-lift has restored the hotel to its 1920s splendor, though it's probably not worth the relatively expensive price tag for rooms that aren't overly spacious, but only adequate. Those on the upper floors provide great views of the Vřídelní Kolonáda.

Divadelní nám. 17, 360 01 Karlovy Vary. www.interhotel-central.cz. © **353-182-630.** Fax 353-182-631. 87 units. 4,400Kč double; 5,100Kč suite. AE, MC, V. **Amenities:** Restaurant; exercise room; spa. *In room:* TV, minibar, Wi-Fi.

MODERATE

Hotel Dvořák ★   As part of the Vienna International hotel chain, the Dvořák has improved immensely over the several years, especially in terms of service. This hotel is within sight of the Pupp, but it's less expensive. The Pupp may have the history and elegance, but the Dvořák has the facilities. The rooms are spacious, with elegant decor and medium-size bathrooms with lots of marble. The staff is very attentive. Business travelers will appreciate the hotel's business facilities.

Nová Louka 11, 360 21 Karlovy Vary. www.hotel-dvorak.cz. © **353-102-111.** Fax 353-102-119. 126 units. 3,375Kč double. AE, DC, MC, V. Parking. **Amenities:** Restaurant; fitness center; pool (indoor); sauna. *In room:* TV, hair dryer, minibar, Wi-Fi.

Hotel Embassy ★   On the river bank across from the Pupp, the Embassy has well-appointed rooms, many with an early-20th-century motif. Set in a historic house, the rooms are medium-size with medium-size bathrooms. The staff here really helps make this hotel worthy of consideration, as does the proximity to the pub, which serves some of the best goulash and beer in the city.

Nová Louka 21, 360 01 Karlovy Vary. www.embassy.cz. © **353-221-161.** Fax 353-223-146. 20 units. 3,130Kč double; 3,990Kč suite. AE, MC, V. **Amenities:** Restaurant, bar; exercise room. *In room:* TV, minibar, Wi-Fi.

Hotel Kolonáda   The Kolonáda, with its lovely facade, was formed by a merger of the Otava and Patria hotels. As the name suggests, it's across from the Mlýnská Kolonáda. The hotel's interior is modern and renovated, as are the rooms, the best of which overlook the Kolonáda.

I. P. Pavlova 8, 360 01 Karlovy Vary. www.kolonada.cz. © **353-345-555.** Fax 353-347-828. 162 units. 3,185Kč double; 3,788Kč suite. AE, MC, V. **Amenities:** 2 restaurants; bar; bikes; health club & spa. *In room:* TV, fridge, minibar, Wi-Fi.

Hotel Krásná Královna (the Beautiful Queen Hotel)   A revitalized property with a familiar face has emerged in the spa zone. The original accents of this 18th-century guesthouse have been revived with fresh colors, classic furniture, and fine accessories. This family-run hotel is again offering comfort and a cozy atmosphere as well as access to spa amenities in the town.

Stará Louka 335/48, Karlovy Vary. www.krasnakralovna.cz. © **353-852-611.** Fax 353-852-612. 21 units. 3,200Kč double; 4,100Kč suite. AE, MC, V. **Amenities:** Restaurant; bar; health club & spa. *In room:* TV, hair dryer, minibar.

SPA CURES & treatments

Most visitors to Karlovy Vary come for a spa treatment, a therapy that lasts 1 to 3 weeks. After consulting with a spa physician, you're given a specific regimen of activities that may include mineral baths, massages, waxings, mudpacks, electrotherapy, and pure oxygen inhalation. After spending the morning at a spa or sanatorium, you're usually directed to walk the paths of the town's surrounding forest.

The common denominator of all the cures is an ample daily dose of hot mineral water, which bubbles up from 12 springs. This water definitely has a distinct odor and taste. You'll see people chugging it down, but it doesn't necessarily taste very good. Some thermal springs actually taste and smell like rotten eggs. You may want to take a small sip at first. Do keep in mind that the waters are used to treat internal disorders, so the minerals may cleanse the body thoroughly—in other words, they can cause diarrhea.

You'll also notice that almost everyone in town seems to be carrying "the cup." This funny-looking cup is basically a mug with a built-in straw running through the handle. Young and old alike parade around with their mugs, filling and refilling them at each thermal water tap. You can buy these mugs everywhere for as little as 80Kč or as much as 300Kč; they make a quirky souvenir. **But be warned:** None of the mugs can make the warmer hot springs taste any better.

The minimum spa treatment lasts 1 week and must be arranged in advance. A spa treatment package traditionally includes room, full board, and complete therapy regimen; the cost varies from about 900Kč to 2,500Kč per person per day, depending on season and facilities. Rates are highest from May to September and lowest from November to February. Nearly all the hotels in town will provide spa and health treatments, so ask when you book your room. Most will happily arrange a treatment if they don't provide them directly.

If you're coming for just a day or two, you can experience the waters on an "outpatient" basis. The largest therapeutic complex in town (and in the Czech Republic) is the **Alžbětiny Lázně-Lázně V,** Smetanovy sady 1145/1 ((℮) **353-304-211;** www.spa5.cz). On its menu are more than 60 kinds of treatments, including water cures, massages, a hot-air bath, a steam bath, a whirlpool, and a pearl bath, as well as use of their swimming pool. You can choose packages of different procedures that run between 430Kč for an anti-cellulite beer bath to 1,200Kč for a hot stone massage. It's open Monday to Friday 8am to 3pm for spa treatments; the pool is open Monday to Friday 9am to noon and 1 to 9pm, Saturday 9am to 9pm, and Sunday 9am to 6pm.

The Castle Spa (Zámecké Lázně), Zámecký vrch 1; ((℮) **353-225-502;** www. carlsbad-plaza.com), is a relatively new (and fancy) spa and wellness house located in a reconstructed site at the foot of the Castle Tower (Zámecká věž) in the old city center. You can make reservations over the website and see a menu of treatments, including both those that require a medical exam and those that don't. The latter include massages, and various baths and aroma treatments.

Hotel Palacký ⚜ This is one of the better deals in town. The hotel is ideally situated on the west side of the river so it gets sun almost all day. The rooms, with their mostly bare walls and low beds, seem huge, especially the ones with a river view. The staff can seem more like furniture than people who help guests, but that's a small price to pay for the relatively good value.

Stará Louka 40, 360 01 Karlovy Vary. www.hotelpalacky.cz. ℰ **353-222-544.** Fax 353-223-561. 20 units. 2,250Kč–2,730Kč double. AE, MC, V. **Amenities:** Restaurant. *In room:* TV, fridge, hair dryer.

Hotel Promenáda ★★ Next door to the Romance-Puškin is the Promenáda. This hotel faces the Kolonáda and has a beautiful view of the old center of the town. Rooms on the lower floors are more spacious than those on the upper levels, but all have an elegant decor highlighted with wrought-iron bed frames and large windows.

Tržiště 31, 360 01 Karlovy Vary. www.hotel-promenada.cz. ℰ **363-225-648.** Fax 353-229-708. 16 units. 3,200Kč–3,700Kč double. AE, MC, V. Parking. **Amenities:** Restaurant; cafe; health club & spa. *In room:* TV, minibar, Wi-Fi.

Hotel Thermal What better way to experience what it was like to stay in Karlovy Vary under Communism? Built in the 1970s, Hotel Thermal towers above the town, rising like a steel-and-glass phoenix from the steam of the river's spas. But because of its size—and the cinema on its ground floor—it becomes a hub during the film festival. All kidding aside, the Thermal also qualifies as a possible place to stay because of its location, services, and size. Don't expect anything exciting, but do take a picture of yourself in the *Star Trek* seats in the lobby bar. While the reception area is still very much a throwback to the 1970s, the guest rooms have been tastefully refurbished and the bathrooms refitted in a modern style.

I. P. Pavlova 11, 360 01 Karlovy Vary. www.thermal.cz. ℰ **359-001-111.** Fax 359-002-603. 273 units. 3,100Kč double. AE, MC, V. Parking. **Amenities:** 2 restaurants; bar; pool (outdoor); room service. *In room:* TV, Wi-Fi.

INEXPENSIVE

Hotel Astoria In the heart of the historic town, the restored Astoria mainly caters to spa guests but, unlike many of its competitors, it is big enough to usually have several rooms available for nontreatment visitors. The staff can be a little gruff at times, but the rooms are big, with satellite TV an added bonus. The restaurant serves standard Czech fare, with a lot of vegetable dishes as well, though I'd recommend trying one of the other places in town for a less bland experience.

Vřídelní 92, 360 01 Karlovy Vary. www.astoria-spa.cz. ℰ **353-335-111.** Fax 353-224-368. 100 units. 2,250Kč double. AE, MC, V. **Amenities:** Restaurant; sauna. *In room:* TV, fridge.

Hotel Romance-Puškin ★★ This place has now been renamed, but for years it's carried the name of the great Russian poet we know as Pushkin. The hotel occupies an intricately ornamented 19th-century Art Nouveau building that has been renovated. It has a terrific location, close to the springs. The rooms are rather basic, but they're comfortable enough. Ask for one that has a balcony facing St. Mary Magdalene Church and enjoy one of the nicest views in the Old Town.

Tržiště 37, 360 90 Karlovy Vary. www.hotelromance.cz. ℰ **353-222-646.** Fax 353-224-134. 37 units. 2,000č–2,940Kč double. AE, MC, V. Parking. **Amenities:** Restaurant; room service. *In room:* TV, hair dryer, minibar, Wi-Fi.

Where to Eat

EXPENSIVE

Embassy Restaurant ★ CZECH/CONTINENTAL   On the ground floor of the Embassy Hotel, this is one of the oldest and best restaurants in town. It offers an intimate dining room with historic interior. If you visit in winter, get a table next to the original hearth. Here you'll find many traditional Czech dishes with slight twists that make them interesting. The grilled loin of pork covered with a light, creamy green pepper sauce makes a nice change from the regular roast pork served by most Czech restaurants. The spicy goulash is more reminiscent of Hungary's piquant flavors than blander Czech fare. The warm strawberries and peppercorns dessert is much better than it sounds.

Nová Louka 21. © **353-221-161.** Reservations recommended. Main courses 220Kč–600Kč. AE, MC, V. Daily 11am–11pm.

Grand Restaurant CONTINENTAL   It's no surprise that the Grandhotel Pupp has arguably the nicest dining room in town: an elegant space with tall ceilings, huge mirrors, and glistening chandeliers. A large menu features equally large portions of salmon, chicken, veal, pork, turkey, and beef in a variety of heavy and heavier sauces. Even the mouthwatering trout with mushrooms is smothered in butter sauce.

In the Grandhotel Pupp, Mírové nám. 2. © **353-109-646.** Reservations recommended. Main courses 290Kč–750Kč. AE, MC, V. Daily noon–3pm and 6–11pm.

Promenáda ★★★ CZECH/CONTINENTAL   This cozy, intimate spot may not be as elegant as the Grand Restaurant, but the cooking is more adventurous. Across from the Vřídelní Kolonáda, the Promenáda offers a wide menu with generous portions. The daily menu usually includes well-prepared wild game, but the mixed grill for two and the chateaubriand, both flambéed at the table, are the chef's best dishes. The wine list features a large selection of wines from around Europe, but don't neglect the Czech wines. An order of crêpes suzette, big enough to satisfy two, rounds out a wonderful meal.

Tržiště 31. © **353-225-648.** Reservations recommended. Main courses 290Kč–750Kč. AE, MC, V. Daily noon–11pm.

MODERATE

Hospoda U Švejka ★ CZECH   This addition to the pub scene plays on the tried-and-true touristy *Good Soldier Švejk* theme. Luckily, the tourist trap goes no further, and once inside, you find a refreshingly nonsmoky though thoroughly Czech atmosphere. Locals and tourists alike rub elbows while throwing back some fine lager and standard pub favorites such as goulash and beef tenderloin in cream sauce.

Stará Louka 10. © **353-232-276.** Main courses 159Kč–319Kč. AE, MC, V. Daily 11am–10pm.

Tandoor ★ INDIAN   And now for something completely different: a relatively authentic (judging by the amount of Indian people in the dining room) Indian restaurant. You'll find all the usual favorites, including a relatively mild *chicken tikka masala* (155Kč), served up by a friendly owner/waiter. Be forewarned: This place is not easy to find. It's hidden in a small alley just to the north (and away from the main spa area) of the Hotel Thermal. Feels as far from the glitz as it gets.

I.P. Pavlova 25 (in an alley). © **608-701-341.** Main courses 140Kč–250Kč. AE, MC, V. Mon–Sat noon–10pm and Sun noon–6pm.

INEXPENSIVE

Café Elefant COFFEE/DESSERT   Who needs to travel all the way to Vienna? Since this is a cafe in the true sense of the word, all you'll find are coffee, tea, alcoholic and nonalcoholic drinks, desserts, and enough ambience to satisfy the hordes of visitors who flock to this landmark. (Be prepared to hear more Russian or German than Czech, as this is a see-and-be-seen haunt.) The Elefant is widely known for its Belle Epoque style and is famous for its freshly baked cakes. Its many outdoor tables overlook the pedestrian promenade.

Stará Louka 32. ⓒ **353-223-406.** Cakes and desserts 60Kč–120Kč. AE, MC, V. Daily 10am–10pm.

MARIÁNSKÉ LÁZNĚ (MARIENBAD) ★

46km (29 miles) SW of Karlovy Vary, 160km (100 miles) W of Prague

When Thomas Alva Edison visited Mariánské Lázně in the late 1800s, he reportedly declared, "There is no more beautiful spa in all the world." Mark Twain, who also stopped by, was slightly more critical. He acknowledged the beauty of the architecture, but in typical Twain style decried what he saw as a "health factory."

Mariánské Lázně now stands in the shadow of the Czech Republic's most famous spa town, Karlovy Vary, but it wasn't always that way. First noted in 1528 by Bohemian historians, the town's mineral waters gained prominence at the end of the 18th and beginning of the 19th century. Nestled among forested hills and packed with romantic and elegant pastel hotels and spa houses, the town, commonly known by its German name, Marienbad, has played host to such luminaries as Goethe (this is where his love for Ulrike von Levetzow took root), Chopin, Strauss, Wagner, Freud, and Kafka (in addition to Edison and Twain). England's Edward VII found the spa resort so enchanting that he visited several times and even commissioned the building of the country's first golf club.

Essentials

GETTING THERE   There are frequent express trains from Prague's main station, via Plzeň, for 240Kč (trip time: 2 hr., 50 min.). There's also decent service to and from Cheb (30 min., 45 Kč) and Karlovy Vary (80 min., about 60 Kč). For up-to-date timetables, go to www.jizdnirady.cz. Mariánské Lázně train station, Nádražní nám. 292, is a good 30-minute walk from the main spa area, so you're best bet on arrival is to take bus no. 5 into town (tickets cost 12Kč; buy them from the driver, coins only).

The **bus** from Prague takes about 3 hours and often requires a change in Plzeň. It costs about 180Kč. The Mariánské Lázně bus station is adjacent to the train station on Nádražní náměstí; take bus no. 5 into town.

Driving from Prague, take Hwy. E50 through Plzeň to Stříbro—about 22km (14 miles) past Plzeň—and head northwest on Hwy. 21. The clearly marked route can take up to 2 hours. Parking is not generally a problem as there's paid street parking on the main drag, Hlavní třída.

VISITOR INFORMATION   Along the main strip lies the **Infocentrum,** Hlavní 47, 353 01, Mariánské Lázně (ⓒ **354-622-474**). Sad to say, the tourist information office here is not very helpful. There are no free maps and not much in the way of useful advice either, other than "buy this." Still, it's a port in the storm stop for basic

THE spa treatment

For those wanting to do a little more than stroll around the grounds and sip the waters from a ceramic cup, nearly all the hotels and spas in town offer some type of "wellness" package, including mineral bubble baths, massages, hot stones, and the like. As is true with any Czech spa or resort, however, it pays greatly to plan and book in advance. Not only will you likely save money, but you'll also be treated much better than as a "walk in." The **Marienbad Kur & Spa Hotels Information Service,**

Masarykova 22, 353 29 (© **354-655-501;** www.marienbad.cz) is a central booking and travel agency with long experience at booking wellness packages of 3 hours or 3 weeks. Another useful website is the main city website, **www.marianskelazne.cz**. It's one-stop shopping for finding spa packages as well as hotel rooms. The website also contains an excellent description in English of the various springs, and which ailments they are intended to "cure."

questions and a good place to buy tickets for events. Open daily 9am to 6pm. For information and tips about what's going on, go to www.marianskelazne.cz.

SPECIAL EVENTS   One of the few places in central Europe not to claim Mozart as one of its sons, Mariánské Lázně has instead chosen to honor one of its frequent visitors, Chopin, with a yearly festival devoted entirely to the Polish composer. The **Chopin Festival** usually runs for 8 to 10 days near the end of August. Musicians and directors from all over the world gather to play and listen to concerts and recitals. In addition, several local art galleries hold special exhibits. Tickets range from 180Kč to 1,500Kč.

Each June, the town plays host to a **classical music festival** with many of the Czech Republic's finest musicians, as well as those from around the world. For more details or ticket reservations for either event, contact **Infocentrum** (see "Visitor Information," above).

Patriotic Americans can show up on **July 4** for a little down-home fun, including a parade and other flag-waving special events commemorating the town's liberation by U.S. soldiers in World War II.

Sports-minded travelers can play one of the country's best golf courses, which staged the early years of the Czech Open international golf tournament in the 1990s.

ORIENTATION   Mariánské Lázně is laid out around **Hlavní třída,** the main street. A plethora of hotels, restaurants, travel agencies, and stores fronts this street. **Lázeňská Kolonáda,** a long, covered block beginning at the northern end of Hlavní třída, contains six of the resort's eight major springs.

Taking the Waters

When you walk through the town, it's almost impossible to miss eye-catching **Lázeňská Kolonáda,** just off Skalníkovy sady. From Hlavní třída, walk east on Vrchlického ulice. Recently restored to its former glory, this colonnade of cast iron and glass is adorned with ceiling frescoes and Corinthian columns. It was built in 1889 and connects half a dozen major springs in the town center; this is the focal point of those partaking in the ritual. Bring a cup to fill or, if you want to fit in with the thousands of guests who are serious about their spa water, buy one of the porcelain mugs with a built-in straw that are offered just about everywhere. Keep in mind that the waters are used to treat internal disorders, so the minerals may act to cleanse the body thoroughly by causing diarrhea. You can wander the Kolonáda any time; water is distributed daily from 6am to noon and 4 to 6pm.

Located just next to the colonnade is the modern landmark of the city. A pool surrounding a flower sculpture of stainless steel and stone is known as **"The Singing Fountain"** and contains a set of 250 water jets. At the top of every odd hour, between 7am and 9pm, and at 10pm, these jets spray in sync to music by different composers.

Learning About the City's Past

There's not much town history, since Mariánské Lázně officially came into existence only in 1808. But engaging brevity is what makes the two-story **City Museum (Městské Muzeum),** Goetheovo nám. 11 (*©* **354-622-740**), worth recommending. Chronologically arranged displays include photos and documents of famous visitors. Goethe slept here, in the upstairs rooms in 1823, when he was 74 years old. If you ask nicely, the museum guards will play an English-language tape that describes the contents of each room. You can also request to see the museum's English-language film about the town. Admission is 60Kč, and it is open Tuesday to Sunday from 9:30am to 5:30pm.

Hiking or Golfing

If the thought of a spa treatment doesn't appeal, you can take a relaxing walk through the woods. The surrounding forest, **Slavkovský les (Slavkov Forest),** has about 70km (43 miles) of marked footpaths and trails through the gentle hills that abound in the area.

If you're a serious golfer or just looking for a little exercise, the **Royal Golf Club of Mariánské Lázně** (*©* **354-624-300;** www.golfml.cz), a 6,135-yard, par-72 championship course dating from 1905, lies on the edge of town. The club takes pay-as-you-play golfers, with a fully equipped pro shop that rents clubs. Greens fees are 1,500Kč to 1,700Kč and club rental is 500Kč. Reservations are recommended on weekends.

Where to Stay

The main strip along Hlavní třída is lined with incredibly grand-looking hotels, many with rooms facing the Kolonáda. But don't be deceived by appearances. Many of the hotels are far more impressive on the outside than they are on the inside. Most of the hotels, in fact, are filled with spa patients and have an atmosphere more akin to an upscale hospital.

If you haven't booked in advance, your best bet is to stroll along Hlavní třída and shop around for a room. You'll likely end up with a better deal than the rack rates.

Also, don't be confused by the room rates. Many of the hotels have complicated pricing menus that include spa treatments and board that you may not want or need. To add to the confusion, many properties break with Czech tradition and list prices per person (not per room). Ask the receptionist for an all-in price before agreeing to take the room.

There is paid parking on the street along Hlavní, and most of the hotels will have their own paid lots.

EXPENSIVE

Falkensteiner Hotel Grand Spa Marienbad ★★   If there's one hotel in Mariánské Lázně that comes close to capturing some of the glamour of the early '60s French New Wave film *Last Year at Marienbad*, it would be this palace that sits atop a long hill at the end of Ruská Street. Unlike many of the other hotels in town, there's no whiff of "hospital" here; it's pure luxury. The rooms strike a nice balance between modern and traditional; many of the baths retain the old tiles. The restaurant is one of the best in town. Check the hotel website for special rates and packages.

Ruská 123, 353 01 Mariánské Lázně. www.falkensteiner.com. © **354-929-396.** Fax 354-929-398. 164 units. 3,600Kč double; 4,600Kč suite. AE, DC, MC, V. Parking. **Amenities:** Restaurant; bar; cafe; wine room; health club & spa; pool (indoor). *In room:* A/C (some), TV, hair dryer, minibar, Wi-Fi.

Grandhotel Pacifik   After a renovation of the building, this hotel has become one of the top establishments on the main strip. Alas, the guest rooms are outfitted with sterile though decent furniture. Ask for a room that faces the street. The restaurant and cafe have also been redone, much for the better. All are now bright and cheery, pleasant for a quick coffee or drink.

Mírové nám. 84, 353 29 Mariánské Lázně. www.marienbad.cz. © **354-651-111.** Fax 354-651-200. 109 units. 3,750Kč double; 4,800Kč suite. AE, V. Parking. **Amenities:** Restaurant; health club & spa; Internet. *In room:* A/C, TV, hair dryer, minibar.

Parkhotel Golf ★   One of the more luxurious hotels in town, the Golf isn't actually in town but across from the golf course about 3km (2 miles) down the road leading to Karlovy Vary. This hotel is busy, so reservations are recommended. The English-speaking staff delivers on their pledge to cater to every wish. The rooms are bright and spacious, and there's an excellent restaurant and terrace on the first floor. Not surprisingly, given the hotel's name, the staff can help arrange a quick 18 holes across the street. The hotel has also opened its own spa center to pamper guests a little more.

Zádub 580, 353 01 Mariánské Lázně. www.parkhotel-golf.cz. © **354-622-651.** Fax 354-622-655. 27 units. 3,800Kč double; 4,900Kč suite. Rates include breakfast. AE, DC, MC, V. Parking. **Amenities:** Restaurant; bar; fitness center; golf course; room service; sauna; spa; tennis courts. *In room:* TV, hair dryer, minibar, Wi-Fi.

MODERATE

Hotel Bohemia ★   In the middle of the action on Hlavní, the Bohemia has several rooms with balconies that overlook the Kolonáda. It has been recently remodeled and improved, rooms tend to be a little larger, and for those looking for location, you can't get more central.

Hlavní třída 100, 353 01 Mariánské Lázně. www.orea.cz/bohemia. © **354-610-111.** Fax 354-610-555. 76 units. 2,800Kč–3,820Kč double. AE, DC, MC, V. **Amenities:** Restaurant; cafe; Internet; spa. *In room:* TV, minibar.

Hotel Excelsior   Across from the Nové Lázně (New Bath), the Excelsior has benefited inside and out from a face-lift. Several rooms have 19th-century period furnishings and ornate balconies overlooking the park that leads up to the Kolonáda. There are two restaurants, including the Churchill, one of the best watering holes on the strip. The hotel staff is also more attentive than those at some other hotels in town.

Hlavní třída 121, 353 01 Mariánské Lázně. www.orea.cz/excelsior. © **354-697-111.** Fax 354-625-346. 64 units. 3,400Kč double. AE, DC, MC, V. **Amenities:** 2 restaurants; cafe; Internet; spa. *In room:* TV, hair dryer, minibar.

😊 family FUN

If you're looking for a weekend break with the family and want to have an enjoyable experience outdoors, book a weekend at the modest **Koliba ★**, Dusíkova 592 (ℂ **354-625-169**). In the summer, dozens of miles of wooded trails are open for hiking and biking. Be careful, though, because many of the paths lead through the golf course, and while golf is becoming more popular in the Czech Republic, the skill level is still such that you need to beware of errant balls. In the winter, try out the mini–ski hill. Two tows at the foot of the hotel take you up a 150m (492-ft.) hill perfect for anyone learning to ski. There are also dozens of kilometers of cross-country ski trails through the local forests that are always in top condition. A 1-day ski pass costs about 400Kč.

The après-ski atmosphere of the lodge, with its giant fireplace and numerous tables, provides the perfect respite from a hectic week. At night, the flames of the open grill roasting all different sorts of game will ease the pain of all those bumps and bruises. In the summer, the trails are ideal for hiking.

Hotel Villa Butterfly ★ One of the many hotels on the main street to be spruced up and expanded, the Villa Butterfly has upgraded to 94 bright and spacious rooms. In fact, from the front hall to the fitness room and even all the way to its new underground parking, the Villa Butterfly has really taken off. An English-speaking staff and a good selection of foreign-language newspapers at the reception area are added bonuses.

Hlavní třída 655, 353 01 Mariánské Lázně. www.marienbad.cz. ℂ **354-654-300.** Fax 354-654-200. 96 units. 2,200Kč double; 3,320Kč suite. Rates include breakfast. AE, DC, MC, V. Parking. **Amenities:** 2 restaurants; bar; cafe; health club & spa. *In room:* A/C, TV, hair dryer, minibar, Wi-Fi.

INEXPENSIVE

Hotel Koliba ★ ♨ Away from the main strip but still only a 10-minute walk from the Kolonáda, the Koliba is a rustic hunting lodge set in the hills on Dusíkova, the road leading to the golf course and Karlovy Vary. The rooms are warm and inviting, with the wooden furnishings giving the hotel the feel of a country cottage. The restaurant is very good too and worth searching out.

Dusíkova 592, 353 01 Mariánské Lázně. http://koliba.xercom.cz. ℂ**354-625-169.** Fax 354-626-310. 15 units. 1,800Kč double Sun–Thurs; 1,960Kč double Fri–Sat. AE, MC, V. Parking. **Amenities:** Restaurant/bar; bikes; ski lift. *In room:* TV, minibar.

Pension Český Dvůr ♨ Walk through the passage from the main street and before you know it, you'll be standing at one of the more recently built accommodations options in town. The Český Dvůr is slightly different from the hotels that line the street in that it is several apartments that have been connected to form a hotel. Inside you find very bright, sunny rooms with small living areas and kitchenettes, as well as spotless bathrooms. This is a find for families, as the hotel is cheap but big enough to allow kids their own space.

Hlavní třída 36c, 353 01 Mariánské Lázně. www.cesky-dvur.com/en. ℂ**354-626-273.** Fax 354-603-150. 6 units. 1,350Kč double. AE, MC, V. *In room:* TV, minibar.

Where to Eat

MODERATE

Churchill Club Restaurant ★ CZECH   Don't let the name fool you—the food is traditional Czech, not British, with a few oddities like "Steak Pampa" served with chimichurri sauce or pasta with spicy chorizo sausage to keep it interesting. A lively bar with a good selection of local and imported beer makes the Churchill one of the few fun places to be after dark in this quiet town.

Hlavní třída 121. ℃ **354-622-705.** Main courses 120Kč–400Kč. AE, MC, V. Daily 11am–11pm.

Classic Café/Restaurant CZECH   A nice place to stop for a light bite, the Classic offers a large assortment of good fresh salads. This open, airy cafe/restaurant has one of the friendliest staffs in town, though a few more tables out front would be welcome. It also brews a decent espresso.

Hlavní třída 131. No phone. Main courses 89Kč–219Kč. AE, DC, MC, V. Daily 9am–11pm cafe, 11am–11pm restaurant.

Medite ★★ TAPAS   A refreshing change of pace for a medium-sized Czech city: an authentic Spanish tapas bar, with very good food and no hint of the tour buses that surround lots of other places in town. You'll find many things to please the palate, including shrimp risotto, grilled veggies, and lightly prepared fish and chicken specialties. There's a good value lunch special weekdays for 120Kč.

Hlavní třída 279. ℃ **354-422-018.** www.medite.cz. Main courses 89Kč–219Kč. AE, DC, MC, V. Daily 11am–11pm.

New York Barcaffe ★ INTERNATIONAL/CAFE   This chic coffee bar by day morphs into a fun and popular cocktail bar at sundown. Truth by told, Mariánské Lazně isn't renowned for its nightlife and what little of it exists usually finds its way here by the end of the night. In addition to coffees, you'll find a small menu of very good food options made up mainly of salads and pastas. The original Caesar salad tastes good and is a good value at 89Kč.

Hlavní třída 233. ℃ **775-167-748.** Main courses 90Kč–200Kč. AE, DC, MC, V. Daily 9am–3am.

Pizzacaffe Express ITALIAN   This modern Italian joint is more than a nice coffee shop, with good and reasonably priced thin-crust pizzas and pasta dishes and a pretty terrace overlooking the main spa area. Also does breakfasts in case your hotel or pension doesn't already lay that on as part of the price. My favorite is Pizza Sorrentina, topped with fresh tomatoes and mozzarella cheese.

Poštovní 5. ℃ **728-202-202.** www.caffeexpress.cz. Pizza 119Kč–145Kč; main courses 129Kč–219Kč. No credit cards. Daily 10am–10pm.

PLZEŇ (PILSEN)

88km (55 miles) SW of Prague

The Czech Republic's fourth-largest city, and the regional capital of Western Bohemia, Plzeň has done a lot to spruce itself up in recent years. The town's central core is rich in historic buildings and surrounded by an arc of lovely gardens that mark where the town walls once stood. Even the tiny riverfront area, these days, is a pleasant place to linger with a clutch of good restaurants and cafes.

And then there's the beer. Some 400 years ago, a group of men formed Plzeň's first beer-drinking guild, and the city still takes pride in its "Birthplace of Beer" moniker.

💬 PLZEŇ'S claim to fame

Founded in 1295 by Václav II, Plzeň was and remains western Bohemia's administrative center. King Václav's real gift to the town, however, wasn't making it an administrative nerve center but granting it brewing rights. More than 200 microbreweries popped up, one in almost every street-corner basement. Realizing that the brews they were drinking had become mostly plonk by the late 1830s, rebellious beer drinkers demanded quality, forcing the brewers to try harder. "Give us what we want in Plzeň, good and cheap beer!" became the battle cry. In 1842, the brewers combined their expertise to produce a superior brew through what became known as the Pilsner brewing method. If you don't believe it, look in your refrigerator. Most likely, the best beer in there has written somewhere on its label "Pilsner brewed."

It's the home to none other than Pilsner Urquell, one of the world's leading lagers. The city draws comparatively few overnight guests (most visitors are day-trippers from Prague in for the beer tour and a meal), but there are compelling reasons to stay longer. There are plenty of nice hotels and places to eat, and the good regional train and bus connections make it a reasonable base for exploring the Western Bohemian spa towns. And then there's the beer.

Essentials

GETTING THERE   Getting to Plzeň from Prague is a cinch, and it's equally easy by bus or train. Several fast **trains** make the trip daily from Prague's Hlavní nádraží in around 90 minutes. The train costs 147Kč second class. To get from the train station to town, walk out the main entrance and take Americká Street across the river; turn right onto Jungmannova, which leads to the main square.

The **bus** operator **Student Agency** (© **841-101-101;** http://jizdenky.student agency.cz) runs hourly buses during the day from Prague's Florenc bus station. The trip from Prague takes 1 hour and costs 100Kč each way.

By car, Plzeň is a straight 70km/42-mile shot down the D5 expressway. Once you've cleared the traffic getting out of central Prague, the trip takes around 45 minutes. Once you get to Plzeň, dump your car in a paid parking lot or use pay parking on the street. Parking rates run about 20Kč an hour.

VISITOR INFORMATION   Trying to be as visitor-friendly as possible, the **City Information Center Plzeň,** náměstí Republiky 41, 301 16 Plzeň (© **378-035-330;** fax 378-035-332; www.icpilsen.cz or www.plzen.eu), is packed with literature to answer your questions. It is open daily 9am to 6pm.

The **American Center in Plzeň,** Dominikánská 9, 301 12 Plzeň (© **377-237-722;** www.americancenter.cz), just off the main square, has English-language books and magazines as well as computer terminals and a handy cafe with Wi-Fi. There's also a "California"-style restaurant in the basement that serves homesick fare like cheeseburgers and club sandwiches. It's open Monday to Friday from 8am to 8pm.

SPECIAL EVENTS   If you're an American or speak English, being in Plzeň in early May is quite an experience. Unlike most of the rest of the country, which was liberated from the Nazis by the Soviet Red Army, Plzeň was liberated by U.S. troops. Soldiers under the command of Gen. George S. Patton took the city on the morning of May 6, 1945. The city still marks the liberation with a big festival in the first week of May, when Czechs drive around in old U.S. Army jeeps, everyone seems to be dressed up like a GI, and the city goes on a 5-day bender.

In mid-August the city hosts a modest music festival called **Jazz on the Streets,** highlighted with several concerts by top-name Czech musicians.

Anxious to capitalize on its beer heritage and always happy to celebrate, Plzeň has started its own Oktoberfest, called **Pivní slavnosti (Beer fest),** which takes place in the end of September and beginning of October.

For more details on festivities for all events, contact the **City Information Center Plzeň** (see above).

ORIENTATION Plzeň's old core is centered on Náměstí Republiky. All the sights, including the brewery, are no more than a 15-minute walk from here.

Touring the Beer Shrines

When in Rome, do as the Romans do; when in Plzeň, take the **brewery tour ★★,** at least that's the motto of most visitors here. It's actually a lot more fun and interesting than it sounds. **The Plzeňské Pivovary (Pilsner Breweries; ✆ 377-062-888;** www.prazdroj.cz/en) at U Prazdroje 7, are the proud home of Pilsner Urquell beer and a Czech national treasure. (Incidentally, this is also where they brew the cheaper, and far-inferior, Gambrinus, which remains the most widely consumed beer in the Czech Republic.)

The main tour lasts about 90 minutes and provides a chance for the current owners of the brewery, SABMiller, to show off their state-of-the-art brewing and bottling facilities and the brewery's long tradition, dating to 1842. The highlight of the tour is the old, underground fermentation cellars and the glass of unfiltered, unpasteurized pale lager you get to drink at the end. Bring a jacket along since it can get pretty cold down there.

Brewery tours in English are held daily at 12:45, 2:15, and 4:15pm. Tickets, which include an English-speaking guide, cost 150Kč for adults and 80Kč for students and seniors. A combined ticket, including entry to the Beer Museum (below), costs 200Kč for adults and 100Kč for students and seniors. There's a small gift shop on the premises. The walk to the brewery from the center takes about 15 minutes.

If you didn't get your fill of beer facts at the brewery, the **Pivovarské Muzeum (Beer Museum; ✆ 377-235-574;** www.prazdroj.cz/en) is a couple of blocks away, closer to the center of town, on Veleslavínova 6. Inside this former 15th-century house, you'll learn everything you wanted to know about beer but were afraid to ask. The displays include a collection of pub artifacts, brewing equipment, and mugs. Most displays have English captions, but ask for a more detailed museum description in English when you enter.

A separate entry to the museum costs 100Kč for adults and 60Kč for children. The museum is open daily from April to December from 10am to 6pm (to 5pm Jan–Mar).

The Beer Museum is also the starting point for an unrelated (to brewing, that is) tour, though they still give you a glass of beer to drink. Here you'll find the entrance to the **Pilsen Historical Underground ★ (✆ 377-235-574;** www.plzenskepodzemi. cz), a series of subterranean passages that was built starting in the 14th century to protect residents of the medieval city from attack as well as other purposes. Tours of the underground cost 90Kč for adults and 60Kč for children and seniors. Daily English-language tours are conducted at 1pm.

Exploring Plzeň

Filled with more knowledge than you may want about the brewing process, proceed to the main square to see what's hopping elsewhere in town. Dominating the center of the square is the Gothic **Cathedral of St. Bartholomew,** with the tallest steeple in the Czech Republic at 100m (328 ft.). A beautiful marble Madonna graces the main altar. The church is open daily from about 7am to 8pm.

You'll see Italian flair in the first four floors of the 16th-century **Town Hall** and in the *sgrafitti* (etchings) adorning its facade. Later on, more floors were added, as well as a tower, gables, and brass flags, making the building appear as though another had fallen on top of it. The Town Hall (✆ **378-032-550**) is open Monday to Friday from 8am to 6pm, Saturday from 9am to 1pm. In front of the Town Hall, a **memorial** built in 1681 commemorates victims of the plague.

Also on the main square at no. 23 is a relatively new attraction, the **Puppet Museum ★ ☺** (Muzeum Loutek; ✆ **378-370-801;** www.muzeumloutek.cz). Younger children will love the puppets and the inventive, interactive exhibitions that let you move the marionettes. Admission is 60Kč for adults and 30Kč for children from 3 to 15. The museum is open from Tuesday to Sunday from 10am to 6pm.

Just west of the square on Sady pětatřicátníků stands the majestic **Great Synagogue (Velká synagoga;** ✆ **377-235-749),** the second-largest Jewish house of worship in Europe after Budapest. It was built in the late 19th century, when the city's then-prosperous Jewish community numbered several thousand. You can tour the interior to admire the painstaking restoration process that has brought back the shrine's beauty. It's now used to host photo and art exhibits. Tickets to enter cost 60Kč for adults and 40Kč for children and seniors. It's open from Sunday to Friday from 10am to 5pm.

Where to Stay

The **City Information Center** (see "Visitor Information," above) can provide a list of private rooms and low-cost pensions around town. Expect to pay about 600Kč per person for this kind of accommodation. Most of the hotels offer paid on-site parking.

Courtyard By Marriott Pilsen ★★ In a city that feels so America-friendly and welcoming, perhaps it's no surprise to see this bright, shining Courtyard Marriott standing just across from the Beer Museum. It's a clean and well-run hotel and very likely a welcome change from the spare pensions and older hotels of other Czech cities. The location is ideal, 5 minutes' walk from the central square and 10 minutes to the Pilsner Urquell brewery.

Sady 5. května 57, 301 00 Plzeň. www.courtyard.com. ✆ **373-370-370.** Fax 373-370-373. 195 units. 2,400č double weekdays; 1,800Kč double weekends. AE, MC, V. Parking. **Amenities:** Restaurant; cafe; bar; concierge; fitness center; room service. *In room:* A/C, TV, hair dryer, minibar, Wi-Fi.

Hotel Central As you look around the historically beautiful Old Town square, one thing stands out: the Hotel Central. This rather sterile building is across from St. Bartholomew's Church. The hotel's a solid choice and surprisingly quiet despite its central location. The rooms have been recently remodeled and all look fresh. Ask for one of the rooms facing east; they have a nice view of the church as the sun rises. The hotel's restaurant and cafe are both smoke free.

Nám. Republiky 33, 301 00 Plzeň. www.central-hotel.cz. ℂ **377-226-757.** Fax 377-226-064. 77 units. 1,990Kč double weekdays; 1,690Kč double weekends. AE, MC, V. Parking. **Amenities:** Restaurant; cafe; bar; exercise room; sauna. *In room:* TV, minibar, Wi-Fi.

Hotel U Zvonu ★ The modern, even slightly aggressive stone-gray exterior hides what in reality is an attractive, clean, and comfortable hotel. The hotel is 5 years old, but still looks brand new inside and out. The rooms are large and modernly furnished. Some have small kitchenettes. The excellent location is just off the small riverside garden area and close to the center, Beer Museum, and beer tour.

Pražská 27, 301 00 Plzeň. www.hotel-uzvonu.cz. ℂ/fax **378-011-855.** 27 units. 2,700Kč double. AE, DC, MC, V. Parking. **Amenities:** Restaurant; bar. *In room:* TV, minibar, Wi-Fi.

Pension City This is an unpretentious, family-run pension with a great location near to the Beer Museum and the sights of the inner town, but also within easy walking distance of the breweries. The house is a lovely, reconstructed 17th-century building, but the rooms are on the plain, though snug and clean. Some look out over the river and the garden in front of the house.

Sady 5. května 52, 301 00 Plzeň. www.pensioncityplzen.cz. ℂ **377-326-069.** 12 units. 1,400Kč double. AE, DC, MC, V. *In room:* TV, Wi-Fi.

Where to Eat

Aberdeen Angus Steakhouse ★★★ STEAKHOUSE With all due respect to the American Center (above), you'll find arguably the Czech Republic's best cheeseburger at this English-style riverside steakhouse. It's served on a home-cooked, oversized bun that resembles an English muffin, with homemade french fries on the side and all for 180Kč. In fact, all the cuts of Angus beef are first-rate and value for money. The downstairs dining room is elegant and perfect for a celebratory meal; in summer, the sunny terrace is a marvelous spot to feel that all is right with the world.

Pražská 23, 301 00 Plzeň. ℂ **371-580-069.** www.angus-farm.cz. Main courses 180Kč–600Kč. AE, DC, MC, V. Daily 11am–10pm.

Restaurace Na Spilce ★ CZECH The Na Spilce looks like a 600-seat tourist trap, but the food is quite good and reasonably priced. The standard *řízky* (schnitzels), goulash, and *svíčková na smetaně* (pork tenderloin in cream sauce) are hearty and complement the beer that flows from the brewery. If you've got a big appetite or just can't decide, try the *Plzeňská bašta,* with ample servings of roasted pork, smoked pork, sausage, sauerkraut, and two kinds of dumplings.

U Prazdroje 7 (just inside the brewery gates). ℂ **377-062-755.** Soups 40Kč; main courses 80Kč–230Kč. AE, MC, V. Sun–Thurs 11am–10pm; Fri–Sat 11am–11pm.

Restaurace Žumbera CZECH A real pub that attracts mainly Czechs, Žumbera has food that's a cut above that of its competitors (of which there are many). If you can't decide, try the *Žumberská mísa,* a dish piled high with roast pork, smoked meat, spinach, cabbage, and several types of dumplings.

Bezručova 14. ℂ **377-322-436.** Soups 35Kč; main courses 80Kč–180Kč. MC, V. Mon–Thurs 9am–10pm; Fri–Sat 9am–midnight; Sun 9am–7pm.

Šenk Na Parkánu ★★ CZECH This very likeable and popular Czech pub is conveniently situated just next door to the Beer Museum (see above). There's a pleasant buzz (or maybe that's just the beer), accentuated by the warm mint-green walls and dark woods. The food includes the standards like goulash and schnitzel, plus more inventive dishes like pork shoulder cooked in dark beer—all at affordable prices. Be sure to book in the evening. There's a small terrace and an enclosed winter garden in case the tavern gets too boisterous.

Veleslavínova 4. ⓒ **377-324-485.** Main courses 80Kč–160Kč. No credit cards. Sun–Thurs 11am–10pm; Fri–Sat 11am–1am.

Simsalabim CZECH   Fun, witch-themed restaurant with very good Czech dishes, mostly pork and beef, served in an evocative cellar setting. The big outdoor terrace with large wooden tables is popular with students and good for groups. It's the perfect place to chill out on a summer night. In addition to food, there are great coffee drinks as well as the usual lineup of wine, beer, and cocktails.

Americká 18. ⓒ **377-222-173.** www.simsalabim.cz. Main courses 180Kč–300Kč. AE, DC, MC, V. Daily 10am–11pm.

U Salzmannů CZECH   This oldest pub in Plzeň, dating from 1637, has been renovated to reincarnate a previous *Jugendstil* rendition of the building. The beer is fresh, but the food is a little disappointing in its standard appearance and taste—you would expect a little flair, given the edifice. However, if you want to stay near the main square and don't want to make the long walk back across the river and up the hill to the brewery pubs, this pub will fulfill your needs admirably.

Pražská 8. ⓒ **377-235-855.** www.usalzmannu.cz. Soups 40Kč; main courses 90Kč–195Kč. AE, MC, V. Daily 10am–11pm.

CHEB (EGER) & FRANTIŠKOVY LÁZNĚ

168km (103 miles) W of Prague, 40km (25 miles) SW of Karlovy Vary

Cheb, the last Czech city of any size before you hit the German border, feels a little forgotten, tucked away in a corner of the country that few people visit. This can have a positive side. The center feels much less touristy and more authentic than do many more popular cities that don't have the intact historic architecture that Cheb has.

Cheb's history is nothing short of fascinating. The city started out 950 years ago as a former stronghold for the Holy Roman Empire on its eastern flank, and was once under the control of the famed Holy Roman Emperor Frederick I Barbarossa.

Eger, as it was then known, changed hands between German and Bohemian rulers several times, before becoming part of the Bohemian crown in 1322. The town found itself on the world stage in 1634, during the height of the Thirty Years' War in Europe, with forces loyal to Habsburg Emperor Ferdinand II squaring off against a mostly Protestant alliance of Swedes and German provinces.

It was here during that year that the gifted commander of the Habsburg forces, Albrecht von Wallenstein, was killed by members of his own army. While it's never been decisively proven what happened, the best theory is that Emperor Ferdinand himself ordered von Wallenstein's assassination after fearing the powerful general may have been negotiating a separate peace with the empire's enemies. You can still visit the bedroom (see below) where the grisly deed took place.

Cheb stayed under Bohemian rule, more or less, until it was forcibly handed over to Germany as part of the 1938 Munich Pact. Soon after the end of World War II, it was returned to Czech hands, when most of the area's native Germans, known as

Sudeten Germans, were expelled for their open encouragement of the invading Nazi army.

You can still see this bilingual, bicultural heritage in the main square, which could be mistaken for being on either side of the border if it weren't for the Czech writing on windows. Among the city's noteworthy sites are the eerie former Jewish Quarter, a small grouping of medieval houses known as the Špalíček, and an enormous Romanesque Chebský Hrad (Cheb Castle).

Only about 10 minutes up the road from Cheb is the smallest and arguably the cheeriest of the three major Bohemian spa towns, **Františkovy Lázně.** Though it pales in size compared with Karlovy Vary and Mariánské Lázně, Františkovy Lázně has taken great strides in the past few years to erase the decline it experienced under Communism. There's not much to see save for the **Spa Museum,** which holds an interesting display of bathing artifacts, but it's a quieter place to spend the night than Cheb. Listed below are places to stay and dine in both Cheb and Františkovy Lázně.

Essentials

GETTING THERE   Cheb is located on the E48, one of the main highways leading to Germany. If you're **driving** from Prague, take the same route you would to Karlovy Vary, which eventually brings you to Cheb. The drive takes about 2 hours.

To get to Františkovy Lázně from Cheb by car, take Hwy. E49. The trip takes about 15 minutes.

Several express **trains** daily make the trip to Cheb from Prague's main station. Trains follow one of two routes, via Plzeň or Karlovy Vary, with the Plzeň trains about 45 minutes quicker, bringing the trip to just over 3 hours. A second-class ticket costs 274Kč. Trains run every 2 hours during the day between Cheb and Mariánské Lázně. The trip takes 30 minutes and costs 45Kč second class. Trains from Cheb to Karlovy Vary run hourly. The trip takes around 1 hour and costs 72Kč.

Buses for Cheb depart Prague's Florenc bus station every 2 hours or so during the day. The trip takes a little more than 3 hours and costs about 200Kč. Buses are the best method for moving between Cheb and Františkový Lázně. Buses leave every 10 to 20 minutes from Cheb's main bus station and make the trip in 15 minutes. Tickets cost 15Kč.

VISITOR INFORMATION   You'll find maps, guidebooks, and lodging at the **Tourist Information Center,** náměstí Krále Jiřího z Poděbrad 33 (© **354-440-302;** fax 354-440-330; www.mestocheb.cz) on Cheb's main square.

ORIENTATION   At the center of the Old Town lies the triangular náměstí Krále Jiřího z Poděbrad. Most of the main sights you'll want to see lie either directly on the square or on one of the many streets leading off it.

Exploring Cheb

The main square, **náměstí Krále Jiřího z Poděbrad,** attracts most of the attention and is a good place to begin a stroll of the Old Town. Though the square is still a little musty in spots, there are several wonderful examples of period architecture, including many still-intact Gothic burgher houses and the baroque **Old Town Hall (Stará radnice).** Toward the south end of the square, the **statue of Kašna Roland,** built in 1591 and a former symbol of capital punishment, reminds people of the strength wielded by justice. At the other end of the square stands the **Kašna Herkules,** a monument to the town's former strength and power. Next to it is a cluster of 11 timber houses, called **Špalíček.** These used to be owned by Jews in the early 14th century, but a fervently anti-Semitic clergy in the area incited such hatred that the Jews were forced up Židská ulice (Jews St.) and into an alleyway called ulička Zavražděných (Murder Victim's Lane), where they were unceremoniously slaughtered in 1350.

Across from Špalíček is the **Cheb Museum** (✆ **739-322-499**) that occupies the house where Albrecht von Wallenstein was murdered in 1634. On the upper level, a display vividly depicts the assassination. The museum's first floor displays many 20th-century paintings, from which you can trace the town's slow demise. Admission is 70Kč for adults and 35Kč for students and seniors. You can buy a combined admission, including entry to the museum and Cheb Castle (below), for 90Kč for adults and 50Kč for students and seniors. From May through October, the museum is open Tuesday to Sunday from 9am to 5pm, and from November through April, Wednesday to Sunday 9am to 5pm.

The Old Town is also packed with churches. The most interesting is **St. Nicholas,** around the corner from the museum. It's a hodgepodge of architectural styles: Its Romanesque heritage, from the 13th century, is reflected in the tower windows, while a Gothic portal and baroque interior round out the renovations over the years. The tower got a makeover in 2008 to repair damage sustained in bombing raids in 1945. The church is open daily from 9am to 6pm.

Touring Cheb Castle

An excellent example of Romanesque architecture in the northeast part of the Old Town is **Cheb Castle** (✆ **739-322-494**). Overlooking the Elbe River, the castle, built in the 12th century, is one of central Europe's largest Romanesque structures. The castle has a storied past going all the way back to German Emperor Barbarossa and extending through the line of Czech kings. The last Czech king to live here was George of Poděbrady in the 15th century.

The complex remains one of the country's best-preserved town-wall and castle-fortification systems. While you can enter the castle only during the day, the area is especially beautiful at night, with the tower (and its white cap) aglow. Strolling the dark empty streets, it's relatively easy to imagine life here in the late Middle Ages.

The castle's main draws are its **Chapel of Sts. Erhart and Uršula** and the **Černá věž (Black Tower).** The two-tiered, early Gothic chapel has a somber first floor where the proletariat would congregate, while the emperor and his family went to the much cheerier and brighter second floor with its Gothic windows.

Across the courtyard from the chapel stands the **Černá věž (Black Tower).** From its 18m-high (59-ft.) lookout, you'll have the best views of the town. The tower's color is mostly black because the blocks from which it is made are lava rocks taken from the nearby Komorní Hůrka volcano (now dormant).

Admission to the castle is 60Kč for adults and 30Kč for students and seniors. The castle and tower are open only in the warmer months from April through October from Tuesday to Sunday. In the months of April and October, the opening hours are 11am to 5pm. From May through September, the complex is open from 9am to 5pm.

Where to Stay

IN CHEB

Hannibal ★ This is a modest, well-run pension about 10 minutes walk from Cheb's historic center. There's not much in the way of facilities, but the rooms are quiet and spotless, and some sport period funky folk furnishing, like wood-carved peasant beds and the like. The little garden terrace downstairs is one of the nicest places in Cheb to eat. The menu offers mostly simple Czech dishes, but the setting is traditional and family friendly.

Májová 10, 350 02 Cheb. www.pension-hannibal.webnode.cz. ⓒ **354-430-475.** 10 units. 1,200Kč double. AE, DC, MC, V. Parking. **Amenities:** Restaurant; Internet. *In room:* TV.

Hotel Barbarossa ★ Cheb's nicest hotel is on a quiet side street just off the main square. Everything is spotless and well maintained, though the furnishings are more in the utilitarian category than outright luxurious. The top-floor apartment has three beds and is a good value for families. The restaurant is arguably the best in the center of town.

Jateční 7, 350 02 Cheb. www.hotel-barbarossa.cz. ⓒ **354-423-446.** 21 units. 1,800Kč double; 2,200Kč top-floor apartment. AE, DC, MC, V. Parking. **Amenities:** Restaurant; Internet. *In room:* TV, minibar.

Hotel Hvězda Don't be put off by the uninspiring facade that's still chipped in places and lending an unfortunate air of decline. The rooms are comfortable and clean and the reception warm. This place is much better operated than it looks and is an excellent value for the money. Ask for one of the more recently remodeled rooms. Breakfast is not included in the price, though there's a nice selection of set breakfasts in the hotel restaurant priced at 60Kč each. There's free parking at the rear of the hotel.

Nám. Krále Jiřího z Poděbrad 4–6, 350 02 Cheb. www.hotel-hvezda.cz. ⓒ **354-422-549.** Fax 354-422-546. 40 units. 900Kč double. AE, MC, V. Parking. **Amenities:** Restaurant; Wi-Fi (lobby only). *In room:* TV, minibar.

IN FRANTIŠKOVY LÁZNĚ
Hotel Tři Lilie (Three Lilies Hotel) The four-star Three Lilies is worth the extra money since it's one of the few luxury hotels in the area. At night, you can relax, blocking out noise in your spotless, spacious room that's outfitted with satellite television. The staff is very attentive and can arrange spa treatments, massages, and other health services.

Národní 3, 351 01 Františkovy Lázně. www.franzensbad.cz. ⓒ **354-208-900.** Fax 354-208-905. 32 units. 2,700Kč double; 4,860Kč suite. AE, MC, V. Parking. **Amenities:** Restaurant; bar; cafe; health club & spa; Internet. *In room:* TV, minibar.

Where to Eat
IN CHEB
There are lots of restaurants and cafes on the central square, Náměstí Krále Jiřího z Poděbrad. The best advice would be to walk around and check menus to see something you like. Some of the better places are listed below.

Bartholomeus ★★ CZECH This is an attractive pub-restaurant with an upscale 1920s look accented by black-and-white and sepia-tone photos of old Cheb on the walls. It's easily the best choice on the main square for a refined evening meal in a town where there aren't that many decent options. The menu is limited mostly to grilled meats and steaks. The rib-eye at 239Kč might just be the best steak in town. Reserve on weekend evenings.

Nám. Krále Jiřího z Poděbrad 36. ⓒ **354-426-179.** www.bartholomeus.cz. Main courses 119Kč–289Kč. AE, DC, MC, V. Daily 9am–10pm.

Kavárna Špalíček CZECH   This kavárna is better for a coffee stop than for a full meal. You can enjoy great people-watching from the terrace, but Špalíček's real charm lies inside the building, which sits like an island in the middle of the square. This special place is a piece of living history.

Nám. Krále Jiřího z Poděbrad. ℂ **354-422-568.** Soups 40Kč; main courses 90Kč–240Kč. No credit cards. Daily 10am–10pm.

IN FRANTIŠKOVY LÁZNĚ

Gourmet Restaurant Goethe ★★ CZECH/CONTINENTAL   This is a great throwback option (as is the Viennese cafe across the hall) to the 19th century, when "Franzensbad" could lay claim to real elegance. Expect waiters decked out in dinner jackets, candlelight, lots of linen, and soothing piano music in the background. In addition to the usual choices, the menu sports more daring options like grilled pike-perch served with asparagus and béarnaise sauce (365Kč) and lamb cutlets served with green beans and gnocchi (495Kč). Book in advance on Friday and Saturday evenings.

Národní třída 1 (in the ICF Casino complex). ℂ **354-500-146.** Main courses 150Kč–520Kč. AE, MC, V. Daily 11:30am–2:30pm, 6–11pm; cafe daily 9am–7pm.

ČESKÉ BUDĚJOVICE

147km (91 miles) S of Prague

This fortress town was born in 1265, when Otakar II decided that the intersection of the Vltava and Malše rivers would be the site of a bastion to protect the approaches to southern Bohemia. Although Otakar was killed at the battle of the Moravian Field in 1278 and the town was subsequently ravaged by the rival Vítkovic family, the construction of České Budějovice continued, eventually taking the shape originally envisioned.

In the 15th century, the Hussite revolution swept across southern Bohemia, with one exception—České Budějovice, which, with its largely Catholic population, remained true to the king. Passing the loyalty test with flying colors, it developed into one of Bohemia's wealthiest and most important towns, reaching its pinnacle in the 16th century. This rise made České Budějovice an architecturally stunning place. As the town prospered, older Gothic buildings took on a Renaissance look. A new town hall was built and the flourishing old market (Masné Krámy) was rebuilt. Towering above it all was a new 72m-tall (236-ft.) turret, the Black Tower. Sadly, the Thirty Years' War (1618–48) and a major fire in 1641 ravaged much of the town, leaving few buildings unscathed. But the Habsburg Empire came to the town's rescue in the 18th century, building baroque-style edifices that stand to this day.

Today, České Budějovice, the hometown of the original Budweiser brand beer, is now more a bastion for the beer drinker than a protector of Bohemia. But its slow pace, relaxed atmosphere, and interesting architecture make it a worthy stop, especially as a base for exploring southern Bohemia or for those heading on to Austria.

Essentials

GETTING THERE   If you're **driving,** leave Prague to the south via the main D1 expressway and take the cutoff for Hwy. E55, which runs straight to České Budějovice. The trip takes about 1½ hours.

Daily express **trains** from Prague make the trip to České Budějovice in about 2½ hours. The fare is 320Kč first class or 213Kč second class. Several express **buses** run from Prague's Roztyly station (on the metro's C line) each day and take 3 hours; tickets cost about 160Kč. Buy tickets from the bus driver.

VISITOR INFORMATION Tourist Infocentrum, nám. Přemysla Otakara II. 1–2 (© **386-801-413**; www.c-budejovice.cz), just next to the historic town hall, provides maps and guidebooks and can help find lodging. It is open Monday to Friday 8:30am to 6pm; Saturday 8:30am to 5pm; and Sunday 10am to 4pm. In winter, it is open Monday and Wednesday 9am to 5pm; Tuesday, Thursday, and Friday 9am to 4pm; and Saturday 9am to 1pm. Don't be fooled by the "Infocentrum" at nám. Přemysla Otakara II. 21. Though it looks like a full-fledged tourist information office, in reality it's a souvenir shop looking to sell maps to unsuspecting tourists.

SPECIAL EVENTS Each August, České Budějovice hosts the largest **International Agricultural Show** in the country (www.vcb.cz), plus many other smaller exhibitions and festivals year-round. Check the website for details.

If you're passing through in the late fall or winter and want to see Czechs at their most emotional, head out to a match of the **Czech Extraliga hockey** league at the hockey arena on ul. F. A. Gerstnera 8/7, where the local team, HC Mountfield, does battle. Arguably some of the best hockey in the world is played in the Czech Republic, which you can see for a fraction of the price—from 100Kč to 180Kč—you'd pay to see players of a similar caliber in the North American National Hockey League. The games are rarely sold out. The box office (© **386-352-705**; www.hokejcb.cz) opens 1 hour before the game. The local newspapers, tourist information center, and posters pasted around the town will tell you what time the next match is.

ORIENTATION České Budějovice's circular Staré Město (Old Town) centers around the Czech Republic's largest cobblestone square, náměstí Přemysla Otakara II.

Exploring the Town

You can comfortably see České Budějovice in a day. At its center is one of central Europe's largest squares, the cobblestone **náměstí Přemysla Otakara II**—it may actually be too large, as many of the buildings tend to get lost in all the open space. The square contains the ornate **Fountain of Sampson,** an 18th-century water well that was once the town's principal water supply, plus a mishmash of baroque and Renaissance buildings. On the southwest corner is the **Town Hall,** an elegant baroque structure built by Martinelli between 1727 and 1730. On top of the Town Hall, the larger-than-life statues by Dietrich represent the civic virtues: justice, bravery, wisdom, and diligence.

One block north of the square is the **Černá věž (Black Tower),** which you can see from almost every point in the city. Consequently, it's worth the climb to the top to get a bird's-eye view in all directions. The most famous symbol of České Budějovice, this 70m-tall (236-ft.) 16th-century tower was built as a belfry for the adjacent **St. Nicholas Church.** This 13th-century church, one of the town's most important sights, was a bastion of Roman Catholicism during the 15th-century Hussite rebellion. You shouldn't miss the church's flamboyant, white-and-cream, 17th-century baroque interior.

The tower is open Tuesday to Sunday (daily Apr–Oct) from 10am to 6pm; admission is 30Kč for adults and 20 Kč for children and seniors. The church is open daily from 9am to 6pm.

Touring a Beer Shrine

On the town's northern edge sits a shrine to those who pray to the gods of the amber nectar. This is where **Budějovický Budvar,** Karolíny Světlé 4 ((✆ **387-705-111**), the original brewer of Budweiser beer, has its one and only factory. Established in 1895, Budvar draws on more than 700 years of the area's brewing tradition to produce one of the world's best beers.

One trolley bus—no. 2—stops by the brewery; this is how the brewery ensures that its workers and visitors reach the plant safely each day. You can also hop a cab from the town square for about 150Kč.

The brewery offers 1-hour guided tours in Czech, English, and German at 2pm from Monday to Friday in season (Apr–Oct) and Tuesday to Friday at 2pm during the rest of the year. Normally, it's okay just to show up, but to be sure call ahead to the **Budvar Visitors' Centre** at the brewery ((✆ **387-705-341**; www.budweiser-budvar.cz) to reserve a place. Tours cost 100Kč per person.

Once you're inside the brewery, the smell may cause flashbacks to some of the wilder frat parties you've attended. This is a traditional brew, and not much has changed at the brewery over the past hundred years or so. The room where everything moves along conveyer belts and goes from dirty old bottles to boxed cartons is fascinating.

Where to Stay

Several agencies can locate reasonably priced private rooms. Expect to pay about 800Kč per person, in cash. The **Tourist Infocentrum,** nám. Přemysla Otakara II. 1–2 ((✆ **386-801-413**), can point you toward a wide selection of conveniently located rooms and pensions.

Grandhotel Zvon Traditionally regarded as the České Budějovice's finest hotel. These days, most of the clients are businessmen traveling on expenses—hence room rates that are a notch above the competition. Rooms are divided into Executive, Business, and Standard rooms, with executive rooms boasting views out over the square and air-conditioning, among other amenities. Executive and business rooms offer sleeker, more modern interiors, while the standard rooms are a bit frumpier. There are several bars and restaurant on the premises and the location, right on the square, is ideal.

Nám. Přemysla Otakara II. 28, 370 01 České Budějovice. www.hotel-zvon.cz. (✆ **381-601-601.** Fax 381-601-605. 75 units. 2,600Kč standard double, 3,400Kč business double, 4,400Kč executive double. AE, DC, MC, V. **Amenities:** Restaurant; cafe; bar. *In room:* TV, minibar, Wi-Fi.

Hotel Budweis ★★ České Budějovice's newest four-star entry, opened in 2010, is a stylish, modern hotel fashioned from the town's former grain mill. Many of the building's original architectural details have been retained, such as the exterior brickwork and wooden ceilings and floors throughout. The rooms are stunning if you like spare futuristic design. The colors are muted, with browns and beiges dominating, and big white comforters draped over huge beds. The management claims all 60 rooms are wheelchair accessible. The riverside location is quiet, and the restaurant is already seen as one of the best in the city.

Mlýnská 6. 28, 370 01 České Budějovice. www.hotelbudweis.cz. (✆ **389-822-111.** Fax 389-822-121. 60 units. 2,990Kč double. AE, DC, MC, V. **Amenities:** Restaurant; cafe; bar. *In room:* A/C (some), TV, hair dryer, minibar, Wi-Fi.

keeping up with the schwarzenbergs:
VISITING A 141-ROOM ENGLISH CASTLE

Only 8km (5 miles) north of České Budějovice lies **Hluboká nad Vltavou** ★★ (© 387-843-911; www.zamek-hluboka.eu). Built in the 13th century, this castle has undergone many face-lifts over the years, but none that left as lasting an impression as those ordered by the Schwarzenberg family. As a sign of the region's growing wealth and importance in the mid–19th century, the Schwarzenbergs remodeled the 141-room castle in the neo-Gothic style of England's Windsor Castle. No expense was spared in the quest for opulence. The Schwarzenbergs removed the impressive wooden ceiling from their residence at Český Krumlov and reinstalled it in the large dining room. Other rooms are equally garish in their appointments, making a guided tour worth the time, even though only about a third of the rooms are open to the public.

The castle is open daily May to August from 9am to 5pm (last tour at 4pm); April, September, and October Tuesday to Sunday from 9am to 4:30pm (last tour at 3pm). There is a lunch break between noon and 12:30pm. Tours in English cost 250Kč adults, 160Kč students.

To complete the experience, the **Alšova Jihočeská Galerie (Art Gallery of South Bohemia; © 387-967-041)** in the Castle's riding hall at Hluboká, houses the second-largest art collection in Bohemia, including many interesting Gothic sculptures from the area, and Dutch painters from the 16th to 18th centuries. It is open daily May to September from 9am to 6pm.

The castle's distance from České Budějovice is short enough to make it a pleasant bike trip from the city or a quick stop either on the way to or from Prague, Třeboň, or Tábor. The town's information center (see below) can help with bike rentals.

If you're driving to Hluboká from České Budějovice, take Hwy. E49 north and then Hwy. 105 just after leaving the outskirts of České Budějovice. Cyclists should follow cycling trail no. 12, which takes you practically to the gates of the castle.

The town's **Information Center** at Zborovská 80 (© 387-966-164; www.hluboka.cz) will provide you with maps, souvenirs, and answers to your questions.

Hotel Malý Pivovar (Small Brewery) ★ Around the corner from the Zvon, this renovated 16th-century microbrewery combines the charms of a B&B with the amenities of a modern hotel. The kind of management found here is a rarity in the Czech tourism industry: They work hard to help out. The rooms are bright and cheery, with antique-style wooden furniture and exposed wooden ceiling beams providing a farmhouse feeling in the center of town. It's definitely worth consideration if being directly on the square isn't a priority.

Ul. Karla IV. 8–10, 370 01 České Budějovice. www.malypivovar.cz. © **386-360-471.** Fax 386-360-474. 29 units. 2,760Kč double; 3,200Kč suite. Rates include breakfast. AE, DC, MC, V. **Amenities:** Restaurant; bar. *In room:* TV, minibar, Wi-Fi.

Hotel U Solné brány Another of the growing number of conveniently located hotels just off the main square, U Solné brány is one of the products of post-Communism: a bright renovated hotel with friendly management. It almost feels like a pension. Most rooms have balconies, making a cold Budvar from the minibar almost mandatory in the early evening or as a nightcap.

Radniční ul. 11, 370 01 České Budějovice. www.hotelusolnebrany.cz. © **386-354-121.** Fax 386-354-120. 11 units. 1,990Kč double; 2,290Kč suite. Rates include breakfast. AE, MC, V. **Amenities:** Restaurant. *In room:* TV, minibar.

Hotel Zátkův Dům ★★ A nice compromise between comfort and price, this family-owned affair is a solid choice. It sits about 3 blocks off the main square, but within easy walking distance of anywhere you'd want to go. The rooms are big and clean and quiet. The baths are modern and comfortably sized. Parking is available in the hotel courtyard, and the reception desk staff is more than happy to help you get your bearings. A solid choice. Some of the rooms off the courtyard are equipped for guests with disabilities.

Krajinská 41, 370 01 České Budějovice. www.zatkuvdum.cz. © **387-001-710.** Fax 387-001-711. 10 units. 1,600Kč double. Rates include breakfast. AE, DC, MC, V. **Amenities:** Restaurant; bar. *In room:* AC, TV, hair dryer, minibar, Wi-Fi.

Where to Eat

Fresh Salad & Pizza ★★ PIZZA A high-quality pizzeria-coffeehouse with a quiet terrace on Piaristické náměstí that's the perfect antidote to the town's hectic main square. The pizzas are filling and well-done. Pizza "U2 Domů" is a crazy combination of bacon, eggs, peppers, chilies, and mushrooms that somehow works beautifully. The salads are big and fresh as advertised. A real find if you're just looking for something quick and easy or are starting to tire of big meals of pork and dumplings.

Hroznova 21 (Piaristické nám.). © **608-258-510.** Pizzas 130Kč; salads 80Kč–100Kč. No credit cards. Daily 11am–10pm.

Indická Restaurace ★ INDIAN Convincingly authentic, delicious Indian restaurant that's sure to awaken your palate after days of milder Czech cooking. The *chicken tikka masala,* in particular, will clear out your sinuses in a hurry. The restaurant is situated one floor up from street level, with two dining rooms. One is cozy and nonsmoking, while the other is a kind of bar-cafe that allows smoking and has the same menu.

Piaristická 22. © **777-326-200.** www.indickarestaurace.cz. Main courses 120Kč–270Kč. No credit cards. Mon–Sat 11am–11pm.

Kavárna Placidus ★ CAFE Every town should have a coffee shop like Placidus, with its serving counter crammed with homemade pastries, cookies, and cakes, as well sandwiches and ice cream. There are several booths to have a seat and enjoy a coffee with your cake. Placidus opens early in the morning, which can be a lifesaver if you're staying at a place that doesn't serve breakfast as part of the deal or you turn up in town before anything is open. If you do stop here for breakfast, try the "hamenex," a Czech version of ham and eggs, where all the ingredients are cooked together in one pan. Delicious.

Na Mlýnské Stoce 11. © **777-312-093.** Main courses 60Kč–120Kč. No credit cards. Mon–Sat 7:30am–9pm.

Masné Krámy ★★ CZECH České Budějovice's fabled watering hole, named after the town's former meat market, just northwest of náměstí Přemysla Otakara II, underwent a thorough face-lift a couple of years ago that left it much cleaner but looking a little bit sterile. Fortunately there's still the same great—and cheap—Czech tavern food, like pork, chicken, and goulash, and the Budweiser beer is straight from the brewery. It's wildly popular, so advance booking is essential if you want to eat. If you're just there for the beer, it's almost always possible to find a seat near the bar.

Krajinská 29. ☎ **387-201-301.** www.masne-kramy.cz. Main courses 120Kč–270Kč. AE, MC, V. Mon–Thurs 10:30am–11pm; Fri–Sat 10:30am–midnight; Sun 10:30am–9pm.

ČESKÝ KRUMLOV ★★★

19km (12 miles) SW of České Budějovice

If you have time on your visit to the Czech Republic for only one excursion, seriously consider making it **Český Krumlov.** One of Bohemia's prettiest towns, Krumlov is a living gallery of elegant Renaissance-era buildings housing charming cafes, pubs, restaurants, shops, and galleries. In 1992, UNESCO named Český Krumlov a World Heritage Site for its historical importance and physical beauty.

Bustling since medieval times, the town, after centuries of embellishment, is exquisitely beautiful. In 1302, the Rožmberk family inherited the castle and moved in, using it as their main residence for nearly 300 years. You'll feel that time has stopped as you look from the Lazebnický Bridge and see the waters of the Vltava below snaking past the castle's gray stone. At night, by the castle lights, the view becomes even more dramatic.

Few dared change the appearance of Český Krumlov over the years, not even the Schwarzenbergs, who had a flair for opulence. At the turn of the 19th century, several facades of houses in the town's outer section were built, as were inner courtyards. Thankfully, economic stagnation in the area under Communism meant little money for "development," so no glass-and-steel edifices (the Hotel Thermal in Karlovy Vary comes to mind) jut out to spoil the architectural beauty. Instead, a medieval sense reigns supreme, now augmented by the many festivals and renovations that keep the town's spirit alive.

Essentials

GETTING THERE   From České Budějovice, it's about a 30-minute **drive** to Krumlov, depending on traffic. Take Hwy. 3 from the south of České Budějovice and turn onto Hwy. 159. The roads are clearly marked, with several signs directing traffic to the town. From Prague, it's a 3-hour drive down Hwy. 3 through Tábor. Once you reach Krumlov, bear in mind that driving in the center is strictly prohibited and if caught you face a stiff fine. Instead, stow your car in one of several numbered, pay parking lots around the city (5Kč/hr.). The best one in my opinion is **parking lot no. 2,** which takes you just to the gates of the Eggenberg brewery and about a 10-minute walk from the main square.

The only way to reach Český Krumlov **by train** from Prague is via České Budějovice, a slow ride that deposits you at a station relatively far from the town center (trip time: 3 hr., 50 min.). Several trains leave daily from Prague's Hlavní nádraží; the fare is 250Kč. If you are already in České Budějovice and you want to make a trip to Krumlov, several trains connect these two cities throughout the day. The trip takes about an hour and costs 50Kč. For timetables, go to **www.jizdnirady.cz.**

The nearly 3-hour **bus** ride from Prague sometimes involves a transfer in České Budějovice. The fare is 100Kč, and the bus station in Český Krumlov is a 10-minute walk from the town's main square.

VISITOR INFORMATION   Right on the main square, the **Information Centrum,** nám. Svornosti 2, 381 01 Český Krumlov (© **380-704-622;** fax 380-704-619; www.ckrumlov.info), provides a complete array of services, including booking accommodations, reserving tickets for events, and arranging travel back to Prague or onward to destinations such as Vienna, Salzburg, and Linz in Austria. There are also terminals here where you can check e-mail (5Kč for 5 min.). It's open daily June through September from 9am to 7pm; in April, May, and October from 9am to 6pm; and from November to March from 9am to 5pm.

Be warned that the municipal hall is in the same building, and it's crowded with weddings on weekends. If someone holds out a hat, throw some change into it, take a traditional shot of liquor from him, and say *"Blahopřeji!"* ("Congratulations!") to everyone in the room.

SPECIAL EVENTS   After being banned during Communism, the **Slavnosti pětilisté růže (Festival of the Five-Petaled Rose)** has made a triumphant comeback. It's held each year during the summer solstice. Residents of Český Krumlov dress up in Renaissance costume and parade through the streets. Afterward, the streets become a stage for chess games with people dressed as pieces, music, plays, and even duels "to the death."

Český Krumlov also plays host to the **International Music Festival** every July and August, attracting performers from all over the world. Performances are held in nine spectacular venues. Tickets and details are available over the festival website (www.festivalkrumlov.cz) or through **Ticketstream** (www.ticketstream.cz) or the event organizer in Prague: **Auviex,** at Perlitová 1820, Prague 4 (© **241-445-404;** www.auviex.cz).

Though much quieter in the winter, the town comes alive on **New Year's Eve** when its spectacular setting is lit up by midnight fireworks shot from a hill next to the center of town. Hotels and pensions fill up quickly, so reservations are recommended. Most restaurants and hotels have a special dinner/dancing deal that is also recommended to ensure you have a place to party when you return from watching the fireworks.

ORIENTATION   Surrounded by a circular sweep of the Vltava River, Český Krumlov is easy to negotiate. The main square, **náměstí Svornosti,** is at the very center of the Inner Town. The bridge that spans the Vltava a few blocks away leads to a rocky hill and the Latrán area, above which is the castle, **Český Krumlov Château.**

Strolling Through Český Krumlov

Bring a good pair of walking shoes and be prepared to wear them out. Český Krumlov's hills and alleyways cry out for hours of exploration, but if you push the pace you can see everything in 1 day. Few cars, thank goodness, are allowed in the historic town, and the cobblestones keep most other vehicles at bay. The town is split into two parts—the **Inner Town** and **Latrán,** which houses the castle. They're best tackled separately, so you won't have to crisscross the bridges several times.

Begin your walk at the **Okresní Muzeum (Regional Museum;** © **380-711-674)** at the top of Horní 152. Once a Jesuit seminary, the three-story museum now contains artifacts and displays relating to Český Krumlov's 1,000-year history. The highlight of this mass of folk art, clothing, furniture, and statues is a giant model of the town that offers a bird's-eye view of the buildings. Admission is 60Kč. The museum is open May to September, daily 10am to 5pm (until 6pm July–Aug); in

ATTRACTIONS ●

Český Krumlov Chateau **6**
- Most Na Plášti **3**
- Gardens **2**
- Theater **5**
Egon Schiele Foundation/
    Egon Schiele Centrum **13**
Former hospital and
    church of St. Jošt **12**
Náměstí Svornosti **17**
Okresní Muzeum **21**
Radnice (Town Hall) **18**
St. Vitus Cathedral **23**

HOTELS ■

Hotel Bellevue **7**
Hotel Konvice **20**
Hotel Růže **24**
Hotýlek & Hospoda u
    malého Vítka **14**
Pension Anna **26**
Pension Barbakán **25**
Pension Na louži **22**
Pension Ve Věži **8**
Zlatý Anděl **16**

RESTAURANTS ◆

Hospoda Na louži **22**
Krčma Markéta **1**
Krčma v Šatlavské **19**
Laibon **15**
Nonna Gina **9**
Papa's Living Restaurant **11**
Zapa Café **10**

A crowd ALERT

Consider yourself warned: Word has spread far and wide about Český Krumlov. (A cover photo on *National Geographic Traveler* magazine a couple of years ago identifying it as one of the "greatest places on earth" didn't help matters.) Late spring to early autumn can be unbearable as thousands of visitors blanket its medieval streets. If possible, try to visit in the off season from November to April, when the crowds recede, the prices decrease, and the town's charm can really shine.

October to December and March to April, it's open Tuesday to Friday 9am to 4pm, and Saturday and Sunday 1 to 4pm. Just to the left of the museum entrance is a small park with arguably the town's most dramatic photo backdrop (which really says something in a place as photogenic as Český Krumlov).

Across the street from the museum is the **Hotel Růže (Rose),** Horní 154 (© **380-772-100;** www.hotelruze.cz), which was once a Jesuit student house. Built in the late 16th century, the hotel and the prelature next to it show the development of architecture—Gothic, Renaissance, and rococo influences are all present. If you're not staying at the hotel, don't be afraid to walk around and even ask questions at the reception desk.

Continue down the street to the impressive late-Gothic **St. Vitus Cathedral.** The church is open daily from 9am to 5pm.

As you continue down the street, you'll come to **náměstí Svornosti.** Few buildings here show any character, making the main square of such an impressive town a little disappointing. The **Radnice (Town Hall),** at nám. Svornosti 1, is one of the few exceptions. Open daily from 9am to 6pm, its Gothic arcades and Renaissance vault inside are exceptionally beautiful. From the square, streets fan out in all directions. Take some time to wander through them.

When you get closer to the river, you still can see the high-water marks on some of the quirky bank-side houses, which were devastated by the floods of 2002. Most of the places have taken the opportunity to make a fresh start after massive reconstruction. **Krumlovský Mlýn (The Krumlov Mill),** Široká 80 (© **736-634-460;** www.krumlovskymlyn.cz), is a combination restaurant, gallery, antiques shop, and exhibition space. For an additional treat, stroll through the exhibition of historical motorcycles. Open daily 10am to 10pm.

One of Český Krumlov's most famous residents was Austrian-born artist Egon Schiele. He was a bit of an eccentric who on more than one occasion raised the ire of the town's residents (many found his use of young women as nude models distressing), and his stay was cut short when the locals' patience ran out. But the town readopted the artist in 1993, setting up the **Egon Schiele Art Centrum ★★** in Inner Town, Široká 70–72, 381 01 Český Krumlov (© **380-704-011;** www.schiele artcentrum.cz). It documents his life and work, housing a permanent selection of his paintings as well as exhibitions of other 20th-century artists. Admission is 120Kč; hours are daily from 10am to 6pm.

After you've seen the museum, stop in at the excellent coffeehouse next door, the **Egon Schiele Café,** Široká 71, 381 01 Český Krumlov (© **725-511-219;** www.

egonschielecafe.com), which specializes in "Fairtrade" coffees, exotic tea drinks, and homemade pastries. Open daily 10am to 7pm.

Exploring the Château

Reputedly the second-largest castle in Bohemia (after Prague Castle), **Český Krumlov Château ★★** was constructed in the 13th century as part of a private estate. Throughout the ages, it has been passed on to a variety of private owners, including the Rožmberk family, Bohemia's largest landholders, and the Schwarzenbergs, the Bohemian equivalent of the Hilton family. Perched high atop a rocky hill, the château is open only from April to October, exclusively by guided tours.

Follow the path for the long climb up to the **castle.** Greeting you is a round 12th-century **Castle Tower**—painstakingly renovated, with its Renaissance balcony. You'll pass over the moat, now occupied by two brown bears. Next is the **Dolní Hrad (Lower Castle)** and then the **Horní Hrad (Upper Castle).**

There are several options for seeing the sights, but be forewarned that prices have crept up in recent years, and a full viewing of the castle (including the three main guided tours) can be an expensive proposition. Family discounts (for up to three accompanying children) can help take the sting out of the prices. One budget option is to simply stroll the grounds (which are free to enter) and climb the Castle Tower (50Kč) for sweeping views out over the town and surrounding countryside. The castle grounds are also open at night, when the views down on the town are even more dramatic and the crowds thin out to a trickle.

The cash desk *(pokladna)* to book one of the three main tours is situated in the main courtyard after you've crossed the moat. Tour 1 begins in the rococo **Chapel of St. George,** and continues through the portrait-packed **Renaissance Rooms,** and the **Schwarzenberg Baroque Suite,** outfitted with ornate furnishings that include Flemish wall tapestries, European paintings, and also the extravagant 17th-century **Golden Carriage.** Tour 2 includes the **Schwarzenberg portrait gallery** as well as their 19th-century suite. Tour 3 presents the Castle's fascinating **Baroque Theater,** though at more than US$20 a ticket, sadly, this is priced more for real theater aficionados than the general public. Tours last about 1 hour and depart frequently. Most are in Czech or German, however. If you want an English-language tour, arrange it ahead of time (© **380-704-711;** www.castle.ckrumlov.cz). The tours in English cost 250Kč adults, 160Kč students, 600Kč family (Tour 1); 240Kč adults, 140Kč students, 500Kč family (Tour 2); 380Kč adults, 220Kč students, 780Kč family (Tour 3). The tickets are sold separately. The castle hours are from Tuesday to Sunday: June to August 8:45am to 5pm; April, May, September, and October 8:45am to 4pm. The last entrance is 1 hour before closing.

Once past the main castle building, you can see one of the more stunning views of Český Krumlov from **Most Na Plášti,** a walkway that doubles as a belvedere to the Inner Town. Even farther up the hill lie the castle's riding school and gardens.

Where to Stay

There are tons of hotels in Český Krumlov and you'll rarely have a problem getting a room, but summer weekends and festival periods can still get tight, so it's always best to book in advance. In addition to the hotels, hundreds of property owners have opened up pensions, and the best of these can rival the hotels for comfort and location—at around half the price. Look for PENSION or ZIMMER FREI signs outside of houses. Two of the best streets for seeking out pensions are tiny Parkán Lane in the center and Rooseveltova, which extends out beyond Horní ulice, to the south and east of the main square. For a comprehensive list of area hotels and help with bookings, call or write to the Information Centrum listed above in "Visitor Information."

VERY EXPENSIVE

Hotel Růže (Rose Hotel) ★   Once a Jesuit seminary, this stunning Italian Renaissance building has been converted into a well-appointed hotel. Comfortable in a big-city kind of way, it's packed with amenities and is one of the top places to stay in Český Krumlov (though prices have risen considerably in recent years and it's not clear it's still really worth this much money). For families or large groups, the larger suites (while still *very* expensive for what you get) have eight beds and at least provide better value.

Horní 154, 381 01 Český Krumlov. www.hotelruze.cz. ℂ **380-772-100.** Fax 380-713-146. 70 units. 5,300Kč double; 6,900Kč suite. Rates include breakfast. AE, MC, V. **Amenities:** Restaurant; bar; health club & spa; pool (indoor); room service. *In room:* TV, hair dryer, minibar, Wi-Fi.

EXPENSIVE

Hotel Bellevue ★★   For years the "City of Vienna" hotel, as the Bellevue was formerly known, was an elegant, crumbling ruin awaiting its white knight. A couple of years ago, that (well-heeled) suitor appeared and now the Bellevue rivals the Hotel Růže as the town's top address. Everything here is spic and span. Some rooms boast spare, chic modern furnishings and beautifully tiled floors, while others favor a 19th-century period look with more fabrics and wood or carpeted floors. Ask to see a few before choosing. There are two restaurants on the premises, as well as a cafe and a spa/wellness center. The location, just within the town gate but outside the main tourist areas, is an advantage away from the hub-bub. Nonsmoking throughout. Some rooms for guests with disabilities.

Latrán 77, 381 01 Český Krumlov. www.bellevuehotels.cz. ℂ **380-720-177.** Fax 380-720-119. 66 units. 2,600Kč double; 4,800Kč suite. Rates include breakfast. AE, MC, V. Parking. **Amenities:** Restaurant; bar; health club & spa; room service. *In room:* TV, hair dryer, minibar, Wi-Fi.

Zlatý Anděl (Golden Angel) ★   After a long reconstruction and renovation of its rooms, including new furniture, the Golden Angel has shed its Communist furnishings for more stylish fittings right down to the marble bathrooms. Think about getting a suite rather than a regular room, since a couple of them are loft apartments that are much more open. The hotel offers a tempting 2-night package for 2,800Kč per person, including two main meals (lunch or dinner).

Nám. Svornosti 10–11, 381 01 Český Krumlov. www.hotelzlatyandel.cz. ℂ **380-712-310.** Fax 380-712-927. 40 units. 2,900Kč double; 4,600Kč suite. Rates include breakfast. AE, MC, V. Parking. **Amenities:** Restaurant; bar. *In room:* TV, minibar, Wi-Fi.

MODERATE

Hotel Konvice ★★   The Konvice wins perennial—justifiable—rave reviews for coziness, cleanliness and location, just a block from the main square. The large suite, room no. 11, has two separate bedrooms and a castle view from the terrace, and is excellent value for money for families. Several other rooms have drop-dead castle views too. Check out the hotel website, which has a helpful photo gallery showing the rooms. There's a very good restaurant on the premises. Book well in advance as this place gets popular in season.

NOT JUST A pretty face

Český Krumlov's charms go beyond those gorgeous Renaissance facades and drop-dead castle views. It's a great base for more active pursuits, such as hiking, boating, cycling, and even horseback riding. Several operators around town can help advise on and outfit you for the activity of your choice. **Vltava,** Kájovská 62, 381 01 Český Krumlov (© **380-711-988;** www.ckvltava.cz), specializes in guided cycling and rafting trips. A great half-day out is to boat down the Vltava to nearby Zlatá Koruna (15km/10 miles) and then cycle back over a very pretty biking trail. The trip takes about 5 hours and costs around 600Kč per person. They also rent bikes (300Kč/day) for independent travel and will drop you off or pick you up at the location of your choice. One popular day outing on the bike is to get a lift out to Hluboka Castle (p. 239) and cycle back to Český Krumlov, passing by the romantic ruins of Dívčí Kámen en-route along marked cycling paths. Figure on about 3 to 4 hours of moderate to intense cycling to make the 40km/25-mile trip. **Expedicion,** Soukenická 33, 381 01 Český Krumlov (© **607-963-868;** www.expedicion.cz), offers a similar array of pursuits, and throws fishing (890Kč/person), rock-climbing (890Kč/person), and horseback riding (300Kč/hr.) into the mix. Equipment, including for fishing and rock-climbing, and transport are included in the prices.

Horní ul. 144, 381 01 Český Krumlov. www.boehmerwaldhotels.de. © **380-711-611.** Fax 380-711-327. 10 units. 1,800Kč double; 3,500Kč suite with castle view. Rates include breakfast. AE, MC, V. **Amenities:** Restaurant. *In room:* TV, hair dryer, minibar, Wi-Fi.

Hotýlek & Hospoda u malého Vítka ★ ⚑ Here's another impossibly cute hotel in Český Krumlov. This one occupies a Renaissance-era house just a few doors up from the bridge that's been remodeled top to bottom by a skilled wood carver. Each of the rooms is snug and clean and has been named after popular Czech cartoon characters. The breakfast downstairs is plentiful, and the little tavern serves excellent Czech specialties.

Radniční 27, 381 01 Český Krumlov. www.vitekhotel.cz. ©/fax **380-711-925.** 20 units. 1,500Kč double; 2,500Kč triple. Rates include breakfast. AE, MC, V. Parking. **Amenities:** Restaurant; bar; Wi-Fi (lobby only). *In room:* TV, hair dryer.

Pension Barbakán After a change in management, the Barbakán, across from the theater, has spruced itself up, inside and out. The owners have redone the inside of the pension completely, putting new bathrooms in all the units and generally keeping the premises spotless. Take breakfast out on the back garden's terrace on warm summer mornings and watch the goings-on below at the river bank. Unlike many other places, parking is available in front of the house and costs 150Kč/night.

Kaplická 26, 381 01 Český Krumlov. www.barbakan.cz. ©/fax **380-717-017.** 8 units. 1,700Kč double; 2,050Kč triple. Rates include breakfast. AE, MC, V. **Amenities:** Restaurant; bar. *In room:* TV.

INEXPENSIVE

Pension Anna ★ ☺ Along "pension alley," this is a comfortable and rustic place. What makes the pension a favorite are the friendly management and homey feeling you get as you walk up to your room. Forget hotels—this is the kind of place where you can relax. The owners even let you buy drinks and snacks at the bar downstairs and take them to your room. The suites, with four beds and a living room, are great for families and groups. Good homemade breakfast and on-site parking available.

Rooseveltova 41, 381 01 Český Krumlov. www.pensionanna-ck.cz. ℂ/fax **380-711-692.** 8 units. 1,250Kč double; 1,550Kč suite. Rates include breakfast. No credit cards. **Amenities:** Bar. *In room:* TV.

Pension Na louži ★ Smack-dab in the heart of the Inner Town, the small Na louži, decorated with early-20th-century wooden furniture, is a charming change from many of the bigger, bland rooms found in nearby hotels. If the person at reception starts mentioning names without apparent reason, don't worry; it's not a language problem. Management has given the rooms human names instead of numbers. The only drawback is that the beds (maybe the people for whom the rooms were named were all short) can be a little on the short side.

Kájovská 66, 381 01 Český Krumlov. www.nalouzi.cz. ℂ/fax **380-711-280.** 7 units. 1,350Kč double; 2,200Kč triple; 2,400Kč suite. No credit cards. **Amenities:** Restaurant; bar.

Pension Ve Věži (In the Tower) ★ 🏨 A private pension in a renovated medieval tower just a 5-minute walk from the castle, Ve Věži is one of the most magnificent places to stay in town. It's not the accommodations themselves that are so grand; none have a bathroom and all are sparsely decorated. What's wonderful is the ancient ambience. Reservations are recommended.

Pivovarská 28, 381 01 Český Krumlov. www.pensionvevezi.cz. ℂ **721-523-030.** 4 units (all with shared bathroom). 1,300Kč double. Rates include breakfast. No credit cards.

Where to Eat
MODERATE

Krčma Markéta ★★ CZECH These days Renaissance-themed restaurants with open-flame grills and "ye olde" atmosphere are all the rage. Marketa's "tavern" (*krčma* in Czech) was one of the first and remains one of the best. The remote castle location keeps foot traffic—and tour buses—to a minimum. To get here, walk all the way up the hill through the castle, continue on through the raised walkway and into the Zámecká zahrada (Castle Garden), where you'll eventually find this pub. Take a peek at the fire to see what's roasting; usually there are a wide variety of meats, including succulent pork cutlets, chicken, and beef. Before the night is over, you'll probably find yourself talking to someone else at the pub's large wooden tables.

Zámek 62. ℂ **775-155-504.** Main courses 120Kč–240Kč. No credit cards. Tues–Sun 11am–9pm.

Krčma v Šatlavské CZECH Popular medieval-style tavern where the food is cooked on a huge grill and diners dine in what was once a dungeon. On a quiet night out of season, this can be a meal to remember, but in the middle of high season, when the tour groups line up out the door, it can feel decidedly like a tourist trap. The food, including grilled meats, pork knee (*koleno*), and a highly recommended garlic soup served in a bread bowl, can make it all worthwhile. Reservations are a must, regardless of the time of year.

Horní 157 (entry from Šatlavská ul.). ℂ **380-713-344.** www.satlava.cz. Main courses 149Kč–349Kč. No credit cards. Daily 10am–10pm.

Papa's Living Restaurant CZECH/INTERNATIONAL Eclectic menu of pastas, grilled meats, including delicious lamb cutlets, and the usual offering of grilled steaks and pork chops. Worth a stop in any season, but particularly nice in summer to dine on the terrace overlooking the river. Great desserts are worth the trip even if you didn't have your main meal here.

Latrán 13 (entry opposite Latrán 14). ℂ **380-711-583.** www.papas.cz. Main courses 180Kč–425Kč. No credit cards. Daily 11am–10pm.

INEXPENSIVE

Hospoda Na louži ★ CZECH   The large wooden tables encourage you to get to know your neighbors at this Inner Town pub, located in a 15th-century house. The atmosphere is fun and the food above average. If no table is available, stand and have a drink; tables turn over pretty quickly, and the staff is accommodating. In summer, the terrace seats only six, so dash over if a seat empties. Be sure to save space for homemade fruit dumplings for dessert.

Kájovská 66. ℂ **380-711-280.** Main courses about 120Kč. No credit cards. Mon–Sat 10am–11pm; Sun 10am–10pm.

Laibon ★ VEGETARIAN   The best vegetarian option in town fuses eastern and local influences. The menu features things like couscous and spiced lentils alongside entrees like traditional *bryndzové halušky* (sheep's cheese and gnocchi), but here without the usual bacon drippings on top. Situated with a view overlooking the river. There's a cute little teahouse next door.

Parkán 105. ℂ **728-676-654.** Main courses about 120Kč. No credit cards. Mon–Sat 10am–11pm; Sun 10am–10pm.

Nonna Gina ★★ ITALIAN/PIZZA   Hands down the best pizza in Český Krumlov and arguably the best in all of Southern Bohemia. The Italian owners have gone out of their way to re-create an authentic Italian dining experience at prices that represent excellent value for money. My favorite is pizza "parmigiano-funghi," fresh mushrooms with shavings of Parmesan cheese on top. There's also a full range of pastas and Italian wines. There are six tables outside for dining in summer. You might even catch an evening concert wafting over the walls of the adjoining cloisters.

Klášterní 52. ℂ **380-717-187.** Pizzas about 140Kč. No credit cards. Daily 11am–11pm.

Zapa Café CAFE   This popular coffee shop can feel like an island of normality in a sea of touristic frenzy. Not much in terms of real food, but very good coffee drinks, pastries, and ice cream make this a welcome pit stop. Separate areas for smokers and nonsmokers, free and reliable Wi-Fi, and a pretty little garden out back add to the pluses. By night, check out the Zapa Cocktail Bar across the street, which maintains the same laid-back vibe into the wee hours.

Latrán 16 (cocktail bar at Latrán 15). ℂ **380-714-578.** Espresso drinks 39Kč, pastries around 40Kč. No credit cards. Cafe daily 8:30am–9pm; cocktail bar daily 6pm–1am.

TŘEBOŇ ★

24km (15 miles) E of České Budějovice

Třeboň is known throughout the Czech Republic as home to the country's beloved carp, a staple on everyone's Christmas Eve menu. The carp—and other fish—are harvested from hundreds of fishponds in the area that were first developed in the late Middle Ages and have survived to this day.

But Třeboň is more than just fish. It's a beautiful walled town that while not quite as breathtaking as Český Krumlov, nevertheless retains much of its Renaissance-era charm, with a lovely pedestrian-only main square, parts of the original town walls still intact, and a brewery, Regent, that dates from 1379 and still turns out—at least in the opinion of this reviewer—some of the best beer in the country.

It's also a major recreational hub for south Bohemia. Cycling and hiking trails fan out in all directions, weaving around ponds and through woods for miles around (see the boxed text below "Stretching Your Legs.") If you've got a few days of downtime and are looking for a way to get some fresh air, look no further than Třeboň, where you can rent bikes, get some cycling maps, and enjoy the region's unspoiled nature.

Třeboň grew slowly from the 12th to the mid–14th century, when four of the Rožmberk brothers (also known as the Rosenbergs) took over, making Třeboň a home away from home (their official residence was down the road in Český Krumlov). Třeboň quickly flourished, attaining key brewing and salt customs rights.

Though war and fires in the 17th and 18th centuries razed some of the town's historic Renaissance architecture, a slow rebuilding process eventually restored nearly every square foot of the walled town to its original state. Under Communism, Třeboň was awarded spa rights, which kept money flowing in and buildings in good repair.

The 4-day festival "Okolo Třeboně" takes place here at the end of June annually. You can experience several street happenings, sport and fun competitions, and listen to Czech folk music performed on stages in the city center and the nearby park. This multigenre event always turns out to be a long party with its unforgettable atmosphere. Check the exact dates at the information center and also ask about the historic Knight Tournament, which, if it occurs, can be a lot of fun, too. Unfortunately, there's no set date for it and it isn't an annual event.

Essentials

GETTING THERE   **Buses** leave from the České Budějovice bus station every hour or so. The trip lasts 30 to 40 minutes and the fare is about 30Kč.

By **train** from Prague, the journey usually requires a change in Veselí nad Lužnicí. The train takes about 3 hours; the second-class fare is 192Kč. Trains and buses also regularly leave for Třeboň from Jindřichův Hradec and Tábor. There also are good connections to and from Vienna through the border town of **České Velenice,** which is reachable from Třeboň via bus or train.

Driving from Prague, take Hwy. E55 through Tábor and turn left onto Hwy. 150 just past the town of Veselí nad Lužnicí. The trip takes at least 1½ hours. From České Budějovice, take Hwy. E551 east to Třeboň.

VISITOR INFORMATION   **Informační Středisko** is in the heart of the Old Town at Masarykovo nám. 103, 379 01 Třeboň (✆ **384-721-169;** fax 384-721-356; www.trebon-mesto.cz). The staff members are excellent and speak several languages, notably German. They provide maps, guidebooks, and information on tours, lodging options, and bike rentals. Open Monday to Friday from 9am to 5pm.

ORIENTATION   There are only three ways to penetrate Třeboň's Old Town walls, short of pole vaulting. To the east is **Hradecká brána (Castle Gate);** on the southern edge of town lies **Svinenská brána;** and to the west is **Budějovická brána.** Once you're inside any of these gates, the six or so streets that comprise the Old Town can be easily navigated.

Exploring Třeboň

City officials, quick to notice that helping visitors helps them, have placed signs guiding visitors to almost every nook and cranny of the center. Since the walled city is relatively small, there's no wrong place to begin a tour, but I prefer to start at the southern gate by the **Svinenská brána,** the oldest of the town's three gates, for reasons that'll become immediately apparent. Just outside the gate and to the right stands the **Regent Brewery,** founded in 1379. Locals will tell you that their brew is every bit as good as Budvar, and they're not lying. On entering Old Town, continue straight through Žižkovo náměstí and you'll arrive at **Masarykovo náměstí,** where the beautifully colored Renaissance facades look as though they were built yesterday.

To the left lies the entrance to Třeboň's showpiece, **Zámek Třeboň ★ (Třeboň Castle; ✆ 384-721-193).** The castle's history is similar to the history of the town. The original Gothic castle was destroyed by fire and reconstructed several times, most recently in 1611. Rather ordinary looking from the outside, it has splendidly decorated rooms that provide a terrific backdrop to the 16th-century furnishings. Admission is by guided tour (in Czech only, English by prior arrangement), with two main tours on offer: Tour A focuses on the castle's Renaissance interiors; Tour B looks at a 19th-century apartment occupied by the noble Schwarzenberg family. Each tour costs 100Kč (150Kč to combine both), with discounts offered for children, seniors, and families. In July and August, a third tour of the cellars and casements is also available. April, May, September, and October hours are Tuesday to Sunday from 9am to 4pm. June through August, it's open Tuesday to Sunday from 9am to 5:15pm.

Walk out the castle gate and straight along Březanova Street to the **Augustinian monastery** and the 14th-century **St. Giles Church** next to it. Inside the church are replicas of some of the finest Gothic works in central Europe; the originals have been moved to the National Gallery in Prague. The church and monastery are open Monday to Saturday from 9am to 7pm and Sunday from 9am to 6pm.

To the south of the Old Town lies **Rybník Svět,** a large pond that locals flock to on hot afternoons. In nice weather, several locations around the pond rent boats. You can also hike or bike the circumference of the pond along marked trails. Figure on about 3 to 4 hours for the hike. On the southeast shore of the pond (about a 20-min. walk from the center) is **Schwarzenberská Hrobka (Schwarzenberg Mausoleum) ★.** Built in 1877, this neo-Gothic chapel and crypt is the resting place for most members of the Schwarzenberg family. To tour the mausoleum costs 50Kč per person. In April, May, September, and October, the crypts are open Tuesday to Sunday from 9 to 11:30am and from 1 to 3:30pm. In June, July, and August, the morning hours are the same, but the afternoon hours are extended to 4:30pm.

Where to Stay

Bílý Koníček (White Horse) ✦ The White Horse Inn offers plain but clean rooms in a 400-year-old Renaissance building on the main square. The rooms are adequately sized and the baths are spotless (showers only). Request a courtyard room if noise is a concern. There's free parking in the rear of the hotel and a big garage out back to store bikes. The restaurant downstairs is a good bet for a quick bite. There's no breakfast, but you can get something small and a cup of coffee in the restaurant. Masarykovo nám. 97, 379 01 Třeboň. www.hotelbilykonicek.cz. ✆ **384-721-213.** 23 units. 1,000Kč double. MC, V. **Amenities:** Restaurant; bar. In room: TV.

Hotel Galerie ★ A step up from the White Horse in terms of charm and comfort, the Hotel Galerie occupies a pretty Renaissance town house on a quiet lane just behind the main square. The rooms are simply furnished, but clean and quiet. The

stretching YOUR LEGS

In the past few years, Třeboň has evolved into one of the Czech Republic's leading cycling centers, drawing hundreds of avid riders each weekend in summer to enjoy the many miles of marked cycling trails. The relatively flat landscape in and around the dozens of fishponds makes the terrain accessible to families with children, older people, and beginning cyclists. There are several operators around town that rent bikes in summer, including the Hotel Zlatá Hvězda. The **Informační Středisko** (Information Center) at Masarykovo nám. 103 can advise on rentals as well as suggest suitable trails and provide detailed cycling maps (a must before you start out). One relatively easy trail suitable for beginners is the 40km/25-mile "Okolo Třeboně" trail that starts out to the northwest of the center of town (look for signs to cycle trail no. 1034) and fans around clockwise, plowing through pond country on mostly quiet country roads. A more ambitious but highly recommended 2-day trek requires an overnight in České Budějovice. On the first day, follow cycle trail no. 1096 along country roads through the pretty town of Rudolfov and into České Budějovice (a distance of about 35km/22 miles). If you get an early start, you'll have the whole afternoon and evening to putter around in Budějovice. On the return to Třeboň, follow cycle trail no. 122 out of České Budějovice (north along the Vltava River) and eventually all the way back to Třeboň (about 40km/25 miles). The trail winds through pristine woods, pretty villages, and dozens of ponds. Allow about 4 hours for the return trip and be prepared for the occasional hilly stretch. If cycling is not your thing, all the trails can be hiked as well. There's a pretty 3-hour hiking trail around the Svět fishpond that starts just south of the town center.

mattresses are on the plusher-than-usual side. The baths are amply sized (showers only). There's a good restaurant on the premises, with a small terrace in nice weather. There's limited street parking, so you'll have to use one of the public lots.

Rožmberská 35, 379 01 Třeboň. www.hotel-trebon.cz. ℂ **384-385-293.** 12 units. 1,400Kč–1,850Kč double; 2,400Kč suite. MC, V. **Amenities:** Restaurant; cafe; bar; Internet. *In room:* TV.

Hotel Zlatá Hvězda ★★ Despite having rather spartan rooms, the Zlatá Hvězda is the most upscale hotel in town, and its location on Masarykovo náměstí can't be beat. An added plus is that the friendly staff can help arrange brewery tours, fishing permits, horseback riding, bike rentals (300Kč/day), and several other outdoor activities. The reception will sometimes cut rates on slow nights.

Masarykovo nám. 107, 379 01 Třeboň. www.zhvezda.cz. ℂ **384-757-111.** Fax 384-757-300. 48 units. 2,600Kč double; 4,000Kč suite. Rates include buffet breakfast. AE, DC, MC, V. **Amenities:** 2 restaurants; spa; bikes; bowling alley. *In room:* TV, fridge, hair dryer; Wi-Fi.

Pension Siesta If all the pensions in the Czech Republic showed up for a contest to see which was friendliest, this one might win. Just outside the Hradecká brána, the Siesta is a small but quiet and clean alternative to the hotels on the square. What makes it special are the owners, who go out of their way to take care of their guests. The pension also has a pleasant terrace in front by the stream, where you can enjoy an afternoon drink and snack.

Hradební 26, 379 01 Třeboň. www.pensionsiesta.cz. ℂ/fax **384-724-831.** 7 units. 1,080Kč double. No credit cards. *In room:* TV.

Where to Eat

Fish & Steak ★★ PIZZA/INTERNATIONAL Arguably the best cooking in town takes place on the ground floor of the Vratislavský dům pension on a corner of the main square, just in front of the castle complex. Expertly grilled trout, carp, and pike-perch (a local specialty) sit alongside equally tempting offerings of grilled pork chops and steaks. There's also a page of pizzas on the menu for the kids (though pizza is not this place's strong suit). There's a tiny terrace out front with a nice view over the square, and free Wi-Fi to check e-mail over your morning coffee.

Březanova 84. ℭ **384-392-595.** Pizzas 130Kč–180Kč; meat and fish dishes 140Kč–280Kč. AE, DC, MC, V. Daily 10:30am–10pm.

Pivovar Bohemia Regent CZECH As with any self-respecting Czech brewery, Třeboň's Regent has an attached beer hall where you can sample the wares, including some harder-to-find wheat beers, as well as order mounds of traditional Czech food at prices that feel like the 1960s. In summer, there's a popular self-serve terrace behind the brewery with the usual beer offerings and lighter food items like sausages and toasted sandwiches. There's frequently live music on Friday nights, but bands tend toward Czech pop classic from the '70s and '80s and country tunes.

Trocnovské nám. Mains 80Kč–130Kč. No credit cards. Daily 10:30am–11pm.

Rožmberska baštá ★ FISH A visit to Třeboň offers the relatively rare option in the Czech Republic to eat excellent local fish for every meal. This little mom-and-pop specializes in the regional dishes like grilled trout and baked or fried pike-perch (*candát*), usually served with a side of parsley potatoes. The front room is snug, nonsmoking, and perfect for a quiet evening meal. There's a small terrace in the back if it's too hot to eat indoors.

Rožmberská 59. ℭ **731-175-902.** Main dishes 180Kč 250Kč. AE, DC, MC, V. Daily 11am–10pm.

TÁBOR

88km (55 miles) S of Prague, 59km (37 miles) N of České Budějovice

The center of the Hussite movement following religious leader Jan Hus's execution in Prague, Tábor was officially founded in 1420 and named by the Hussites after the biblical Mount Tábor. Forsaking their property, the Hussites came here to receive Christ on his return to earth. The group of soldiers leading Tábor, some 15,000 in all, felt that they had been commanded by God to break the power of the Catholics at that time.

Legendary warrior Jan Žižka led the Taborites, as this sect of Hussites was known. Time and time again, Žižka rallied his troops to defeat the papal forces, until he was struck down in battle in 1424. For 10 more years the Hussites battled on, but their loss at Lipany signaled the end of the uprising, and an agreement was reached with Emperor Sigmund of Luxembourg of the Holy Roman Empire. Later, the town submitted to the leadership of Bohemia's Jiří z Poděbrad (George of Poděbrad) and blossomed economically, creating the wealth needed to construct the Renaissance buildings now found in the historic Old Town.

Essentials

GETTING THERE If you're **driving,** leave Prague by Highway D1 and turn off at the E55 exit (signs BENEŠOV, ČESKÉ BUDĚJOVICE). Hwy. E55 runs straight into the city of Tábor. It's a 1-hour drive. Once you're in Tábor, parking can be a problem. Try to snag a paid spot along the street as you approach the center.

Tábor is about 90 minutes by express **train** from Prague or close to an hour from České Budějovice. The train station has a baggage check, and you can get to the center of town by taking bus no. 11, 14, or 31. From Prague, the fare is 210Kč first class, 134Kč second class.

The **bus** trip to Tábor lasts about 1½ hours from Prague and costs 88Kč. To get to the center, it's about a 20-minute walk; go through the park and then bear right at its farthest corner to walk along třída 9. května into town.

VISITOR INFORMATION   Next to the Hussite Museum, **Infocentrum města Tábor,** Žižkovo nám. 2, 390 01 Tábor (✆ **381-486-230;** fax 381-486-239; www. tabor.cz), is stocked with information of all types: from maps, film, and postcards to advice about lodging, restaurants, and the best place for ice cream. The center's staff has volumes of pamphlets, phone numbers, and good advice. It's open May to September, Monday to Friday from 8:30am to 7pm, Saturday and Sunday from 9am to 4pm; and October to April, Monday to Friday from 9am to 4pm.

SPECIAL EVENTS   In September, the **Táborská Setkání (Tábor Meeting)** takes place. Each year, representatives from towns worldwide named after Mount Tábor congregate for some medieval fun—parades, music, and jousting. The 4-day event even reenacts the historic battle of Tábor, with brilliantly clad warriors fighting one another "to the death."

> ### 💬 An A-Maze-ing City
>
> If you get confused by roads that twist, turn, and then end as you leave the square, the Taborites have caught you exactly as planned—the town was designed to hold off would-be attackers with its maze of streets.

For more details on the Tábor Meeting and summer cultural events, see **www.tabor.cz**, or contact **Infocentrum města Tábor** (see "Visitor Information," above).

ORIENTATION   Staré Město (Old Town) is situated around Žižkovo náměstí, site of the town church and the Hussite Museum. Medieval walls surround the entire Old Town core. The Kotnov Castle, now one of the town's museums, is at the southwest corner. Outside the historic town, there's little to see in Tábor besides factories and the ubiquitous *paneláky* (apartment buildings) that ring most every big Czech town and city.

Exploring Tábor

Most of the city's sights are on or around **Žižkovo náměstí.** On the square's west side is the **Museum of the Hussite Movement** (✆ **381-254-286;** www.husitske-muzeum.cz). The late-Gothic former town hall now chronicles the movement that put Tábor on the map and in the history books. In front of the building lie stone tables where Hussite ministers gave daily communion. Leading from the museum's entrance, twisting and turning 650m (2,133 ft.) underneath the square, is a labyrinth of **tunnels** dating from the 15th century. After visiting the museum, take one of the guided tours that snakes through the underground maze, which has housed everything from beer kegs to women imprisoned for such dastardly things as quarreling with men. The tunnels also doubled as a way to sneak under enemy guards if the town ever fell, allowing Hussite soldiers to launch an attack from behind. Admission to the museum is 60Kč for adults and 40Kč for children and seniors 65 and over. Opening hours are April to October daily 9am to 5pm, and November to March Wednesday to Saturday 9am to 5pm.

When you emerge from the tunnels, you'll be on the opposite side of the square, facing the **Church of Transfiguration of Our Lord** (℃ 381-251-226), with its vaulted impressive stained-glass windows and Gothic wooden altar. Climb the tower for one of the best views of the town. Open daily from 10am to 5pm May through August, and Saturday and Sunday 10am to 5pm in September and October. Admission is 25Kč.

You can pay homage to the Hussite military mastermind Jan Žižka at his **statue** next to the church. For a wondrous avenue of Renaissance buildings, stroll down **Pražská ulice,** off the southeast corner of the square. From here you can turn down Divadelní and head along the Lužnice River toward **Kotnov Castle** (℃ 381-252-788). If your feet aren't up to the walk, you can take a more direct route to Kotnov by heading straight down Klokotská ulice, which runs away from the square next to the Hussite Museum.

A 14th-century castle that forms the southwest corner of the town wall, Kotnov Castle is most recognizable for its round **tower,** with another great view of the town. Inside the castle is a well-organized collection on the Middle Ages, with old farming tools, armor, weapons, uniforms, and other artifacts. Admission is 50Kč, and it's open April to September daily from 8:30am to 5pm.

Where to Stay

The number of quality hotels in Tábor continues to grow; still there are several good privately run pensions in town, and this is a good place to experience going "local." Expect to pay about 800Kč per person. The information center next to the town hall at Žižkovo nám. 2 can provide a list of recommendations or call and book a room for you (see "Visitor Information," above). Many of the hotels will not have on-site parking but rather offer access to a nearby paid garage or lot.

Hotel Nautilus ★★★ Easily the most stylish and comfortable hotel in town, though slightly pricier than most of the other places nearby. The owners have taken a former run-down town house on the square and transformed it into a lovely four-star boutique hotel, complete with original artwork and eye-catching design touches that extend from the lobby to the light and airy rooms. Even if you don't stay here, stop by for a meal, the nicest place on the square to eat. The presidential suite is priced as a honeymoon-only affair. They recently opened a "wellness" center, essentially a sauna and small whirlpool.

Žižkovo nám. 20. května 617, 390 02 Tábor. www.hotelnautilus.cz. ℃ **380-900-900.** Fax 380-900-999. 22 units. 2,800Kč double; 7,800Kč presidential suite. AE, MC, V. **Amenities:** Restaurant; bar; health club & spa; room service. In room: TV, hair dryer, minibar, Wi-Fi.

Hotel Dvořák ★★ Located in a reconstructed historic building of Tábor brewery, which is part of the Kotnov Castle complex, this addition to the list of hotels in Tábor is a good choice not only for families but for business travelers as well. The colorful interior design is inviting, and the rooms are a good size with comfortable beds.

Hradební 3037. 390 01 Tábor. www.dvoraktabor.ca. ℃ **381 207 211.** 72 units. 2,000Kč double; 3,600Kč suite. AE, MC, V. **Amenities:** Restaurant; bar; pool; room service; sauna. In room: TV, hair dryer, minibar, Wi-Fi.

Pension 189 Karel Bican   This atmospheric, family-run pension is just a short walk from the central square. Book well in advance or ring the buzzer and hope for the best, as this place tends to fill up fast. The rooms are furnished in traditional style and are cute and quiet, though nothing extravagant. Some have modest efficiency kitchens. There's a pleasant garden and terrace, and the owners rent bikes.

Hradební 189/16, 39001 Tábor. www.globalnet.cz/bican. ⓒ **381-252-109.** Fax 381-254-109. 5 units. 1,500Kč double. AE, MC, V. **Amenities:** Bikes. *In room:* TV.

Where to Eat

Bowling Club CZECH   Yes, really. There's a bowling alley here, too. The pub upstairs serves good Czech food and beer all day, and since there's not too much to do in town at night, you may want to go bowling downstairs. Don't worry, they serve beer downstairs as well—you can't have one without the other.

Třída 9, května 678. ⓒ **381-498-308.** Soups 40Kč; main courses 80Kč–280Kč. No credit cards. Mon–Thurs 3pm–2am; Fri 3pm–3am; Sat 2pm–3am; Sun 2pm–midnight.

Restaurace Beseda CZECH   Beseda is a good place to stop after you slink through the tunnels and climb the tower at the Church of Transfiguration of Our Lord. You've probably seen this menu in just about every town so far, but the food is above average if not new. Their *svíčková* (sirloin in a cream sauce with dumplings) is a favorite. On hot summer days, the patio is great for people-watching while drinking a cold Budvar.

Žižkovo nám. 5. ⓒ **381-253-723.** Main courses 70Kč–260Kč. No credit cards. Daily 10am–10pm.

THE BEST OF MORAVIA

W hile Bohemia is the traditional home of a beer-favoring populace and the seat of Czech industrial muscle, the less-visited kingdom of Moravia to the south and east has spawned a people more attuned to the farmland and the potent wines it creates. For 1,000 years, Moravians have watched as the wealth of their Czech brethren has been put on display in numerous palaces and factories, but Moravians have plenty of their own accomplishments.

The provincial capital of Brno is the home of modern genetics; the place where a curious monk named Gregor Mendel discovered the building blocks of life while playing with pea plants in his monastic garden 150 years ago. It is also the birthplace of one of the most famous novelists of the latter half of the 20th century, Milan Kundera. The Czechs' own favorite author, Bohumil Hrabal, coincidentally, was born here as well. While Brno is definitely in Prague's shadow when it comes to historic architecture, it is home to some of the country's finest early modern and Functionalist buildings built in the 1920s and '30s.

Smaller towns maintain their real Moravian character, with lively song and dance and colorful traditional costumes that have fallen by the way-side in Bohemia. Even the food's a bit different: The bland goulash in Prague becomes a little spicier in Moravia, owing to the Hungarian influence that's seeped in from neighboring Slovakia.

Here, winemaking is taken as seriously as it is in most other European grape-growing regions. Many wine bars throughout Moravia serve the vil-lage's best straight from the cask, usually alongside traditional smoked meats. While the Bohemians have the sweet taste of Becherovka to sip at meals, Moravians have the sharp taste of *slivovice* (plum spirits) to cleanse the palate (sometimes for hours on end if it's *domácí*—home-brewed).

Having seen its fair share of history, Moravia conjures up a different image than Bohemia: Here, too, castles and picture-perfect town squares exist. But the friendly people and slower lifestyle set Moravia apart.

BRNO: THE REGION'S CAPITAL

224km (139 miles) SE of Prague, 128km (79 miles) N of Vienna

An industrial city with an industrial-strength image as "boring," Brno suf-fers the fate of many second cities around the world—no respect. Sure, as you approach from the highway, the sight of dozens of concrete apartment buildings may give you second thoughts. But bear with the Communist-inspired urban sprawl—the bad rap is undeserved. In fact, Brno is a vibrant and interesting city with a panache all its own.

Since Brno came of age in the 19th century on the back of its textile industry, the city's architecture, for the most part, lacks the traditional Gothic, Renaissance, and baroque elements that are part of the fabric of cities like Prague. But spend a day or two here, and the beauty of the old city center will become apparent. Empire and neoclassical buildings abound. For fans of early modern architecture, Brno is an unexpected delight. In the 1920s and '30s, the city was a leading center of Functionalist design. The high point of any tour is the Villa Tugendhat, a masterpiece by the German Mies van der Rohe, one of the giants of modern architecture.

Quirky sights like the Brno Dragon and the Wagon Wheel add character. Špilberk Castle and the Gothic cathedral of Saints Peter and Paul give historical perspective. And lush streets and parks make aimless wandering a pleasure.

Essentials

GETTING THERE   **Driving** to Brno from Prague is simple but nerve-wracking. The country's main freeway, the D1 (also called the E50), in theory, whisks you the 200km (120 miles) from Prague to the center of Brno in around 2 hours, but traffic can be heavy and road-construction delays are frequent. Be especially careful in winter when icy roads make the drive particularly treacherous.

If you're not a fan of white-knuckle driving, **train** travel between Prague and Brno is much more relaxing and takes just 2¾ hours. Special high-speed Pendolino trains (www.pendolino.cz) cut the journey to about 2½ hours. **Trains** from Prague leave Prague's Hlavní nádraží (main station) approximately once every half-hour during the day and hourly in the evenings. Any train heading to Budapest and Bratislava and the majority of Vienna-bound trains will stop in Brno. Second-class express fare is around 300Kč. Brno is an excellent jumping-on spot for onward trains to Bratislava (1 hr.), Budapest (4 hr.), and Vienna (2 hr.).

Brno's aging train station is long overdue for a thorough face-lift, and there's even talk of shutting down the station altogether and moving it to another location. The good news is that it's within an easy walk of the center of the city, at the foot of the main pedestrian walk, Masarykova ulice. To reach the center from the train station, follow the signs to "centrum," first descending into a confusing passageway of shops and kiosks and then climbing the stairs on the other side, which brings you into the Old Town.

Buses are as convenient as trains and have the added advantage of being cheaper. Most buses depart from Prague's Florenc station to Brno at least every hour. The trip takes 2½ hours and costs around 170Kč. Reservations are recommended during peak hours. Buses will either drop you at the city's main bus station (located behind the train station) or, more usually, at a small stop in front of the Grandhotel Brno (see "Where to Stay," later in this chapter). **Student Agency** (✆ **800-100-300**), which in spite of the name sells tickets to travelers of any age, is the leading local operator for buses to Brno and back to Prague.

VISITOR INFORMATION   The **Turistické Informační Centrum** (Tourist Information Center/TIC; ✆ **542-211-090;** www.brno.cz or www.ticbrno.cz; Radnická 8; 9am–5pm Mon–Sat, 9am–3pm Sun) is situated in the Old Town Hall. The English-speaking staff hand out free maps with excellent walking tours already

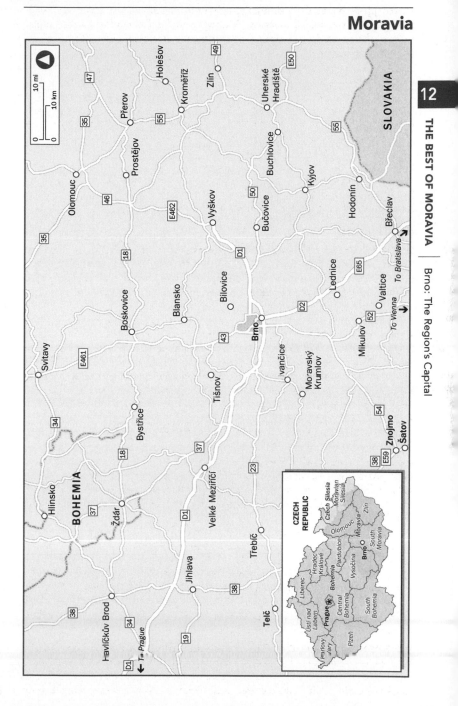

sketched out. The staff can also advise on hotels but usually will not book rooms. There are also a couple of computers on hand for checking e-mail. The tourist office has branches at Nádražní 8 (© **542-221-450;** Mon–Fri 9am–1pm and 1:30–5pm), across from the main train station, and at the Exhibition Grounds, Hall E (open during fair times).

SPECIAL EVENTS   Usually when the words *special events* and Brno are mentioned in the same sentence, the phrase *trade fair* isn't too far behind. Many fairs held at Brno's BVV exhibition grounds are world-class displays of technology, industrial machinery, and even well-groomed pets. One word of warning at fair time: Hotels tend to jack up rates shamelessly. So if you're not coming to see a tractor or a dog show, best to avoid fair times altogether. You'll find a calendar of events at www.bvv.cz.

Brno celebrates music as well, hosting the **Janáček Music Festival** each June and the **Brno International Music Festival (Moravský Podzim)** in September and October. However, probably the most attended event occurs each August when the **Motorcycle Grand Prix** tour rolls into town to tackle the Brno Circuit.

ORIENTATION   Brno is a large rambling city, but most sights are concentrated in its inner core. At the center is **náměstí Svobody (Freedom Square),** connected to the train station by Masarykova ulice. Just west of Masarykova is **Zelný trh (Cabbage Market),** the largest square in town. Cars can't pass through the Old Town, but tram no. 4 barrels through with little regard for the pedestrians in its way.

The city is small enough for walking. All hotels, restaurants, and sights are close to each other, so you will likely not have to use public transportation. The only exception may be shuttling to and from your hotel.

If you need information on public transportation, the Tourist Information Office can provide a good map. Brno has a comprehensive network of trams and buses (www.dpmb.cz). Tickets range in price from 14Kč for 10 minutes of travel on one tram or bus without any transfers, to 18Kč for 15 minutes including transfers and 22Kč for 60 minutes with transfers. You can buy tickets at kiosks and tobacconists, or from yellow ticketing machines at some stops. You can also buy 30Kč tickets from the drivers, allowing for 60 minutes of traveling including transfers. Be sure to validate your ticket on entering the tram or bus.

Strolling Around Brno

The Old Town holds most of the attractions you'll want to see, so it's probably best to start at the former seat of government, the Old Town Hall on Radnická 8. To get there, walk from the train station along Masarykovo and make a left at Orlí Street; if you're coming from náměstí Svobody, head toward the train station and turn right on either Panská or Orlí.

Brno's oldest secular building, from the 13th century, the **Old Town Hall** is a hodgepodge of styles—Gothic, Renaissance, and baroque elements melding together, demonstrating Brno's development through the ages. Almost everything in the building has a story or legend attached to it, beginning with the front door and its crooked Gothic portal. Designed by Anton Pilgram, who lists Vienna's vaunted St. Stephen's Church on his résumé, the door was completed in 1510. Town officials supposedly reneged on their original payment offer, and a furious Pilgram took revenge by bending the turret above the Statue of Justice.

On the second floor, a modest collection of armor, coins, and photos is displayed in the same room where town councilors met from the 13th century right up until

Brno

THE BEST OF MORAVIA | Brno: The Region's Capital

ATTRACTIONS ●
Cathedral of Saints Peter
  and Paul **26**
Denisovy Sady **25**
Kapucínský Klášter
  (Capuchin Monastery) **27**
Kostel Nalezení
  svatého Kříže **27**
Moravian Regional
  Museum **22**
Old Town Hall **19**
Parnas Fountain **20**
Reduta Divadlo **23**
Špilberk Castle
  (Brno City Museum) **13**
Villa Tugendhat **1**
Zelný trh (Cabbage Market) **19**

HOTELS ■
Comsa Brno Palace **15**
Grandhotel Brno **24**
Holiday Inn **28**
Hotel Brno **29**
Hotel Continental **1**
Hotel Europa **3**
Hotel Pod Špilberkem **14**
Hotel Royal Ricc **16**
Hotel Santander **29**
Hotel Slavia **10**

RESTAURANTS ◆
Brabander **5**
Café Podnebi **8**
Koishi **6**
Pivnice Hotel
  Pegas **11**
Pivnice U Richarda **7**
Rebio **21**
Špalíček **18**
U Kastelána **2**
Zemanova
  Kavárna **12**

SHOPPING ●
Antikvaríat Alfa **9**
Velký Špalíček **17**

1935. Climb the stairs of the tower for an interesting, if not beautiful, city view; smokestacks and modern buildings battle for attention.

Before you leave Old Town Hall, examine two of Brno's most beloved attractions: the **Brno Dragon** and the **Wagon Wheel.** The "dragon" hanging from the ceiling is actually not a dragon, but an alligator given to the city by Archprince Matayás in 1608. Here also stands the Wagon Wheel, a testament to Brno's industrious image. Local lore has it that a carpenter named Jiří Birek from nearby Lednice wagered with locals that he could chop down a tree, fashion a wheel from it, and roll it the 40km (25 miles) to Brno all in a single day. Well, he managed to do it, but the townspeople, certain that one man couldn't do so much in a day, decided that Birek must have had assistance from the devil. With this mindset, they refused to ever buy his works again.

Just south of the Old Town Hall is **Zelný trh (Cabbage Market),** a farmers' market since the 13th century. You can still buy a head or two of the leafy vegetable at the market today as entrepreneurs sell their wares under the gaze of **Hercules,** depicted in the **Parnas Fountain** in the square's center. The fountain used to be a vital part of the market; quick-thinking fishermen let their carp swim and relax in the fountain until the fish were chosen for someone's dinner.

At the southern corner of **Zelný trh** lies the 17th-century **Reduta Divadlo,** a former home of Mozart. Another block closer to the train station, on Kapucínské náměstí, are the **Kostel Nalezení svatého Kříže (Church of the Sacred Cross)** and the **Kapucínský Klášter ★★ (Capuchin Monastery; ⓒ 542-213-232).**

The Capuchin Monastery is best known for its fascinating (if gruesome) crypts, which along with Kutná Hora's Bone Church count among the most ghoulish sights in the Czech Republic. Kids will either love or be terrified by (parental discretion advised) the mummified remains of dozens of former monks and Austrian noblemen lying on the floor in their final repose. The basement's special ventilation helps maintain the corpses in their original state. The noblemen paid large sums of money to be interred here in the hope that proximity to the monks might improve their prospects in the afterlife. The monastery is open May to September Monday to Saturday from 9am to noon and 2 to 4:30pm and Sunday from 11 to 11:45am and 2 to 4:30pm (Feb–Apr and Oct–Dec closed on Mon; closed Jan).

Dominating **Zelný trh** at its southwest corner is the **Moravian Regional Museum,** Zelný trh 8, Brno (ⓒ **542-321-205;** www.mzm.cz), housed in the Dietrichstein Palace. Completed in 1620, the palace was used by Russian Marshal Kutuzov to prepare for the battle of Austerlitz in 1805. These days, the museum displays a wide array of stuffed birds and wild game, as well as art, coins, and temporary exhibits. Admission is 50Kč adults, and 25Kč students and children. It's open Tuesday to Saturday from 9am to 5pm.

From the museum, head up Petrská Street to the **Cathedral of Saints Peter and Paul.** Perched atop a hill overlooking the city, the cathedral was built in the late 12th and early 13th centuries. In 1743, it was rebuilt in a baroque style, only to be re-Gothicized just before World War I. The resulting melding of styles gives the cathedral a unique character. The cathedral is open Monday to Wednesday and Friday and Saturday from 6:30am to 6pm, Thursday from 6:30am to 7:30pm, and Sunday from 8:30am to 6pm.

Take a break at **Denisovy sady,** the park behind the cathedral, and prepare to climb the hill to get to Špilberk Castle. If you're not up for it, tram nos. 6, 9, 14, and 17 go near the castle, but you'll still have a short but strenuous walk from there. If you want to walk all the way, head along Biskupská, where **interesting houses**

WHAT time IS IT?

If you tour the cathedral in the late morning, you may think that you've switched time zones. Don't worry: The cathedral bells strike noon an hour early in remembrance of a quick-thinking bell ringer who, seeing that the city was on the verge of attack by the Swedes during the Thirty Years' War, found out that the army was planning to take the city by noon. If not successful by then, Swedish commander General Torstenson is said to have decided the attack would be called off and the army would beat a hasty retreat. The bell ringer, sensing that the town couldn't repel the Swedes, rang the cathedral bells an hour early at 11am, before the army could attack. True to his word, Torstenson packed up and went home.

provide a nice foreground to the bustling city. Make a left on Starobrněnská to Husova, and then left onto Pellicova. At Pellicova 11 is a fine example of František Uherka's cubist architectural vision.

But the real reason for this climb is **Špilberk Castle ★★**. If there's one building in the Czech Republic that's ready to be overrun by visitors, it's Špilberk—and it's had practice. It was built in the 13th century, and the Hussites controlled the castle in the 15th century. The Prussians saw the castle's position as an excellent lookout when they occupied it in the early 17th century. It was a fearsome prison during the Habsburg occupation in the 18th and 19th centuries. The Nazis converted it into a barracks and prison for holding and torturing Czech political prisoners during World War II.

At Špilberk's **Brno City Museum ★** (© 542-123-611; www.spilberk.cz), you can see several permanent exhibitions such as "Prison of Nations" or "History of Brno" and others. Admission to all exhibitions, casemates, and the lookout tower is 160Kč adults, 90Kč students. It's open Tuesday to Sunday from 9am to 6pm May to September, and from 9am to 5pm October to April.

More to See & Do

MUSEUMS   At first glance, this sleek villa looks like just another stylish modern home, but many count the **Villa Tugendhat ★★**, Černopolní 45 (© 545-212-118; www.tugendhat.eu; admission Kč120 adult and 60Kč child; 10am–6pm Wed–Sun) among early modern architect Mies van der Rohe's best works. Mies broke new ground here in the late 1920s with—among other things—a fully open floor plan and huge wall-sized windows at the back. He used expensive woods and marbles, rather than ostentatious decoration, to give the house its character. Visits are only allowed with a guided tour that must be arranged in advance. The tourist office can help with this, or call the number above or visit the website. *Note:* The villa was closed to visitors in 2011 to carry out long-overdue renovations, but was expected to open by 2012 (check with tourist office before venturing out). To visit, take tram no. 3, 5, or 11 from the center to the Dětská nemocnice (Children's Hospital) stop.

SHOPPING   Once back in the city center, take some time for a quick meal and browse along the **pedestrian shopping zone,** which unfolds between náměstí Svobody and the train station. Prices for goods are often cheaper here than in Prague, so you may find a better deal for the crystal vase or pair of earrings you were thinking of buying. Brno has several large shopping malls; the most impressive one in the center is the **Velký Špalíček** shopping center (Dominikánská 5; ℰ 543-237-385; www. velkyspalicek.cz) that starts at the top of the Zelný trh (Cabbage Market). For rare maps, lithographs, and posters, plus an unusual selection of autographed photos of Czech superstars, including one of crooner Karel Gott (p. 29), the country's answer to Tom Jones, peek in at **Antikvariát Alfa** (Veselá 39; ℰ 542-211-947; Mon–Fri 10am–6pm; Sat 10am–1pm).

SOCCER   Sports fans can partake in a Sunday ritual as dear to Czechs as football is to Americans by taking the 20-minute walk north from the main square to Brno stadium, where first league **soccer team 1. FC Brno** plays its home games. Grab a beer and a sausage and cheer along. Tickets, beginning at around 80Kč, are always plentiful and can be bought at the stadium on game day.

Where to Stay

Brno's bread and butter are regular trade fairs held at the exhibition grounds outside the center. Try to avoid arriving during a major fair (usually in May and Sept), when hotels raise rates 50% or more. The organizer carries a fair schedule on its website (www.bvv.cz). Parking can be a problem in Brno, but most hotels listed below offer some sort of on-site parking, usually for a fee from 200Kč to 400Kč a night.

EXPENSIVE

Comsa Brno Palace ★★★   Arguably Brno's nicest hotel occupies a stunningly restored 19th-century town palace, within easy walking distance of the Špilberk Castle or the city center. The four-story atrium will take your breath away. The rooms maintain the same high standard, artfully blending old-world charm and modern convenience.

Šilingrovo nám. 2, 602 00 Brno. www.comsabrnopalace.com. ℰ **532-156-777.** Fax 532-156-711. 119 units. 3,500Kč–4,500Kč double. AE, DC, MC, V. Parking. **Amenities:** Restaurant; bar; concierge; exercise room. *In room:* A/C, TV, hair dryer, minibar, Wi-Fi.

Holiday Inn ★   The modern Holiday Inn Brno, on the fairgrounds, caters mainly to the trade-fair crowd, so be warned that prices jump steeply when events are scheduled. Everything, from the rooms to the restaurant to the bars, looks similar to its counterparts in other Holiday Inns around the world. Still, the beds are more comfortable than most, and the rooms are spotless, with large writing desks and showers that have no problems with water pressure. The staff is friendly and speaks English.

Křížkovského 20, 603 00 Brno. www.ichotelsgroup.com. ℰ **543-122-111.** Fax 543-246-990. 200 units. 3,120Kč double; 3,600Kč suite. AE, DC, MC, V. Parking. **Amenities:** Restaurant; bar; exercise room (limited); sauna. *In room:* A/C (some), TV, hair dryer, minibar, Wi-Fi.

Hotel Royal Ricc ★★   A small, quiet inn set just off the Cabbage Market, the Ricc is part of the Romantic Hotel chain, combining the rustic appeal of a bed-and-breakfast with the service of a top-quality hotel. Rooms vary in size, but all are decorated with antiques that lend a warm feeling lacking in most competing hotels. Many of the rooms have beautifully restored ceilings with intricate artwork. The sitting rooms, wine bar, and restaurant all live up to the surroundings. Paid parking and high Wi-Fi fees, though, add to the room price.

Starobrněnská 10, 602 00 Brno. www.romantichotels.cz. ℰ **542-219-262.** Fax 542-219-265. 30 units. 3,600Kč double; 6,000Kč suite. AE, MC, V. Parking. **Amenities:** 2 restaurants; wine bar. *In room:* TV, hair dryer, minibar, Wi-Fi (fee).

MODERATE

Grandhotel Brno ★   Since it was taken over by the Austria Hotels International chain in the mid-1990s, the Grandhotel has lived up to its name. Its rooms are spacious and well appointed, though some rooms located at the front get a little noisy due to the major street running past with its never-ending stream of trams; ask for a room that has windows facing north, away from the commotion. The rack rate puts this hotel in the expensive category, but the daily rate posted on the hotel's website can push this hotel down into the moderate range. The location right from the train station is especially convenient if you're arriving by train.

Benešova 18–20, 602 00 Brno. www.austria-hotels.at. (𝄢 **542-518-111.** Fax 542-210-345. 105 units. 2,875Kč double; 3,400Kč suite. AE, DC, MC, V. Parking. **Amenities:** 2 restaurants; casino; exercise room; room service. *In room:* A/C (some), TV, hair dryer, minibar, Wi-Fi.

Hotel Continental ★   This high-rise Communist-era hotel is trying to capitalize on its funky '60s design, and fans of Jetsons'-style futurism will feel right at home. The rooms on the top floor, outfitted with flatscreen TVs and high-end toiletries, have gotten a full design makeover and are as hip as anything you're likely to find in Prague, or New York's East Village for that matter. The helpful staff is approachable for advice on how to reach the sights. The Continental is north of the city center, so you'll get some cleaner air and enjoy a pleasant, short walk into the center.

Kounicova 6, 602 00 Brno. www.continentalbrno.cz. (𝄢 **541-519-111.** Fax 541-211-203. 230 units. 2,100Kč–2,500Kč double. AE, DC, MC, V. Parking. **Amenities:** Restaurant; bar; concierge. *In room:* A/C, TV, hair dryer, minibar, Wi-Fi.

Hotel Europa ★★   One of a new generation of business hotels occupying a remodeled town house about 10 minutes' walk from the center of the city. It's a good compromise choice, being high-end enough to attract corporate clientele, yet affordable for leisure travelers. The corridors are a little drafty, but the rooms are snug and bright. The lobby, decorated by local artists, can be charitably described as exuberant, with lavish pink walls and funky plastic chairs. The rooms are more business-like, with low-slung beds, big workstations, and flatscreen TVs. You'll find LAN connections in the rooms and free Wi-Fi in the public areas. There's free street parking out front or pay 200Kč per night for guarded parking in the rear courtyard.

Tř Kapitane Jaroše 27, 602 00 Brno. www.hotel-europa-brno.cz. (𝄢 **545-421-400.** Fax 545-421-403. 45 units. From 2,100Kč double; 3,000Kč suite. AE, DC, MC, V. Parking. **Amenities:** Restaurant; bar. *In room:* A/C, TV, Internet, minibar.

Hotel Slavia   This is a big, refurbished 19th-century hotel with a wisp of lingering Communist-era neglect about it. Nevertheless, it's the best location for the money in Brno, just off the main square. Rooms are spartan, with bland furniture, but clean. The rooms are not uniformly sized, so take a look at a couple before choosing.

Solniční 15, 602 00 Brno. www.slaviabrno.cz. (𝄢 **542-321-249.** Fax 542-211-769. 82 units. From 2,290Kč double. AE, DC, MC, V. Parking. **Amenities:** Restaurant; cafe. *In room:* TV, minibar, Wi-Fi.

INEXPENSIVE

Hotel Brno   Once a run-down dive, the Brno has been given a face-lift and a new lease on life. The Communist-era rooms, while small and sparsely furnished, have been freshened up. Near the city center, the hotel even has its own tennis courts, but its main attraction is as a quiet place to lay down your head at the right price.

Horní 19, 639 00 Brno. www.hotelbrno.cz. (𝄢 **543-214-046.** Fax 543-215-308. 90 units. 1,390Kč double. AE, DC, MC, V. Parking. **Amenities:** Restaurant, Internet. *In room:* TV.

Hotel pod Špilberkem ★   This is a small, family-run hotel with an excellent location, within easy walking distance of the center and Špilberk Castle. The name means "under the Špilberk," and indeed several rooms, while plainly furnished, at least have views up toward the castle. Though the street is busy, the rooms are set back. There's off-street parking, but watch the narrow doorway into the parking courtyard.

Pekařská 10, 602 00 Brno. www.hotelpodspilberkem.cz. © **543-235-003.** Fax 543-235-066. 25 units. 1,650Kč double (free for children 5 and under). MC, V. Parking. **Amenities:** Restaurant. *In room:* TV, Wi-Fi.

Hotel Santander ★★   Hotels in trade-fair towns are anonymous places, so it's a nice surprise to be greeted by name when you arrive at this family-owned villa on the western edge of town. The rooms are large and clean, if a bit sterile. Ask for no. 7, a rustic double with its own private entrance to a lovely back garden. The breakfast buffet, included in the room rate, is the best in town.

Pisárecká 6, 603 00 Brno. www.hotelsantander.cz. © **547-220-233.** Fax 543-220-375. 15 units. 1,800Kč double. AE, DC, MC, V. Parking. *In room:* TV, Wi-Fi.

Where to Eat
EXPENSIVE
Koishi ★★★ JAPANESE   The Czech Republic's best sushi restaurant just happens to be in Brno. In fact, some reviewers put Koishi among the country's top 10 restaurants in all categories. The specialties here are nigiri and maki sushi, but there's also a wide range of other types of fish, steaks, and even pastas to satisfy all palates. The refined interior, with dark woods and white leather banquettes, makes a nice choice for an intimate dinner. There's a small terrace out back in nice weather.

Udolní 11. www.koishi.cz. © **777-564-744.** Reservations recommended. Main courses 280Kč–600Kč. AE, DC, MC, V. Daily 11am–11pm.

U Kastelána ★★ CZECH/CONTINENTAL   Since opening its doors a few years ago beside a nondescript shopping center, U Kastelána has been winning awards and garnering the attention of Czech foodies with creative dishes like shoulder of veal served with shiitake mushrooms or grilled venison served in a chestnut puree. Start off a meal to remember with a shrimp "cappuccino" soup or a Czech "kulajda"—a traditional sweet and sour egg-drop soup that's usually served with sausage, but here with smoked salmon and quail egg. While prices for evening meals can climb pretty high, the daily luncheon specials make this an affordable treat.

Kotlářská 51a. © **541-213-497.** www.ukastelana.cz. Reservations recommended. Main courses 260Kč–530Kč; lunch specials 250Kč–300Kč. AE, DC, MC, V. Mon–Sat noon–midnight; Sun noon–10pm.

MODERATE
Brabander ★ CZECH   The Brabander Living Restaurant is a local favorite, both for the expertly prepared food and for the relaxed but refined setting. It's a good choice for either lunch or dinner, with a central location within easy walking distance of Brno's main square. The menu features a broad selection of mostly Czech specialties, including venison, duck, and pork tenderloin, at reasonable prices for the quality of the cooking. There's an extensive wine list.

Joštova 4. © **542-211-922.** www.brabander.cz. Reservations recommended. Main courses 180Kč–300Kč. AE, DC, MC, V. Daily noon–11pm.

Pivnice U Richarda ★★ CZECH A popular microbrewery with an impressive selection of homemade beers, including a relatively rare (in the Czech Republic) unpasteurized, unfiltered wheat beer. There's a full range of delicious grilled meats and steaks, plus salads and pasta dishes. Buy bottles of your favorite beer to take back to the hotel for later.

Udolní 7. ⟡ **775-027-918.** www.uricharda2.cz. Reservations recommended. Main courses 150Kč–300Kč. AE, DC, MC, V. Daily 11am–11pm.

Zemanova Kavárna ★ CZECH This fully restored 1920s-era Functionalist cafe now has a multipurpose role as highly stylized cultural center, atmospheric restaurant, and, naturally, a cafe. Stop in for the excellent-value lunch specials, where soup and a very well done traditional main like roast pork or schnitzel runs around 100Kč. The black-and-white photos on the wall complete the fun period-piece feel.

Jezuitská 6. ⟡ **542-218-096.** www.zemanka.cz. Main courses 100Kč–150Kč. AE, DC, MC, V. Mon–Sat 10am–11pm.

INEXPENSIVE

Café Podnebi ★ CAFE A great spot for a very good coffee or a cheap, quick bite (menu offerings include mostly sweet and savory pancakes priced for student wallets). The real draw here, though, is the hidden terrace at the back, in the shadow of the Špilberk Castle.

Udolní 5. ⟡ **542-211-372.** www.podnebi.cz. Main courses 30Kč–100Kč. No credit cards. Daily 9am–11pm.

Pivnice Pegas CZECH This central microbrewery is a regular spot for visiting British stag parties (courtesy of Ryanair), but don't let that put you off. Sample the wheat beer—a relative rarity in the barley-only Czech Republic. The tables are usually fully booked by 8pm, so go early to get a spot. This pub also has an in-house hotel with clean rooms at decent prices.

Jakubská 4. ⟡ **542-210-104.** www.hotelpegas.cz. Main courses 90Kč–160Kč. AE MC, V. Daily 9am–midnight.

Rebio VEGETARIAN There are not many truly vegetarian restaurants in Brno. This inviting self-service place, about 10 minutes walk from the main square, serves large portions of vegetarian rice and pasta dishes as well as soups and sandwiches. It's nonsmoking throughout, and popular with students.

Orlí 26. ⟡ **542-211-130.** www.rebio.cz. Main courses 50Kč–80Kč. No credit cards. Mon–Fri 8am–7pm; Sat 10am–3pm.

Špalíček ★ CZECH A rustic, traditional Czech pub situated just off a main square, the "Cabbage Market" serves local specialties like roast pork and dumplings, along with very passable mugs of Brno's home beer, Starobrno. It offers a daily lunch special with soup and main course for 79Kč. Sit out on the terrace in nice weather.

Zelný trh 12. ⟡ **542-211-526.** Main courses 100Kč–150Kč. No credit cards. Mon–Sat 10am–11pm.

Brno After Dark

While it may lack Prague's energy, Brno still has plenty to offer at night. A strong cultural program dominates, with a local theater and symphony offering world-class entertainment. Go to www.brno.cz to find out what's going on at major venues, or visit the Informační Centrum (see earlier in this chapter) to get tickets.

For the young at heart, the **Metro Music Bar** (Poštovská 6, Alfa-Pasáž; ✆ 515-533-452; www.metromusic.cz; Mon–Sat 7pm–5am) is the place to dance. The program changes daily from live bands to DJs and back. Concerts start at 8:30pm.

Otherwise, make like a Brno resident and go to any number of local pubs, which are located on nearly every street corner. **U Blahovky** ★ (Gorkého 54; ✆ 543-233-310) is a Brno classic, an old-school pub with reputedly the best Pilsner Urquell beer in the city. Both microbrewers listed above (see "Where to Eat"), **Pivnice Pegas** and **U Richarda,** are excellent drinking choices. I lean toward U Richarda for its light lager, one of the best beers in the country for my money.

TELČ ★

149km (92 miles) SE of Prague, 86km (53 miles) W of Brno

As you go through towns while traveling in Moravia, you may be tempted to pass up Telč, dismissing it as yet another "small town with a nice square." Don't. Those who make the trip to Telč strike gold. Telč is one of the few towns in Europe that can boast of not being reconstructed since its original edifices were built. It now enjoys the honor of being a United Nations (UNESCO) World Heritage Site. Its uniformly built houses and castle give it an almost too-perfect look, as though no one ever really lived here.

Due to its small size, you can explore Telč in a just a couple of hours. Those traveling by car to Brno or Vienna should stop here on the way. I recommend spending the night to admire the **illuminated castle and square,** especially if there's an evening recital or concert at the castle. You can also combine a stop here with a visit to Znojmo (see below).

Essentials

GETTING THERE   Located about halfway between České Budějovice and Brno, Telč can be reached by taking Hwy. 23. **Driving** from Prague, take Hwy. D1 in the direction of Brno and exit at Jihlava, where you pick up Hwy. 38 after going through the town. Then head west on Hwy. 23. You can leave your car in one of three large parking lots at the town's northern and southern gates. It's a 2-hour drive from Prague.

Train connections to Telč aren't great, so be patient. First-class fare from Prague costs 320Kč, and second-class fare is 252Kč. The town lies on the Havlíčkův Brod, Kostelec u Jihlavy line, where you'll have to change in Kostelec u Jihlavy. Once you get there, you'll find several trains departing daily to Telč. The train station offers storage, though its hours aren't the most dependable. Figure on a journey time of 4 to 5 hours if you are lucky.

Better than the train is the **bus,** which costs around 150Kč. Several buses daily leave from Prague's Florenc bus station in the direction of Telč. The journey, including usually a change of bus in Jihlava, takes about 3 hours. The castle and town square are a 10-minute walk from the bus station. To get to town, exit through the station's back entrance, turn right on Tyršova, and then turn left on Rudnerova. Follow this street as it bears left, and turn right at the second small alley. This will guide you to the main square.

VISITOR INFORMATION   Since UNESCO gave its backing to Telč in 1992, services for visitors have blossomed, and none more so than the information center on the main square. At the **Informační Středisko,** nám. Zachariáše z Hradce 10

(✆ **567-112-407;** www.telc-etc.cz), you'll find bountiful information on accommodations, cultural events, guided tours, and even hunting; brochures are in Czech, German, and English. The staff is eager to arrange reservations. Open May to October Monday to Friday 8am to 5pm, Saturday and Sunday 10am to 4pm; November to April Monday and Wednesday 8am to noon and 1 to 5pm, Tuesday and Thursday 8am to noon and 1 to 4pm, and Friday 8am to noon and 1 to 3pm.

SPECIAL EVENTS The **Prázdniny v Telči (Holidays in Telč),** a season of concerts, recitals, and fairs, runs from the end of July to the middle of August. For details, contact the **Informační Středisko** (see "Visitor Information," above) or www.prazdninyvtelci.cz.

ORIENTATION Telč's historic center is shaped like a trapezoid and is surrounded by lakes on three sides. At the center is a very large square named after the town's former owner, Zachariáš z Hradce.

Exploring Telč

Start with a tour of **Telč Château ★** (✆ **567-243-943;** www.zamek-telc.cz) at the northwest end of the main square. Zacharias of Neuhaus, whose name now graces the main square, was so enamored of the Renaissance style rampant in Italy that in 1553 he commissioned Antonio Vlach, and later Baldassare Maggi de Ronio, to rebuild the château, originally a 14th-century Gothic structure. This castle's exterior, however, cannot prepare you for its interior—hall after hall of lavish rooms with spectacular ceilings.

Highlights inside the château include the **Africa Hall,** with rhino heads, tiger skins, and other exotica from expeditions accumulated by Karel Podstatky, a relative of the castle's last owner, in the early 1900s. The **Banquet Hall's** *sgrafitti* seems to mock those who overindulge, and the **Marble Hall of Knights** features a wood ceiling decorated with bas-reliefs from 1570, plus a fine collection of armor. In the **Golden Hall,** where balls and ceremonies once took place, 30 octagonal coffers with mythological scenes stare down at you from the ceiling.

Visits are by guided tour only. The main tour, Tour A outlined above, costs 110Kč adults, 70Kč students, free for children 5 and under. The fee for an English-language guide is an additional 100Kč per person. A second tour, Tour B, focuses on the interiors of the 19th-century residential apartments and takes an additional 45 minutes. Tour B costs 90Kč, 60Kč students. The castle is open Tuesday to Sunday: May to September from 9am to noon and 1 to 5pm; October and April from 9am to noon and 1 to 4pm; the castle is closed November to March.

Next to the castle is the **Church of St. James (Kostel sv. Jakuba),** its walls adorned with late-15th-century paintings. Next to St. James is the baroque **Jesuit Church of the Name of Jesus.**

After strolling the castle grounds, head back to the main square, where a sea of soft pastel facades awaits. If you find yourself wondering how the entire square can be so uniform, you're not alone. After rebuilding the castle, Zacharias realized that the rest of the place looked, well, out of place. To rectify the situation, he promptly rebuilt the facade of each building on the square, though Gothic columns belie what once was. Of particular note is the building referred to as **House 15,** where a round oriel and *sgrafitti* portraying the crucifixion, Saul and David, Christopher, and faith and justice jut onto the street corner. And watching over it all are the cherubs on the Marian column, built in 1718.

Where to Stay

If you haven't arranged lodging ahead of time, head straight to the information center in the main square, where the staff has a complete list of what's available. For hotels, expect to pay upwards of 1,400Kč for a double.

Private accommodations are also available, and for the most part, these rooms are comparable to hotel rooms (if not better and less expensive), though there are far fewer amenities. The information center staff will call and arrange for you to meet the room's owner so you can check out the place. Several rooms located directly on the square are available. Rates will be about 600Kč per person. On slow days, owners will usually negotiate a better price.

Hotel Celerin ★   Located in a small corner of the square, the Celerin is a little hard to find, but worth the effort. The rooms themselves are only average, but the real selling point is the view out over the square of the front rooms. By all means try to get a room with a view. Looking out over the square at night when it's bathed in light will remind you why this town is a UNESCO treasure. Travelers with disabilities will find the staff here helpful, and some rooms are fully accessible.

Náměstí Zachariáše z Hradce 43, 588 56 Telč. www.hotelcelerin.cz. ✆ **567-243-477.** Fax 567-213-581. 12 units. 1,750Kč double with a castle view. Rates include continental breakfast. AE, DC, MC, V. Parking. **Amenities:** Restaurant; bar. *In room:* TV, minibar, Wi-Fi.

Hotel Černý Orel (Black Eagle Hotel)   On the main square overlooking the Marian column, the Black Owl is a favorite among visitors. The room has a lingering old-fashioned feel and the rooms are a bit faded but clean. Ask for a view of the square; the staff will usually accommodate this request if a room is available. One room on the ground floor is barrier-free. A lively restaurant downstairs serves good Czech fare.

Náměstí Zachariáše z Hradce 7, 588 56 Telč. www.ucernehoorla.eu. ✆ **567-243-222.** Fax 567-243-221. 33 units (5 rooms without toilet). 1,800Kč double. AE, MC, V. Parking. **Amenities:** Restaurant. *In room:* TV, Wi-Fi.

Hotel Telč   Just off the main square, the Telč has rooms that feel spacious because of their high ceilings. The park next to it adds to the effect and provides a sense of being out in the country, a good choice if you've had enough of staying in noisy city centers. Rooms facing the street are brighter but louder than those to the rear. The all-wood furnishings add some ambience, but the bathrooms are cramped.

Na Můstku 37, 588 56 Telč. www.hoteltelc.cz. ✆ **567-243-109.** Fax 567-223-887. 10 units. 1,550Kč–1,840Kč double. AE, DC, MC, V. **Amenities:** Restaurant. *In room:* TV, fridge.

Where to Eat

Caffe Antoniana CZECH   Hands-down the best coffee in Telč, served in a hip, laid-back space that does double duty as a photo gallery. Come back at night for a glass of wine or beer. The large back room is a fun place to hang out (in a town with admittedly not much nightlife), with both a foosball and a pool table.

Náměstí Zachariáše z Hradce 23. ✆ **603-519-903.** Drinks 30Kč–60Kč. No credit cards. Daily 8am–midnight.

Švejk CZECH   With very good Czech staples like goulash and roast pork, this is the place to go if the Black Eagle is too crowded. Sit on the terrace in the summer with a commanding sweep over the entire square. The location, just around the corner from Telč Château, is convenient for a hearty after-tour lunch.

Náměstí Zachariáše z Hradce 1. ✆ **567-213-151.** Main courses 90Kč–180Kč. No credit cards. Daily 10am–midnight.

U Černého Orla (At the Black Eagle) ★ CZECH   If it looks as though every visitor in town is trying to get in here, it's because they are. The Black Eagle is worth the effort. This is one of the few restaurants in Telč that can be trusted to serve good food consistently. Crowd in at any free space and enjoy a wide range of Czech meals. The hearty soups are especially welcome on days when the sun isn't shining. When it is, get a table on the terrace out front—though the service, which is quick if you're inside, usually slows down considerably.

Náměstí Zachariáše z Hradce 7. ✆ **567-243-222.** Reservations recommended. Main courses 80Kč–190Kč. AE, MC, V. June–Sept daily 9am–10pm; Oct–May Tues–Sun 9am–10pm.

ZNOJMO

190km (118 miles) SE of Prague, 64km (40 miles) S of Brno

The ancient royal town of Znojmo, with its castle overlooking the Dyje River valley, for centuries marked an important border between Moravia and Austria. During the Cold War, when the border region was effectively transformed into a no-man's land, the town withered, cut off from its Lower Austrian hinterland.

These days with the frontier now wide open—you won't even find passport formalities any more—Znojmo is busy re-establishing and redefining itself as a regional cultural hub. The town's traditional strong suit, wine production, has been augmented by a series of wine and music festivals that now take place throughout the year, as well as the development of extensive hiking and biking trails that take advantage of the area's natural beauty. For maps and tips, go to Informační Středisko (below).

Several exceedingly cute pensions have opened up in recent years, making Znojmo a natural choice for a couple of days' downtime after hectic Prague or a convenient stopping-off point if you're traveling between Prague and Vienna.

Znojmo was settled as far back as the 7th century, and the town gained prominence in the 9th century, when the Great Moravian Empire took over. In the 11th and 12th centuries, Prince Břetislav I constructed a fortress here; in 1226, the town was granted rights (including collecting taxes and making wine) by the king—even before the Moravian capital of Brno. Znojmo's position on the border made it a natural location as a trading center, and Czech kings ensured that the town was taken care of.

In addition to the castle and adjoining Romanesque rotunda, dating from the 11th century, the kids will enjoy exploring the town's extensive underground passageways, the Znojemské podzemí (Znojmo Underground). Over the centuries, the townspeople here carved out nearly 30km (19 miles) of underground tunnels that were used for everything from hiding from marauders to storing pickles, wine, and munitions. Around a kilometer of the old tunnel system has been excavated and opened to public (see below).

Znojmo has two other claims to fame: It's considered the pickle capital of the Czech Republic. They're made from the best cucumbers the country has to offer. And when put into a spicy sauce, as they are in *Znojemský guláš*, these sweet-and-sour pickles really taste great.

Znojmo is also home to pretty good beer. The town's traditional brewer, Hostan, has won more than its fair share of national accolades. Unfortunately, the local brewery was shut down a couple of years ago and production moved elsewhere. Nevertheless, several pubs still proudly serve the hometown lager.

Essentials

GETTING THERE Znojmo is most easily reached by **car** and is especially convenient for those heading to or from Vienna or Telč. Take the D1 motorway south from Prague and exit at Hwy. 38 in the direction of Jihlava. As you enter the town, you're already on the right highway, so just pass by the town center and follow the signs. From Prague, the trip should take about 2½ hours.

By public transportation, buses are usually quicker and cheaper than trains, both from Prague and Brno. Several **buses** from Prague's Florenc station make the daily run to Znojmo in about 3 hours. The one-way fare is around 200Kč. From Brno, the trip is much quicker (around an hour) and costs about 65Kč one-way.

By **train** from Prague, the complete trip takes at least 5 hours via Brno and costs around 500Kč. You'll usually have to change in Břeclav. From Brno, several trains make the trip throughout the day, though again you'll usually have to change in Břeclav. The ride takes a little over 2 hours and costs about 160Kč.

VISITOR INFORMATION In the center of Znojmo, **Informační Středisko,** at Obroková 10, Znojmo (*C* **515-222-552;** www.znojmocity.cz), can help with accommodations, maps, and directions. They also sell cycling maps and can advise on rentals. Ask what's on in town, and they can book tickets for you on the spot. The office is open in May, June, September, and October, Monday to Friday from 8am to 6pm, and Saturday and Sunday from 10am to 5pm; July and August daily 9am to 7pm; and November to April, Monday to Friday from 8am to 4pm.

SPECIAL EVENTS In late August and early September, residents of Znojmo celebrate their vintages at the **Znojmo Wine Festival.** Taste wine, eat pickles, and listen to traditional Moravian music late into the night, which is normally tranquil on other nights. For details, contact **Informační Středisko** (see "Visitor Information," above). Outside of the main wine festival, Znojmo hosts around a dozen smaller festivals, usually centered on music or wine.

ORIENTATION Znojmo's main square is **Masarykovo náměstí,** and pretty much everything you'll want to see is on or near it. **Zelenářská Street,** which runs off the square's northwest corner, leads to the castle and St. Nicholas Church.

Strolling Through Znojmo

A walking tour of Znojmo takes about 2 to 3 hours. Begin at **Masaryk Square,** where the **Art House** (**Dům umění,** Masarykovo nám. 11; *C* **515-226-529**) holds a small collection of coins, plus temporary exhibitions. It is open Tuesday to Saturday from 9am to 6pm. Admission is 40Kč. The southern end of the square is one of the few historic areas that hasn't been maintained well; the dilapidated **Capuchin Monastery (Kapucínský klášter)** and **Church of St. John the Baptist** show few signs that they were once focal points of the town.

Impossible to miss is the **Town Hall Tower** (*C* **515-216-297**), the only remaining piece of what was once referred to as Moravia's prettiest town hall. The actual town hall met misfortune during World War II, but the late-Gothic 70m-high (230-ft.) tower still stands guard. For 30Kč, you can climb up to the lookout, which offers a picturesque view of the castle and the Dyje River. Try not to let the nondescript department store that occupies the spot where the town hall once stood wreck the picture. The tower is open May to September, daily 9am to 5pm; April, Monday to Friday from 9am to 5pm, Saturday 9am to 1pm; and October to March, Monday to Friday 9am to 5pm, Saturday 9am to noon.

THE wine trails OF VALTICE-LEDNICE

While Znojmo may be considered the Czech Republic's winemaking hub, it's not the only area to offer great wine in a breathtaking setting. About 60kms (36 miles) due east of Znojmo (40km/24 miles south of Brno) are the UNESCO-protected towns of **Valtice** and **Lednice.** Both are part of an important wine-producing region as well as home to some interesting historical curiosities, courtesy of the Liechtenstein family, and more than a thousand kilometers of cycling and hiking paths through hills and dales known collectively as the **Moravian Wine Trails** ★ (Vínařské Stezky; www.stezky.cz). If you've got a couple of days to relax or you haven't yet drunk your fill in Znojmo, it's well worth a detour.

Start your exploration in the small border town of Valtice, dominated by the enormous **Valtice Castle,** Valtický Zámek, Zámek 1 ((℃) **519-352-423;** www.zamek-valtice.cz). The castle dates from the beginning of the 18th century and was designed by a group of leading architects of the day, including the baroque master Johann Bernhard Fischer von Erlach. Tour the castle to see the restored interiors and furnishings. It's open in April, Tuesday to Sunday from 9am to 4pm, and May through September, Tuesday to Sunday from 9am to 5pm. Admission is 120Kč adults, 90Kč students.

For accommodations options, you need look no further than the **Hubertus Hotel,** Zámek 1, 691 42 Valtice (www.hotelhubertus.cz; (℃) **519-352-537**), conveniently situated in a wing of Valtice Castle. While the 31 rather ordinary doubles can't measure up to the splendid setting, the central location is a plus and there are plenty of great places to taste wine nearby.

Lednice lies about 8km (5 miles) north of Valtice and boasts another spectacular one-time Liechtenstein residence, **Lednice Castle,** Zámek Lednice ★ ((℃) **519-340-128;** www.zamek-lednice.info). A variety of tour options (check out the castle website for details) offer the chance to wander through the castle interiors. Stroll the lovely grounds to find one of Europe's oldest greenhouses and even a mock minaret. The castle is open in April and October on weekends from 9am to 3:15pm, and May through September on Tuesday to Sunday from 9am to 5pm. Admission for most of the tours runs about 100Kč for adults, 70Kč students.

The helpful **Tourist Information Office,** Turistické informační centrum, Zámecké nám. 68 (www.lednice.cz; (℃) **519-340-986**) in Lednice can give you an overview of what's on, as well as hiking and biking information, and advice on bike rentals and where to eat and stay.

The best way to reach the Valtice-Lednice area is by **car.** From Znojmo, head east on Hwy. 53 in the direction of Pohořelice, turning south on Hwy. 52 to Mikulov, and then following the signs south to Valtice. From Brno, head south on the D2 highway, exiting on road 422, following the signs to Lednice. By **public transportation,** take the train from either Prague or Brno to Břeclav. From the Břeclav train station, buses leave pretty much on the hour in season to Lednice. To move between Valtice and Lednice, you can hike or bike along a pretty marked trail. The 8km (5-mile) trip on foot takes about 3 hours at a leisurely pace. There's also local bus service.

Follow the small alleyway called **Kramářská** to **Slepičí trh 2** (the former Hen Market) to find the entrance to the **Znojemské podzemí (Znojmo Underground)** ☺★★. If there's a tour just leaving or a few people waiting, arrange to join them, since the tours (which are in Czech only, though English-language pamphlets are provided) are given only to groups of more than six. From May to September, admission is 90Kč adults, 60Kč students, 200Kč families (up to three accompanying children). From October to April, the rates are 60Kč adults, 40Kč students, 140Kč families. The Underground is open May to September, daily 9am to 5pm; October to April, Monday to Saturday 10am to 5pm, Sunday 1 to 4pm. For reservations call ✆ **515-221-342.**

Head back 1 block west to Zelenářská ulice and follow it away from the square to Malá Mikulášská ulice, which leads to the Gothic **St. Nicholas Church** and behind it the bi-level **St. Wenceslas Chapel.** The church is supposed to be open only for services and the occasional concert, but check the door just in case. In any event, the panorama here out over the valley is breathtaking.

Farther on, at the edge of the embankment, lies **Znojmo Castle** and the 11th-century **Rotunda sv. Kateřiny** ★ (✆ **515-282-211**), one of the oldest and best examples of Romanesque architecture still standing in the Czech Republic. Note the path to the castle and rotunda starts just to the left of the entrance to the old Hostan brewery. Inside the rotunda are painstakingly restored frescoes of the Přemyslid rulers dating back to the mid–12th century. The rotunda is accessible by guided tour only (in Czech but headphone translation available) May to October, Tuesday to Friday, 9am to 5pm. Admission is 90Kč, with no discounts. Tours depart all day on the quarter hour and last around 20 minutes. Znojmo Castle is open from May to October, Tuesday to Sunday, from 9am to 5pm. Admission costs 20Kč.

Where to Stay

The quality of lodging in Znojmo has drastically improved in recent years. In addition to the properties listed below, there's now a raft of small family owned pensions behind the main square in and among the tiny lanes that overlook the river valley. The best bet if you turn up without a room is to roam around the center and see if something strikes your fancy. Except during wine festivals in the fall, you're unlikely to have a problem finding a room.

Althanský palác ★ This romantic and tastefully reconstructed town palace is one of the nicest hotels in town. The location is dead center, and perfect for exploring the main squares or the tiny alleyways that overlook the river valley. Many of the rooms have retained their period details, like hardwood floors and beam ceilings. Ask to see a few before deciding. The beautiful "Blue Room," with pale blue walls and wood floors, goes for the price of an ordinary double. The in-house restaurant is one of the best around.

Horní nám. 3, 669 02 Znojmo. www.althanskypalac.cz. ✆ **731-441-090.** 22 units. 1,950Kč double; 3,500Kč suite. AE, DC, MC, V. Parking. **Amenities:** Restaurant; bar; wine cellar; bikes; exercise room. *In room:* TV, Internet, minibar.

Hotel Lahofer ★★★ 🍴 One of the country's smartest and best-run small hotels, the Lahofer occupies a renovated town house dating back to the 13th century, just a block from the main square and in the middle of what was once the city's Jewish Quarter (in the 15th c.). The rooms are done out in high-end contemporary furnishings. The lighting, for example, is from the Italian designer Lucente. The rooms have immaculate baths, big flatscreen TVs, and large, low-slung beds with thick but firm mattresses. The hotel is owned by the Lahofer winery, and there's a small wine shop in the reception area. The in-house restaurant is arguably the best in Znojmo, and each menu item has been paired with a Lahofer wine. Book ahead.

Veselá 13, 671 00 Znojmo. www.lahofer.cz. ℂ **515-220-323.** Fax 515-220-332. 15 units. 1,900Kč double; 3,000Kč suite. AE, DC, MC, V. Parking. **Amenities:** Restaurant; bar. *In room:* A/C (some), TV, hair dryer, Internet, minibar.

U Mikuláše This "cyclopenzión" (meaning recommended for touring cyclists) got a face-lift in 2010, leaving the rooms with a delightful period-piece look that feels welcoming. Ask to see a couple of rooms, since some have pretty views and a terrace out over the valley. The pension occupies a quiet lane just above the river and down from St Nicholas Church. Opposite the hotel is a good spot for lunch or coffee, the U Mikuláše restaurant.

Mikulášské nám. 8, 669 02 Znojmo. www.penzionumikulase.cz. ℂ **607-555-202.** 8 units. 600Kč–1,200Kč double. No credit cards. Parking. **Amenities:** Restaurant (across the street).

Where to Eat

Znojmo may have the pickles, but finding a decent rest of the meal is still tricky. The dining revolution that has swept much of the rest of the country has yet to be felt here, and most of the restaurants in town have the look and food of a Communist-era throwback. Fortunately, there's plenty of good wine on hand, and the beer—courtesy of brewer Hostan—isn't bad either. The restaurants in the Althanský palác and Hotel Lahofer (see "Where to Stay," above) are both very good.

Na České CZECH This popular family restaurant is a solid choice for well-cooked, if ordinary, Czech dishes, including several choices with fish and duck, at affordable prices. For hearty appetites, try the potato pancakes stuffed with chicken and pork. For dessert, the potato noodles sprinkled with poppy seed and plum sauce is a local specialty and a filling meal in itself. There's a small, enclosed garden in the back in nice weather.

Dolní Česká 6. ℂ **515-260-155.** Main courses 90Kč–180Kč. No credit cards. Daily 11am–10pm.

Na Věčností ★ CZECH This is a wine cellar, beer hall, and art gallery rolled into one. The food is simple but good and the laid-back vibe is the best in town. Lunchtime offers a rotating menu of traditional foods with modern updates and lots of vegetarian offerings. The place is completely nonsmoking.

Velká Mikulášská 11. ℂ **515-221-814.** Main courses 70Kč–180Kč. No credit cards. Mon–Sat 11am–9:30pm.

PLANNING YOUR TRIP TO PRAGUE & THE CZECH REPUBLIC

13

As with any trip, a little preparation is essential before you start your journey to Prague. This chapter provides a variety of planning tools, including information on how to get there; tips on accommodations; and quick, on the ground resources.

In preparing for Prague, there are no unusual packing requirements. Your suitcase or backpack will look pretty much as it would for any U.S. or Continental European destination with four distinct seasons. If you forget anything, rest assured that just like at home, there's likely to be a shopping mall or convenience store down the street where you can find a suitable substitute.

A couple of items to pack that you might not think about would include an eye mask for sleeping that blocks out the early morning light. For some reason (unknown to me, at least), many Czech hotels (and especially many cheaper pensions) don't have light-blocking curtains. Additionally, mosquito repellent in summer and fall is always a good idea to have handy. Mosquitoes are no more a problem here than anywhere else, but in woods or near rivers, you'll find them to be a nuisance.

Even in midsummer, you'll want to pack some warm clothes, like a sweater or jacket for evening. And always prepare for rain at any day, any time. Lastly, don't forget to bring a pair of comfortable walking shoes and be ready to use them. Although there's great public transportation everywhere, you're probably going to do a lot more walking than you think, and the cobblestones can be especially unforgiving in uncomfortable shoes.

GETTING THERE

By Plane

Prague Airport (code PRG; ✆ **220-113-314;** www.prg.aero) is the main international air gateway to the Czech Republic. The airport lies in the suburb of Ruzyně, about 18km (12 miles) northwest of the center. The airport has two main passenger terminals: 1 and 2. Terminal 1 handles destinations outside the European Union's common border area (known in E.U.-speak as the *Schengen Zone*), including overseas flights to and from the U.S. as well as flights from Ireland and the U.K. Terminal 2 handles what are considered to be internal flights within the European Union (inside the Schengen Zone), including flights to and from France, Germany, Italy, and Switzerland.

Prague is well served by the major European and international carriers, including several budget airlines. The Czech national carrier, **CSA** (www.csa.cz) operates regular direct service to New York's JFK airport, as well as, in high summer season, to Atlanta. **Delta Airlines** (www.delta.com) also offers regular direct service between Prague and both New York JFK and Atlanta (summer only).

GETTING INTO TOWN FROM THE AIRPORT

Taxis are the quickest but most expensive option. Several cab companies are licensed to operate at the airport. The most reliable of the lot is **AAA Radiotaxi** (© 222-333-222; www.aaa-taxi.cz). Look for yellow AAA cabs lined up outside both main terminals: 1 and 2. Fares with AAA average about 600Kč to the center. The trip normally takes about 25 minutes, but the drive can run as long as an hour during rush hour.

If you're staying in the immediate center of town, a cheaper alternative is to take a minibus operated by **CEDAZ** (© 221-111-111; www.cedaz.cz). Minibuses depart from both terminals every 30 minutes from 7:30am to 7pm and drop you at V celnici street in central Prague (near Náměstí Republiky) for 120Kč per person, including one piece of luggage. Use the V celnici stop for the return trip to the airport as well. Schedules are similar in both directions. The CEDAZ minibus can also take you to the Dejvická metro station (on line A) for onward travel on the metro, for 90Kč per person.

The most affordable option is public transportation. City bus no. 119 stops at both terminals and runs regularly from the airport to the Dejvická metro station (on line A), from where the center is just three metro stops away. Bus no. 100 runs south from the airport to the area of Zličín and connects to metro line B. Travel on both requires a 32Kč ticket purchased from yellow ticketing machines at the bus stop (note that the machines only accept change). Buy two tickets if you're carrying large luggage. A special **Airport Express** (designated "AE" on buses) runs to and from Prague's main train station and costs 50Kč per person each way. Buy tickets directly from the driver. This is convenient if you are connecting directly to an international train.

By Car

Prague is easily accessible by major highway from points around Europe. The main four-lane highways leading into and out of the city include the D1 expressway, which runs south and east from Prague and links the city to Brno (2 hr.), Bratislava (3 hr.), and with onward connections to Kraków, Poland (8 hr.), and Budapest, Hungary (6 hr.). The D5 motorway runs southwest from Prague to the Czech city of Plzeň (Pilsen; 1 hr.) and onward to Nürnberg, Germany (3 hr.), with connections to Italy and points in southern and western Europe. The D8 runs north out of Prague to Dresden, Germany (2 hr.) and eventually to Berlin (5 hr.) and points north. Road connections to Vienna, alas, are not what they should be. The trip takes about 5 hours by car, with most of the way along crowded two-lane highway.

For information on car rentals and gasoline (petrol) in Prague, see "Getting Around by Car," later in this section.

By Train

Prague lies on major European rail lines, with good connections to Dresden (2 hr.) and Berlin (5 hr.) to the north, and Brno (2–3 hr.), Vienna (4–5 hr.), Bratislava (3 hr.), Budapest (7 hr.), and Kraków (8 hr.) to the east. New high-speed rail service, the Pendolino, has been introduced on the Prague-Vienna run, shortening the travel time on some trains to as little as 4 hours. More high-speed rail links are on the drawing board.

Prague has two international train stations, so make sure to ask which station your train is using when you buy your ticket. Most international trains arrive at the main station, **Hlavní nádraží** (Wilsonova 8, Prague 1; ℂ **840-112-113;** www.cd.cz; metro stop: Hlavní] nádraží, line C). Some trains to and from Berlin, Vienna, and Budapest, however, may stop at the northern suburban station, **Nádraží Holešovice** (Vrbenského ul., Prague 7; ℂ **840-112-113;** www.cd.cz; metro stop: Nádraží] Holešovice, line C). Train information is available at the telephone numbers indicated or on the web at www.jizdnirady.idnes.cz.

Of the two main stations, Hlavní nádraží is more central and better equipped. It's undergone a massive face-lift in the past few years and these days is bustling with useful shops, bank ATMs, currency exchanges, restaurants (including a Burger King), and a left luggage office. From the train platform, you'll walk down a flight of stairs and through a tunnel before arriving in the ground-level main hall, which contains ticket windows, a useful **Prague Information Service** office that sells city maps and dispenses information, and restrooms. Also useful is the **ČD center** (ℂ **840-112-113;** www.cd.cz) run by the Czech Railways. It provides domestic and international train information as well as currency exchange and accommodations services. It is open daily 7 to 11am, 11:30am to 2pm, and 2:30 to 5:45pm. Visa and Master-Card are accepted.

After you leave the modern terminal hall, a 10-minute walk to the left puts you at the top of Wenceslas Square and 20 minutes by foot from Old Town Square. Metro line C connects the station easily to the other two subway lines and the rest of the city. Metro trains depart from the lower level, and tickets are available from one of several newsstands in the station's main lobby. Gouging taxi drivers line up outside the station and are plentiful throughout the day and night but are not recommended.

Prague has two smaller train stations. **Masaryk Station,** Hybernská ulice, Prague 1 (ℂ **840-112-113**), is primarily for commuters traveling to nearby Bohemian cities. Situated about 10 minutes by foot from the main train station, Masaryk is near Staré Město, just a stone's throw from náměstí Republiky metro station. **Smíchov Station,** Nádražní ulice at Rozkošného, Prague 5 (ℂ **840-112-113**), is the terminus for commuter trains from western and southern Bohemia, though it's a convenient station for getting to popular day trip destinations like Karlštejn and Plzeň. The station has a 24-hour baggage check and is serviced by metro line B.

By Bus

The **Central Bus Station–Florenc,** Křižíkova 4–6, Prague 8 (ℂ **900-144-444;** www.florenc.cz for timetable info), is a few blocks north of the main train station. Most local and long-distance buses arrive here. The adjacent Florenc metro station is on both lines B (yellow) and C (red). Florenc station is relatively small and doesn't have many visitor services. There are even smaller bus depots at **Želivského** (metro line A), **Smíchovské nádraží** (metro line B), and **Nádraží Holešovice** (metro line C).

GETTING AROUND

On Foot

Prepare to do plenty of walking. Most of the center of the city is closed to vehicles, including taxis, meaning you'll have to walk pretty much everywhere. Distances are relatively close, but always wear comfortable shoes since many of the streets are *paved* (if that's the right word) with cobblestones.

By Public Transportation

Prague's highly efficient public transportation network of metros (subways), trams, and buses (© 296-191-817; www.dpp.cz) is one of the few sound Communist-era legacies. In central Prague, metro stations abound. Trams and buses offer a cheap sightseeing experience but also require a strong stomach for jostling with fellow passengers in close quarters.

TICKETS & PASSES

For single-use **tickets,** there are two choices. The first is a short-term ticket, which costs 24Kč, or 12Kč for kids from 6 to 15 (children 5 and under ride free) and seniors (70 and over). This allows for unlimited travel on metros, trams, and buses for a period of 30 minutes from the time the ticket is validated. A long-term ticket costs 32Kč, 16Kč for 10- to 15-year-olds and seniors, and allows for unlimited travel on public transit for up to 90 minutes after validation. The cheaper ticket is usually sufficient for most trips within the center.

You can also buy a **1-day pass** for 110Kč, kids from 6 to 15 and seniors pay 55Kč, which is good for unlimited travel on metros, buses, and trams for 24 hours from when the ticket is validated. A similar **3-day pass** costs 310Kč, with no discounts for children or seniors.

You can buy tickets from yellow coin-operated machines in metro stations or at most newsstands marked TABÁK or TRAFIKA. The machines have English instructions but are a little clunky to operate. First push the button for the ticket you want (either 24Kč or 32Kč), and then insert the money in the slot. Validate your ticket in the little stamping machine before you descend on the escalator in the metro or as you enter the tram or bus. Hold on to your validated ticket throughout your ride—you'll need to show it if a ticket collector (be sure to check for his or her badge) asks you. If you're caught without a valid ticket, you'll be asked, and not so kindly, to pay a fine on the spot while all the locals look on, shaking their heads in disgust. The fine is 700Kč if paid on the spot and 950Kč if paid later.

BY METRO

Metro trains operate daily from 5am to midnight and run every 2 to 10 minutes depending on the time of day. The three lines are identified by both letter and color: A (green), B (yellow), and C (red). The most convenient central stations are Muzeum, on both the A and C lines at the top of Václavské náměstí (Wenceslas Square); Můstek, on both the A and B lines at the foot of Václavské náměstí; Staroměstská on the A line, for Old Town Square and the Charles Bridge; and Malostranská, on the A line, serving Malá Strana and the Castle District. Refer to the metro map on the inside back cover for details.

BY TRAM & BUS

The city's 24 tramlines run practically everywhere, and there's always another tram with the same number traveling back. You never have to hail trams; they make every

riding the rails **IN THE CZECH CAPITAL**

While Prague has a fine metro and an extensive bus network, it's the tram—*tramvaj* in Czech—that sets the transportation tone for the city. Any visitor will be familiar with the sight of these (mostly) red-and-cream whales on rails, gliding smoothly over the cobblestones and pushing their girth through impossibly narrow streets that were originally built to accommodate horses but are now packed with cars, trucks, buses, and an endless stream of streetcars.

Tram no. 22 is a visitor's favorite. For the price of a 90-minute ticket—32Kč—you can ride all the way from Prague Castle, down through the Lesser Quarter, across the Vltava River (with stunning views of Charles Bridge to the left), and into the very center of town. Stay on the line and you're transported in minutes through the gentrifying suburb of Vinohrady, and out to the Communist-era, high-rise housing projects of Hostívař and beyond. You may even have some time left on your ticket to return to the center free of charge.

Prague's trams remain a repository of civility that long ago vanished from other aspects of city life. Visitors—forced mostly to interact with waiters and shop clerks—can sometimes get the impression that Czechs are a little gruff. But step onto a tram and it's like going back 50 years in time. For example, it's still considered bad manners on a crowded tram for a man to fail to offer his seat to women of a certain age. This societal nicety doesn't apply as strictly to the city's newer and less-mannered metro.

Prague's trams are usually quiet and there's not much banter among the riders. This changes after 11pm, when the city's day fleet retires to the garages, and special night trams are brought into service to ferry revelers from pubs in the center to the housing projects on the outskirts. The mood at 3am can get raucous, and night trams are often little more than pubs on wheels. There are no laws against carrying open containers of alcohol (at least none rigorously

stop. The most popular tram, no. 22 (aka the "tourist tram" or the "pickpocket express"), runs past top sights like the National Theater and Prague Castle.

Regular bus and tram service stops at midnight, after which selected routes run reduced night schedules, usually only once per hour. Schedules are posted at stops. If you miss a night connection, expect a long wait for the next.

Buses tend to be used only outside the older districts of Prague and have three-digit numbers. Both the buses and tramlines begin their morning runs around 4:30am.

BY FUNICULAR

The funicular (cog railway) makes the scenic run up and down Petřín Hill every 10 minutes (15 min. in winter season) daily from 9am to 11:30pm with an intermediate stop at the Nebozízek restaurant halfway up the hill, which overlooks the city. It requires either a valid 24Kč or 32Kč ticket or any of the same transport passes as other modes of public transport and departs from a small house in the park near the Újezd tram stop (trams no. 12, 20, and 22) in Malá Strana.

By Car

Driving in Prague isn't worth the money or effort. The roads are crowded and the high number of one-way streets can be incredibly frustrating. What's more, parking in the enforced). Unlike in New York, for example, there's no need to swill from a paper bag.

Prague's extensive tram network sprang up in the early years of the 20th century, more or less concurrent with the country's independence from the Austro-Hungarian Empire. The original electronic genius behind the system was a Czech, František Křížík, though it must be admitted the tram culture shares much in common with the empire's former capital, Vienna. Anyone who's spent much time there will feel at home here.

In a city that's in the throes of remarkable change, the trams add a welcome sense of permanence. Looking at old tram maps from the 1920s and '30s, it's reassuring to see how little the basic layout has changed. The no. 12 tram still wends its way northward from the suburb of Smíchov in the southwest across town to the neighborhood of Holešovice and beyond—just as it did 70 years ago.

The no. 17 tram still hugs the eastern bank of the Vltava for much of its run, as it always has. It's no stretch to say that a Czech Rip Van Winkle returning to the city from the 1930s would, in turns, be horrified and amazed to hear about the Nazi occupation, the Communist period, the Velvet Revolution, and now the European Union, but would have no trouble at all making his way home that night on the tram.

The future for Prague's trams looks secure. After a long period of neglect, the city appears committed to improving the tram infrastructure, including adding a new generation of super-sleek cars designed by none other than the Porsche group. These oversized, red-and-gray cars recall a kind of comic-book bullet train (even though trams top out at just 30 mph).

—*Mark Baker*

center is often restricted and available only to residents with pre-paid parking stickers. The only time you *might* want a car is if you only have a few days and plan to explore other parts of the Czech Republic.

RENTAL COMPANIES

Try **Europcar,** Elišky Krásnohorské 9, Prague 1 (© **224-811-290;** www.europcar.cz). There's also **Hertz,** Evropská 15, Prague 6 (© **225-345-031;** www.hertz.cz), with a branch at Prague Airport (© **225-345-021**). **Budget** is also at Prague Airport (© **220-560-443;** www.budget.cz) and at the main train station, Hlavní nádraží, Wilsonova 8, Prague 1 (© **222-319-595**).

Local car-rental companies sometimes offer lower rates than the big international firms. Compare **CS Czechocar,** Kongresové centrum (Congress Center at Vyšehrad metro stop on the C line), 5. května 65, Prague 4 (© **261-222-079** or 261-222-143; www.czechocar.cz), or at Prague Airport, Prague 6 (© **220-113-454**); or try **SeccoCar,** Přístavní 39, Prague 7 (© **220-802-361;** www.seccocar.cz).

Car rates can be negotiable. Try to obtain the best possible deal with the rental company by asking about discounts. Special deals are often offered for keeping the car for an extended period, for unlimited mileage (or at least getting some miles thrown in free), or for a bigger car at a lower price. It also usually helps to book over the Internet as far in advance as possible.

ROADWAYS & EMERGENCIES

Major roadways radiate from Prague like spokes on a wheel, so touring the country is easy if you make the capital your base. The Prague-Brno (D1) motorway (*dálnice*) is the most traveled, but the Prague–Nürnberg (D5) motorway has opened a 2-hour express route into western Germany. In addition, the D8 motorway is now complete all the way to Dresden to the north. You are advised to check the most recent map before you travel. Alternatively, see www.ceskedalnice.cz, where you will find updates on the newly built motorways. If you are going to use any of these, you have to purchase a special stamp-sticker (*dálniční známky*), which goes on your windshield. Most gas stations and post offices sell them. The sticker costs 250Kč for 10 days, 350Kč for 1 month, or 1,200Kč for the calendar year. Rental cars should come with a valid stamp already.

Always exercise care when driving. Czech roads are often poorly designed, narrow, and overcrowded. Drivers are of the aggressive variety, and can always be counted on to try to overtake no matter what the road condition or situation with oncoming traffic is. The few superhighways that do exist are in good shape, so whenever possible, stick to them, especially at night. If you have car trouble, major highways have **SOS emergency phones** to call for assistance, located about every 1km (half-mile). There's also the **ÚAMK,** a 24-hour auto club like AAA that can provide service for a fee. You can summon its bright yellow pickups on the main highways by using the emergency phones. If you're not near an SOS phone or are on a road without them, you can contact ÚAMK at ✆ **1230** (www.uamk.cz), or **ABA,** another emergency assistance company, at ✆ **1240** (www.aba.cz). If you do encounter problems and have to call road service, have all the necessary information at hand for the operator, including the make, model, and year of the car, license number, and other technical details. Rest assured, the operator will ask for them.

In theory, foreign drivers are required to have an international driver's license, though this is often overlooked in practice and short-term visitors are fine with a valid national driver's license. Cars must also carry **proof of insurance** (a green card issued with rental cars), **registration** (in Czech *technický průkaz*), as well as a **first-aid kit** in the trunk.

Czech police are infamous for stopping cars with foreign plates, and the "fines" they exact are often negotiable. If you're stopped, expect to pay at least 1,000Kč for speeding or other common infractions like not having your headlights on during the day. Those caught by the police should ask for some type of receipt (*účet* in Czech, pronounced *oo*-chet); this can help cut down on overpayment.

GASOLINE

Gasoline (*benzín*) in the Czech Republic is expensive. Prices in 2011 averaged around 35Kč per liter, or about 140Kč per gallon. Filling stations can be found on all major highways. Most are open 24 hours, and many have minimarkets with food and drink as well. If you're leaving the country, fill up near the border, as the price of gas in Austria and Germany can be higher still.

PARKING

Finding a parking spot in Prague can be more challenging than driving in this maze of a city. Fines for illegal parking can be stiff, but worse are "Denver Boots," which immobilize cars until a fine is paid. If you find your car booted, call the number on the ticket, tell them where you are, wait for the clamp removers, and pay them 1,500Kč or more, depending on the violation. Much of the center of Prague has restricted parking available only to residents (these are marked out by blue lines painted on the curb and street). Here and there, you'll find a few zones where paid street parking is permitted (marked out in white lines painted on the curb and street). In these areas, you will have to feed coins into a central parking meter, which will then issue a slip that you place on the dashboard so that it is visible through the windshield. Parking rates in the center average around 40Kč per hour; rates are cheaper outside the center.

SPECIAL DRIVING RULES

Drivers are required to use headlights night and day year-round. Seat belts are required, and you *cannot* legally make a right turn when a traffic light is red. Automobiles must stop when a pedestrian steps into a crosswalk (however, they often don't, as you'll find when you're walking around). Children under 1.5m (about 5 ft.) tall are not permitted to ride in the front seat. On major highways, the speed limit is 130kmph (81 mph). The yellow diamond road sign denotes the right of way at an unregulated intersection. When approaching an intersection, always check to see who has the right of way, since the "main" road can change several times within blocks on the same street. Drinking and driving is strictly prohibited and the allowable blood-alcohol content is zero. You'll get a very steep fine if you're caught.

By Bike

Prague has a growing number of specially marked bike lanes, including a long and popular run that follows the Vltava River south of the center from the National Theater, and another that starts around the Prague Zoo and follows the Vltava northward toward Germany. The city's ubiquitous cobblestones make mountain bikes (with fat tires) the natural choice. Two companies in central Prague specialize in rentals (and also give organized bike tours): Praha Bike, Dlouhá 24, Prague 1 (✆ **732-388-880;** www.prahabike.cz), and City Bike, Královdvorská 5, Prague 1 (✆ **776-180-284;** www.citybike-prague.com).

[FastFACTS] PRAGUE & THE CZECH REPUBLIC

Area Codes There are no area or city codes in the Czech Republic. Each telephone number is a unique nine-digit number, usually written xxx-xxx-xxx. Numbers that begin with a "6" or "7" indicate a mobile phone. See "Telephones," later in this section.

Business Hours Normal business and banking hours run from 9am to 5pm Monday to Friday. Stores in central Prague are typically open weekdays from 9am to 7pm and on Saturday from 9am until at least 1pm;

larger stores and shopping centers are likely to be open on Sundays and holidays as well. Post offices are open from 8am until 7pm Monday to Friday. Some larger post offices have limited Saturday hours. Castles and museums are usually closed on Mondays. Tourist attractions usually have shorter hours or shut down altogether during the winter (Nov–Apr).

Car Rental See "Getting There by Car," earlier in this chapter.

Cellphones See "Mobile Phones," later in this section.

Crime See "Safety," later in this section.

Customs The Czech Republic is a member of the European Union's common border and customs zone, the Schengen Zone, meaning there are no customs checks at border crossings or airports when traveling between most E.U. member states (excluding the U.K. and Ireland). If you're flying in from the U.S., Canada,

Australia, U.K. or Ireland, after you've collected your luggage, at the customs point, walk through the "green" lane if you have nothing to declare. This is usually a formality and you'll rarely be asked to even open your suitcase. Travelers are permitted to import freely modest amounts of tobacco products, alcoholic beverages, gifts, and perfume for personal use. Restricted items include meat, milk and dairy products, certain plants, and wildlife as well as illegal narcotics (including marijuana), weapons, explosives, and pornographic materials. Travelers entering the country with more than 10,000€ in cash are required by law to make a currency declaration.

Travelers with Disabilites Prague remains a difficult city for travelers with disabilities. Few sidewalks have curb cuts, the cobblestones are difficult to walk and wheel over, and many older buildings do not have elevators (or if they do, the elevator is not wide enough to accommodate a wheelchair). New hotels and buildings built in the past 10 years must conform to new standards, but they remain in the minority. The main umbrella organization for the rights of people with disabilities is the **Prague Association of Wheelchair Users** (Pražská organizace vozíčkářů) at Benediktská 6, Prague 1 (© **224-827-210;** www.pov. cz). The website is in Czech

only but has several useful maps showing wheelchair-friendly parts of the city. The Prague public transit company (DPP) continues to expand facilities for passengers with disabilities. Several, but not all, metro stations have accessible elevators. A handful of new trams and buses have street-level doors to allow wheelchair entry. For further information, contact the DPP website with information on barrier-free travel in English (www.dpp.cz).

Doctors See "Hospitals," later in this section.

Drinking Laws Alcoholic beverages (including beer, wine, and spirits) are widely available at supermarkets, convenience stores, cafes, and bars. The legal age for buying and consuming alcohol is 18, though ID checks are not common. There are no set hours for when bars can operate. Traditional Czech pubs close around 11pm. More modern bars and clubs in Prague usually stay open until at least 1 or 2am. The blood-alcohol limit for driving a car is zero, and motorists face a stiff fine and loss of their driving license if caught.

Driving Rules See "Getting Around," earlier in this chapter.

Electricity The Czech Republic operates on the standard European 220v using a two-pronged plug with round pins. Most U.S. appliances, like hair dryers, will need a transformer and a plug adaptor. Laptops will

usually only require a plug adaptor.

Embassies & Consulates All foreign embassies are located in the capital, Prague. The embassy of the **United States** is located at Tržiště 15, Prague 1, Malá Strana (© **257-022-000;** http:// czech.prague.usembassy. gov). The embassy of **Canada** is at Muchova 6, Prague 6, Dejvice (© **272-101-800;** www.canada international.gc.ca/czech-tcheque). The embassy of the **United Kingdom** is at Thunovská 14, Prague 1, Malá Strana (© **257-402-111;** http://ukinczech republic.fco.gov.uk). The local consular office of **Australia** is at Klimentská 10, Prague 1, Nové Město (© **296-578-350**).

Emergencies Dial the following numbers in an emergency: **112** (general emergency, equivalent to U.S. 911); **155** (ambulance); **158** (police); **150** (fire); **1230, 1240** (emergency road service).

Family Travel Prague and the Czech Republic are not particularly family- or kid-friendly. Kids will enjoy the metros, trams, trains, and castles, but are likely to tire of endless museum visits or castle tours focused on unfamiliar history. That said, there are lots of things for younger visitors to do. To locate accommodations, restaurants, and attractions that are particularly kid-friendly, look for the "Kids" icon throughout this guide.

Gasoline Please see "Getting There By Car," earlier in this chapter.

Health A visit to the Czech Republic presents no unusual health risks aside from the usual good advice of not to overdo it with food and drink. Medical care is very good and on par with western Europe. Pharmacies are abundant and sell both over-the-counter (OTC) medications, like aspirin, as well as prescription drugs. OTC medicines are usually not available in grocery stores, convenience stores, or gas stations and must be purchased at a licensed pharmacy. Stock up on prescription drugs before leaving home, as a Czech pharmacist may not recognize your doctor's prescription. In any event, use generic names instead of trade names when describing drugs (such as acetaminophen instead of Tylenol), as trade names change from market to market and may not be the same in the Czech Republic.

Dietary Red Flags Czech food tends to be heavy and not advisable for anyone on a low-fat or low-cholesterol diet. Vegetarian restaurants are few and far between, but Prague has a couple of decent vegetarian options.

Bugs, Bites & Other Wildlife Concerns Ticks are common in wooded areas, and if you plan on camping or hiking in wilderness areas, you're best advised to get vaccinated against tick-bite encephalitis, a rare but serious disease caused by a bite from an infected tick. Mosquitoes are a problem in wooded and wet areas. Poisonous spiders and snakes are very rare.

Sun/Elements/Extreme Weather Exposure Prague receives its share of sunny days, and it's always best to put on sunscreen before heading out for the day. This is particularly advisable if you're planning a boating trip or hike or some other activity that will increase your exposure.

Hospitals For emergency medical treatment, go to Nemocnice Na Homolce (Na Homolce Hospital) at Roentgenova 2, Prague 5, Smíchov (© 257-271-111; www.homolka.cz). If you need nonurgent medical attention, practitioners in many fields can be found at the Canadian Medical Care center at Veleslavínská 1, Prague 6, Dejvice (© 235-360-133; www.cmcpraha.cz). For dental service, call American Dental Associates at V Celnici 4, Prague 1, Nové Město (© 221-181-121; www.americandental.cz), open 9am to 7pm Monday to Friday.

Insurance U.S., Canadian, and Australian citizens should obtain medical insurance with international coverage prior to arrival in the Czech Republic, as any doctor or hospital visit must be paid for out of pocket. Hospitals may demand cash pre-payment before rendering services, but be sure to save all the paperwork for later reimbursements. The Czech Republic and the E.U. have a reciprocal health insurance agreement that covers U.K. citizens provided they have a European Health Insurance Card (EHIC).

For information on traveler's insurance, trip cancellation insurance, and medical insurance while traveling, please visit http://www.frommers.com/planning.

Internet & Wi-Fi Prague and the Czech Republic are well-wired. Nearly every hotel above a basic pension will have some form of Internet access: either a LAN (Ethernet) cable in the room or Wi-Fi. Even if Wi-Fi isn't offered in the rooms, many hotels will have a free Wi-Fi connection for guests in the lobby. Around town, many bars and cafes offer free Wi-Fi for customers (usually password-protected), which can come in handy if you're carrying a laptop or Wi-Fi enabled smartphone. The only drawback is that Wi-Fi tends to be spotty, and networks seem to be down about as often as they are up. Coffee Fellows, at Dlouhá 20, Prague 1, Staré Město (© 222-310-200), is centrally located just off of Old Town Square and has a reliable, free Wi-Fi connection and good coffee. They are open daily from 8am to 9pm.

Central Prague has several Internet cafes with their own computers for checking e-mail, printing out documents and timetables, or making Skype or VOIP telephone calls. Rates typically run from 1Kč to 2Kč per minute. Near Old Town Square, try Bohemia Bagel at Masná 2, Prague 1, Staré Město (☎ **224-812-560;** www.bohemiabagel.cz). They have a dozen PCs in a pleasant setting for 2Kč per minute; open daily from 8am to 11pm. Spika at Dlážděná 4, Prague 1, Nové Město (☎ **224-211-521**) is open Monday to Friday 8am to midnight and Saturday and Sunday 10am to 11pm, and charges 20Kč for 15 minutes.

Prague Airport offers both free and paid Wi-Fi. The free connection is notoriously slow and overburdened, which helps them push customers to the paid service. Rates start at 60Kč for 1 hour, billed through a credit card.

Language Czech is a Slavic language, a distant cousin to Russian but similar to Slovak and Polish. Nearly anyone who works in a hotel, restaurant, or tourist center will be able to speak at least some English. Outside of the capital, English ability decreases, though nearly anyone under the age of 30 has had (in theory, at least) several years of English instruction in school. German may also prove useful, particularly with older people.

Legal Aid There are no specific agencies that offer legal services for visiting foreigners. For serious infractions, contact your embassy as soon as you can. In general, it's best to keep your cool if you are stopped by the police. Acting angry or defensive is almost certain to backfire. Be sure to carry your passport and driver's license and produce them when asked by a law-enforcement officer. Traffic violations are usually settled through a spot fine paid directly to the police officer. Ask for a receipt as a way of keeping the officer honest.

LGBT Travelers Prague and the Czech Republic are tolerant destinations, and gay and lesbian travelers are not likely to encounter any problems. Overt discrimination on the basis of sexual preference is against the law. Same-sex partnerships are protected under law and contain many of the same legal protections as marriage. The Prague neighborhood of Vinohrady is particularly gay-friendly, and several gay clubs and bars have opened up there in recent years. For a list of popular gay clubs, see "Gay & Lesbian Clubs" on p. 187. In addition, there are a couple of hotels and

guesthouses around town that cater to a largely or exclusively gay clientele. The Czech *GayGuide* (www.czechgayguide.org) and *GayGuide Prague* (www.prague.gayguide.net) are both helpful resources for happenings, bars, restaurants, and clubs. Both are in English and written with visitors in mind. The latter site includes information on Budapest, Warsaw, Kraków, and Sofia, as well as Prague.

Mail Postcards and light letters sent within the E.U. cost 18Kč. Those going outside the E.U. (to the U.S., Canada, and Australia) cost 21Kč, though rates vary by weight, and letters should always be weighed at the post office to ensure proper postage. Mail service is reliable and unless you're sending something very important or fragile, there's usually no need to use a trackable service like FedEx or DHL. Letters to destinations within Europe take 3 to 5 days, and to the U.S. 7 to 10 days. Most post offices are open Monday through Friday from 8am to 7pm. The main post office (Hlavní pošta), at Jindřišská 14, Prague 1 (☎ **221-131-111**), is open 24 hours. You can receive mail, marked "Poste Restante" and

THE VALUE OF THE CZECH CROWN VS. OTHER POPULAR CURRENCIES

Kč	Aus$	Can$	Euro€	NZ$	UK£	US$
100	5.40	5.60	4.00	7.00	3.50	5.70

WHAT THINGS COST IN PRAGUE	CZECH CROWNS (KČ)
Taxi from the airport to downtown [destination]	650
Double room, moderate	2,200
Double room, inexpensive	1,600
Three-course dinner for one without wine, moderate	500
Bottle of beer	30–50
Cup of coffee	50
1 gallon/1 liter of premium gas	140/35
Admission to most museums	150

addressed to you, in care of this post office.

Medical Requirements
The Czech Republic presents no unusual health concerns and proof of vaccination is not required to enter the country. See "Health," earlier in this section.

Mobile Phones Czech mobile phones operate on a GSM band of 900/1800MHz. This is the same standard in use throughout Europe but different from the one used in the U.S. American mobile phones will work here provided they are tri- or quadband phones (not all phones are) and that you've contacted your service provider to allow for international roaming. Keep calls to a minimum, however, since roaming charges can be steep. U.K. mobiles should work without any problem provided that you've contacted your service provider to activate international roaming (the same precautions about steep roaming charges apply to U.K. mobile phones).

A good way to avoid international roaming charges is to purchase a pay-as-you-go SIM card for your mobile and a prepaid calling card. This provides you with a local number and allows you to make calls and send text messages at local rates. All the major local telephone operators, including Telefónica 02 (www.o2.cz); T-Mobile (www.t-mobile.cz); and Vodafone (www.vodafone. cz), offer pay-as-you-go SIM cards and telephone number services.

The situation is more complicated if you're carrying a **smartphone** like an iPhone, Android, or Black-Berry that can't be easily unlocked. With these phones, it's best to contact your home telephone provider to discuss international calling and data plans appropriate for your phoning, text, and data needs. Most operators offer some kind of short-term international plan that will allow for a certain number of calls and megabytes of data downloads. An alternative is

to switch your phone to "Airplane" mode on arrival, which blocks calls and text messages but still allows you to enable Wi-Fi use, and simply use your phone as a Wi-Fi device. You can use Skype over local Wi-Fi at very low cost provided you've downloaded the Skype app beforehand. Always be sure to turn off your smartphone's "Data Roaming" setting on arrival to avoid extortionist data download fees.

Money & Costs The Czech currency is the crown (*koruna* in Czech). It is usually noted as "Kč" in shops and "CZK" in banks. One crown, in theory, is divided into 100 haler, though halers no longer circulate. Coins come in denominations of 1, 2, 5, 10, 20, and 50 crowns. Bills come in denominations of 100, 200, 500, 1,000, and 5,000 crowns. The euro is not in circulation in the Czech Republic, though some hotels and larger shops will accept euros (though they usually provide change in crowns). Most hotels and stores will not accept U.S. dollars as payment for goods.

Frommer's lists exact prices in the local currency. The currency conversions provided were correct at press time. However, rates fluctuate, so before departing consult a currency exchange website such as **www.oanda.com/currency/ converter** to check up-to-the-minute rates.

The Czech Republic is not as cheap a destination as it was a few years ago but remains generally less expensive than western Europe. Prices for everyday travel expenses like food and drink (especially beer), hotels, and museum admissions are substantially less than they would be in Paris or London. The exceptions are rental cars (and gasoline), hotels, and imported clothing and other luxury goods, for which prices are as high as anywhere else.

Changing money is not a problem in the Czech Republic. If you're arriving at Prague Airport, skip the currency-exchange booths and instead use one of the ATMs located in arrival halls of both main terminals. Banks and ATMs generally offer the best rates and lowest commissions. Local ATMs work with a four-digit PIN; before leaving home make sure that you have a four-digit PIN and let your bank or credit card company know that you will be abroad so they don't protectively block your account once they see a few foreign transactions come through.

Whatever you do, resist the temptation to use one of the private currency-exchange offices that line Václavské náměstí and other areas with heavy tourist concentrations. These outfits seldom pay the rates they advertise on the outside and the commissions (and hidden commissions) can be prohibitive, especially on relatively small amounts of money. If you must use one of these private currency exchanges, before surrendering your bills, show them to the teller through the window and then ask him or her to write down the amount in Czech crowns that you will receive. Once you've handed over the money, it's too late.

You will find ATMs on practically every street corner in central Prague. Komerční banka has three convenient Prague 1 locations with ATMs that accept Visa, MasterCard, and American Express: Na Příkopě 33, Spálená 51, and Václavské nám. 42 (© **800-111-055,** central switchboard for all branches; www.kb.cz). The exchange offices are open Monday to Friday from 8am to 5pm, but the ATMs are accessible 24 hours.

Credit and debit cards are increasingly common and many shops, restaurants and hotels accept them. Stores may impose a minimum purchase amount for using a card. Traveler's checks, on the other hand, have become much less common in recent years and much harder to use. As a

rule, only large banks will cash traveler's checks; hotels and restaurants are not likely to accept them.

Beware, though, of hidden credit card fees while traveling. Check with your credit or debit card issuer to see what fees, if any, will be charged for overseas transactions. Recent reform legislation in the U.S., for example, has curbed some exploitative lending practices. But many banks have responded by increasing fees in other areas, including fees for customers who use credit and debit cards while out of the country—even if those charges were made in U.S. dollars. Fees can amount to 3% or more of the purchase price. Check with your bank before departing to avoid any surprise charges on your statement.

For help with currency conversions, tip calculations, and more, download Frommer's convenient Travel Tools app for your mobile device. Go to http://www.frommers.com/go/mobile and click on the Travel Tools icon.

Newspapers & Magazines

The Prague Post (www.praguepost.com) is a decent English-language newspaper that comes out once a week every Wednesday. It provides a good overview of political and social life in the Czech Republic, as well as excellent restaurant, film, and culture reviews. It's usually available free on flights to Prague as well as at some hotel reception desks. It costs 79Kč at newsstands. The *Prague Daily Monitor* (www.praguemonitor.com) is a daily online newspaper, with both original content and reprints from other publications. *Czech Position* (www.ceskapozice.cz/en) is another online newspaper that focuses mainly on politics and economics and has a good "Czech Living" section with dining and cultural recommendations.

Packing Be sure to bring along a nice sport coat (men) or dress (women) for a concert or tablecloth dinner in the evening. Plan for cool nights, even at the height of summer, and don't forget to bring an umbrella or raincoat no matter what time of year. Other packing needs depend on what you intend to do. Definitely bring a pair of opera glasses, for example, if concerts or opera are on the schedule. If you plan on renting a car, consider bringing your car's GPS or sat-nav system (like Garmin or TomTom). Download the Czech or European maps before you travel and use it in your rental just like you would at home. For more helpful information on packing for your trip, download our convenient Travel Tools app for your mobile device. Go to http://www.frommers.com/go/mobile and click on the Travel Tools icon.

Passports A passport valid for at least 6 months is required to enter the Czech

Republic. To replace a lost or stolen passport, contact your embassy immediately; see "Embassies & Consulates," above.

See www.frommers.com/planning for information on how to obtain a passport. For additional information, contact the following agencies:

Australia Australian Passport Information Service (☏ **131-232,** or visit www.passports.gov.au).

Canada Passport Office, Department of Foreign Affairs and International Trade, Ottawa, ON K1A 0G3 (☏ **800/567-6868;** www.ppt.gc.ca).

Ireland Passport Office, Setanta Centre, Molesworth Street, Dublin 2 (☏ **01/671-1633;** www.foreignaffairs.gov.ie).

New Zealand Passports Office, Department of Internal Affairs, 47 Boulcott St., Wellington, 6011 (☏ **0800/225-050** in New Zealand or 04/474-8100; www.passports.govt.nz).

United Kingdom Visit your nearest passport office, major post office, or travel agency, or contact the **Identity and Passport Service (IPS),** 89 Eccleston Sq., London, SW1V 1PN (☏ **0300/222-0000;** www.ips.gov.uk).

United States To find your regional passport office, check the U.S. State Department website (travel.state.gov/passport) or call the **National Passport Information Center** (☏ **077/487-2778**) for automated information.

Petrol Please see "Getting Around by Car," earlier in this chapter.

Police Dial the European Emergency Number ☏ **112** from any phone in an emergency. For Czech police, dial ☏ **158.**

Safety In Prague's center you'll feel generally safer than in most big cities, but always take common-sense precautions. Be aware of your immediate surroundings. Don't walk alone at night around Wenceslas Square—one of the main areas for prostitution and where a lot of unexplainable loitering takes place.

All visitors should be watchful of pickpockets in heavily touristed areas, especially on Charles Bridge, in Old Town Square, and in front of the main train station. Be especially wary on crowded buses, trams, and trains. Don't keep your wallet in a back pocket and don't flash a lot of cash or jewelry. Petty crime, especially car break-ins and bike theft, are serious problems and are underreported in official statistics. Don't leave valuable items in parked cars overnight or leave bikes, even if they're securely locked, unattended for more than a few minutes.

Drug laws tend to be more lenient than in other countries. Marijuana has been decriminalized; possession of a few marijuana cigarettes is a low-level misdemeanor and the police are usually tolerant about outdoor smoking (though most bars and clubs will not allow you to smoke pot indoors). Possession of larger amounts of cannabis or any amount of harder drugs can land you in big trouble. If you're caught, you are best off phoning your embassy to figure out your legal options.

Prostitution is technically legal, though it's only loosely regulated and potentially high-risk. Václavské náměstí (Wenceslas Square), at night, is filled with touts pushing various "cabarets" and "nightclubs," code words for strip clubs and occasionally bordellos. If you choose to patronize one, don't take in lots of big bills with you and leave your credit cards back at the hotel. Most of the women working at these places are not likely to be Czechs, but Russians, Romanians, Ukrainians, and others, some brought here via organized crime networks. Public health checks are infrequent, if ever, so exercise extreme caution.

There are very few serious discrimination issues and most travelers won't have any problems. The only exception may be Roma (gypsies) or travelers with darker skin and dark hair who could conceivably be mistaken as Roma. Anti-Roma discrimination in the Czech Republic runs deep, and while such travelers are unlikely to meet with any overt violence, they might experience unfriendly treatment at the hand of shop owners.

Czechs are remarkably tolerant when it comes to homosexuality, and while same-sex hand-holding is rare, gay and lesbian travelers are not likely to experience any overt discrimination. See "LGBT Travelers," above.

Women traveling alone are not likely to experience any serious problems or unwanted attention. Women are generally safe walking alone at night, though of course bad things can happen anywhere and if there's any doubt, proper precautions should be taken.

Senior Travel Seniors, usually defined as 70 years of age and older, nearly always qualify for discounts at castles, museums, and other attractions and pay half-fare on public transportation. Simply ask for a senior ticket and show your passport if asked. In practice, you'll rarely be challenged.

Smoking As of 2010, all restaurants, bars, and cafes must post their smoking policies at the door. A yellow triangle with the words *kouření povoleno* indicates the establishment has a separate smoking section, while a red circle with a line through the middle means no smoking allowed or there is a separate nonsmoking section. Smoking rules are noticeably more lax than in the United States or Britain, though many better restaurants have gone completely nonsmoking in response to customer preferences. Casual places and pubs are likely to have more liberal smoking rules (and can get quite smoky), though in theory all places must be able to offer nonsmoking tables on request. Most hotels are completely nonsmoking or will have only a limited number of smoking rooms. Note that it's illegal to smoke outdoors near bus and tram stops. This rule is rarely enforced, but the fine, 1,000Kč, is steep.

Taxes All goods and services in the Czech Republic are levied a value-added tax (VAT, or *DPH* in Czech), charged at 10% or 20%, depending on the item. This tax is almost always included in the price.

Telephones The country code for the Czech Republic is 420. To dial the Czech Republic from abroad, dial your country's international access code (for example, 011 in the United States) plus 420, and then the unique nine-digit local number. Once you arrive, to dial any number anywhere in the Czech Republic, simply dial the unique nine-digit number. There are no area or city codes in the Czech Republic.

To make a direct international call from the Czech Republic, dial 00 plus the country code of the country you are calling, and then the area code and number. The country code for the U.S. and Canada is 1; Great Britain, 44; and Australia, 61. You can dial abroad from any pay phone using a prepaid magnetic card (see below) or from the main post office (see "Mail," above). The cheapest alternative is simply to use Skype on a Wi-Fi–enabled smartphone or from a PC at an Internet cafe (see "Internet & Wi-Fi," above).

Working public phones are rare thanks to the rapid growth of mobile phones. There are a few surviving coin-operated pay phones around town, but most public phones require a prepaid magnetic card. Find the cards at tobacco and magazine kiosks (cards are available for 200Kč–500Kč). Simply insert the card, listen for the dial tone, and dial.

For directory inquiries regarding phone numbers within the Czech Republic, dial © **1180.** For information about services and rates abroad, call © **1181.**

Time The Czech Republic is in the Central European time zone, the same as Paris, Berlin, and Vienna, and 1 hour ahead of London (GMT), 6 hours ahead of New York (EST). **Daylight saving time** is in effect from early spring until fall (the actual date varies from year to year). Daylight saving time moves the clock 1 hour ahead of standard time. The switch is made at 2am on a Sunday morning to cause the least disruption.

Tipping In hotels, tip **bellhops** 20Kč per bag (more if you have a lot of luggage), and though it's not expected, it's a nice gesture to leave the

chamber staff 20Kč per night (depending on the level of service). Tip the **doorman** or **concierge** only if he or she has provided a specific service (for example, calling a cab for you or obtaining difficult-to-get theater tickets).

In restaurants, bars, and nightclubs, tip **service staff or bartender** 10% of the check to reward good service. On smaller tabs, it's easiest just to round up to the next highest multiple of 10. For example, if the bill comes to 72Kč, hand the waiter 80Kč and tell him or her to keep the change.

As for other service personnel, tip **cab drivers** 5% to 10% of the fare (provided he hasn't already overcharged you). Tip **hair dressers** and **barbers** 10% to 15%.

For help with tip calculations, currency conversions, and more, download our convenient Travel Tools app for your mobile device. Go to http://www.frommers.com/go/mobile and click on the Travel Tools icon.

Toilets Acceptably clean pay toilets are scattered around tourist areas and can be found in every metro station. Expect to pay 5 Kč to 10Kč for the privilege. You'll find generally cleaner free toilets in restaurants, hotels, and fast-food outlets, but these are usually reserved for customers.

VAT See "Taxes," earlier in this section.

Visas As of this writing, citizens of the U.S., Canada, the U.K., Ireland, Australia,

and New Zealand are not required to obtain a visa for short-term stays of 90 days or less within a 6-month period, though a lingering dispute with Canada could change this for Canadian travelers. Contact the **Czech Ministry of Foreign Affairs** website (www.mzv.cz) for up-to-date visa information or how to obtain a visa if required.

Visitor Information
The official tourist information service for the Czech Republic is the Czech Tourist Authority, known as **CzechTourism** (www.czech-tourism.com). They have offices in several countries abroad and can help make basic travel arrangements and answer questions. The website is a treasure-trove of useful information.

In the U.S., CzechTourism is located at 1109 Madison Ave., New York, NY 10028 (© **212/288-0830, ext. 101**). Note that Czech-Tourism closed its Canada office at the end of 2010 and Canadian citizens are advised to use the U.S. office. **For the U.K. and Ireland,** contact CzechTourism at 13 Harley St., London W1G 9QG (© **0207-631-0427**). The agency has no formal representation in Australia or New Zealand.

Once in Prague, the main tourist information center is the **Prague Information Service (Prague Welcome)** (© **221-714-444;** www.praguewelcome.cz), with offices at the Old Town Hall on Old Town Square, several other points around the

13

city, and at the main train station and airport. Prague Welcome hands out maps, organizes tours, and can help book rooms.

Helpful websites include www.mapy.cz, an online map and journey planner that covers Prague and the entire Czech Republic. Simply type in an address and a map shows you exactly where it is. For the ins and outs of Prague's public transportation system, including maps and info on tickets and travel passes, go to www.dpp.cz/en.

The site www.idos.cz provides an online timetable for trains and buses, including international destinations. Type in the city (using the Czech spellings, such as "Praha" for Prague, but note diacritical marks are not required), and you'll get a complete listing of train and bus connections. The main website for the National Gallery in Prague, including practical information, admissions fees, and opening times for many of the city major museums, is www.ngprague.cz.

Water Tap water is fine to drink, but most restaurants won't serve it, preferring instead to charge for bottles of mineral water. Carbonated water is *"perliva voda."* To order still water, say *"neperlivou vodu."*

Wi-Fi See "Internet & Wi-Fi," earlier in this section.

USEFUL TERMS & PHRASES

Although Czech is a difficult language to master, you should at least make an attempt to learn a few phrases. Czechs will appreciate the effort and will be more willing to help you out.

BASIC PHRASES & VOCABULARY

Czech Alphabet

There are 32 vowels and consonants in the Czech alphabet, and most of the consonants are pronounced about as they are in English. Accent marks over vowels lengthen the sound of the vowel, as does the *kroužek*, the little circle that usually appears only over a "u."

A, a *f*ather
B, b *b*oy
C, c *gets*
Č, č *choice*
D, d *d*ay
Ď, d' *Dior*
E, e *n*e*ver*
F, f *f*ood
G, g *g*oal
H, h un*h*and
Ch, ch Lo*ch* Lomond
I, i *n*eed
J, j *y*es
K, k *k*ey
L, l *l*ord
M, m *m*ama

N, n *n*o
Ň, ň Ta*ny*a
O, o *aw*ful
P, p *p*en
R, r slightly trilled *r*
Ř, ř slightly trilled *r* + *zh* as in Pe*r*sian
S, s *s*eat
Š, š cru*sh*
T, t *t*oo
Ť, t' *not y*et
U, u *r*oom
V, v *v*ery
W, w *v*ague
Y, y funn*y*
Z, z *z*ebra
Ž, ž a*z*ure, plea*s*ure

Czech Vocabulary
EVERYDAY EXPRESSIONS

English	Czech	Pronunciation
Hello	**Dobrý den**	*doh*-bree den
Good morning	**Dobré jitro**	*doh*-breh *yee*-troh
Good evening	**Dobrý večer**	*doh*-bree *veh*-chair
How are you?	**Jak se máte?**	*yahk* seh *mah*-teh
Very well	**Velmi dobře**	*vel*-mee *doh*-brsheh
Thank you	**Děkuji vám**	*dyek*-ooee vahm
You're welcome	**Prosím**	*proh*-seem
Please	**Prosím**	*proh*-seem
Yes	**Ano**	*ah*-no
No	**Ne**	neh
Excuse me	**Promiňte**	*proh*-min-teh
How much does it cost?	**Kolik to stojí?**	*koh*-leek taw *stoh*-ee
I don't understand.	**Nerozumím.**	*neh*-roh-zoo-meem
Just a moment.	**Moment, prosím.**	*moh*-ment, *proh*-seem
Goodbye	**Na shledanou**	*nah* skleh-dah-noh-oo

TRAVELING

Where is the . . . ?	**Kde je . . . ?**	*gde* yeh . . .
bus station	**autobusové nádraží**	*au*-toh-boos-oh-veh *nah*-drah-zhee
train station	**nádraží**	*nah*-drah-zhee
airport	**letiště**	*leh*-tyish-tyeh
baggage check	**úschovna zavazadel**	*oo*-skohv-nah *zah*-vahz-ah-del
Where can I find a taxi?	**Kde najdu taxi?**	*gde nai*-doo *tahks*-eh
Where can I find a gas station?	**Kde najdu benzínovou pumpu?**	*gde nai*-doo *ben*-zeen-oh-voh *poomp*-oo
How much is the fare?	**Kolik je jízdné?**	*koh*-leek yeh yeesd-neh
I am going to . . .	**Pojedu do . . .**	*poh*-yeh-doo doh . . .
One-way ticket	**Jízdenka**	*yeez*-den-kah
Round-trip ticket	**Zpáteční jízdenka**	*zpah*-tech-nee *jeez*-den-kah
Car-rental office	**Půjčovna aut**	*poo*-eech-awv-nah ah-oot

ACCOMMODATIONS

I'm looking for . . .	**Hledám . . .**	*hleh*-dahm . . .
a hotel	**hotel**	*hoh*-tel
a youth hostel	**studentskou ubytovnu**	*stoo*-dent-skoh *oo*-beet-ohv-noo
I am staying . . .	**Zůstanu . . .**	*zoo*-stah-noo . . .
a few days	**několik dnů**	*nyeh*-koh-leek dnoo
2 weeks	**dva týdny**	dvah tid-*neh*
a month	**jeden měsíc**	*yeh*-den *myeh*-seets

English	Czech	Pronunciation
I have a reservation.	**Mám zamluvený nocleh.**	mahm *zah*-mloo-veh-ni *nohts*-leh
My name is . . .	**Jmenuji se . . .**	*meh*-noo-yee seh . . .
Do you have a room . . . ?	**Máte pokoj . . . ?**	*mah*-teh *poh*-koy . . .
for tonight	**na dnešek**	*nah* dneh-sheck
for 3 nights	**na tři dny**	*nah* trshee dnee
for a week	**na týden**	*nah* tee-den
I would like . . .	**Chci . . .**	khtsee . . .
a single	**jednolůžkový pokoj**	*jed*-noh-loosh-koh-vee *poh*-koy
a double	**dvojlůžkový pokoj**	*dvoy*-loosh-koh-vee *poh*-koy
I want a room . . .	**Chci pokoj . . .**	khtsee *poh*-koy . . .
with a bathroom	**s koupelnou**	*skoh*-pehl-noh
without a bathroom	**bez koupelny**	*behz* koh-pehl-nee
with a shower	**se sprchou**	*seh* spur-choh
without a shower	**bez sprchy**	*bez* sprech-eh
with a view	**s pohledem**	*spoh*-hlehd-ehm
How much is the room?	**Kolik stojí pokoj?**	*koh*-leek *stoh*-yee *paw*-koy
with breakfast?	**se snídaní?**	*seh* snee-dan-nyee
May I see the room?	**Mohu vidět ten pokoj?**	*moh*-hoo *vee*-dyet ten *paw*-koy
The key	**Klíč**	kleech
The bill, please.	**Dejte mi účet, prosím.**	*day*-teh mee oo-cheht, *praw*-seem

GETTING AROUND

I'm looking for . . .	**Hledám . . .**	*hleh*-dahm . . .
a bank	**banku**	*bahnk*-oo
the church	**kostel**	*kohs*-tell
the city center	**centrum**	*tsent*-room
the museum	**muzeum**	*moo*-zeh-oom
a pharmacy	**lékárnu**	*lek*-ahr-noo
the park	**park**	pahrk
the theater	**divadlo**	*dee*-vahd-loh
the tourist office	**cestovní kancelář**	*tses*-tohv-nee *kahn*-tseh-larsh
the embassy	**velvyslanectví**	*vehl*-vee-slahn-ets-tvee
Where is the nearest telephone?	**Kde je nejbližší telefon?**	gde yeh *nay*-bleesh-ee *tel*-oh-fohn
I would like to buy . . .	**Chci koupit . . .**	khtsee *koh*-peet . . .
a stamp	**známku**	*znahm*-koo
a postcard	**pohlednici**	*poh*-hlehd-nit-seh
a map	**mapu**	*mahp*-oo

EMERGENCIES

English	Czech	Pronunciation
I need a doctor	**Potřebuji lékaře**	*poh*-trzhe-boo-yee *leh*-kahrz-e
Hospital	**nemocnice**	nay-*mohts*-nee-tse
Help!	**Pomoc!**	poh-*mohts*
Call the police	**zavolejte policii**	*zah*-vo-lay-te *pol*-ee-tsee-yee
I'm lost	**atratil jsem se**	ztrah-*teel* sem seh

SIGNS

No Trespassing	**Cizím vstup zakázán**	*see*-zeem *ve*-stoop *zah*-kah-zahn
No Smoking	**Kouření zakázáno**	*koh*-zhen-ee *zah*-kah-zahn-oh
No Parking	**Neparkovat**	ne-*park*-oh-vaht
Arrivals	**Příjezd/Přílet**	*pchee*-yezd/*pchee*-let
Entrance	**Vchod**	v-*khod*
Departures	**Odjezd/Odlet**	*od*-yezd/*od*-let
Exit	**Východ**	vee-khod
Toilets	**Toalety**	*toe*-ah-let-ee
Information	**Informace**	*in*-form-*ah*-tse
Danger	**Pozor, nebezpečí**	*poh*-zor, *neh*-bez-*pech*-ee

NUMBERS

1	**jeden** (*yeh*-den)		16	**šestnáct** (*shest*-nahtst)
2	**dva** (dvah)		17	**sedmnáct** (*seh*-doom-nahtst)
3	**tři** (trzhee)		18	**osmnáct** (*aw*-soom-nahtst)
4	**čtyři** (*chtee*-rshee)		19	**devatenáct** (*deh*-vah-teh-nahtst)
5	**pět** (pyet)		20	**dvacet** (*dvah*-tset)
6	**šest** (shest)		30	**třicet** (*trshee*-tset)
7	**sedm** (*seh*-duhm)		40	**čtyřicet** (*chti*-rshee-tset)
8	**osm** (*aw*-suhm)		50	**padesát** (*pah*-deh-saht)
9	**devět** (*deh*-vyet)		60	**šedesát** (*she*-deh-saht)
10	**deset** (*deh*-set)		70	**sedmdesát** (*seh*-duhm-deh-saht)
11	**jedenáct** (*yeh*-deh-nahtst)		80	**osmdesát** (*aw*-suhm-deh-saht)
12	**dvanáct** (*dvah*-nahtst)		90	**devadesát** (*deh*-vah-deh-saht)
13	**třináct** (*trshee*-nahtst)		100	**sto** (staw)
14	**čtrnáct** (*chtur*-nahtst)		500	**pět set** (*pyet* set)
15	**patnáct** (*paht*-nahtst)		1,000	**tisíc** (tyee-seets)

DINING

Restaurant	**Restaurace**	*rehs*-tow-rah-tseh
Breakfast	**Snídaně**	*snee*-dah-nyeh
Lunch	**Oběd**	*oh*-byed
Dinner	**Večeře**	*veh*-chair-sheh
A table for two, please. (Lit.: There are two of us.)	**Jsme dva.**	*ees*-meh dvah
Waiter	**Číšník**	*cheess*-neek
Waitress	**Servírka**	ser-*veer*-ka

Basic Phrases & Vocabulary

USEFUL TERMS & PHRASES

English	Czech	Pronunciation
I would like . . .	Chci . . .	khtsee . . .
a menu	jídelní lístek	*yee*-del-nee *lees*-teck
a fork	vidličku	*veed*-leech-koo
a knife	nůž	noosh
a spoon	lžičku	lu-*shich*-koo
a napkin	ubrousek	*oo*-broh-seck
a glass (of water)	skleničku (vody)	*sklehn*-ich-koo (vod-*dee*)
the check, please	účet, prosím	*oo*-cheht, *proh*-seem
Is the tip included?	Je v tom zahrnuto spropitné?	yeh *ftohm*-zah *hur*-noo-toh *sproh*-peet-neh

MENU TERMS
General

Soup	Polévka	*poh*-lehv-kah
Eggs	Vejce	*vayts*-eh
Meat	Maso	*mahs*-oh
Fish	Ryba	*ree*-bah
Vegetables	Zelenina	*zehl*-eh-nee-nah
Fruit	Ovoce	*oh*-voh-tseh
Desserts	Moučníky	*mohch*-nee-kee
Beverages	Nápoje	*nah*-poy-yeh
Salt	Sů1	sool
Pepper	Pepř	*peh*-psh
Mayonnaise	Majonéza	*mai*-o-neza
Mustard	Hořčice	*hohrsh*-chee-tseh
Vinegar	Ocet	*oh*-tseht
Oil	Olej	*oh*-lay
Sugar	Cukr	*tsoo*-ker
Tea	Čaj	chye
Coffee	Káva	*kah*-vah
Bread	Chléb	khlehb
Butter	Máslo	*mahs*-loh
Wine	Víno	*vee*-noh
Fried	Smažený	*smah*-sheh-nee
Roasted	Pečený	*pech*-eh-nee
Boiled	Vařený	*vah*-rsheh-nee
Grilled	Grilovaný	*gree*-loh-vah-nee

SOUP

Potato **Bramborová**

Lentil **Čočková**

Goulash **Gulášová**

Tomato **Rajská**

Chicken **Slepičí**

Vegetable **Zeleninová**

MEAT

Steak **Biftek**

Goulash **Guláš**

Beef **Hovězí**

Liver **Játra**

Lamb **Jehněčí**

Duck **Kachna**

Sausage **Klobása**

Rabbit **Králík**

Mutton **Skopové**

Veal **Telecí**

Veal Cutlet **Telecí kotleta**

Pork **Vepřové**

FISH

Carp **Kapr**

Caviar **Kaviár**

Fish Filet **Rybí filé**

Herring **Sleď**

Pike **Štika**

Cod **Treska**

Eel **Úhoř**

Oysters **Ústřice**

EGGS

Scrambled Eggs **Míchaná vejce**

Fried Eggs **Smažená vejce**

Boiled Eggs **Vařená vejce**

Soft-boiled Eggs **Vejce naměkko**

Bacon and Eggs **Vejce se slaninou**

Ham and Eggs **Vejce se šunkou**

SALAD

Bean Salad **Fazolový salát**

Mixed Green Salad **Hlávkový salát**

Cucumber Salad **Okurkový salát**

Beet Salad **Salát z červené řepy**

VEGETABLES

Potatoes **Brambory**

Celery **Celer**

Asparagus **Chřest**

Onions **Cibule**

Mushrooms **Houby**

Cauliflower **Květák**

Carrots **Mrkev**

Peppers **Paprika**

Tomatoes **Rajská jablíčka**

Cabbage **Zelí**

DESSERT

Cake **Koláč**

Cookies **Cukroví**

Chocolate Ice Cream **Čokoládová zmrzlina**

Apple Strudel **Jablkový závin**

Pancakes **Palačinky**

Vanilla Ice Cream **Vanilková zmrzlina**

FRUIT

Lemon **Citrón**

Pear **Hruška**

Strawberry **Jahoda**

Apple **Jablko**

Plum **Švestka**

BEVERAGES

Tea **Čaj**

Coffee **Káva**

Milk **Mléko**

Wine **Víno**

Red **Červené**

White **Bílé**

Water **Voda**

Beer **Pivo**

Index

See also Accommodations and Restaurant indexes, below.

General Index

A

B

C

302